LIVES AND TIMES:
PRACTICE, POLICY AND PEOPLE WITH DISABILITIES

Lives and times:
Practice, policy and people with disabilities

Edited by
Patricia Noonan Walsh
and
Hugh Gash

Rath*down*

First published in 2004 by
Rathdown Press
(A division of Wordwell Ltd)
PO Box 69, Bray, Co. Wicklow
www.wordwellbooks.com

Library of Congress Cataloging-in-Publication Data are available for this book.

A CIP catalogue record for this book is available from the British Library.

ISBN 0-9548207-0-3

Cover design: Rachel Dunne
Cover illustration: 'Downtown Bangkok' by Geraldine McEvoy and Mary
Francis Leahy, reproduced by kind permission of the owner Justin Hanley.

Copy-editing: Emer Condit
Typesetting and layout: Wordwell Ltd

Book design: Nick Maxwell

Printed by E.G. Zure, Bilbao

CONTENTS

FOREWORD

In 2003, the highest number yet of people with intellectual disability in receipt or in need of services was recorded in Ireland and stands at nearly 26,000 (Report of the National Intellectual Disability Database, Health Research Board, 2004). This growth is largely due to the increased longevity of people with an intellectual disability and has occurred slowly as a result of improved care, more effective medical intervention and a better quality of life. It is something of which our society can be proud.

This book — *Lives and times; practice, policy and people with disability* — is a timely reminder of the wealth of issues that arise in considering the life course of people with intellectual disability, the protection of their human rights, the development of their talents, their needs in old age and their relationship with those who are more intellectually gifted. While we speak of people with intellectual disability, the reader is constantly reminded in this book of the diversity of life experiences and expectations and the need to respect the choice and individuality of every person.

Professor Patricia Noonan Walsh of the Centre for Disability Studies in University College Dublin and Hugh Gash of St Patrick's College are to be commended on their foresight as editors and contributors in bringing together so much experience, wisdom and expertise about issues relevant to intellectual disability in one book and in presenting the material in a highly readable way. The book comprises sixteen chapters written by experts in practice and/or research related to people with intellectual disability from Ireland, Northern Ireland and Britain. It will be an indispensable handbook of evidence-based practice for the increasing number of students now enrolled in interdisciplinary courses related to disability. Many contributors also lecture on postgraduate courses for nurses, therapists, managers and others who work with people with intellectual disability. It is to this next generation of carers, mentors, planners and advocates, who face the challenge of maintaining and enhancing the progress of the previous generation, that this book is primarily addressed.

Congratulations are also due to the Rathdown Press of Wordwell Ltd, the publishers of the book, on a most handsome production.

Ruth Barrington Ph.D
Chief Executive
Health Research Board

July 2004

Acknowledgements

The editors acknowledge the generous financial support provided by the following organisations: the National Association for People with Disabilities Ireland; the Academic Publications Scheme at the National University of Ireland, Dublin; National Lottery funds made available through the Department of Health and Children; the St Patrick's College Research Fund; and Eason & Son Ltd.

The editorial assistance provided by Richard Molloy and Marie O'Connor at UCD is very gratefully acknowledged. We also want to thank Nick Maxwell of Wordwell for his support and encouragement, without which this volume would not have appeared.

Finally, the opinions expressed do not necessarily reflect those of the organisations that provided financial support and their endorsement should not be inferred.

1. Introduction

PATRICIA NOONAN WALSH AND HUGH GASH

Most of the people with intellectual disabilities alive at the start of this century will grow into middle and old age. Increasingly, they will attend school, live, work, enjoy social life and retire alongside their peers in their own communities. These social changes are the result of government policies in Ireland, the United Kingdom and the rest of Europe, and mirror global trends. In addition, fresh thinking about good practice in providing supports for people with intellectual disabilities is founded on a human rights perspective and in research evidence. Sea changes in policy and practice have swelled demands for new approaches to teaching and professional development. One result is a proliferation of interdisciplinary courses in the field of disabilities at third-level institutions.

The target audience for this book includes an increasing number of students enrolled in interdisciplinary and professional courses in special education at certificate, diploma and degree levels throughout Ireland and the UK. Readers in these groups are the service commissioners, managers, developers, practitioners and evaluators for today and tomorrow. Additional readership includes many students in programmes such as clinical psychology or special education who must have a solid, evidence-based foundation source in the field of intellectual disabilities. Finally, as social inclusion widens, teachers, health-care professionals, service-providers, employers, co-workers and other members of the community are more likely to meet people with intellectual disabilities for perhaps the first time: it is hoped that this book will inform these readers also.

This text is designed to meet the needs of these students by presenting chapters on key issues in this area. It adopts a global perspective yet focuses on the Irish context. Many of the authors work in this area in Ireland or the United Kingdom, where there are often exchanges of ideas about inclusive practice and other issues. The book is organised in three sections.

SETTING THE CONTEXT

The first section focuses on three groups of leading players who define the context of service provision: individuals with intellectual disabilities in society, families and professionals. Bob McCormack has contributed a detailed and valuable history of service provision for people with intellectual disabilities in Ireland. He shows how the initial services were heavily dependent on voluntary organisations and how the State has become increasingly involved in provision of services. McCormack's chapter guides the reader through distinct yet overlapping phases of response to the presence of people with intellectual disabilities in Irish life over the past 250 years.

Roy McConkey (Chapter 3) writes about staff development and support for people with intellectual disabilities. His chapter reminds readers that staff involved in intellectual disability services are a disparate group, ranging from low-paid, untrained staff through to specialists receiving substantial salaries, and working in a vast array of settings. They are diverse, too, in their attitudes, knowledge and experiences of people with intellectual disabilities. McConkey discusses the essential elements for effective staff, and suggests that it is worthwhile to promote their empathy as well as their skills.

Mark Mulrooney and Mark Harrold have written about the expectations of the parents of people with disabilities by letting their voices reach a wide audience through this chapter. Recently, parents in Ireland have sought to redress shortcomings in educational and other service provision for their children through the courts: to date, these issues have yet to be resolved to general satisfaction. Expectations of parents have changed radically over the past generation and this chapter provides insight into parents' difficulties, needs and expectations.

SUPPORTS ACROSS THE LIFESPAN

The second section of the book is concerned with supports across the lifespan. Stephen Kealy writes about the provision and influence of early childhood intervention in this area. It is well known that the timing of intervention has dramatic implications for its effects. Research has shown, for example, that at two years, the more severe the neonatal condition and complications, the greater the deficiencies in development socially, intellectually, and in health. However, the intellectual deficits were closely related to the environmental opportunities: for children in unstable poor families with mothers with low IQ, the group with severe complications were 19–37 IQ points lower than the group with mild or no complications, whereas for children in stable high-SES families, the group with severe complications were only 5–7 IQ points lower than the group with mild or no complications (Werner 1989). Kealy reviews the types of interventions that may be offered to families and proposes strategies for more effective supports for families with young children.

During the 1990s the concept of integrated education shifted to one of inclusive education. The key issue was to conceptualise education as including children who were different. This meant that it was no longer sufficient to have them in the same building, but rather that they should be included as partners in the school's activities. How this takes place is influenced by school policy and the severity of the disability a child experiences. Michael Shevlin from Trinity College Dublin and Barry Carpenter, Sunfield School, England, write about the developments in this area. Teachers now have access to assistants who can help with a child with a disability in the classroom: as recently as 1998 this was not the case. At that time, children with disabilities—children with Down Syndrome, for example—were placed in some schools in ordinary classes without classroom assistants to help them. This situation has dramatically changed for the better in Ireland, as Shevlin and Carpenter describe in this dynamic chapter.

Sexuality is an area that requires great sensitivity and practicality in Ireland for individuals as well as their parents and their carers. Shay Caffrey has given workshops for staff and has experience of working with parents in this area for over a decade. In the past the simple answer was abstinence and separation of men and women with intellectual disabilities. Now, however, with increased opportunities for meeting and forming relationships, it is very important to help people with disabilities to understand how to have more intimate relationships with their partners. Caffrey's chapter is a sensitive, compassionate and insightful discussion of the difficulties and challenges that this topic presents to staff and parents.

This section concludes with a chapter on ageing—a theme with tremendous importance as men and women with intellectual disabilities experience greater life expectancy. Walsh and Conliffe adopt a perspective encompassing older people with intellectual disabilities on the island of Ireland. Their chapter reviews evidence on typical characteristics of older people with intellectual disabilities during the course of their lives, including age-related developmental change. They discuss factors related to healthy ageing of older men and women; well-being and vulnerability; family issues; and effective personal and social supports for individuals in this growing, more visible cohort.

BEST PRACTICE

The third section of the book is devoted to providing examples of best practice in a number of areas. Finding employment of some form or other provides a person with disability with an opportunity to increase their independence and to participate more fully in society. To a certain extent the opportunities depend on the economy and the need for staff. However, the employment of a person with an intellectual disability is often a matter for careful planning and efforts to engage the willing commitment of employers and co-workers. Some companies have policies that facilitate the employment of people with intellectual disabilities. Walsh and Lynch review the policies and trends in developing more inclusive models of employment in a European context, drawing on recent research findings and policy statements.

Policies and trends in employment, concerning sexuality, and in relation to inclusive practice in relation to persons with an intellectual disability all depend on the attitudes of the people in the society. Hugh Gash, with colleagues in Spain at the University of Murcia, presents a series of empirical studies on attitudes towards children with a disability and their education. In Ireland children in ordinary schools have quite positive and sympathetic attitudes towards a child with a disability. However, experience of meeting a child with a disability often results in a differentiation of attitude towards these children. There are variations depending on the type of disability and between Irish and Spanish children. These variations often seem to depend on the opportunities to get to know children with a disability, and also on the quality of the contacts experienced. As part of this chapter parents and adults were also surveyed and their attitudes to inclusive practice were largely positive, though more so for children with a mild disability than for children with Down Syndrome.

John McEvoy has centred his chapter on behavioural supports on the story of Jimmy, a young man whose behaviour threatens to diminish his life opportunities. A central theme of the chapter is that behaviour support is not simply a matter of eliminating problem behaviour: rather, it involves teaching new skills, changing and enriching the environment, and providing increased choice for individuals. The chapter closes with a discussion of some of the implications of adopting behaviour-support principles for carers and service-providers so as to ensure that interventions fit with the person's natural surroundings.

Alan Carr has contributed a chapter written from a family systems perspective. Family dynamics change depending on the constituent members of the family. His chapter adopts a family life-cycle approach and outlines how an integrative model of family therapy may benefit families with a son or daughter who has intellectual disabilities. Intervention may be sought at transitional points within the life cycle marked by events such as the birth of the child, entry into primary school, entry into secondary school, leaving secondary school and launching into adulthood.

The last three chapters of this section provide information on some social, economic and legal issues related to the status of people with intellectual disabilities in society. Emerson, Walsh and colleagues in the UK and Ireland summarise briefly current trends in patterns of residence and present some key research findings related to the quality and costs of residential supports for adults with intellectual disabilities. They conclude that policy-makers should build residential supports with the aim of achieving valued outcomes for individuals in terms of greater opportunities to make choices, to experience healthy ageing in their own communities, and generally to achieve an enhanced quality of life.

Shivaun Quinlivan's chapter on the rights of people with disabilities in Ireland leads with an inspiring statement from Article 1 of the UN Universal Declaration of Human Rights (UN 1948): *All human beings are born free and equal in dignity and rights.* Today, while it may be accepted that people with disabilities hold rights within society in Ireland, grave difficulties remain in translating the rights ideology into enforceable legal rights. Quinlivan's chapter contributes a detailed, illuminating review of recent policy and legislation landmarks in Ireland, offering vital information for all who work in this field.

To bring the book to its close, Gerard Quinn and Anna Bruce address human rights in an international context. In their view, the human rights revolution in the context of disability has to do with making the human being visible. Their chapter outlines the new human rights agenda in the field of disability, particularly how rights may be harnessed to enable people with disabilities to take their place in the mainstream. The authors focus on steps toward a UN Convention on the Rights of Persons with Disabilities. Finally, they set current developments in Ireland within the global context of the human rights agenda.

A WORD ABOUT WORDS

Readers of this book will be aware that diversity and debate thrive in the field of disability about what terms are apt. To give justice to all views is beyond the scope of this book. We have adopted the term *intellectual disabilities*, endorsed in the Irish Government's policy document *Needs and abilities* (1990) and increasingly used internationally. Thus students using this book will see references to publications using *intellectual disabilities* as well as *developmental disabilities, learning disabilities* or—chiefly in the United States—*mental retardation.* We are aware that other terms are preferred in practice in Ireland and respect these preferences.

FOR READERS OF THIS BOOK

Finally, we salute you, the readers of this book, and acknowledge the challenges you meet from all sides. Global bodies urge you to place the human rights of people with intellectual disabilities at the forefront—not always easy where institutional walls hold fast. Regionally, you must strive for greater social and vocational inclusion in an expanding and increasingly diverse Europe. At home, the voices of policy-makers, evaluators and advocates themselves do not always sing in harmony. Calls for fiscal parsimony are constant, and service-providers wonder where the next funding axe will fall. Even within service organisations, some practices may be set in stone and resistant to change even in the light of fresh research evidence. But among you, too, are tomorrow's agents of change, now set on a course to improve the quality of interventions on behalf of people with intellectual disabilities and their families. Our hope is that this book will be a resourceful companion on your journey.

Patricia Noonan Walsh
Hugh Gash
Dublin, April 2003

REFERENCES

Bennett, J., Gash, H. and O'Reilly, M. (1998) Integration as appropriate: segregation where necessary. In Tony Booth and Mel Ainscow (eds), *From Them to Us: an international study of inclusion in education*, 149–64. London. Routledge.
Needs and abilities (1990) Dublin. Government Publications Office.
UN (1948) *Universal Declaration of Human Rights*. New York. United Nations.
Werner, E.E. (1989) High risk children in young adulthood: a longitudinal study from birth to 32 years. *American Journal of Orthopsychiatry* **59**, 72–81.

2. TRENDS IN THE DEVELOPMENT OF IRISH DISABILITY SERVICES[*]

BOB MCCORMACK

INTRODUCTION: DISABILITY—THE IRISH RESPONSE

In reviewing the development of disability services over the past two and a half centuries in one brief chapter the challenge is to balance the detail with the wider picture, to identify the significant developments which took place and to relate these historical developments to the present situation. Indeed, it is a truism to say that we study the past in order to understand the present better.

This chapter sets out to answer the question: How has Irish society responded to individuals with learning disabilities over the past two and a half centuries? We can identify six distinct strands to this response, strands which emerged in the sequence outlined below but in many cases overlapped with each other. Arguably all these strands are evident to this day.

RESPONSE NO. 1: A PROBLEM?

Before Irish society decided to respond to disability in any particular way, it had first to decide that having a disability was a problem—or at least a big enough problem to require a societal response. For centuries children have been born with Down Syndrome and with brain damage. Society responded in various ways—by creating myths to explain the birth of a less-than-perfect child, by keeping the child out of sight in the home, or by letting the young adult wander or fend for itself. Many children with severe impairments did not survive long in a world with poor living conditions, poor hygiene and without antibiotics. Some new-born infants were killed or allowed to die. But it seems that for the majority of children and adults with disabilities a communal, agricultural socie-

---

[*] Some material in this chapter previously appeared in Module 1 of the Open Training College's Diploma in Applied Social Studies.

ty could offer a role, meaningful activity and some level of acceptance. Acceptance was not assured, and the 'village idiot' was presumably a source of fun and ridicule, as in the film *Ryan's daughter*.

But there were accepted roles—the visually impaired travelling musician, illustrated by the eighteenth-century O'Carolan; the hearing-impaired tailor; and so on. (Today a comparable role is that of telephone switchboard operator.) The shock and genetic insults—'there was always a weakness in that family'— were mitigated by supporting myths such as the changeling which the fairies put in place of the real infant, as in Yeats's poem *The stolen child*, and the old wives' tales of frights in late pregnancy.

Being a slow learner only came into focus as a problem with the advent of universal elementary education from the 1830s on, following the establishment of the national school system in Ireland. Only then could a child be sent home for failing to master basic academic skills—a formal and public judgement of learning disability before IQ tests were even thought of.

Once the focus is on disability, it seems to be difficult to be ordinary. The person tended to be viewed quite negatively, or extremely positively—a devil or an angel. The middle ground was unavailable.

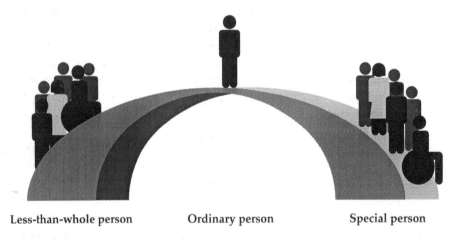

Less-than-whole person   Ordinary person   Special person

Fig. 1—Public perceptions of people with learning disabilities.

Families struggled to cope with having a son or daughter with a disability. Overlap and confusion between disabilities was rife. In practical terms, the difference between a frustrated, aggressive and destructive son with learning difficulties and a son with mental health problems may have seemed somewhat academic. Coping strategies were not always admirable; one nineteenth-century commission witness reported finding a man kept in a hole in the kitchen floor of a cottage, covered over with a strong wicker basket (Kirkpatrick 1931); one poor Dublin woman chained her imbecile child to a bed while she went to work every day to support the two of them (Robins 1992). The more docile individuals were sometimes allowed to wander, begging, and according to one nineteenth-century report were 'often teased, often goaded to frenzy by thoughtless children, often the victims of ill-treatment' (Robins 1986, 165).

On the other hand, there were some tough characters who were well able to look out for themselves. One such eighteenth-century Dublin character was Billy in the Bowl (Moylan 1938). Billy had no legs and, using a large wooden bowl, propelled himself around with his hands; he was accused of robbery and successfully eluded capture on at least one occasion.

Some children with obvious learning disabilities did attend ordinary schools, as Clifford's 1930s study of north Dublin city schools demonstrates. Undoubtedly some became the class dunce rather than the village idiot, vulnerable to a cruel teacher and mocking classmates. In a period when teachers were judged on the academic performance of their pupils, 'backward' children with disabilities were hardly welcomed (Clifford 1940).

RESPONSE NO. 2: A SOCIAL PROBLEM?

Two hundred years ago Ireland had just undergone a twenty-year boom period under Grattan's Parliament. Most of Georgian Dublin's fine squares and public buildings, including James Gandon's Custom House, were built in this period. But the prosperity of the city brought its own problems, with a growing number of 'vagabonds and sturdy beggars' roaming the streets, pestering—and sometimes even threatening—the wealthy citizens with their demands for money. The city fathers responded by opening the Dublin House of Industry in 1773, and wagons were sent out to round up these healthy beggars, resulting in some lively encounters between bailiffs and beggars!

The House of Industry was hardly open when ten cells were set apart for lunatics and idiots, who soon formed a significant proportion of the inmates. A few years later an adjoining bridewell (prison) was taken over, and the infamous 'Hardwicke cells' were located there.

The Dublin House of Industry in North Brunswick Street was a typical catch-all institution, a one-stop solution to every social problem: a place for beggars, for the ill, the disabled, the destitute and the troublesome.

Of course there were other catch-all institutions in this period—the prisons (bridewells and marshalseas), the poorhouses and later the workhouses, and the asylums. In one early Dublin reference to individuals with specific disabilities, it was reported that in 1774 there were 'one mad woman, one foolish ditto, one ditto subject to fits and one boy fool' in James's Street bridewell (Moylan 1938).

In one of the key decisions of the early nineteenth century, the Westminster parliament decided not to offer 'outdoor relief' in Ireland. If you were destitute, the only way you could get help from the State was to enter a workhouse; as long as you stayed at home, you could receive no help. There were 163 workhouses in Ireland by the time of the Great Hunger. Families were split up, with

Part of the Celbridge workhouse, one of the three Kildare workhouses.

separate sections for men, women and children. Each workhouse had a small number of 'lunatic cells' at the back of the complex for those who needed to be restrained.

By the end of the nineteenth century there were 22 'distinct lunatic asylums', each with a catchment area of one or two counties. These resembled Goffman's 'total institution', where both the inmates and the staff lived, with no interaction with the outside world. This isolation removed outside influences; it gave the keepers unchecked powers and it allowed abuses to thrive. It also allowed society to be happily ignorant of how fellow human beings were being treated, to continue to under-resource these institutions, to blame keepers and inmates for their lot, and to ignore the need for change. The following description of the Limerick House of Industry in 1805 reflects the horror of a visitor from the outside world:

> '... under the roof of this house, I saw madmen stark naked, girded only by their irons, standing in the rain, in an open court ... their cells upon the ground-floor, scantily supplied with straw, damp and ill-secured' (Carr 1806, 412).

Another visitor described the facilities 'as we would not think appropriate for dog kennels' (Spring Rice 1817, 12). Their outrage was shared by others and some reforms were implemented.

The under-funding, segregation and isolation which characterised the nineteenth-century institutions continue right up to the present in some cases.

> 'A [women's] dormitory with seven beds had no curtains. Many patients were in bed for the night at the time of our visit, 5:15 p.m. Another dormitory housed ten patients and was also without curtains . . . on the opposite wall a structure had been erected in which five patients were separately incarcerated. Each unit was roofed in the manner of a stall and each door was closed by three farmyard bolts. Mattresses were generally on the floor. These units did not have external windows or fresh air . . .
>
> The Dining Room is a vast high-roofed structure which seats 200 at one sitting . . . the overall impression is one of anonymity, vastness and gloom . . . Potatoes, of poor quality, had been placed on the tables even though patients had not by then begun to take their places . . . The use of plastic cups, saucers and plates of inferior quality serves only to worsen a bad situation. No effort was made to make eating an enjoyable experience. Milk and sugar are frequently included with the tea in the pot' (Our Lady's Hospital Cork 1990, 22).

This report of the Inspector of Mental Hospitals, Dr Dermot Walsh, on Our

The Richmond Lunatic Asylum (later part of St Brendan's Hospital, Grangegorman), built at the back of the Dublin House of Industry—part of the process of specialisation.

Lady's Hospital Cork, which he visited on 8–10 February 1988, reminds us that almost two centuries have not changed the vulnerability of dependent people with disabilities.

The phrase 'put away'—whether into a prison or an institution—implies being forgotten about, taken charge of by keepers (Glouberman 1990). Dealing with a social problem by putting it away, handing over your child to the keepers, left no role for the family, for neighbours or friends, or for the local community. Life 'on the inside' was different; it bore no relationship to life on the outside. This black-and-white segregation continued in disability services until the first parent-and-friend groups started in the late 1950s. The first day-attender in Stewart's Hospital started almost a century after the institution opened. Even as late as 1974, 41% of those living in Irish residential centres were rarely or never visited by anyone (Mulcahy and Ennis 1974).

It is worth reflecting on the upset and heartbreak such 'putting away' caused both families and the persons themselves—a sense of being utterly abandoned, suddenly bereft of family and friends, of familiar places and routines, of individuality and personal choices. Staff coped by assuming that the person would 'settle in' after a time.

One of the earlier reasons for putting people with disabilities away was based on an assumption of promiscuity, a fear that women with learning disabilities would encourage sexual advances and have numerous children, all of

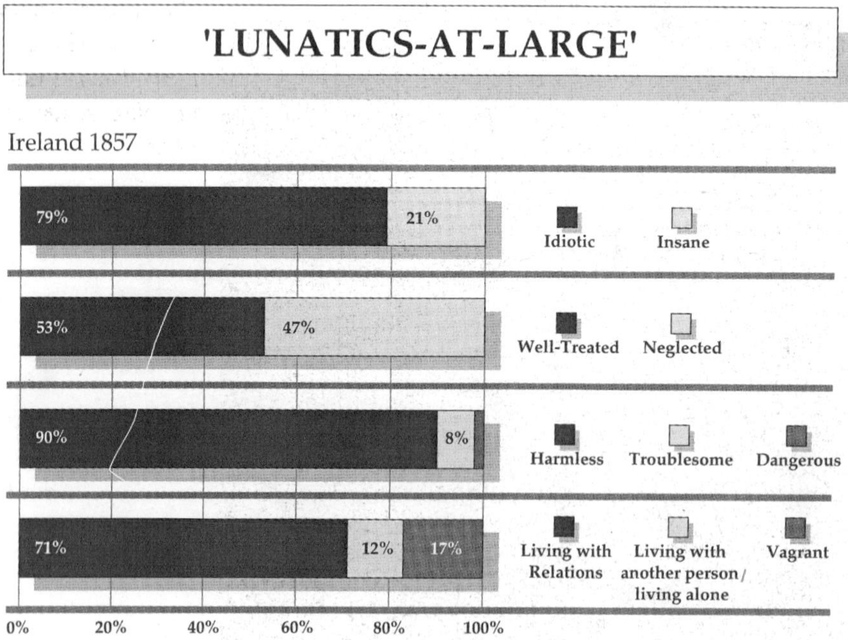

Fig. 2—State of lunatics at large in Ireland, 1857.

whom would be of low ability. Recent revelations in Sweden and the United States show that sterilisation of sexually active women with disabilities was a State policy for many years (Cleary 1997). It was seen as a choice between sterilisation and segregation as the preferred means of controlling the breeding of the 'unfit' (Radford 1991).

RESPONSE NO. 3: A SPECIAL PROBLEM?

During the 1850s a focus on the 'special' needs of idiots and mental defectives developed. In the only examination of the state of 'lunatics at large' during that century, the Commissioners on Lunacy presented their analysis of the situation in 1857, summarised in Fig. 2.

It is notable that the position of people with learning disabilities living in the community ten years after the Great Famine was not universally bleak, despite no support, funding or expertise. Fewer than one in five were vagrant, and only one in ten were considered troublesome or dangerous.

Interest in learning disabilities at this time was partly influenced by the

The Stewart Institute relocated to Lord Donaghmore's estate in Palmerstown in 1879.

development of small facilities in England for idiotic children, which followed on from the work of Itard and Seguin in France. The early facilities had a strong instructional focus and a belief that 'the idiot can be cured'—or at least be taught to lead a useful life.

In Ireland, a few prominent Dublin citizens lobbied for government funding and for public subscriptions to set up an institution in Ireland; these included the Quaker philanthropist Jonathan Pim; Lord Charlemont; Cheyne Brady, a governor of the Meath Hospital; and George Kidd, a physician at the Coombe Hospital. Pamphlets were published and some funds were raised in Dublin and Belfast for a national Protestant institution, but the project only got off the ground when Dr Henry Hutchinson Stewart, the last governor of the Dublin House of Industry, handed over to the committee the lease on part of his private asylum at Lucan and a donation of £4000. The Stewart Institution for Idiotic and Imbecile Children opened in 1869, and moved to its present site in Palmerstown ten years later. Four teachers were appointed and a programme of instruction drawn up.

The Stewart Institution was intended for about 100 'educable' imbecile children; the assumption was that, following training, they would return at eighteen to their families. Because it depended on voluntary donations, donors were allowed to nominate or 'elect' children to be sent to the institution. Over time, more severely disabled children were elected, despite the exhortations of the governors, and most children did not return home at eighteen. Accordingly, few vacancies arose.

Within the lunatic asylums a different debate went on, mostly about the spiralling numbers being admitted into the asylums and the costs of maintaining them there. While asylums were financed from central funds, workhouses were supported by local rates. So while the Boards of Guardians of the workhouses were happy to move any 'lunatics' on to the district asylum (more than 1000 were moved in 1904), the government proposed providing less expensive care for incurable lunatics—mostly people with learning disabilities. They suggested auxiliary asylums, but only in Cork was the suggestion taken up, when Youghal opened. In Dublin, Portrane opened at the turn of the century as an overflow asylum from Grangegorman, taking mainly 'incurables'. In most asylums the incurables were put into the back wards and the poorest accommodation—a primitive form of specialisation.

More than 50 years passed before a second special institution opened. From 1892 the Daughters of Charity had run the workhouse school in Cabra in Dublin. While the workhouses were abolished by the new Free State government in 1922, the Cabra school remained open and in 1926 there were more than 500 children there, 53 of whom had a learning disability. At the suggestion of Archbishop Byrne, and following negotiations with the new government, the Daughters agreed to make it a home and school for children with learning disabilities (Robins 1992).

The Daughters of Charity took over nearby properties in Clonsilla (1943) and

The workhouse school in Cabra became the first Catholic institution in 1926.

the Guinness house in Glenmaroon (1950). Other religious orders followed, and special centres were opened by the St John of God order at Blackrock (1931), Stamullen (1942), Drumcar (1946) and Celbridge (1952); by the Brothers of Charity at Glanmire outside Cork (1939) and Kilcornan near Galway (1952); by the Sisters of La Sagesse in County Sligo (1955); and by the Sisters of Charity of Jesus and Mary at Delvin in Westmeath (1954).

Specialisation
The development of special centres marked the start of a process of specialisation. Special centres and special schools required specialised staff, and the drive for specialisation got under way in earnest in the 1960s with the development of a range of new professions—mental handicap registered nurses, special teachers, occupational therapists, speech therapists and physiotherapists, in addition to the small but growing number of psychiatrists, psychologists and social workers working in the learning disability services. Various therapies were devised and special equipment required—therapy pools, multisensory rooms, and so on.

The underlying assumption in this drive towards specialisation was that people with learning disabilities had special needs—so much so that these words became a catch-phrase, especially in Britain. But is the assumption true? Surely people with a disability have the same needs as everyone else—for somewhere to live, for a job, for an income, for friends and for intimacy. In other words, people with disability have ordinary needs but often need support in having these ordinary needs met.

The growth of the professions

1958: University College Dublin course in Applied Psychology started; by 1960 there were four recognised university courses. By 1982 more than a third of psychologists employed in the health and education areas were employed by learning disability agencies.

1960: First mental handicap nurses registered from St Joseph's Clonsilla and St Mary's Drumcar nursing schools; by 1979, 975 nurses were working in mental handicap organisations and a further 470 were in training. By the 1980s, ten nursing schools had been established in residential institutions.

1961: The Special Education Diploma course was established in St Patrick's College, Drumcondra. By 1984, 522 teachers had obtained the Diploma.

1961: NAMHI, the National Association for the Mentally Handicapped of Ireland, was founded as an umbrella group for the voluntary agencies; within a year there were 23 affiliated organisations.

1961: The government Commission of Inquiry was set up; it published its report in 1965, proposing a major expansion of special education provision.

1963: The College of Occupational Therapy was established by the National Organisation for Rehabilitation (later the NRB). In 1974 there were six OTs working in learning disability services; 183 were employed by 1981.

1969: College of Speech Therapy, later to become the School of Speech and Language, was established at Trinity College.

In common usage, 'special' either means better than usual or second-rate. In disability services, the term means different and less desirable. In other words, parents of average children are not trying to get them into special schools; indeed, parents of children with learning disabilities are in some instances looking for access to ordinary schools, despite the better pupil–teacher ratio, better resourcing and more highly qualified staff in special schools.

In a religious context, special meant apart. The religious perspective presented the special child as innocent, angel-like and close to God, as seen in their spontaneity and lack of responsibility for their actions. In working with people with learning disabilities, religious orders imbued their services with the desirable qualities of religious life—removed from the hustle and bustle of everyday life, freed from the cares and distractions of ordinary living. The country manor houses purchased between 1930 and 1955 would have suited equally for a religious community, with their removed, peaceful settings. In services modelled on the religious life, 'secular' contact was not valued.

The Camphill communities have incorporated some of the values of the religious communities and some of the values of a shared communal life, in which everyone's contribution is needed and valued in a shared, accepting, egalitarian community.

One of the effects of specialisation was the disempowerment of the family, who were expected to unquestioningly accept the advice of the expert; indeed, teams of up to ten experts frequently sat around the table deciding what was best for a child or adult in the absence of parents or family members. The shortage of 'places' in services meant that parents were expected to feel grateful for whatever was offered and to accept that everyone was 'doing their best'. The result was sometimes a struggle between the family, the individual and the various professionals. Sometimes it seemed that the agency 'owned' the person, even assuming that they had the final say. In any event, families were easily overawed in the face of professional pronouncements.

RESPONSE NO. 4: A LOCAL PROBLEM?

The development of Parent and Friend Associations began in 1955 with the placing of a personal notice in the *Irish Times* by a Mrs Farrell, a well-to-do Westmeath parent with a young son with learning disabilities who was frustrated by the fact that there were no daytime educational or remedial facilities available for children whose parents did not wish them to be admitted to one of the few existing institutions, all of which had long waiting-lists. She arranged a meeting in the tearooms of the Savoy Cinema to which nine or ten people came; further meetings were held in the ICA's Country Shop on St Stephen's Green. Patricia Farrell was encouraged by barrister and Dáil member Declan Costello and advised by Lady Valerie Goulding to hold a press conference, at which she announced a public meeting for interested parties in Dublin's Mansion House. To their surprise, 186 people—mostly parents—attended the meeting. A committee was formed and the Association of Parents and Friends of Mentally Handicapped Children was set up as 'a strictly non-sectarian lay organisation' (Robinson 1987).

Two years later, in response to a local polio epidemic, an Association was established in Cork to provide after-care facilities. In 1959, when this epidemic had waned, the Cork Polio and General Aftercare Association (now the COPE Foundation) extended its activities to provide for children with brain damage or mental handicap in Cork city and county.

The 1960s saw a remarkable growth in similar local groups, in Mayo, Galway, Longford, Wexford, Kildare and elsewhere (see Ryan 1999). In Newbridge, Dan and Mary O'Donovan 'discovered through extensive enquiries that there were no facilities available in the locality which could cater for their daughter' (Weller

---

Getting off the ground

'In the autumn of 1965 a one-year-old child, Tom Fallon Junior, was diagnosed as being severely mentally handicapped at the Children's Hospital, Crumlin, Dublin. His father, Mr Tom Fallon, an insurance representative in the Castlebar area, was advised by the medical social worker, a Miss Sonia Smyth, to go back to Mayo and form a "Parents and Friends Association" which might make a start on the provision of some services for the mentally handicapped in the county.

Just at this time, Johnny Mee (later a Castlebar Urban Councillor), as a parent of a mentally handicapped child, sent a letter to *The Connaught Telegraph* newspaper, calling for the formation of such an organisation. These two parents went to see Mr Michael Egan of Mountainview, Castlebar, who also had a mentally handicapped child.

All three decided to call a public meeting in Castlebar early in January 1966 to test local opinion and try to get an organisation off the ground. Tremendous work was done prior to this meeting. Local children distributed the St John of God Brothers' Football Pools each week; printed notices were stapled to the Results Sheets each week telling people of their intentions and providing information on mental handicap. Two hundred letters of invitation were sent to people of influence and community workers in Castlebar. A draft constitution for the new organisation was prepared.

There was a gratifying attendance at the meeting in the Imperial Hotel on the night of 10th January 1966. Many were unable to get into the double lounge of the hotel. Mr John Garavan (now a District Justice) chaired the meeting. The draft constitution was adopted and "The Association of Parents and Friends of Mentally Handicapped Children in Mayo" was formed' (Carney 1981, 14–15).

1992, 9). They spoke to their friends about the problem, they made contact with other parents who found themselves in a similar position, and they spoke with the county Chief Medical Officer. The first meeting took place in their home at 13 Ballymany Park. Support was forthcoming from many local organisations and groups, including the local army barracks.

The involvement of local communities was strong during this pioneer stage. Almost immediately, a 3-day-week school started in the local GAA hall (which was given free of charge); there were 'around 30 drivers, mostly women, who came in the mornings with the children and went back with them in the afternoons' (Weller 1992, 12); local sheep-farmers subsequently waived their grazing rights to enable a school to be built on the Curragh (with the agreement of the Minister for Defence and the County Council).

Within six years the County Kildare Association, KARE, had eighteen branches and 4000 members. Today KARE has 22 local branches throughout the county and its board consists of two representatives selected by each branch.

This kind of local initiative involved the 'coming out' of many families—highlighting the fact that their child had a disability—and a search for local support. The first priority was to raise some funds, and in many organisations this became the dominant role of parent-and-friend groups. But the local nature of these organisations created grass-roots support and greatly heightened the awareness of learning disability. This in turn politicised the issue, resulting in statutory funding for these local groups. In 1961 Declan Costello, then a leading young politician and president of the Dublin Association, tabled a Private Member's Bill in the Dáil on learning disability, in turn prompting the first government inquiry into the issue since the establishment of the state.

In time, the recreational needs of young adults with learning disabilities were recognised. The first ARCH Club started in 1977 in Dundrum; six years later there were thirteen such clubs up and running. CASA (Caring and Sharing Association) Clubs spread around the same time, with fourteen clubs throughout Dublin and around the country. In 1983 the CASA organisation took 150 individuals and helpers to Lourdes at a cost of £70,000.

RESPONSE NO. 5: NO PROBLEM!

The move from the institutional homes located behind walls or in isolated manor houses to the use of the local town hall for people with disabilities heralded a significant shift in thinking—from protecting people to accepting people.

In reality the shift was less dramatic and more illusory because the model

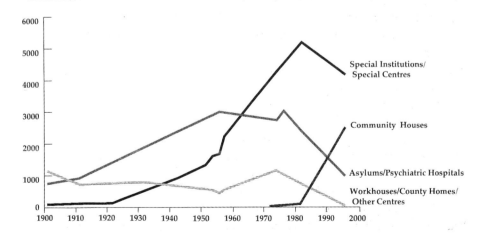

Fig. 3—Out-of-family provision for people with learning disabilities in the twentieth century.[1]

The language debate

An early term for someone with a learning disability was 'fool' and is found in Dublin in 1774 in phrases such as 'a boy fool' or 'a foolish woman'. We still use the phrase 'a foolish person', meaning someone lacking common sense. We also use the phrase 'playing the fool', meaning pretending to be a fool.

This reminds us of the common dramatic device of the court jester or fool, found, for example, in Shakespeare's *King Lear*. Here the fool is saying important things to the king in a light-hearted way so as not to offend him, obliquely commenting on the king's poor judgement, and later trying to lift him out of his despair.

Sometimes the term is set in juxtaposition to madness, as in Swift's quatrain: 'He gave the little Wealth he had / To build a House for Fools and Mad', effectively distinguishing between learning disabilities and mental health problems. This distinction goes back to fifth-century Irish Brehon law, which provided different penalties for leading a fool or a madman into trouble (drunkenness, pregnancy, or stealing). In English law, the *De Praerogitiva Regis* (1325) of King Edward II made separate arrangements for the estates of fools and madmen based on the congenital and permanent nature of the fool's condition.

Later English law dealt mainly with the insane, and the early medical distinction was between curables and incurables, the latter including individuals with learning disabilities, on whom less resources and effort should be spent!

The term 'idiot', from the Greek word meaning a private person, has found a colloquial form in Ireland in phrases such as 'acting the eejit', which has similar connotations to 'playing the fool'. Both 'fool' and 'idiot' still have a familiar ring to them, though we seldom now make the connection with learning disability.

Later terms such as 'moron' and 'imbecile' are still commonly used by teenagers to berate their peers; they are found in Victorian legislation and government reports and, when used in the context of learning disability, seem very dated. The terms 'feeble-minded', 'dullard' and 'defectives' seem more quaint and offensive to modern ears and did not enter into popular usage in the same way as earlier terms.

In the nineteenth century, the term 'lunatic' was sometimes used to refer to both people with mental health problems and those with learning disabilities. The phrase

being aspired to was still that of the specialised service. It was not until the early 1980s that the writings of Wolf Wolfensberger and John O'Brien were to reach an Irish audience, most effectively through the week-long PASS courses. This American influence was complemented by a powerful series of policy documents emanating from the King's Hospital Fund in London—the 'Ordinary Life' series (1980; 1984). These publications challenged the assumption that people had 'special needs' which could not be met in ordinary settings.

This questioning of the efficacy of special provision had started more than a decade earlier with two seminal papers from the US on the poor outcomes of special education pupils with mild learning disabilities (Johnson 1962; Dunne 'lunatics at large' meant people not in asylums, workhouses, prisons or other institutions—mostly individuals with learning disabilities.

A new category of learning disability came to the fore around the turn of the century. 'Moral defectives' could include anyone whose social behaviour was at odds with accepted social norms. Unmarried women who became pregnant were a prime target, and well as any unruly member of the family.

This new category was probably influenced by the eugenic movement of the period, which raised concerns through pseudo-scientific studies about the likelihood of parents with mild learning disabilities having large families, all of whom would have similar problems, thus leading to widespread 'degeneracy', both moral and intellectual. Owing to the lack of special provision in Ireland in the early part of the twentieth century, and the political preoccupation of the period with Irish nationalism, the concept was not widely used here, though the treatment of young single mothers throughout the first half of the twentieth century was secretive and shameful, with forced adoptions and other abuses.

In the mid-twentieth century, terms such as 'mentally subnormal' and 'educationally subnormal' were common in the UK, to be followed by 'mentally handicapped', 'mentally retarded' (USA), and 'intellectually disabled' (Australia). Since the early 1990s the terms 'learning difficulties' and 'learning disabilities' have been in common use, though Irish government reports since *Needs and abilities* use the more awkward term 'intellectual disability'.

In more recent times the language has perhaps been kinder and the intentions good, but as Wolfensberger (1975) has pointed out, a different set of assumptions has been promoted—the person with a learning disability as a holy innocent, a burden of charity, an object of pity and an eternal child. These images have often unconsciously been reinforced by the names of services and centres—St Michael's House, Sunbeam House, Holy Angels, and so on. The public must also have been confused by the changes in clientele (usually from psychiatric services to learning disability services) and the confusing titles of some services (McCormack 1986).

1969). However, the King's Fund papers went considerably further; they argued that an ordinary life was an aspiration for everyone, irrespective of the severity of their disability. The assumptions of the 'ordinary life' philosophy were that individuals with learning disabilities:

- have the same needs as everyone else;
- need support in having their needs met.

This philosophy was developing in some areas. By 1981 there were 97 pre-schools in Ireland which had at least one child with a disability; a speech disorder was the most common disability, followed by a learning disability (Hayes and McConkey 1981). In the same year there were 241 individuals living in houses in the community (Mulcahy and Reynolds 1984); four years later this figure had more than doubled (Kellegher *et al.* 1990).

Many families wished their son or daughter to remain at home, but the lack of support systems—planned breaks, home help and so on—meant that the State has abused these families who desperately needed help. This abuse of families, especially mothers, continues to this day and is exacerbated by the lack of suitable places for their son or daughter to live (Woods 1997).

The human rights debate

It has been suggested that the disability rights movement is the last of the great civil rights movements of our time. These started with the rights of workers and the trade union movement in the early part of the century, and continued with the women's rights movement (the suffragettes and the later feminist movement) and the gay rights movement. It is only in the last decade or so that people with disabilities have publicly protested for the first time in this country.

The right of people with disabilities to a service from the State, for example, is only now being addressed. Recent Supreme Court cases have established the right to a public education for every child, irrespective of their degree of impairment (O'Donoghue v. Department of Education, 1993; Synott v. Department of Education, 2000). Dependence on charity and on fund-raised monies demeans people while wasting the energies and commitment of local communities. Anti-discrimination legislation is now in place (Ireland, Office of the Director of Equality Investigations 1998; Ireland, Office of the Director of Equality Investigations 2000) and a Disabilities Act is promised which will help establish clear rights in relation to public transport, employment and other areas.

RESPONSE NO. 6: YOUR PROBLEM!

The disability movement has developed considerably in the past decade. Those with physical and sensory disabilities have led the way in developing their own analysis of society's response to their disability. People with disabilities have invested hugely in accommodating themselves to society as it presently operates. Now they are arguing that people with disabilities are not the problem, that non-disabled society is the problem through its fear and ignorance, its unwillingness to accommodate people with disabilities in its public and private life— public buildings that are not accessible, inaccessible public transport, inaccessible public and private housing, inflexible public services and discriminatory employment practices.

In effect what people with disabilities are saying is that society has a problem being comfortable with disability and it should start to acknowledge that. The model being proposed here is not just integration (meaning 'to make whole') but to have no fracturing in the first place. An inclusive society is one in which it is OK to be different, where standardisation and conformity are not the passports to full citizenship. In an inclusive society, diversity is welcomed and valued.

This perspective is part of a much wider response from a wide variety of groups to the increasing social stratification of Irish life, which now has increasing ethnic diversity, rising unemployment, public housing shortages and a widening gap between an increasingly affluent and self-satisfied middle class and a marginalised, unemployed or low-paid class.

In this context the development of 'community' is increasingly spoken of and the notion of 'social capital' has given the concept economic validity (Putnam 2000). In Ireland, the opportunity to maintain and develop local community spirit and practice is still there—but for how much longer?

This reversal of focus—from the individual to society—is a sign of the increasing self-empowerment of people with disabilities.

For society to begin to listen to people with disabilities, it must find the source of the voice. Who speaks for people with disabilities? Too often it is still professionals; only recently have people with learning disabilities begun to claim the microphone; only now are they gaining the confidence and experience to speak more freely—not just in the media, but to the professionals and agencies which were set up to support them. Determining the design and delivery of the services they want is still an aspiration for most people with learning disabilities (Atkinson *et al.* 1997).

And that is the biggest challenge currently facing staff in agencies—how to give service-users the primary say in what support is provided and how it is to be provided.

AN EVOLVING MODEL OF SERVICE

Looking back on the various trends which have shaped provision in Ireland, what kind of service provision is now emerging? The short answer is that it is too early to define this emerging model, but the recent trends in service development have the potential to coalesce into a new model of service for which the underpinning principles are as follows.

1. The service is delivered locally

Just as any other person living in any town in Ireland might hope to go to school locally, get a job fairly close by, and have their social life largely centred in the town, so would someone with a disability expect to have most of their needs met locally. Indeed, someone with a disability has more reason to focus locally because of the presence of family and neighbours, transport difficulties, and the importance of being supported informally by people who know them.

2. The service views the individual in a holistic way

The service supports the individual in any aspect of his or her life where support is needed and sought. The traditional divisions between what you do during the day and what you do in the evening are gone; it is not a nine-to-five service. Similarly, support staff work closely together whether they support the person in their working, leisure or living arrangements.

3. The service is designed afresh for each individual

As each person with a disability is unique, their interests and aspirations, the difficulties they have and the help they need may be very individual. A personal planning system, such as Personal Futures Planning (Mount 1994) or Personal Outcomes Planning (Council on Quality and Leadership 1998), offers a tool to design individual services rather than designing services for groups of people. To be effective, it assumes a central role for the individual and his/her family, and support from unpaid or other-paid individuals (neighbours, friends, community workers, etc.).

4. The service is delivered by people, not by places

Wherever someone is being supported, that is where the service is happening at that time. In youth service literature, 'boot-strap' services refer to services without specific buildings or facilities—if a youth worker meets a teenager for coffee in a coffee-shop to discuss how they are getting on in their new job, then that is where the service is being delivered. One way of ensuring that the service happens in ordinary places is not to own a 'special' place. With the advent of mobile phones, and operating a very local patch, this model becomes more feasible.

5. The service is for everyone

It is not just for a certain age range or level of disability. The service aspires to support everyone with a disability in the defined local area—children, adults, older people, wheelchair-users. The word 'aspires' is used advisedly, as it is far more challenging to deliver this model for individuals with more severe or multiple disabilities.

6. The service is in a support role

Commonly professionals decide what is to be offered to any family or individual. The options are limited—often there is only one option on offer: 'We have a place at the moment in … which we can offer your son/daughter if they were to take it now'! A combination of shortages in services and an inflexible model have reduced choices to a 'you're-lucky-we-happen-to-have-a-place' approach, even with the best will in the world.

7. The service is managed locally

The service has strong local roots and is strongly identified with a geographic patch, both by the paid staff of the service and by the local community. This requires a high degree of local autonomy; in other words, the local service manager makes day-to-day decisions without getting clearance from outside, while operating within well-defined parameters in terms of budgets and accounting procedures, personnel policy, and a clearly stated value system.

8. The service promotes community development

Traditionally, agencies have seen community facilities and services as opportunities to be used for the benefit of the individuals they work with. In this emerging model, the service is involved in give and take; it has such a vested interest in the local community that it contributes to its development. In other words, if an individual wanted to go plane-spotting every Sunday morning, the local service might help to bring together a plane-spotting group where none existed. If it owned a meeting-room, it would make it available to other community groups when not in use.

This emerging model, described as the Local Support Service (McCormack 1997), hands power back to families and individuals, and provides more alternatives through using existing ordinary services and through allowing more creativity in how we deploy people and resources.

The Local Support Service model draws on service developments which have taken place in Irish services over the past decade or more. Almost all elements of the model have already been implemented in services. For example, agencies support large numbers of pre-school children attending local playgroups and pre-schools; they support a growing number of children attending their local primary school and, in some instances, second–level schools; they have encouraged or supported teenagers attending mainstream CERT, FAS and FETAC training courses; and they are supporting a large number of young adults in finding and keeping work in ordinary workplaces, living in apartments, flats or shared accommodation, and attending evening classes, clubs and other leisure interests.

What makes the Local Support Service a model is that it brings all these disparate elements together in a coherent way. In other words, it offers model coherency. This means that the diverse elements brought together in this model are compatible with one another and are mutually supportive. In all cases the 'service' happens in ordinary places with people who don't have disabilities, and people not employed by the agency are a significant part of the service—as teachers, instructors, co-workers, neighbours, acquaintances or friends. Agencies don't 'own' the service, they support it.

The strength of this emerging model is that it avoids mixing new approaches with old approaches which are at odds with each other, pulling in opposite directions or cancelling out the impact each strand might have. By implementing a model in which philosophy, values and practice are explicit, agreed and in unison, the maximum impact is achieved.

SUMMARY

The response of Irish society to people with learning disability has evolved through six phases over the past two and a half centuries. This response developed from no provision or support whatever to placement in catch-all institutions such as prisons, workhouses and asylums. There followed specialised services to meet 'special needs' by increasingly specialised staff. Paralleling and overlapping with this was the development of locally based parent-and-friend groups around the country. Recent years have seen the evolution of some integrated and inclusive services, with increasingly articulate service-users who are beginning to challenge Irish society on its acceptance of people with disabilities.

Recent trends in service development point to the emergence of a new coherent model, the Local Support Service, whereby an inclusive, holistic service is managed and delivered locally, designed afresh for each individual, with a focus on people rather than buildings, and in which the agency supports local community development in the interests of the individuals with disabilities who live there.

REFERENCES

Atkinson, D., Jackson, M. and Walmsley, J. (1997) *Forgotten lives: exploring the history of learning disability.* Kidderminster. British Institute of Learning Disabilities.

Byrne, M.M. (1979) The origins and development of services for the mentally handicapped in Ireland 1700–1960, with special reference to educational provision. Unpublished M.A. thesis, Education Dept, UCD.

Carney, T.J. (1981) The development of treatment and services for the mentally handicapped in County Mayo. Unpublished M.Ed. thesis, UCG.

Carr, J. (1806) *The stranger in Ireland; or a tour in the southern and western parts of that country in the year 1805.* London. T. Gillet for Richard Phillips.

Cleary, C. (1997) Dark shadow on a 'model' state. *The Irish Times* (30 August 1997), 10.

Clifford, L. (1940) Investigations into the incidence of mental deficiency among Dublin school children. *Journal of the Statistical and Social Inquiry Society of Ireland* **16**, 29–48.

Council on Quality and Leadership (1998) *Planning with Personal Outcomes.* Towson, MD. Council on Quality and Leadership.

Dáil Report, 19/11/1957 Minister for Health reply to Dáil question.

Department of Health (1965) *Report of the Commission of Inquiry on Mental Handicap.* Dublin. Stationery Office.

Department of Health (1990) *Needs and abilities: report of the Review Group on Mental Handicap Services.* Dublin. Stationery Office.

Department of Health (1992) *Green Paper on Mental Health.* Dublin. Stationery Office.

Department of Health (1994) *Shaping a healthier future: a strategy for effective healthcare in the 1990s.* Dublin. Stationery Office.

Dunne, L. (1969) Special education for the mildly retarded—is much of it justifiable? *Exceptional Children* **35** (1), 5–22.

Glouberman, S. (1990) *Keepers: inside stories from total institutions.* London. King Edward's Hospital Fund for London.

Hayes, N. and McConkey, R. (1981) The informal integration of pre-school children with handicaps: a national survey. Unpublished report. Dublin. St Michael's House Research.

Ireland, Office of the Director of Equality Investigations (1998) *Employment Equality Act 1998.* Dublin. Office of the Director of Equality Investigations.

Ireland, Office of the Director of Equality Investigations (2000) *Equal Status Act 2000.* Dublin. Office of the Director of Equality Investigations.

Johnson, G.O. (1962) Special education for the mentally handicapped—a paradox. *Exceptional Children* **8**, 62–9.

Kellegher, A., Kavanagh, D. and McCarthy, M. (1990) *Home together: a study of* community based residences in Ireland for people with mental handicap. Dublin. Medico-Social Research Board.

King's Hospital Fund (1980) *An ordinary life.* Project Paper No. 24. London. King's Hospital Fund.

King's Hospital Fund (1984) *An ordinary working life.* Project Paper No. 50. London. King's Hospital Fund.

Kirkpatrick, T.P.C. (1931) *A note on the history of the care of the insane in Ireland.* Dublin University Press.

McCormack, B. (1986) Facing up to and removing organisational barriers to full participation and equality. In *Full participation and equality—the realities,* 67–75. Dublin. Union of Voluntary Organisations for the Handicapped.

McCormack, B. (1997) Developing a new service in north County Dublin: a preliminary proposal. Unpublished report. Dublin. St Michael's House Research.

Mount, B. (1994) *Making futures happen: a manual for facilitators of personal futures planning.* St Paul, MN. Minnesota Governor's Planning Council on Developmental Disabilities.

Moylan, T.K. (1938) Vagabonds and sturdy beggars. *Dublin Historical Record* **1** (3), 65–73.

Mulcahy, M. and Ennis, B. (1974) *Census of the mentally handicapped in the Republic of Ireland (residential).* Dublin. Medico-Social Research Board.

Mulcahy, M. and Reynolds, A. (1984) *Census of the mentally handicapped in the Republic of Ireland 1981.* Dublin. Medico-Social Research Board.

Mulvaney, F. (2001) *National Intellectual Disability Database, annual report, 2000.* Dublin. Health Research Board.

O'Donoghue v. Department of Education, Ireland. (HC) O'Hanlon, J. Judgement delivered 27 May 1993.

Our Lady's Hospital Cork—February 1988. In *Frontline* **4** (Winter 1990), 22.

Putnam, R.D. (2000) *Bowling alone: the collapse and revival of American community.* New York. Simon and Schuster.

Radford, J.P. (1991) Sterilization versus segregation: control of the 'feeblemind-ed', 1900–1938. *Social Science and Medicine* **33** (4), 449–58.

Robins, J. (1986) *Fools and mad: a history of the insane in Ireland.* Dublin. Institute of Public Administration.

Robins, J. (1992) *From rejection to integration: a century of service by the Daughters of Charity to persons with a mental handicap.* Dublin. Gill and Macmillan.

Robinson, L. (1987) Patricia Farrell and the miracle of St Michael's. *The Irish Press* (12 August 1987), 8.

Ryan, A. (1999) *Walls of silence.* Chapter 6: People Power. Callan, Co. Kilkenny. Red Lion Press.

Spring Rice, T. (1817) *Evidence to: Report of the Select Committee appointed to Inquire into the Expedience of Making Further Provision for the Relief of the Lunatic Poor of Ireland 1817.* British Parliamentary Papers VIII 33, 12.

Synnott v. Department of Education, Ireland & Attorney General. (HC) Barr, J.

Judgement delivered 4 October 2000.

Weller, V. (1992) *An extraordinary voluntary commitment—25 years of KARE.* Newbridge. KARE.

Wolfensberger, W. (1975) *The origin and nature of our institutional models.* Syracuse. Human Policy Press.

Woods, M. (1997) *Costing the halo—effects of compulsory altruism on the lives of mothers and severely handicapped adult children.* Occasional Paper. Dublin. National Rehabilitation Board.

Note

1   Based on figures from Census Reports of 1901 and 1911 in Byrne 1979; Mulcahy and Reynolds 1984; Department of Health 1965; Dáil Report, 19/11/1957; figures supplied by the Department of Health/MSRB (pers. comm.); Kellegher *et al.* 1990; Department of Health 1990; 1992; 1994; Mulvaney 2001.

3. THE STAFFING OF SERVICES FOR PEOPLE WITH INTELLECTUAL DISABILITIES

ROY MCCONKEY

INTRODUCTION

Most Irish people with an intellectual disability live with family carers. This is certainly true for nearly all children but it remains the case even for older adults. Hence the numbers living in some form of residential accommodation and looked after by paid staff are a minority, but nonetheless they form a sizeable and growing population and their carers constitute a substantial part of the service workforce. Many of these carers will have had no formal training and often they receive low wages.

Likewise there are sizeable numbers of people employed in what can be broadly termed 'family support services', most of whom work in schools and day centres as teachers, instructors or care assistants. But this grouping also includes staff involved in supported employment schemes or leisure projects and domiciliary support workers who assist in the family home.

Then there is a myriad of different professionals who attend to the specific needs of people with disability and their carers. These include doctors from a range of specialisms but mostly general practitioners and psychiatrists, nurses, psychologists, social workers, peripatetic teachers, various types of therapists, dentists, podiatrists and dietitians. Some of these professionals are employed in agencies solely for persons with intellectual disabilities while others are accessed through mainstream health and community services. They must have a professional qualification in order to practice, although in Ireland only nurses and consultant psychiatrists have the opportunity to take a qualification specifically in intellectual disabilities.

Finally, all services have managerial, administrative and secretarial staff to support the running of the service, although these individuals may have limited contact with the users of the service.

PROFILE OF STAFF

This brief synopsis highlights a number of features about staff involved in intellectual disability services. First, they are a disparate group, ranging from low-paid, untrained staff through to specialists receiving substantial salaries. Second, they work in a variety of settings and often have limited contact with other staff from outside the residence, day centre or school where they work. Third, they come from diverse backgrounds with different attitudes, knowledge and experiences of people with intellectual disability. Fourth, the staff are employed to fulfil many different functions; some of these are very precise (e.g. dentists), while others are very broad (e.g. home leader in a residence). In addition, they may be employed by different service systems—education, health board, voluntary body and so on.

The numbers of paid staff in Irish services have grown dramatically in the last two decades and they have taken over many of the jobs previously done by 'volunteers' (see McCormack, this volume). Although services still seek to recruit volunteer helpers they are few in number; they work limited hours and are often deployed on specific tasks such as befriending and leisure activities.

Finally, as the population of Irish people with intellectual disabilities continues to grow and the services become more individualised, the numbers of staff employed in these services will rise in the coming years—government funding permitting!

TRUISMS ABOUT STAFFING

Despite the diversity of staffing, we can state a number of truisms.

The quality of any service is dependent on the quality of its staff. Buildings, facilities and equipment play some part, but the service is pre-eminently delivered by people. It is their attitudes, knowledge and skills and the relationships they forge with the service-users that make for a good service.

The bulk of the costs in intellectual disability service is taken up with staff salaries. On average upwards of 80% of the running costs of services are spent on staffing. If services are going to achieve the government's aspirations for them to be more effective and efficient in cost terms, then staffing will have to deliver the bulk of improvements.

There are insufficient staff to meet the needs of service-users. People with intellectual disabilities need extra help and support throughout their lifespan. As more people live longer, these demands invariably increase, both in numerical terms as well as in terms of an individual person needing more help. In addition, more people with more complex health-care needs are surviving longer and they too aspire to live in ordinary settings. However, international experience tells us that most services are constantly underfunded and staff have to cope with the strains that arise from this.

In sum, the key issue for all intellectual disability services must be the recruitment, deployment and management of effective staff. This chapter attempts to summarise what this involves.

CHRISTY'S STORY

But let's begin with a true story recounted by an Irishman, Christy Nolan (1987), in his award-winning autobiography. Christy is physically disabled and totally dependent on others for all his personal care. He cannot communicate verbally but with assistance he uses a computer to converse with others and to write poetry and prose. In his reminiscences of childhood he tells of the day in County Clare when the family went swimming in the Atlantic Ocean—his mother and father, his sister and himself (whom he calls Joseph in the book). He wrote:

> 'All hands joined forces to help Joseph swim and float . . . he felt totally relaxed and safe in their hands and through their efforts he sampled the joys of the able-bodied' (1987, 104).

The frail boy being supported in the ocean waves is a fitting metaphor for all staff working in intellectual disability services. Many in the wider society would dismiss their work as impossible, as wasted effort or as unnecessarily risky. Yet staff face the challenges of billowing waves every day in their work.

But Nolan's story is also a parable for what makes for effective staffing. In it he identifies five key elements. We will examine each in turn.

'All hands joined forces'

Teamwork was needed. Each individual had a particular contribution to make, but by joining forces they achieved what one person alone could not. Yet we still have a great deal to learn about how to create effective teamwork in intellectual disability services among staff within the same agency as well as across different agencies.

Obviously opportunities for staff to meet one another are essential but not always possible, given the different hours people work. Yet these meetings will allow team members to build a common identity and, crucially, to create a shared vision of their service aims, whether it be for one client or for all clients. From this basis, agreed work practices and protocols can be developed so that staff know what is expected of them in their role and service-users receive continuity and consistency in their service. All of this is much easier to say than to achieve in practice. A common obstacle is the absence of good leadership from those charged with managing services.

Teamwork is even more necessary among the diverse specialists—be they psychologists, social workers or therapists—who are now available to advise families and carers. In one area of Northern Ireland, one third of children aged 0–19 years saw four or more different professionals in one year, and the highest number was ten (McConkey and McAteer 1999).

Common complaints from parents include the conflicting advice given and the jargon used. Here the concept of 'key worker' or 'named worker' has much to commend it. One member of the team is assigned to one client or family. They provide an immediate point of contact for the users but also serve to integrate the inputs from different specialists into a common action plan and to support front-line carers in its implementation.   This model has worked particularly well in the pre-school years, especially when the 'key worker' is also available to visit the family home regularly, but it is applicable throughout the lifespan. Teachers in special schools or staff in day centres often fulfil this coordinating role by default but there is scope to formalise it (McConkey, in press). Likewise, staff teams in centres and residences can benefit from having a named person from the clinical support team with whom they can build up a relationship and who can advise them on a range of issues.

In recent years a new concept has emerged of a support worker whose aim is to help an individual or a family to access help from the range of resources available within most communities and not just from specialist agencies. In Western Australia, for example, a local area coordinator works with around 50 persons of various ages and disabilities to determine their specific needs and to connect them into existing community services and facilities so that their particular needs can be met (Disability Services Commission, no date). This can include education, respite breaks, leisure, employment and housing. Indeed, one of the main functions of the coordinators is to work with local agencies and personnel to increase their confidence and competence in working with people who have disabilities. Although this model was pioneered in more remote rural communities it has been successfully extended to urban areas. It achieves high satisfaction ratings from its users and is highly cost-efficient. The recent review of learning disability services in Scotland has proposed the adoption of this staffing model by all local authorities (Scottish Executive 2000).

Similar strategies have to be used in developing countries which cannot afford the range of specialist services found in western societies. A 'community-based rehabilitation' worker receives training in basic procedures for overcoming disabilities and accessing local services so that they in turn can educate families and local communities to respond to the needs of their disabled members (Helander 1993). The emphasis is on empowering people with disabilities, their families and communities to find their own solutions.

Some would argue that it is only these new styles of staffing that will fully achieve the objective of equal opportunities for, and the social inclusion of, people with disabilities, and that the very existence of specialist agencies and professionals prevents this from occurring as often they fail to join forces with mainstream agencies in producing a socially valued life (Schwartz 1992).

'. . . to help Joseph'

The role of all staff can be simply stated: it is to help an individual person. We now appreciate that this help can take many different forms, although in past years services tended to restrict their help to caring for people's personal needs and keeping them safe. Indeed, this ethos may still dominate over other forms of help that people require, such as accessing appropriate health care, education, leisure and employment opportunities, and helping people to form relationships, perhaps to marry and to have children.

Nor is it a case of doing things for people but rather of helping people to learn to do things for themselves. One of the great success stories of intellectual disabilities services has been enabling people to become more independent in their personal care, in looking after themselves at home and in holding down a job. Staff need not only to provide service-users with opportunities to learn in realistic settings but also to actively support them in mastering new skills. This involves creating daily schedules of activities with identified teaching goals, having teaching plans to assist the learner and using appropriate instructional techniques. When these methods were used in community residences marked increases were found in staff engagement with residents and in their participation in various household and leisure pursuits (Jones *et al.* 1999). This research concluded that it is not just the availability of staff that is crucial but how they go about their job.

Staff help needs to be tailored to individuals, yet it is only in recent years that services have attempted to respond to individuals through personally tailored services such as supported living. More usually people are grouped within service settings and staff are expected to cope with the needs of the group, with little scope to individualise their attention. For example, the amount of attention and assistance that staff gave to residents in fifteen community residences (mostly hostels accommodating an average of nineteen residents) was directly observed during a three-hour period centred around the evening meal (Felce *et al.* 1999). Overall it was found that residents received attention from staff for an average of fourteen minutes per hour and assistance for an average of two minutes per hour, confirming a pattern found in several previous studies. However, this varied greatly across the different residences, with some groups receiving virtually no assistance and others having four times the average assistance. Surprisingly, individuals with greater support needs did not receive more attention or assistance than their more able counterparts.

The results from observations in day centres were similar: only 13% of person-hours were organised as individual activities; most time was spent in groups. Users had staff attention for around sixteen minutes in each hour and were engaged in activities for 54% of the time, but this fell by half in sessions for people with high support needs. The researchers concluded that people with high support needs within typical day centres had only about five hours of constructive occupation per week.

Person-centred planning approaches offer a useful way of helping staff in such settings to create more individualised supports to a service-user (Sanderson and Kilbane 1999). Unlike care planning, which reflects staff views of what the 'client' needs, person-centred planning is based around the individual's needs and aspirations as articulated by the person or through an advocate. The staff involved with the individual, along with family and other involved persons, then draw up a plan as to how they could all work together to meet these needs and aspirations. As yet there is sparse evidence that these approaches make a demonstrable difference to the quality of services that people receive, but it has been argued that they are necessary for ethical and moral reasons, notably promoting the person's autonomy and rights (O'Brien *et al.* 1997).

'. . . totally relaxed and safe in their hands'

Service-users must have trust in their staff. The crucial issue, then, is how this trust is built and maintained. An important starting-point is to recruit staff who have the personal qualities required for the job as some of these cannot be easily learned or acquired through training. Prime among these are good interpersonal skills (Hall and Hall 2002). Taylor *et al.* (1996) identified seven competences, including the ability to empower the service-user, being a sensitive communicator, and being able to conduct crisis intervention in ways that defuse the situation and preserve the service-user's dignity.

Equally, staff coming into posts may need particular assistance in communicating effectively with people who have intellectual disabilities. Research has shown that front-line staff in day and residential settings are inclined to rely too much on verbal communication rather than using non-verbal methods. Their language is too complex; they ask too many questions; they fail to leave sufficient time for service-users to respond; and often they fail to respond to their initiations (McConkey, Morris *et al.* 1999). These issues are even more crucial when staff do not have English as their first language.

All staff have a 'duty to care' for their clients, which means not exposing them to unnecessary risk or abusive practices. Sadly, evidence is accumulating that this client group is particularly vulnerable to abuse, from name-calling by teenagers through to sexual assault by peers, family members and staff (Mencap 2001). Hence all staff have a duty to protect individuals in their care from physical or verbal assaults from other clients with whom they share a home or day facility, and possibly also from the actions of other staff members. It is essential that all services have guidelines for their staff on the prevention, detection and reporting of abuse. This should also cover what has been termed 'whistle-blowing', the expectation that staff will report colleagues who are abusing service-users and that they will not be penalised for doing so.

Staff need training if they are to do their job effectively. Recently the emphasis has shifted from not just imparting information and knowledge to also ensuring that staff have developed and are using the practical competences needed for their work. In Britain, National Occupational Standards have been developed for social care workers (as for many other industries) which specify performance indicators of good practice for different levels of staff (Training Organisation for the Personal Social Services 1999). Staff are assessed in work situations to see whether they meet these standards and if so they are awarded a National Vocational Qualification in Social Care. These awards are intended to remove, or at least blur, the distinction between trained and untrained staff and more crucially to provide a mechanism for increasing the probability that service-users will receive a better-quality service. However, the sheer ambitiousness of the undertaking has been its greatest weakness and the number of staff qualifying remains a small proportion of the workforce. Nonetheless the intention behind such schemes is wholly laudable and the government remains strongly committed to it. Competence-based training is here to stay.

A more controversial issue relates to professional practice. In simple terms, can service-users 'trust' the assessments and treatments offered by specialists? The move towards evidence-based practice, particularly in health services, places the onus on clinicians to defend their choice of assessment tools and treatments by citing evidence for their effectiveness. Sadly this is often lacking with intellectually disabled populations.

Emerson *et al.* (2000a) provide a particular example in relation to the management of challenging behaviours in a variety of residential settings in England that had been chosen to represent 'good' or 'better' services. They found that residents with challenging behaviours were three times more likely to receive anti-psychotic medication than behavioural interventions. They note that there is considerable evidence that the latter are effective in the short and medium term in helping people to overcome challenging behaviours but that there is no reliable evidence that anti-psychotic medication has any specific beneficial effect. Moreover, they found that nearly 50% of residents who exhibited challenging behaviour were subject to physical restraint, a procedure that exposes staff and clients to risk of injury, and recent departmental guidance (Department of Health 2002) cautions against using restraint except in very controlled circumstances.

In future all staff will need to be better informed about the outcomes of research and encouraged to re-evaluate their practice. Then service-users can have more confidence and trust that they are getting the help they need.

'. . . through their efforts'

Helping people with disabilities requires efforts from staff; it is not easy work. Indeed, a topical issue at present in most western countries is the turnover among front-line service staff and the difficulty in recruiting to these posts. In the United States annual turnover rates in community facilities have ranged from 34% to 71%, compared to 18% turnover in large public institutions (Larson and Lakin 1999).

A survey of over 500 staff working mostly in NHS community services in the UK found that almost one third showed high levels of distress indicative of mental health problems (Hatton *et al.* 1999). This proportion was higher than for other NHS employees, other employed persons or adults generally. Just over half of the staff had taken sick leave in the past six months, and approximately one eighth had applied for another job within the last three months.

Organisational culture has been shown to have an impact on staff stress, sickness and turnover in many businesses. In a study of 450 British workers in a range of learning disability services they rated their organisations as relatively high in achievement orientation and in fostering social relationships but relatively low in managing conflict and providing rewards for staff (Hatton *et al.* 1999). Moreover, the latter featured strongly in staff ratings of an 'ideal' organisation.

The three factors most predictive of job satisfaction for these workers were stress linked to a low-status job, support from supervisors and having influence over work decisions (Hatton *et al.* 1999). Paying front-line staff more money for the job may not solve all the staffing problems of organisations but it is an obvious starting-point given these research findings. Likewise managers need to expend more effort on supporting front-line staff, in particular specifying service goals, clarifying staff roles, providing training and feedback, involving staff in decision-making, and reducing job strains such as not working longer than contracted hours. Indeed, some have suggested that the main weakness is the lack of strategic planning and human resource management among administrators of intellectual disability services (Hall and Hall 2002).

It is noteworthy that these findings apply to staff at all levels in organisations and across a range of job titles. Moreover, they hold irrespective of the characteristics of the client groups served. Hence a major effort in the future must be to create a better understanding of the organisational characteristics required to produce a relatively stable and productive workforce. Put bluntly, many of our existing agencies were created to look after the helpless, yet that is not the task facing us in the new millennium, with the emphasis on citizenship, equal opportunities and human rights. Handy (1995) anticipates an end for mass organisations in modern technological societies, noting that they have not been with us long and that maybe we will be better off without them. He concludes that 'change comes from small initiatives which work, initiatives which imitated, become the fashion' (1995, 271).

In the field of intellectual disability we already have the evidence to support this. Indeed, try as we might, professional services cannot easily replace the family as the most effective care and development organisation for people with an intellectual disability. But those services that come closest often share the same characteristics—small-scale, local, personal and committed. In this respect, then, Handy's advice is apposite: 'We cannot wait for great visions from great people . . . it is up to us to light our own small fires in the darkness' (1995, 271).

'. . . sampled the joys of the able-bodied'

The outcome of all our service activities is neatly captured in Nolan's phrase. Note too the word 'sample': he accepts that he will never become able-bodied but from time to time he aspires to share in the joys the non-disabled too easily take for granted—swimming in the sea, meeting friends in the pub, living in your own home, getting paid employment, having a sexual partner. The list can go on and on, yet the critical question is how good staff are at letting people sample these joys.

Sadly, the answer must be 'not very'. Services remain dominated by a care culture that frequently denies the user the chance to be treated as able-bodied. Imagine if Christy had lived in a progressive Belfast nursing home for disabled people that did person-centred planning, and which had a stable and well-trained workforce whose goal was to give their residents as normal a life as possible. In response to Christy's desire to swim in the Atlantic when on holiday, it is likely that a case conference of his doctor, therapists and social workers would be required to approve it; a trained nurse would need to accompany him, as this is a condition under government regulations for nursing homes; the staff would have to abide by the Moving and Handling regulations under the European Directives when lifting him from his wheelchair into the sea and make use of a mechanical hoist to do it; and a life-saver with suitable qualifications would need to be on hand because of his disability. In sum, it is very unlikely that Christy would ever have got to swim in the Atlantic! He might just manage a dip in an indoor pool provided that it is fully equipped for his needs, and thereby he would sample the joys of being *disabled*!

Of course service-users must not be exposed to unnecessary risk, but as services become more dominated by procedures that aim to minimise risk, a culture develops in which risks are no longer managed but simply avoided. Is this the outcome that service-users—the people with the disability—want? Probably not. Hence we need to make staff more adept at making realistic risk assessments and becoming more competent in managing risks (Alaszewski and Manthorpe 1998).

Moreover, a growing body of research evidence clearly demonstrates the failure of many residential services in particular at achieving social inclusion for their users. This is particularly marked for residents living in congregated settings such as residential homes or complexes made up of separate houses. By contrast, those living in small group homes or in supported living arrangements had larger social networks, including both disabled and non-disabled people; they were able to have routine day activities such as attending day centres and adult education, and to experience a greater number and variety of recreational and community-based activities (Emerson *et al.* 2000b). These findings held when the severity of the person's disability was taken into account. Hence the style of service provided can make it harder or easier for staff to do a good job.

New styles of services have likewise proved to be more successful in achieving social inclusion than traditional services. For example, people who avail of respite breaks with a 'host' family rather than staying in a special residential centre are more likely to make use of more community facilities and to meet other people (McConkey, McConaghie *et al.* 2003). Similarly, supported employment schemes that provide a job coach for individuals in ordinary work settings have been much more successful at getting people into paid employment than were vocational training centres (Beyer and Kilsby 1997).

As governments spend ever more money on health and social services in general and intellectual disability services in particular, they are increasingly examining whether they get value for money. This means having a clear statement as to the outcomes that a service attempts to achieve so that there is a yardstick against which performance of services can be judged. Various schemas and methods have been proposed for doing this but the outcomes-based approach promoted by the Council for Quality and Leadership in the United States has attracted much interest in Irish services (*Council on Quality and Leadership*, available at www.thecouncil.org). In brief, the service is judged on the numbers of clients who have been helped to attain personally defined outcomes in seven areas, including Autonomy, Attainment, Rights, and Health and Wellness. An example of a personal outcome measure is: 'people have time, space and opportunity for privacy'. Trained assessors talk to a sample of service-users (or their advocates) to determine whether this outcome is present. They may ask questions such as 'Where do you go when you want to be alone?' or 'If you need help with personal hygiene how do you decide who will help you?' There are also 21 organisational performance measures to assess whether the agency meets standard requirements in areas such as health and safety, staff recruitment and financial accounting but also in terms of organisational learning and communication with users, families and communities.

This system is designed to encourage and assist agencies to improve by identifying their strengths and weaknesses, but when an agency attains a minimum standard as verified by external assessors the Council will accredit it as a 'quality service'. Such accreditation is necessary in the United States for agencies to obtain government funding.

In other countries different types of accreditation systems are used, but again the intent is to ensure a consistency in service delivery and a means of producing better-quality services (Federation of Voluntary Bodies 1998).

Evaluating services in terms of the outcomes they secure for their clients is likely to be the dominant philosophy in this decade. It encourages services to make explicit their goals and priorities, it provides staff with a clear focus for their work and, most importantly, service-users can make comparisons within and across services as to their effectiveness in producing the intended outcomes for their clients.

Implicit in this is a redefinition of the role of the staff. They will become more accountable to the users; they will need to focus more on the outcomes of their work rather than on the activities they undertake; they need to acquire the skills of monitoring and adapting their inputs to achieve the desired outcomes. These add to the many challenges already facing service administrators and managers but in many ways they form part of the solution.

FUTURE SERVICES

This review of staffing issues has identified the major changes that are required in intellectual disability services to make them 'fit-for-purpose' in the coming decades of this new century.

Some of these will involve radical changes in the structure of services, with more people being served through a collection of smaller, locally based and person-centred services, each with a discrete function.

Some of the changes will involve the creation of new staff posts with a variety of different support functions. For example, more staff will support families and people in their own homes and more staff will be employed to help people to access education, employment, training and leisure pursuits in mainstream settings.

Some of the changes will introduce new forms of funding services. In Britain particular emphasis is being placed on 'direct payments' in which government monies are given directly to the service-user, who then employs the support staff as needed. The intention is to make the employee more accountable to the user than is the case at present.

As the saying goes, the only constant is change. But experience has taught us the ingredients in producing a competent workforce. These are:

- *Attitudes:* Staff who respect the dignity and worth of all persons and who advocate for equal opportunities and human rights.
- *Knowledge:* Staff who have acquired a knowledge and understanding of the disabling effects of environments as well as biological impairments and how these can be removed or minimised through positive action with individuals, families, communities and governments.
- *Skills:* Staff need to be skilled practitioners in different spheres of work and this comes through supervised practice and feedback from competent

mentors, but their interpersonal and communication skills are central.

- *Empathy:* Staff need the capacity to empathise with those they try to help, and in particular to listen to their concerns, needs and aspirations. They need to empower their clients so that they can have greater choice and control over their own lives.
- *Commitment:* The impact of disability cannot be solved by short-term solutions; support has to be ongoing and possibly life-long. This requires continuity and commitment from agencies especially through the rough seas as well as the calm waters.

And so we end where we started, with Christy's story. Many families epitomise these five attributes better than the best services. The reason is not hard to see. It is their *loved one* for whom they care. In English the word 'love' has many meanings, but modern culture emphasises romantic and sexual attachment. Yet a deeper meaning of love is the altruistic, self-sacrificing actions most parents show to their children or lovers to each other. In modern society, with its business and career ethos, is it too much to expect paid staff to display this kind of love? If we do not aspire to keeping such feelings alive, I suspect we have little hope of truly meeting the needs of people with intellectual disabilities.

REFERENCES

Alaszewski, A. and Manthorpe, J. (1998) Welfare agencies and risk: the missing link? *Health and Social Care in the Community* **6** (1), 4–15.

Beyer, S. and Kilsby, M. (1997) Supported employment in Britain. *Tizard Learning Disability Review* **2** (2), 6–14.

Council on Quality and Leadership. Available at: http://www.thecouncil.org [March 2003].

Department of Health (2002) *Guidance for restrictive physical interventions: how to provide safe services for people with learning disabilities and autistic spectrum disorder.* London. HMSO.

Disability Services Commission (no date) *Local area coordination.* Available at: http://www.dsc.wa.gov.au/uploads/LAC_Metro.pdf [March 2003].

Emerson, E., Robertson, J., Gregory, N., Hatton, C., Kessissoglou, S., Hallam, A. and Hillery, J. (2000a) Treatment and management of challenging behaviours in residential settings. *Journal of Applied Research in Intellectual Disabilities* **13** (4), 197–215.

Emerson, E., Robertson, J., Gregory, N. *et al.* (2000b) The quality and costs of village communities, residential campuses and community-based residential supports for people with learning disabilities. *Tizard Learning Disability Review* **5** (1), 5–16.

Federation of Voluntary Bodies (1998) *Interim report of Task Group on Quality Measurement Systems in Learning Disability Services.* Galway. Federation of Voluntary Bodies.

Felce, D., Lowe, K., Perry, J., Jones, E., Baxter, H. and Bowley, C. (1999) The quality of residential and day services for adults with intellectual disabilities in eight local authorities in England: objective data gained in support of a Social Services Inspectorate inspection. *Journal of Applied Research in Intellectual Disabilities* **12** (4), 273–93.

Hall, P.S. and Hall, N.D. (2002) Hiring and retaining direct care staff: after fifty years of research what do we know? *Mental Retardation* **40** (3), 201–11.

Handy, C. (1995) *The empty raincoat.* London. Arrow Books.

Hatton, C., Rivers, M., Mason, H. *et al.* (1999) Organizational culture and staff outcomes in services for people with intellectual disabilities. *Journal of Intellectual Disability Research* **43** (3), 206–18.

Helander, E. (1993) *Prejudice and dignity: an introduction to community-based rehabilitation.* New York. UNDP.

Jones, E., Perry, J., Lowe, K. *et al.* (1999) Opportunity and the promotion of activity among adults with severe intellectual disability living in community residences: the impact of training staff in active support. *Journal of Intellectual Disability Research* **43** (3), 164–78.

Larson, S.A. and Lakin, K.C. (1999) Longitudinal study of recruitment and retention in small community homes supporting persons with developmental disabilities. *Mental Retardation* **37** (4), 267–80.

McConkey, R. (in press) Information needs of parents about learning disabilities. *Journal of Learning Disabilities*.

McConkey, R. and McAteer, D. (1999) The contacts which families and children with learning disabilities have with health and social services. *Child Care in Practice* **5** (2), 67–73.

McConkey, R., McConaghie, J., Roberts, P. and King, D. (2003) *Adult family placement schemes for older carers of people with intellectual disabilities: final report to Foundation of People with Learning Disabilities*. Bangor. Positive Futures and University of Ulster.

McConkey, R., Morris, I. and Purcell, M. (1999) Communications between staff and adult persons with intellectual disabilities in naturally occurring settings. *Journal of Intellectual Disability Research* **43** (3), 194–205.

Mencap (2001) *Behind closed doors: preventing sexual abuse of adults with a learning disability*. London. Mencap.

Nolan, C. (1987) *Under the eye of the clock*. London. Pan Books.

O'Brien, C.L., O'Brien, J. and Mount, B. (1997) Person-centred planning has arrived . . . or has it? *Mental Retardation* **35** (6), 480–4.

Sanderson, H. and Kilbane. J. (1999) *Person centred planning—a resource guide*. Clitheroe. North West Training and Development Team. Available at: http://www.nwtdt.com/pdfs/pcp.pdf [March 2003].

Schwartz, D. (1992) *Crossing the river: creating a conceptual revolution in community and disability*. Cambridge, MA. Brookline Books.

Scottish Executive (2000) *The same as you? A review of services for people with learning disabilities*. Edinburgh. Scottish Executive.

Taylor, M., Bradley, V. and Warren, R. (1996) *The Community Support Skills Standards. Tools for managing change and achieving outcomes*. Cambridge, MA. Human Services Research Institute.

Training Organisation for the Personal Social Services (1999) A Summary of the S/NVQ Awards in Care, Caring for Children and Young People, Diagnostic and Therapeutic Support and Promoting Independence. Available at: http://www.niscc.info/pdf/sum.pdf [March 2003].

4. Parents' voices

MARK MULROONEY AND MARK HARROLD

INTRODUCTION

In this chapter we talk to parents of persons with intellectual disabilities and summarise their views. Our thanks go to these parents, and we hope that this chapter will prove to be of help to all parents who read it. If the views of parents come across as negative at times, that is probably because the experience of raising a child with intellectual disability very often is just that. It is clear from the parents we meet that raising a disabled child is hard work. The 'Heaven's Special Child' syndrome is dead and buried. It is evident that parents are no longer prepared to be silent about the types of support required to raise a child with intellectual disability. These requirements are great and do not diminish as the child grows older. Indeed, it is now clear that the needs of the child and their family become greater as the person grows towards adulthood and beyond.

We posed a number of questions to parents when researching this chapter. Here is Jim and Ann's response to a question about the positive aspects of raising a child with intellectual disability (their daughter is in her mid-twenties):

> 'This question is like asking a one-legged man what is nice about not having two legs. Maybe he would say that he only has to polish one shoe.'

Hard work was a recurring theme in many of the responses from parents. Rather than interpreting these themes as overwhelming or negative, we believe that the first step in taking action to do something about your own situation is to recognise the scale and nature of the problem in the first place. By the time you finish reading this chapter, you may have realised that you are not alone in some of your thoughts and feelings, and that there are parents out there whose hopes and fears are the same as yours but who are not prepared to accept the crumbs from the table or any charitable interpretation of the services provided for their disabled child. As Fiona, whose daughter is in her early twenties, stated:

'The days when parents of people with a mental handicap were prepared to settle for the "loose change" approach to mental handicap are over. We want rights for our children and for ourselves, and we want those rights expressed in proper, professional, planned structures.'

Fiona went on to say:

'Protest is necessary for us as parents. But parents are not just interested in protest—we want to contribute too. And we don't just believe this is about money, although money is certainly an issue. We believe that the rights of our children deserve and demand an entirely new approach— new structures, better management, better use of resources, a fuller commitment to their long-term education and training, and the right to live an independent life when we are gone.'

Pauline prefaced her response to our questions thus:

'I think one's response to having a child with mental handicap is in part determined by the nature and severity of the handicap, the age of the child, number of other children, birth order, and family circumstances. Our eight-year-old has Down Syndrome. She does require more time and care but we treat her in so far as possible as just another member of the family. Her health is excellent and has been so since birth. She attended a mainstream playgroup from the age of three, began in Montessori at age five and has just entered Junior Infants where she has settled well. Her speech is fairly good which makes life a lot easier for us. I know if our child had a moderate to severe disability, had poor communication skills, presented with challenging behaviour or had attendant health problems which necessitated a lot of extra care our concerns would be different.'

We elicited responses from parents of children with intellectual disabilities of all ages and differing circumstances. The sentiments expressed were remarkably consistent. This chapter will endeavour to reflect a range of viewpoints on a range of topics which, we hope, will be of relevance to all parents who are raising a person with an intellectual disability.

HEARING THE NEWS

We have not yet met a parent who could not relate in the finest detail how they were informed that their child had an intellectual disability. 'Devastation' is the word that describes the experience for most parents. Many parents described the insensitivity of the manner in which they were informed about their child's handicap, while all expressed the view that there is no easy way to be told that your child will be dependent for the rest of his/her life. The most notable comment was about the lack of support and/or counselling for them after hearing the news. Maura and Brian described their experience:

> 'There was a lot of difficulty with the medical profession. The consultant said "Your baby is severely handicapped mentally and physically and will never achieve anything!" Very badly put. There is no easy way to tell parents but arrangements should be made to have someone available to talk the implications through. No support at all was offered or available to us in the early years.'

Mary and Eoin had a similar experience:

> 'We were told very brutally by a neurologist and left to flounder afterwards. We should have been told gently in a very supportive atmosphere over a few consultations. We should immediately have had bereavement counselling as we were grieving for the child we expected but did not have. It would have been helpful to have been put in touch with other parents in a similar position. Being told of the services available and of the possible life plan would have helped. If I see a person with a handicapped child I make a point of telling them about the achievements of children like theirs.'

Pauline wishes she had been given the news differently:

> 'After the birth I was in the recovery room and my husband had gone to make the "good news" phone calls. A doctor I had never met before came in holding the baby and asking the medical staff where "the husband" was. On my husband's return he proceeded to inform us in broken English that our baby had Down Syndrome. His grasp of the English language grew more tenuous with every passing moment. Nobody likes getting bad news. No matter how it is delivered there is always a tendency to shoot the messenger. I don't think there is any way of telling a parent that their newborn infant is handicapped that softens the blow. That said, such news should not be given in a public area surrounded by nurses and other medical staff. If at all possible it should be given by a doctor the parents know and have formed some kind of relationship with—for most women that would be the doctor who cared for them during pregnancy and birth. Need I add that the doctor giving the news should have sufficient grasp of the English language to be able to explain himself clearly and answer the questions put to him?'

Kate had a different experience:

> 'Brona was born at home and started having seizures within 48 hours of
> birth. She was in the Children's Hospital under observation for
> approximately six weeks. An appointment was made with the consultant
> for results and prognosis. He told us—without any show of emotion, but
> gently and sensitively—that tests had shown that our child had brain
> damage, caused probably by a tiny brain haemorrhage, and that an
> operation was not recommended even if they could find the location as
> more damage might result from same. He told us to rear her as normal as
> possible and only in time would we know the extent of her handicap. We
> never had any problem with the forthright manner in which we were told.
> We still believe this was best.'

It is clear that hearing the news that your child has an intellectual disability
is one of the most traumatic experiences a parent could encounter. The sense of
isolation and unexpressed grief and anger which emanated from the responses
about hearing the news was as striking as it was sad. Strangely enough, Mike,
who is the parent of four children who do not have a disability, probably catches
the mood:

> 'What do you say when you meet your friends and their new baby who
> has been diagnosed with a mental handicap? If I say how beautiful the
> child is, they might feel I am being patronising. If I express sympathy,
> they may be insulted. It is very awkward.'

It is clear that awkwardness exists on all sides. The reality is that numerous
conflicting emotions are experienced by parents when the news that their child
has an intellectual disability is confirmed. It takes time to work through these
and to make the necessary adjustments to family life.

ADJUSTING TO LIFE WITH A CHILD WITH AN INTELLECTUAL DISABILITY

The overriding theme of the responses to this section was one of lost
opportunities. Monica summarised her feelings thus:

> 'At first we were in shock and "went through the motions" of normal
> living for a long time. We felt isolated as our child was developing at a
> slower rate than our friends' children. As our child possibly had suffered
> anoxia at birth, we decided not to have any more children. In fact, we had
> two more children two and four years later. When our children were small
> the gap between our first child and the others was not so noticeable. But

over the years the gap widened dramatically and we found it difficult to find things to do as a family which suited everybody. It often ended up with one parent with our mentally handicapped child and the other parent with the others in tow. Our handicapped child needed more time and attention and as a mother I felt pulled in different directions and felt my attention was spread very thinly between the children. Personally, having a handicapped child has robbed me of choices I probably would have had in my life. My son is now 30 years old and my routine hasn't changed. I would have liked to pursue further studies or returned to the work force but my life still has to be built around my handicapped son. As his general health is not good, I often have to change plans if he is ill and when he has holidays at Christmas, Easter and the month of August I have to be home.'

John described his family's experience:

'You don't consciously "adjust". In our case Helena was a year old at the time so she was no different after we knew than she was before. You muddle along and gradually get used to it. However, you do it alone, or at least we did. Our families gave a little sympathy and a little help but really didn't know how to handle it so by and large tried to ignore it. This might have been influenced by the fact that, up to a few years ago, we tended to keep our trouble to ourselves. We were both interested in walking and intended taking the children walking with us when they were old enough. This we never really did as it was not possible with Helena. Certain things were not possible because of Helena's tantrums. For example, my wife was reluctant to take her to many places because she would make a show of her. As I could control her I tended to make myself available for these "dangerous jaunts". So, a visit to Santa for all the family needed my presence, particularly because we went to a restaurant after. I was needed to drag her away from all the neighbouring tables and to quell the tantrum which invariably threatened when she realised that she could not eat everything in the restaurant.'

Pauline has tried to get the balance right:

'We have tried in so far as possible to minimise the effects on family life. We have three other children who have their own needs and demands. We try not to let it prevent us taking part in activities we would otherwise have enjoyed. The main cost to family life has been on time. Caring for our special needs child is more time-consuming, particularly to the extent to which we have worked with him on social and educational skills. This means there is less time for the other children.'

Kate described her adjustment:

'As a mother it meant that whilst I could deal with the other children in quite a routine way, Brona always needed special care and arrangements. Physically and mentally this was an extra strain. This, for us, was normal family life.'

Alan described the adjustment quite succinctly:

'It took years to come to terms with it. It has changed our whole family life in every way.'

Jim again:

'At the moment we have gone through three/four months free from tantrums. In one sense this has been wonderful. However, like the old phrase used in the cowboy films—"It's quiet! TOO QUIET!" We have a constant feeling of unease. She has never lasted this long and so every time the phone rings when she is out we expect it to be word of the latest tantrum. (When she has them it has the effect of shattering our lives for weeks after.) Still, waiting for the next one certainly beats her having it.'

Alice described her family's adjustment as difficult:

'Because Leoni is our first child, we did not have anyone to compare her to. The others find her hard going at times. I tried to keep her happy but the others didn't always agree with what I was trying to do. I think they felt they have missed out on things. Because of her, you have to make sure that all outings are going to keep her interested. If not, your and the other children's outing is gone up in smoke.'

It was the adjustment of others which proved difficult for Stella:

'The main thing that would have made things easier for me would have been the support of my immediate family. They had and still have a lot of difficulty dealing with the reality of having a handicapped child in their midst. Society itself is not welcoming to persons with disabilities. If we lived in a society which had a positive and inclusive attitude to disability it would have been much easier for us to accept a child who was "different". As it is, it is a struggle to win for him a place in his community and his society.'

Peter found the special occasions such as birthdays particularly poignant:

'We cannot put our finger on it but when she made her Holy Communion and then later had her twenty-first party we were quite low. What should have been the happiest occasions of Evelyn's life just seemed to make the difference that much more obvious. It is as if these milestones made it patently clear that Evelyn will never function independently, will never get married, and will always depend on us.'

It is evident that life with a child who has an intellectual disability does not get easier as children grow older. Indeed, the differences become more marked as time moves on. This will become more obvious in the next section, which looks at the comparison between the intellectually disabled children and their brothers and sisters.

THE OTHER CHILDREN

We asked the parents about the differences in raising an intellectually disabled child in comparison to their other children. While it is impossible to estimate the extent of those differences, it is clear that they are significant. Maura described the difference in one word—guilt.

'You are consumed with guilt with regard to the handicapped child. Guilt if you are cross with him as you cannot explain, guilt if you are too tired to do stimulating exercises with them, guilt if they are very ill when you get to the doctor. Forever and ever you have to do everything for this child.'

Pauline also has one word to describe the difference:

'Time. Our non-handicapped children effortlessly reach their developmental milestones. With or without our extra help they will walk, talk, develop skills, make friends. Our child with a disability takes so much longer to learn everything, each step is so much harder for him. You try to integrate your teaching skills so far as possible into ordinary family life but sometimes it can feel as if you are permanently "working". It can be hard to relax and just be a parent, which is, after all, what your child primarily needs you to be.'

Avril provided a new perspective:

'Don't think that because your other children are "normal" that they don't need you also. In fact, they are the special children.'

Jim and Ann made the comparison thus:

> 'When you raise a non-handicapped child you have expectations and hopes for the future for them and for your relationship with them. With a handicapped child you dread the future. The future is when you will be old and unable to cope and your handicapped child will no longer be controllable. Or the future is when you die and you don't know what will happen to this person that you love, dislike, and fear all at the same time. With the non-handicapped child there is a kind of blueprint for raising him. Custom, experience and what other people are doing or have done all give ideas that we might not be perfect but that things are fairly OK. With the handicapped child the rule book does not exist. No matter how good you are you have no way of gauging your own success. Every lesson is first begun with huge amounts of planning. For example, the process of teaching Aoife to put on her jumper. It became an analysis session on how people dress themselves. In short, you never feel you are "getting there", you never really know what "there" is and you never relax.'

Phil cannot help making the comparison with what might have been:

> 'A child with a mental handicap doesn't absorb skills or messages about their environment automatically and have to have the skills broken down into stages and practised often. One needs enormous patience for this. To make my child confident I have to listen closely to every word he says, to get the context, and then help develop the conversation. When a person has imperfect speech this can be very tiring. My son needs help with showering and dressing and everything takes a long time to do. I often wonder what my disabled son would have been like and I occasionally get a glimpse. For example, I think he would have been musical and liked poetry. I live a life of "if only" and never lose that huge sense of loss.'

Monica gets to the point:

> 'It's hard. You end up telling the child to do the same thing over and over. With the others, once or twice and they get the message.'

Kate identified some positive aspects:

> 'The differences are both mental and physical. With non-handicapped children each day is a new day of development, new horizons, new requirements. From an early age, they have been geared towards a life of self-determination with good common sense and moral values as decent human beings. The handicapped child requires a greater amount of time

spent looking after physical needs. Each step forward is slow and requires much patience and hope. Perhaps the one worry I don't have with Brona is that she is not capable of disappointing anyone or hurting her fellow man.'

Tom and Eithne have found that as time goes on they have been better able to get the balance right:

'While we have always tried to raise Aine in the same way as the other children, it *is* very different. At this stage we have learned how to handle most situations with her and try and avoid the major tantrums. However, this took a long time and was very trying at times, particularly when she began acting up in public places. With non-handicapped children there are guidelines—there is a sense of going along a predictable path with them whereas with Aine there was always a sense of the unknown. There is also the whole issue of expectations. "Normal" children are expected to conform to certain patterns as regards feeding, toilet training etc., etc. With a handicapped child there is a constant reviewing of expectations. One thing I find extremely touching is how understanding the other two children are. Although they get annoyed and embarrassed at times they are incredibly generous and patient with Aine.'

We will leave the last word to Maura:

'There is a huge restriction of freedom to go places and do normal things with the other children and family members. I have a concern about our other children who are older than the handicapped child. I think they are too adult, concerned, and good! Isn't that ridiculous!'

PERSONALLY SPEAKING

The impact on family life of raising an intellectually disabled child is being recognised more and more both in the literature and in organisations which serve families. An area which still requires attention is the impact of having an intellectually disabled child on the personal life and outlook of parents. May's account is both moving and very real:

'I find the burden heavier now than ever before. My younger two sons have set up their own careers and homes so we don't have the benefit of their help as much. They were always enormously helpful and supportive and would mind their older brother in the evenings when at home. As a couple we are isolated and sidelined from our friends because we can't join in activities that they pursue and go away for weekends etc. The last group of "sitters" I had are now past the sitting age so getting out in the evening is a major problem. Having a weekend or holiday away is nearly impossible. When someone does take our mentally handicapped son for a day we live like people "on parole" and cram in all we can in these precious hours. When we were young parents we had a great "network" with our friends and we all minded each other's children and had a week's holidays on our own. My friend's children are all grown up so we don't now have this support. As a couple we feel cheated of these years couples typically get after rearing a family. We share a lot of interests but are forced to pursue them separately. Getting time together is harder now than ever. We used to dream of travelling to see the world but these will never be fulfilled. We avail of any respite care offered but it is scarce and of short duration and we are given very short notice of it.'

Tom and Eithne found the going very difficult at the start:

'Because of the very slow diagnosis we initially felt a sense of relief that at least we now knew what the problem was. However, we both became very depressed at different times. My self-esteem was very, very low—I tortured myself looking at other women with normal healthy babies wondering what I had done wrong that they hadn't. We both really went in on ourselves and lost a lot of previous social contacts. I found it very difficult to face people. We also got very little family support. They found it difficult to come to terms with.'

Maura describes her situation in a pragmatic way:

'On a day-to-day basis we are very well. As the level of care can be demanding from time to time we are tired. Our other children are at the exam stage so I feel our life has more drudgery than other people's lives.'

It was a struggle for Pauline to come to terms with her situation:

'I adjusted with great difficulty. The first few months were a blur of strong emotional responses—grief, resentment, self-pity, anger. The first year was probably the most difficult period—I would not like to experience it again. I found counselling to be of enormous benefit. It allowed me to express a depth of negative feeling which society does not encourage mothers to admit to. It allowed me to be angry and to explore my own preconceptions and prejudices. Being able to get angry empowered me to deal with life more positively.'

A number of parents have commented on their dislike of patronising comments by people who have no idea what they are dealing with. Breda had this to say:

> 'It drives me mad when well-meaning people tell you how marvellous you are and that you will get your rewards in heaven. I did not choose for my child to have a handicap and I do not want to wait until I get to heaven to have a good time.'

Eithne described it thus:

> 'A good listening ear without all the painful platitudes—such as my mother-in-law's favourite, "God fits the back for the burden"—is helpful. The one that used to annoy me most—"only special people are chosen"— best translated as "so long as it doesn't happen to me".'

Jim identified the hardest aspects of caring for his intellectually disabled daughter:

> 'First, the feeling of being a failure as a parent. Second, the feeling of isolation. That is, isolated in the job of raising her. Also, isolated from our friends because we cannot do what they do because we are minding her and it is often awkward to bring her to events because of her unusual approach to social intercourse.'

Seamus perhaps summarises the feelings of all parents:

> 'We never get used to having a child with a mental handicap. In a sense, it leaves a pain that never goes away. And in a sense, the whole family becomes handicapped. Sometimes the pain is so small we don't know it is there. Sometimes it is so great we can hardly bear the ache of it. But it never leaves us. This we live with and expect to live with. It's like the rain. It is just part of life. However, we do not expect to have also to live in an uncaring system which adds its own pain by its careless, unfeeling attitude to the whole disabled family.'

Experiences of the caring services

The message coming through from parents in this section is that services are generally good once families can avail of them. Most of the difficulties lie in the fact that it is often quite problematic to gain access to the appropriate service. And then there are the inefficiencies within the services themselves. Jim and Ann capture the mood:

'Our experience with the service-providers has been very mixed. We have met a lot of well-intentioned people who clearly have the good of the client at heart. However, there is often a lack of professionalism and very often a huge lack of organisation and knowledge. Brona first had a tantrum when she was less than five years old and could not sleep at night because she was cold. At that point and on all occasions since we have sought help. Many times we were just ignored. We have listened to the advice given to us (when it was given) and made serious attempts to act on it. We never made an issue of it when different people gave conflicting advice. We are not stupid people and were always serious about taking whatever steps were necessary to solve the problems. Nevertheless, we were given the clear impression from the start that the problem was of our own making and that if we just "behaved ourselves" things would be OK. We even got this impression during a period when the majority of the tantrums occurred while she was with the care service. Somehow our bad parenting resulted in the teacher's poor control. For example, it seemed to be assumed that if she had a tantrum at the centre, this was the result of a row at home before she left the house. This was almost never the case.

One example of bad organisation was where Brona had six different teachers in the one year. Another was the issue of Brona's weight. We were constantly being advised that she was overweight and that we should take steps to reduce it. The result was that we fed her mouse-size meals. On the other hand, when she was in school she was allowed to eat any meals that other children did not want as well as her own.

The final crib! We always believed she was the WORST student ever seen in the school or training centre. While she was (and is) definitely in the A league it is only in recent years that we discovered that there are many more like her. It would have done a lot for our peace of mind and our self-esteem as parents to know that we were not alone in our uselessness. Yet it is true to say that the majority of the people we dealt with were honourable hard-working people.'

Tom and Eithne found a new lease of life when they were able to access the facility of regular breaks for Aine:

'When one has access to the services, the quality has been excellent. The difficulty lies in accessing services, particularly speech therapy. We are extremely lucky in that we now have a person who takes Aine on outings about once each week and she is brilliant. She has become like an auntie to Aine—she is a very caring person. Also over the past year, the same person and her family have taken Aine for regular breaks—generally only for one night or occasionally two. I feel that they have fulfilled an essential need that we have had for a number of years, i.e. a place for Aine to go where she is loved and cared for and an opportunity for us to give more attention to our other two children. In my view, respite care is essential for certain families particularly where there is very little extended family support. Because we now have these short breaks the whole family is coping much better. I believe services must begin to address the needs of the whole family unit. The other children in the family have needs which must be met and they also have to cope with the additional burden of having a handicapped sibling.'

Maureen would like to see an improvement in attitude from her service:

'Most of the personnel have given generously of their time and talents. However, I feel services are run to suit the staff more than the clients. The opinions of parents are often undervalued and sometimes ignored. I would like to see parents consulted more and included in decisions about their children. When my son was eighteen and had to leave school I felt the service-provider was not informed about services and options outside their own. We did our own research.'

Fiona has become intolerant of the 'fashionable ideologies' which appear to be so prevalent among care service agencies:

'I think it's time we stopped operating on the basis that the person with a mental handicap has to do all the integrating into normal society—and time we started thinking about normal society integrating with them instead. I think they might enjoy that!'

She further expresses her frustration:

'None of our children exist just from 9 to 5 from Mondays to Fridays. They are 24-hours-a-day, 365-days-a-year, real people, and as parents we understand that only too well.'

Fiona has this advice for service-providers:

'The ideas of parents must be taken into account in deciding types and standards of residential accommodation. Parents have never been asked, for example, whether they would consider a single group home in a housing estate to be a preferable alternative to a village or a small community environment.'

Monica would like to be more involved in the planning stages:

'The care workers are fantastic. They are very interested in the child and the progress being made. However, there is no consultation between management and parents regarding future plans and location for my child. Management needs to be improved. I have a general concern that if you complain, nobody listens to you and you have nowhere to go. It is very difficult to plan ahead.'

May has this advice for service-providers:

'They should provide:
- Counselling after diagnosis.
- More information on services available.
- More contact with other parents with similar problems.
- More involvement with school, special care unit or workshop.
- A parents' council in every special unit or school.
- Stating children's needs and a life-plan set out and reviewed regularly.
- Activities organised during the long summer holidays. These holidays are dreaded by the children and parents equally. It is my perception that while a little structure might exist for children of school-going age, it all seems to stop at eighteen years of age. When mentally handicapped children are younger they can sometimes join siblings and their friends or other children on the road for play. But by the time they are eighteen, this is not so and disabled adults are nearly always lonely. This is particularly so when they are the only one at home with parents.
- Planned, regular respite care and plenty of notice of it. Recently, I got a few days' respite care for my son but the notice of it was so short my husband could not change business commitments. So it really was a waste of an opportunity for us as a couple.
- Phased-in residential care. There should be funding for seven-day residential houses. Some people could live there for five days (Mon–Fri) and then other people living at home could go there for the weekend. This would also facilitate looking at different mixes of people with a view to them forming a permanent home together.'

Kate has had a very productive relationship with her service-provider:

'I have always found them helpful. They seem to be continually reassessing and improving the quality of life for their charges and I have found we have worked hand in hand together.'

FEARS FOR THE FUTURE

Many parents of people with intellectual disabilities express the wish that their child will die half an hour before they do. Parents do not wish to pass on the responsibility for a life they have created to anyone. This is a sad but very real predicament for parents of a child with intellectual disability. It was notable while going through the responses that parents who were already availing of residential care or who had a range of options with regard to respite care were less frightened about the future. Indeed, some of those parents felt that their offspring were happier in residential care than if they were living at home. The gaping hole with regard to parents' concerns for the future is the complete lack of flexibility with regard to when and how their disabled offspring will eventually avail of residential care. Seán, like most parents, has many questions yet to be answered:

> 'What will happen to my mentally handicapped daughter when I die? Who will look after her? Will it be the "caring agencies" who did such a dismal job during my lifetime? Will it be a family member? Which one? Where will she live? Will it be in the house in which she has spent all her life thus far? If so, how will it be supported? Will it be by the community which she knows intimately and which knows her? If not, where? If she moves somewhere else who will help her adjust to alien surroundings and strange people? Should I will my house to her? If so, who might share it with her, to help with expenses and oversee the smooth running of her affairs? Should I set up a trust for her? If so, who should administer the trust? Family solicitor or family member? Would such a trust interfere with her Disability Allowance money? What are her rights in law? What would happen to the trust when she dies?'

Andrew takes a more optimistic view:

> 'A view to the future. But first a look back in time. Our efforts for our son have been to enable him to become an independent person, able to look after himself. This would be ideal but is unfortunately not realistic. He will need support for life. This will become an increasing burden on us, his parents. Up until now this has not been a problem. The way forward in the future I see as a gradual transfer of support to the caring agency. They would eventually take over and maintain his lifestyle. This can be achieved over a period of time by using respite places and eventually to full residential placement. I would like to see my son happily settled in my lifetime.'

Tom and Eithne have one word to describe their thoughts about the future:

'FEAR—Who will take care of Aine when we die? I lie awake at night worrying about this. She is so vulnerable. It's frightening to think about. Fear also that the burden of care will become intolerable. While those around us will move on when their children become independent, we will be caught in a "time warp"—endlessly caring even when we are no longer able to.'

Maura expresses a similar view:

'I hope he dies before we do. Other than that, I dread the future.'

Kate is a parent who has seen her daughter settle into residential care and her views are quite contrasting:

'As Brona is already in residential care, I'm happy that she will always be looked after. I see lots of caring people in the profession and know that now such work is respected and facilities and services are improving all the time. As she has spent 15 years fully at home in the family, I know that should she outlive me, they will be there for her. I don't think she will make any great improvement, but has reached her potential and has a good life.'

ADVICE

We asked the parents what advice they would have for other parents of people with intellectual disability, particularly those who are just starting out. A recurring theme was the importance of taking 'one day at a time', as the song says. The other important point worth highlighting is the fact that you, the parent, are the real expert about your child. Both professionals and parents themselves must acknowledge this fact. The first piece of advice from Maura is as simple as it is insightful:

'Be helpless and not too capable. Life is hard but by no means is it all that bad.'

Pauline cautions about worrying too much:

'When our daughter was born I imagined all kinds of awful scenarios, none of which materialised. So one thing I have learned is that if you sit and worry about the future, the picture you paint is invariably worse than the reality.'

Jim offers some very worthwhile advice:

> 'Remember you are the expert. The professional will never know the reality of living with a mentally handicapped person, will never have to accept ultimate responsibility, will eventually shake your hand and move on. Take no shit. You don't have to get caught up in the "little gift from heaven" syndrome. You are taking on something which is hard work and which will possibly take a lot out of you. However, it can be done and you can have a reasonable life despite the drawbacks.'

May listed her advice as follows:

> '1. Get bereavement counselling.
> 2. Be very careful of your relationship with your partner and nourish it well over the years.
> 3. Build up huge support systems and use them regularly.
> 4. Never call your handicapped child your "special child". This could imply that your other children aren't special.
> 5. Value your own expertise regarding your child and insist that professionals value it too.
> 6. Scream and shout at the government to properly fund appropriate services.'

Barbara's view appears to concur with many of the others:

> 'Accept all the help you can get. Enjoy the good days and forget the bad ones.'

Kate cautions against trying too hard:

> 'After having your child assessed, don't go from one source to another looking for possibly better results. Get in touch with any services in your district. Always listen but make the final decision yourself. Don't look for reasons to blame yourself. Don't get offended by some friends' attitudes of pity, avoidance, or advice. They also are trying to come to terms with it. Take time and don't try to accomplish the impossible.'

May sees the positive side also:

> 'While a lot of the comments are negative we have gained a lot from our handicapped child and other parents do too. There is no security with life and people so I cope by taking it day by day. If you worry about the big issue you'll miss so many nice things every day.'

For a unique and, we believe, very helpful perspective, Eithne offers this advice:

'When responding to these questions, I felt it was important to make what is for me, at any rate, a fundamental distinction between the person that Aine is and her handicap. What causes all the worry and difficulty for *us* is not her as a person but the fact that she has this handicapping condition. This might appear a stupid thing to say but if, in an ideal world, the needs of the handicapped person were met adequately and without hassle on the part of the families, the burden would be eased greatly. So much of the grief families experience is bound up in the absence or inadequacy of services. And this inevitably interferes in the child–parent relationship. Since we have recently been able to avail of a number of breaks for Aine, it has made a great difference to our lives, because for the first time there was a sense of having the burden lifted— that there was a recognition of Aine's needs and also our needs as a family. This service is very cost-effective and yet it makes a great difference to us. I also feel that if we had had counselling at the time of Aine's diagnosis it would have made a great difference to us.'

Looking back, Monica says she should have sought and received help much sooner:

'I, mother, coped very badly, but as I put a good face on things nobody asked me ever how I felt or how I was. Contact with other parents in a support group situation would have been great. Better support in his early days to identify his condition and requirements would have made all the difference.'

SUMMARY

Probably the first reaction of any parent of an intellectually disabled person upon reading this chapter is 'and I thought I was the only one'. Well, now you know you are not. For those not raising a disabled person, the message is that we will never appreciate quite how hard parents have to work in order to maintain and develop their dependent offspring. Perhaps this is why neither governments nor service-providers have provided sufficient supports for families to date. However, it is evident that parents are no longer prepared to accept piecemeal services. They will demand the kinds of support services that will enable them to enjoy 'normal' family life with a minimum of adjustment owing to the needs of the intellectually disabled child. Only in recent years have parents been coming forward and specifying exactly what these needs are. This must continue.

If this chapter sparked any emotion in you or struck a chord, then that is because the people who contributed to it are the ones who understand best what parents are going through. The best therapists, counsellors, confidants and supporters are other parents. If you are a parent who is feeling overwhelmed by your current circumstances, or even if you are not, make the effort to contact other parents. The most likely place to do that is the unit/school which your child attends. You will be amazed at how much you have in common with other parents. That is where you can give out about things which few others will understand.

It is also important for parents to remember that they are the experts with regard to the needs of their intellectually disabled child. It is no longer necessary for parents to be intimidated by professionals of any discipline. Professionals are paid by the State to provide the best possible care for your offspring. Without your child, they would not have a job. Parents must demand the best possible service and never accept rudeness or buck-passing. If you do not insist on a professional and comprehensive support structure, the services will not develop to the level that is so clearly required.

Another message that came through the survey loud and clear is that parents must learn to accept whatever help and support is offered. Being 'helpless and not too capable' sounds like very sensible advice. Parents themselves may be slow or unable to recognise the level of stress and burden of care which comes with raising a child with an intellectual disability. It is also important to insist that they are provided with regular support services. For most parents, regular breaks have proven to be of enormous benefit to all the members of the family. It is critical that parents learn to have a life that is sometimes without the disabled child. The intellectually disabled person also needs to learn that the umbilical cord was cut at some point. So if parents will not take this time out for themselves, they should do so in the long-term interests of their disabled child. It is clear that there is simply not enough of this type of support available.

All parents worry about the future. However, it is rarely discussed with their other children or with the service-providers. If there is to be a smooth transition of the intellectually disabled person into that phase of their life when the parents are no longer around, early planning is essential. As it is likely that the siblings will be around to oversee the outcome of that transition after the parents have passed away, it is essential that they are involved in these negotiations at an early stage. Open communication lines across all boundaries are essential if intellectually disabled people and their families are to enjoy life to the full. This means regular contact with the personnel in the caring service and open discussion about the pertinent issues within the family.

Finally, it is very evident that, despite all the trials and tribulations of raising an intellectually disabled child, most parents are coming out the other side. They are learning to adapt to a life that they did not anticipate. They are now demanding their own rights and those of their intellectually disabled offspring. And it is about time.

5. EARLY INTERVENTION

STEPHEN KEALY

INTRODUCTION

The years of infancy and early childhood are a time of great importance for all children and their families. Current theories of human lifespan development suggest that many factors—the child's temperament, parenting styles, opportunities for learning, and the family's social and economic environment, among others—help to shape patterns of growth and learning (Santrock 1995). The presence of a condition leading to disability is an additional source of influence on the development of some children. Early intervention programmes set out to ameliorate the impact of disability and/or disadvantage on children from birth to the age of four years. These programmes have been very effective in changing the thrust of service development, not only for children but also for their families. For most parents the birth of a son or daughter is anticipated with great joy and excitement. A child who is born with an apparent disability can radically challenge and alter parents' expectations. Diagnosis at birth is possible if an infant is born with an identifiable syndrome or medical condition. Other children may develop disabilities later, and their needs will emerge only during the first few years of life.

This chapter provides an overview of current services in Ireland, examines the impact of disability, the rationale and effectiveness of early intervention services, their recent history in Ireland, and some of the ongoing challenges which have to be addressed in early services programmes in order to ensure that good practice operates equitably at a national level.

EARLY CONTACT

For some parents, first contact with early services takes place in the hospital maternity unit or when the birth notification reaches their local health board. Children aged up to two years who have disabilities are also identified through the public health home visiting programme, while general practitioners (primary care medical doctors) may refer some young children for special intervention. Parents may also contact service agencies directly if they have concerns about their children's development.

Families in Ireland

Family composition today reflects recent social change and greater cultural diversity. The family as a unit of father and mother as married partners and their children is no longer the norm. In 1996 just 39% of Irish households comprised a married couple with children, and 28% of all births in Ireland were outside marriage—more than the average EU rate (Kennedy 2001). Recently, too, Ireland has been seen by women from abroad as a desirable place to give birth, and the numbers of infants born in Ireland to mothers from outside Europe has increased. Immigration into Ireland has generated a cultural diversity not easily mapped onto services provided to date by the regional health boards. Whatever the composition of a family, its members must grapple with the presence of a child with apparent disabilities and what this means for them. Providers of special services and national associations increasingly recognise the needs of the brothers and sisters of a child with disabilities and are aware of cultural diversity.

Formal supports

The Domiciliary Care Allowance (DCA) introduced in Ireland in the 1970s is an acknowledgement of the financial demands of disability. This understanding is alluded to in the health strategy document *Shaping a healthier future* (Department of Health 1994). This allowance becomes available when a child reaches two years of age on the basis that a child with disabilities may require care and attention above the norm.

Irish government strategy had earlier emphasised the desirability of a range of supports in its policy document *Needs and abilities* (Review Group on Mental Handicap Services 1990). Unfortunately the lack of clear national directives and the insufficient allocation of resources have meant uneven service delivery in spite of detailed planning by regional health boards (Southern Health Board 1997).

Flexibility

Not all families have the same capacity to adjust, adapt and manage their responsibilities. Respecting this variation in family capacity has shifted the focus of early services towards considering flexible supports: for example, such an approach has enabled some families to take home with them young children with serious life-support needs. Home support programmes endeavour to reduce the impact of disability in practical ways by providing flexible, instrumental supports. These range from home nursing to in-house child cover for a number of hours each day or week, which in turn enables parents to spend time together, address the needs of their other children or complete essential jobs. Voluntary groups such as the Jack & Jill Foundation, an initiative started by a parent, provide additional support to the statutory services (Redmond 1999).

At its simplest, such provision allows personal space and time for either parent. However, the impact of disability is likely to be lessened if there is a collaborative understanding between parents and professionals based on trust, mutual respect, and open and clear communication (Bailey *et al.* 1998). Anecdotal evidence suggests that the impact of disability is likely to be lessened if services are equitably provided. To date, the unevenness of how new resources are allocated in Ireland can often mean in practice that those in greatest need may be the last to receive an appropriate service.

EFFECTIVENESS OF EARLY INTERVENTION

Evaluating the effectiveness of early intervention programmes can be difficult and occasionally elusive. Many studies have focused on the gains children make in cognitive, social, motor and language development. Evaluation of family intervention includes effectiveness and appropriateness of the intervention for the family and the ensuing quality of life (Bailey *et al.* 1998). Long-term outcomes are also key indices as to whether or not an intervention has been effective (Kellaghan *et al.* 1995). The increase or decrease of family distress, parent–child interactions and the achievement of greater community involvement are other measurable outcomes (Guralnick 1998).

Effective early intervention programmes may be said to share a number of components, as they help to:
- *enable* parents to optimise the time spent with their children;
- *complete* specific pieces of work with a child based on identified need;
- *develop* the relationship between parent and child;
- *make* services more accessible;
- *provide* a collaborative working structure for parents, professionals and service-providers.

There is, accordingly, a compelling requirement to monitor and evaluate whether early intervention programmes are delivered to plan, implemented equitably and achieve a quality standard. At a minimum, each substantive element of early services should, it is proposed, be tracked under the headings listed below (Rush 2002).

Effectiveness
- What are the key results or outcomes of the service?
- Is the service delivered against defined objectives and goals?

Efficiency
- Are the core processes or activities being delivered in a way that minimises the costs incurred?
- Are redundancies of appointments, meetings and family and service resources minimised?
- Is there attention to value for money in service arrangements?

Quality and service levels
- Are there consistent standards in how services are delivered?
- Are these standards defined and measured?

SERVICES IN IRELAND

Early intervention services in Ireland have developed over the past 30 years in tandem with sweeping changes in both the policy underpinning services and the structure of services for families who have children with disabilities or who experience other forms of disadvantage.

Community care
The Commission on Mental Handicap in Ireland (1965) recommended the setting up of regional diagnostic teams to ascertain the presence of mental handicap (the term used at that time). These teams were available to regional health boards to provide assessment and advice in respect of children presenting with a significant intellectual delay or a recognisable syndrome of mental handicap. A team consisted of a psychologist, psychiatrist and social worker. Once established, the teams provided little more than an assessment and placement service: ongoing support to families was not seen as part of their brief.

The establishment of diagnostic and assessment teams coincided in some areas with the setting up of the regional health boards under the 1970 Health Act (Government of Ireland 1970), which gave the regional health boards a role in developing services for people with a mental handicap. The structure of the regional health boards reflected the emerging emphasis on community services. No clear philosophy of community services was then in place but rather an awareness that the health services should be based in local communities and accessible there. Each regional health board inherited a number of community-based services from the county councils. The 1970 Health Act set out a structure for the development of community services which built upon and augmented those services already in place. Debates at the time about the configuration of services questioned whether those delivered in the community were more cost-effective than institutional care. It was argued at the time that even if good-quality community care might be more costly than alternatives it was nonetheless the preferred option (Mittler 1982). In the United Kingdom the process of dismantling large institutions had commenced, influenced significantly by the thinking of Wolfensberger (1972), among others (Felce *et al.* 1998).

First steps

In Ireland the first official programme of early intervention was the Rutland Street Project of the late 1960s and early 1970s which was intended to provide structured learning opportunities for children in Dublin's inner city. It developed along lines similar to the American 'Headstart' programme. Its aims were to augment and enrich early learning for marginalised children with few educational opportunities.

By 1994, Headstart programmes in the United States had served some 700,000 children. A re-analysis of data from the original Headstart longitudinal study found that these children made gains when compared with children who attended other programmes and pre-schools (Lee *et al.* 1988). Gains were not always sustained, possibly because of poor-quality follow-on programmes. But it was striking that when there was greater participation of parents in the process, outcomes were greater (Parker *et al.* 1987). By contrast with today's more family-centred approaches, clinical teams in Ireland in the 1970s did not often perceive parents as active participants in the development of their children's lives. In the area of intellectual disabilities, parents were slowly making demands on professionals, not only for more information on the nature of their son or daughter's intellectual disability but also on how to help and stimulate them. Parents began to question traditional attitudes and practices in the care of their children. They often reported negative experiences about how they were informed about their child's disability. Some were told in very brutal terms, often with the suggestion that institutionalisation was the best option. Children with disabilities were not always seen as valued, and consequently there was little in the way of official supports either in urban or rural areas.

Changed focus

Regional assessment teams in Ireland began to move from their role of assessment and diagnosis to one of meaningful supportive intervention with families. Voluntary bodies such as St Michael's House in Dublin and the Brothers of Charity Services in the west of Ireland were at the forefront of this change (McCormack, this volume). At St Michael's House Research in Dublin, the first incumbent of a dedicated research position, Roy McConkey, brought a fresh perspective to service development by emphasising the primary role of parents in the lives of children with disabilities.

At the same time, a number of researchers at the Hester Adrian Research Centre, Manchester, were working innovatively with children who had an intellectual disability, notably on strategies recognising the key role of parents in the development of their children (Cunningham and Sloper 1978). Brimblecombe (1974; 1976) introduced flexible access for parents to professional staff and services, all of which challenged traditional thinking (Goddard and Rubissow 1977).

A programme originating in the United States, the Doman-Delacato Method of training (Doman 1974), set out to develop lower brain structures through a range of patterning and physiotherapy exercises, in the belief that higher cortical functions could not develop unless primitive and basic neurological responses were facilitated. This programme was identified by some parents in Ireland as a way in which they could become more actively involved with their son or daughter. The programme gained popularity through the national media (e.g. the *Irish Press* of 2–4 April 1973). The method enabled parents to harness the goodwill of their friends and neighbours in putting in place very active exercise and stimulation programmes each day.

At an official level some support was given to the Doman-Delacato method, and at least one family was sponsored to visit the United States to partake in the assessment process and to follow an intervention programme. However, no unambiguous evidence emerged to support the hypothesis that such an intensive physical intervention had a significant and sustained impact on a child's future development (American Academy of Paediatrics 1982). The intensity of the programme reportedly had a negative impact on some families. By the start of the twenty-first century the Doman-Delacato method was no longer prominent in Ireland, although similar volunteer-based initiatives, such as the 'Brainwave' programme, continued to be seen by parents as effective for some children.

ACCESS TO EARLY INTERVENTION

By the 1990s, parents of young children with disabilities in Ireland could find advice and information about appropriate interventions in a range of materials.

National Association
Both the Down Syndrome Association and the National Association for the Mentally Handicapped of Ireland (NAMHI) prepared information packs on disabilities for parents. These provide important personal and practical information on disabilities so often absent from clinical textbooks. These Associations have also announced their intent to extend information services by providing them on-line.

Unfortunately, good practice guidelines on breaking the news to parents about their child's disability are not readily accessible or available from the regional health boards in Ireland. As a consequence, practice varies a good deal from region to region, or even among agencies. A telephone survey of hospital maternity units in January 2003 suggested that it is not clear whether written guidelines are in place as a matter of policy. However, all respondents affirmed the key role of the resident paediatrician in informing parents about their son or daughter's condition. Doran (2000) reported that the National Maternity Hospital follows guidelines from a document provided by the Royal College of Paediatrics and Child Health entitled *Right from the start: breaking bad news to parents*. These guidelines insist that both parents should be told together in a private place and as soon as possible.

Parents have reported a continuum of experience from very positive to extremely negative as to how the news was broken to them. Arbitrary practices mean that a core question posed earlier by Peter Mittler in Tullamore, Co. Offaly (Mittler 1982), has not lost its relevance. The question—'What happens in the local maternity unit when a child with Down Syndrome is born?'—is relevant to all children born with a disability and should provide a focus for early services.

Parent groups

Parent groups are a resource within any programme of early services. Over the last 20 years specialist parent groups have developed in response to specific syndromes (e.g. Joubert's, Fragile X). Some programmes run specific workshops for parents, while others facilitate mutual support groups. The Down Syndrome Association of Ireland has very active branches which support parents and link them with each other at critical periods, as does the Irish Society for Autistic Children. Providing support for brothers and sisters has now become an integral part of many early services. Brothers and sisters have identified the impact that the presence of a family member with disability can have on others. The challenge, then, for early support service-providers is to stay in touch with parents and family members and learn from their feedback while being sensitive to cultural and family differences.

NATIONAL SURVEY

A national survey on early intervention identified the uneven extent of services for young children with intellectual disabilities (NAMHI 1995). The survey identified nearly 2000 children (1924) between the ages of birth and six years in receipt of a service. The total number of children referred to the responding agencies in the survey year was 804, most with an identifiable syndrome or developmental delay. What emerged from analysis of the survey data was the unevenness of services around the country. In some places programmes were innovative and of good quality, while elsewhere this was not so. At the time of the NAMHI survey no data were available from longitudinal follow-up studies of children with a very low birth weight in Ireland.

The survey identified the pivotal roles of the Director of Community Care and the Medical Officer of Health in the regional health boards in the process of routing all referrals for early intervention services. Area Medical Officers (AMOs) reported to these officers and managed developmental clinics, and contacted children seen by public health nurses as they visited homes in the area. Children who attended these clinics were also tracked during the school medical visit.

In summary, it was evident that throughout the country many innovative approaches in service delivery were in place. Where this was so, services arose and, today, continue to flourish in the absence of any coherent national policy on the aims and outcomes of early intervention for young children with developmental delay. As developmental delay may also be associated with educational difficulty (Guralnick 1998) and increased rates of health, psychological and neuro-developmental problems (Blair *et al.* 1995), prospective studies are indicated. For example, paediatric programmes linked to hospital maternity units should gather relevant data on at-risk infants as a priority.

LOCAL SERVICES

The apparent success of some early intervention services dramatically changed the nature of provision for young children. First, an educational approach to address the learning needs of children gathered force. Interventions were made very early, shortly after the birth of a child with a recognisable syndrome. The greater involvement of parents in meeting the needs of their children led in turn to pressure for more locally based services. Many parents had previously faced the stark choice of either sending their child away to a residential facility or keeping them at home. Staying at home, in the absence of any local provision, meant in practice that some children received little or no support. Some parents, because of prevailing attitudes or through a lack of understanding, denied their children any contact with the greater community.

The demand for local early services led to the establishment of special day care services and pre-schools, some located in assessment clinics managed by voluntary bodies. As younger children attending these centres grew older, parents sought day schools and classes. The ongoing change in attitudes created a demand for more inclusive learning opportunities. Children with special needs began to attend their local community pre-schools and national (primary) schools on the basis of inclusion. Current policy is to strengthen the resource base to achieve inclusion (Department of Education and Science 2002). Pre-school inclusion is more likely to take place in an urban setting than in a rural one. The White Paper on Education (Department of Education 1995, 16) identified the importance of early childhood experiences for a child's development: 'Early disadvantages affect the child's enduring experiences within formal schooling, because such disadvantages tend to be both persistent and cumulative'. The policy agreement *A government of renewal* (Government of Ireland 1994) committed the government to further expansion of pre-school education. As yet, public supported pre-school education has not achieved any urgency. In rural areas a scattered population makes it difficult to provide pre-school services, particularly in the absence of mandated government policy.

NEW APPROACHES

Recently, awareness has grown about the need to involve and collaborate with parents as partners in the care of their young children. Parents have become more assertive in demanding local services, inclusion and participation in decisions about their children. The network of non-residential educational support programmes, particularly in rural areas, is a direct response to the stated needs of parents. The inclusion of children with disabilities in mainstream pre-schools and schools suggests a greater openness and understanding of disability. Although the Visiting Teacher Service is over-subscribed, demand for it indicates to some extent the success of early services programmes. Each of these improvements demands evaluation to ensure that resources are targeted effectively. Each reflects, too, a growing awareness of the family context of early intervention.

Family functioning

Adopting a systemic approach helps to illuminate the benefits of good early intervention (Carr, this volume). Early services may foster the relationships between parents, child and other family members. The quality of the relationship will often determine how any intervention is made within the family. Child characteristics contribute to outcomes. Biological conditions express a child's developmental vulnerability. And yet vulnerability also interacts with behavioural and other family factors, for example in families with poor social competencies and inadequate support structures (Crnic and Stormshak 1997). Intervention programmes that improve a mother's capacity to interact more appropriately and effectively with her child have lasting positive effects on both mother and child (Krauss 1997). Knowledge of the disabled child means that parents relate to the person and adapt to the disability. This knowledge facilitates an understanding of the child's needs, not only as a member of the family but also in the community. Such an understanding, built on early positive experiences, sets clear objectives for the future with a greater possibility of more desirable outcomes.

Increased competence

Building social competencies of child and parents is central to future progress and a core component of effective intervention programmes. Such competencies are more likely to be achieved where there are positive parent interactions that provide warmth and predictability in meeting identified need (Bowlby 1980).

MEETING NEEDS

Parents of young children seek information about their child's condition and the likely prospects as the child grows and develops. Most frequently, they ask about what their child's diagnosis—if there is one—may mean, and the range of available services. More immediately, the questions parents ask continue to have the same urgency:

- Will my child sit up?
- Will my child walk?
- Will my child go to the local school?
- What sort of life will my child have?

Regardless of how much difficulty a child has, parents continue to ask very similar questions. In response, early service agents set out to address these issues through the provision of home-based or centre-based support, community services or some combination of each of these formal supports.

Recent developments

What is clear, however, is that while services have developed nationally throughout Ireland, they have not done so in response to an explicit national policy. Rather they have sprung up haphazardly in both voluntary and statutory organisations. Each initiative has met identified needs in different but flexible ways with the primary aim of reducing for parents their sense of isolation and of encouraging a more proactive working relationship with their son or daughter. Since the early 1990s the Department of Health has endorsed a wide range of supports to enable young children to live in the family. These supports explicitly recognise the impact a disabled child can and does have on all family members. The success of the Home Support Scheme is one of the most significant outcomes at a policy level for early services. However, the scheme has been implemented and delivered unevenly. Some attempt is now being made to quantify outcomes for families who have a child with a diagnosed disabling condition (Department of Health 1994).

Respite services

Respite care is provided on a planned basis to enable families to have a break from the 24-hour care of their son or daughter. This service is a key factor in enabling some parents to care for the child within the family home, particularly those children with multiple handicaps. Some respite services are based in special centres, while others use adapted houses in the community. Most parents who use respite services speak positively of their experiences. For all parents, leaving their son or daughter in the care of another person can be upsetting, evoking strong feelings of guilt. They may find it helpful to place the short-term respite opportunity in the wider context of planning shared care—where family carers work with professional bodies or volunteers to meet their childrens' needs over time (McConkey and Adams 2000).

Respite services are provided in most community care areas in Ireland, usually on a contract basis with a local service-provider, either a voluntary agency or the local health board. An innovation in respite care was the development of 'Share a Break' schemes (Fay 1999). These schemes, initially started as holiday breaks, are essentially short-term fostering arrangements whereby children stay with host families in the community. The relationship established between both families enables bilateral arrangements to be put in place to address specific needs.

A more difficult need to address is that of emergency care. This need usually arises when a specific crisis presents, e.g. the death of a parent, sickness, etc. In different community care areas throughout the country solutions emerge, often painfully, to address this need. As with all service provision flexibility is a key component.

CHALLENGES

Providers who undertake to deliver early intervention for children in Ireland face challenges in coordinating services, achieving equity, targeting specific needs of some groups of children, and adhering to guidelines for good practice.

Coordination

Successful early services depend on the effective coordination of scarce resources. This process should begin, if not in the maternity unit soon after birth, at least from the time the birth notification reaches the local regional health board. A designated service coordinator may contribute by liaising between families and various professionals. However, neither coordinating activity has a legal basis. In the United States federal legislation mandates states to provide and resource an individual family support programme. Closer to home, legislation directs local authorities to provide statements of children's needs. By contrast, the 1970 Health Act does not place an equivalent responsibility on regional health boards.

The abolition of the position of Director of Community Care and the reduced role for Area Medical Officers has led to some confusion as to who has the overall responsibility for ensuring good-quality, effective early services programmes. Each health board now has a Director of Disabilities, who in turn has operational Disability Managers. It remains to be seen what role these managers will play in coordinating scarce resources to ensure that effective programmes operate on the ground. Nationally, the government's strategy on primary health care (Department of Health and Children 2001) is a challenge for the coordination of different intervention strands. The ten pilot sites in each regional health board area will provide an opportunity to ensure that the needs of people with disabilities are kept to the fore, particularly the young infant in the family.

Equity

A key concept in the health strategy document (Department of Health 1994) is equity. Equity is also a substantive underlying theme of the report of the Commission on the Status of People with Disabilities (1996). Equity can only be achieved by effective coordination and management of scarce resources, human and material, in each community care area.

A local coordinator will:

- link statutory and voluntary agencies, locally and nationally;
- evaluate intervention programmes;
- ensure that resources reach parents as needed;
- promote community awareness;
- ensure that a library of information is available to parents;
- have in place an individual programme for each family;
- source resources, such as pre-school education in the local community;
- listen to parents;
- ensure flexibility in service provision;
- endeavour to customise the supports to the child in the family.

In putting in place an individual family support programme plan, a coordinator should consult with parents in the knowledge that they are stakeholders and that each family is unique in how members perceive or adapt to disability. Some parents will understand their child's disability more swiftly than others and consequently will seek intervention supports at an earlier stage. For a small number of parents, uncertainty about using services can place their disabled child at risk. Uncoordinated management of clinic attendance can be needlessly stressful, with some parents spending a disproportionate amount of time visiting different clinics, sometimes at a great distance from the family home. This can be particularly demanding in rural areas in the absence of a local public transport system. Parents from rural areas also receive appointments at Dublin-based clinics where interventions are planned similar to those which take place locally. This results in poor use of limited resources, adding additional stress on families.

Structuring early services demands a collaborative effort between a large number of professionals and agencies:

- the public health service;
- maternity units;

- paediatric services;
- children's hospitals;
- pre-school services;
- special units;
- all professionals involved in children's services.

Children with particular needs

Some young children have very special life needs which are additional to their intellectual disability and consequently require intensive medical follow-up, not only in a paediatric unit but also in the family home. Supporting such children within the family home requires collaboration between members of early services, the paediatric unit and local health personnel. One of the outcomes of better neonatal care is the survival of children with specific syndromes whose life needs place very great demands on family carers. Many homes become overcrowded with the amount of equipment needed to sustain life. Some syndromes have very specific consequences for care and learning. The provision of such intensive care does have a major impact on family members. Simple everyday activities such as feeding and washing can become time-consuming and when completed have to commence again. Balancing the needs of other children in the family against those of the child with particular needs can introduce an additional burden.

Other children may show behavioural challenges from an early age which can become very disruptive to the functioning of the family home. The ongoing challenge for early service-providers is to provide a programme of support which reflects the needs of the child within the family.

Education

In the past decades residential placement has become the exception for young children with intellectual disabilities: most children live with their families (Mulvany 2000). An inclusive model of service provision sets out to identify the many resources available within a child's local community and to access these either by right or through negotiation. For some years, children who have a diagnosis of Down Syndrome and cerebral palsy have been attending local pre-schools and national (primary) schools on an inclusive basis. The approach to children with intellectual disability is now primarily educational, displacing older models of care or custody. However, cognisance must be taken of a medical or diagnosed condition with specific effects on the child's health or functioning.

Educational opportunities in the community for a child with disabilities vary and can often reflect more the commitment of individual schools or principals than active coherent government policy (Shevlin and Carpenter, this volume). However, some early service programmes have reported anecdotally on the reluctance of some schools to include children with disabilities. This reluctance is often linked to lack of knowledge of disability. In addition, school boards of management are acutely aware of the financial constraints under which the Department of Education must operate. The Review Committee report (Special Education Review Committee 1993) identified inclusion as a choice for parents. More recently, additional resources have been made available to schools to support children with disabilities in their local schools. Resource support teachers and special educational needs assistants have eased the inclusion process (Department of Education and Science 2002). However, serious consideration has also to be given to substantially reducing class size. In rural areas, the choice of the local national (primary) school is often not a realistic option, given class sizes and competing demands. Where children have been successfully integrated, the decisive component is the willingness, motivation, interest and 'can-do' attitude of teachers and schools.

For children attending their local schools, there is a recognition that ongoing visiting support is needed. However, the emerging National Educational Psychological Service is not in a position to support all teachers who have a child with disabilities in their class.

To date, no Education Act has spelled out the responsibilities of the Department of Education and Science. This has meant that while children with disabilities may have more readily accessible supports in the classroom, such supports are not seamlessly provided and may not reflect specific needs. Recent high court cases in Ireland involving decisions instructing the Department of Education and Science to provide services for certain types of children suggest that a coherent, well-executed national education policy is not yet being implemented.

Guidelines

Recommendations for further development of early intervention services, based on evidence from the published literature and from practitioners working with families in Ireland, are proposed here.

- Develop a national policy on early intervention services as a matter of priority.
- Mandate each regional health authority to have in place a local early intervention policy in line with national policy.
- Ensure that each regional health authority area has early intervention teams which will link closely with local services, including maternity, paediatric and genetic units.
- Resource early intervention services adequately.
- Coordinate early intervention services to provide the maximum benefit to the child and the family.
- Monitor each child's development from birth to three years, as some delays are not evident until the child reaches his/her second or third year.

Partnership between professionals and parents should be the theme of early

intervention services and should include the following elements (NAMHI 1998):
- home-based and/or centre-based programmes as appropriate;
- family counselling services;
- adequate crisis and respite services;
- flexible and intensive home support services;
- flexible systems to support the child in the local pre-school;
- specialist pre-school services;
- support groups for parents, siblings and extended families;
- adequate funding for resource materials, e.g. reading materials, audio-visual materials, information technology, and toy library equipment.

SUMMARY

The community-based service model of early support services has been recognised for some time as a decisive factor in fostering the development of parent–child relationships. Children who have opportunities for more consistent, satisfying interactions with their parents tend to be better in their development, particularly where an emphasis is placed on improving their social competencies.

The structure of family life has changed dramatically in Ireland, as has the richness of cultural diversity. Families, regardless of their composition, have a continuum of needs which challenge the effective delivery of services. Disability does have a significant impact on mothers, fathers, grandparents, brothers and sisters. Expectations are changed, sometimes to the extent that they are too low, which in turn is unhelpful to the child with disabilities.

Disability brings, for some parents and families, a sense of isolation and social exclusion, which in turn can foster a sense of helplessness. Support services and intervention programmes have to be delivered equitably, with their content incorporating strong evidence-based data.

The Department of Health and Children and the Department of Education and Science must start implementing programmes of early services on the basis of a visionary national strategic policy. This task is not insurmountable, given the relatively small population of the Republic of Ireland—3.9 million persons. Recognition of the emotional, financial and time demands of a disabled child in the family should be expressed in mandated national policies. Regional health boards should have a mandated responsibility to put in place individual and adequately resourced family support programmes which in turn would make a significant contribution to strengthening national programmes of family support based on equity and need. Early support services at all levels need a statutory commitment linked to adequate resources. But more importantly, planners should listen to parents, read the data and take action.

REFERENCES

American Academy of Paediatrics, Committee on Children with Disabilities (1982) Policy statement: the Doman-Delacato treatment of neurologically handicapped children. *Pediatrics* **70**, 810–12.

Bailey, D.B. Jr, McWilliam, R.A., Darkes, L.A., Hebbeler, K., Simeonsson, R.J., Spiker, D. and Wagner, M. (1998) Family outcomes in early intervention: a framework for program evaluation and efficacy research. *Exceptional Children* **64** (3), 313–28.

Blair, C., Ramey, C.T. and Hardin, J.M. (1995) Early intervention for low birth weight, premature infants, participation and intellectual development. *American Journal on Mental Retardation* **99** (5), 542–54.

Bowlby, J. (1980) *Attachment and loss, Vol. 3. Loss: sadness and depression.* New York. Basic Books.

Brimblecombe, F.S.W. (1974) Exeter Project for Handicapped Children. *British Medical Journal* **4**, 706–9.

Brimblecombe, F.S.W. (1976) *Pediatricians and parents as partners in early management of handicapping disorders.* Review of Research and Practice No. 19. Amsterdam. Associated Scientific Publishers.

Commission on Mental Handicap in Ireland (1965) *The report of the Commission on Mental Handicap in Ireland.* Dublin. Government Publications.

Commission on the Status of People with Disabilities (1996) *A strategy for equality: report of the Commission on the Status of People with Disabilities.* Dublin. Stationery Office.

Crnic, K. and Stormshak, E. (1997) The effectiveness of providing social support for families of children at risk. In M.J. Guralnick (ed.), *The effectiveness of early intervention,* chapter 10. Baltimore. Paul H. Brookes Publishing Co.

Cunningham, C. and Sloper, P. (1978) *Helping your handicapped baby.* London. Souvenir Press.

Department of Education (1995) *Charting our education future: White Paper on Education.* Dublin. Stationery Office.

Department of Education and Science (2002) *Circular to boards of management and principal teachers of National Schools: Circular Special Education 08/02.* Athlone. Department of Education and Science.

Department of Health (1994) *Shaping a healthier future: a strategy for effective health care in the 1990s.* Dublin. Stationery Office.

Department of Health and Children (2001) *Primary care: a new direction: quality and fairness—a health system for you.* Dublin. Stationery Office.

Doman, G. (1974) *What to do about your brain injured child.* New York. Double Day.

Doran, J. (1999) When babies are born with special needs: What assistance maternity hospitals and community care give in helping their parents to cope and getting the child intervention services. Unpublished MSc thesis, Trinity College, Dublin.

Fay, B. (1999) *Draft report of project team on evaluation of the Share-a-Break and Room-to-Share schemes.* Tullamore. Midland Health Board.

Felce, D., Grant, G., Todd, S. *et al.* (1998) *Towards a full life: researching policy innovation for people with learning disabilities.* Oxford / Boston / Johannesburg / Melbourne / New Delhi / Singapore. Butterworth-Heinemann.

Goddard, J. and Rubissow, J. (1977) Meeting the needs of handicapped children and their families. *Child Care, Health & Development* **3** (4), 261–74.

Government of Ireland (1970) *Health Act, 1970.* Dublin. Stationery Office.

Government of Ireland (1994) *A government of renewal: a policy agreement between Fine Gael, the Labour Party, and Democratic Left.* Dublin. Stationery Office.

Guralnick, M.J. (1998) Effectiveness of early intervention for vulnerable children: a developmental perspective. *American Journal on Mental Retardation* **102** (4), 319–45.

Kellaghan, T., Weir, S., O'Huallachain, S. and Morgan, M. (1995) *Educational disadvantage in Ireland.* Dublin. Combat Poverty Agency, Department of Education, Educational Research Centre.

Kennedy, F. (2001) *Cottage to crèche: family change in Ireland.* Dublin. Institute of Public Administration.

Krauss, M.W. (1997) Two generations of family research and intervention. In M.J. Guralnick (ed.), *The effectiveness of early intervention,* 611–24. Baltimore. Paul H. Brookes Publishing Co.

Lee, V.E., Brooks-Gunn, J. and Schnur, E. (1988) Does Headstart work?: a one year follow-up comparison of disadvantaged children attending Headstart, no pre-school and other pre-school programmes. *Developmental Psychology* **24** (2), 210–22.

McConkey, R. and Adams, L. (2000) Do short breaks services for children with learning disabilities match family needs and preferences? *Child: Care, Health and Development* **26** (5), 429–44.

Mittler, P. (1982) *Proceedings of seminar on Early Intervention.* Tullamore. Midland Health Board.

Mulvany, F. (2000) *National Intellectual Disability Database. Annual report of the National Intellectual Disability Database Committee.* Dublin. Health Research Board.

NAMHI (1995) *Survey on early services.* Dublin. NAMHI.

NAMHI (1998) *A position paper on early intervention services.* Dublin. NAMHI.

Parker, S.L., Piotrkowski, C.S. and Peay, L. (1987) Headstart as a social support for mothers: the psychological benefits of involvement. *American Journal of Orthopsychiatry* **57** (2), 220–3.

Redmond, B. (1999) *A report on the needs of carers of fragile babies and young children with severe developmental disability.* Dublin. Centre for the Study of Developmental Disabilities, University College Dublin.

Review Group on Mental Handicap Services (1990) *Needs and abilities: a policy for the intellectually disabled.* Dublin. Stationery Office.

Rush, D. (2002) *Review of early services, County Kildare and West Wicklow. Draft report to South-Western Area Health Board.* Galway. The Performance Partnership.

Santrock, J.W. (1995) *Life-span development.* Madison, WI. Brown and Benchmark.

Southern Health Board (1997) *Services to persons with a mental handicap — development plan.* Cork. Southern Health Board.

Special Education Review Committee (1993) *Report of the Special Education Review Committee.* Dublin. Stationery Office.

Wolfensberger, W. (1972) *The principle of normalization in human services.* Toronto. National Institute on Mental Retardation.

6. CREATING AN INCLUSIVE CURRICULUM

BARRY CARPENTER AND MICHAEL SHEVLIN

INTRODUCTION

Internationally, increased numbers of children with learning difficulties (a term used in the UK to describe those with intellectual and other developmental disabilities) are attending mainstream schools. However, the transition from separate categorical provision for children with learning difficulties to inclusive forms of provision has been controversial and is far from complete. Within this chapter the rationale for developing inclusive provision will be explored and the creation of inclusive curricula will be examined.

Following the publication of the seminal Warnock Report (DES 1978) in the United Kingdom the term 'integration' became common language for teachers in all schools. This report outlined three main forms of integration, which were characterised as locational, social and functional. Locational integration referred to a situation where special classes/units are attached to mainstream schools; social integration involved social interaction between children from the special setting and their mainstream peers; the inclusion of the children from the special setting in regular classes alongside their mainstream peers was characterised as functional integration. These definitions of locational, social and functional integration were exemplified in practice over the next two decades.

The advent of the National Curriculum in the UK provided teachers with a common curriculum framework and language. This enhanced dialogue led to the establishment of some creative projects, often at the initiative of the Special School, but lack of long-term funding meant that many of these projects did not survive beyond the endeavours of their originators (Steele and Mitchell 1992). The quality of the integration experiences offered was variable; the most original and creative examples had a clear focus on the quality of relationships through genuine shared learning experiences between children of all abilities (Carpenter 1994). Attitudinal development was an important dimension of the collaborative learning projects reported between special and mainstream schools (Beveridge 1996; Lewis 1995). However, the capacity of integration opportunities to now be rooted in the curriculum certainly contributed to reducing the marginalisation of pupils with SLD (Sebba and Ferguson 1991). The legislated curriculum principle of differentiation offered teachers an underpinning for planning learning experiences that celebrated diversity, and enabled teaching to be adjusted to meet a range of individual needs within the classroom.

Without doubt opportunities for integrated provision have increased substantially over the intervening period, and the number of children with learning difficulties in mainstream provision has increased exponentially. However, early in this process concerns were expressed that the minority group of children with learning difficulties were expected to conform to mainstream expectations. Commentators characterised the process as resembling assimilation rather than real integration (Gartner and Lipsky 1997). The major protagonist for integration throughout this period was education, through its schools. The dimension that was missing, and probably undermined the sustainability of some good integration work, was the societal level. Schools are a reflection of their society. As such, society must be in harmony with the ethos of its schools. This element was lacking in relation to integration: there was little or no attempt to embrace the worthiness of the integration endeavour between special and mainstream schools, or to value the tremendous contribution that these shared learning opportunities were making to the citizenship development of children.

INCLUSION APPEARS

Over time, Lewis (1995) suggests, integration became a too narrowly interpreted concept. It had failed to align itself to the more socially permeated concept of normalisation, and thus educationalists sought a concept that was more holistic in its outlook. The concept of inclusion emerged and advocated the belief that children with learning difficulties belong in mainstream schools. Assimilation was rejected in favour of the notion that children at a disadvantage, whatever the source, should be included in mainstream provision (Avramidis et al. 2002; Thomas et al. 1998). Outside the UK a move was afoot to look at inclusive schools as organisations capable of accepting diversity and, through school improvement, to meet a range of individual needs in pupils (Forest and Pearpoint 1992). For pupils with learning difficulties, the full opportunity to participate in the educational activities that typify society will ultimately require education reform policies that do not treat them as members of a minority group (Florian 1998).

Such social constructions may be beyond the perceived remit of the classroom teacher, and her desire may be to design her learning environment in such a way that it embraces all children as active participants. For as Mittler (2000, 7) points out:

'Inclusion is not about placing children in mainstream schools. It is about changing schools to make them more responsive to the needs of all children. It is about helping all teachers to accept responsibility for the learning of all children.'

THE IRISH CONTEXT

Until the 1970s and 1980s in Irish education policy and practice, children were categorised as either 'handicapped' or 'normal', and the categories were educated separately. Until the 1970s all special provision was located in separate special schools; provision has diversified since then, so that it now includes special schools, special classes, and supported integrated placement of disabled pupils in mainstream classes. The integration debate in Irish education has tended to become polarised between advocates of increased integration and supporters of special education in special schools.

Ireland in the 1990s witnessed increased attention to special-needs issues, as illustrated by the SERC report (Special Education Review Committee 1993), the government White Paper on Education *Charting our education future* (Department of Education 1995), the CSPD report *A strategy for equality* (Commission on the Status of People with Disabilities 1996), the Education Act (Government of Ireland 1998), and the NCCA discussion document *Special educational needs: curriculum issues* (National Council for Curriculum and Assessment 1999).

The Irish government is committed to the principle of equity in relation to education for young people with disabilities. However, the translation of this principle into education practice has proved difficult. The Irish government has contributed to these difficulties through a clinical/pathological approach to disability issues (McDonnell 2000). This is amply illustrated in the definition of disability employed in the 1998 Education Act (Government of Ireland 1998), the 1998 Employment Equality Act (Office of the Director of Equality Investigations 1998) and the 2000 Equal Status Act (Government of Ireland 2000). It is a precise medicalised listing of 'conditions'—loss of bodily or mental functions, disease, deformities—that result in impeded mental, physical or communicative functioning and/or learning difficulties. This definition serves to justify the category-based approach to provision for disabled people. It does not capture the complex intersection of physical, psychological and social factors in the life experience of disabled people, and therefore it is a wholly inadequate framework for planning and provision to ensure equity for people with disabilities (Shevlin *et al.* 2002). By contrast, the *Report of the Commission on the Status of People with Disabilities* (Commission on the Status of People with Disabilities 1996) stipulates that legislation and policy be informed by a social model of disability, within a civil rights perspective based on principles of equality and human rights. In addition, children with the severest disabilities are not guaranteed access to education and families have had to avail of the courts to try to ensure this type of basic access for their child.

Other factors have militated against the integration of children with learning difficulties, including the large class sizes at primary level (Bennett *et al.* 1998) and teachers' perceived inadequacies in teaching these children (Lynch 1995). Also, the education system had been seriously under-resourced, which resulted in the lack of a coherent infrastructure to support the integration of children with learning difficulties within mainstream schools. Despite these difficulties a number of valuable integration programmes have been undertaken. Participants from mainstream and special settings have collaborated in the development of creative arts programmes (Shevlin and O'Moore 1999; Walsh *et al.* 1996). Also, a limited number of children with Down Syndrome have been successfully included in mainstream provision in many parts of Ireland (Buckley 1999; Butler and Shevlin 2001). Integration programmes of this type have tended to be *ad hoc* and lack the systemic and philosophical commitment required to sustain these initiatives and ensure lasting change in the Irish education system. As a consequence, a fuller exploration of inclusion issues will be particularly valuable as Irish families and educators begin to develop educational responses that respect and value the diversity among our children.

THE INCLUSIVE CURRICULUM

The societal debates around inclusion over the last fifteen years or more (Tomlinson 1982; Skrtic 1991) now need to be translated into dynamic curriculum practice if they are truly to have an impact on the lives of children and subsequently upon our future society. Tilstone *et al.* (1998, 1) adopt a pragmatic line and state:

> '. . . special educators, meaning those with expertise in the education of pupils who experience difficulty in learning at school, are important players in promoting more inclusive practice.'

As Tilstone *et al.* (2000, 12) point out, developing a responsive curriculum is a critical element in creating an inclusive ethos within schools:

> 'For the curriculum to be genuinely inclusive, it needs to take serious account of educational diversity and recognise the heterogeneity of educational needs that all pupils, including those with a range of learning difficulties, present to their teachers.'

Central to this debate should be the rights of the child as a learner. How do we design learning environments and learning activities that will ensure that each child is an active participant in the learning process and not a bystander, a peripheral participant, watching the activity of others? Carpenter *et al.* (2001) have clearly articulated how pupils with learning difficulties can be included in all aspects of the curriculum, and how those closest to them, particularly their families, teachers and other professionals, can be supported in achieving this goal. They state that we must together seek to build an inclusive curriculum.

Social exclusion is a constant threat to some children with significant degrees of learning difficulty. Their challenging behaviour may lead some schools to decide that such pupils can no longer be effectively educated in that school (Evans and Lunt 2002). Disenfranchisement from the education system may loom large. Therefore it is important in our definitions of inclusion to think of children with all kinds of special needs and learning difficulties remaining within the education system regardless of the setting.

It has to be recognised that in giving access to inclusion for all there are many challenges which face teachers, not least of which is how to promote inclusive learning styles (Read 1998). There is increasing diversity in many classroom situations, and an ever-widening ability range within these classrooms, whether in special or mainstream schools. We need a critical re-examination of the pedagogy that will enable teachers to remain focused on the needs of their pupils and to ensure that equality of education opportunity exists for all at a time of rapid change. Our goal should be that children learn and learn well, and this can only be achieved through a curriculum of the highest quality, and teachers with the skills and convictions to deliver it effectively.

Children with learning difficulties will need specific learning pathways to be charted for them if they are to be given access to the curriculum. They are pupils for whom imaginative and creative programmes of study are necessary to enable them to receive their curriculum entitlement; pupils who, without a well-differentiated curriculum, would be alienated from the flow of learning experience in the classroom; pupils who need specific engagement strategies to be employed to ensure their participation in the curriculum; and pupils who, without learning routes which mirror their learning styles, would remain on the periphery of curriculum activity when they have the right to be active participants at the heart of the learning process (Howley and Kime 2003). Alongside access to the curriculum now comes access to inclusion. This still relies upon the innate creativity and personal skill of the teacher working with the pupils with learning difficulties.

The specific guidance offered for curriculum planning for pupils with learning difficulties in England and Wales (DfEE/QCA 2001) proposes aims and purposes for the curriculum and suggests that the school curriculum for pupils with learning difficulties might, therefore, aim to:

- enable pupils to interact and communicate with a wide range of people;
- promote self-advocacy or the use of a range of systems of supported advocacy;
- enable pupils to express preferences, communicate needs, make choices, take decisions and choose options that other people act upon and respect;
- prepare pupils for an adult life in which they are enabled to exercise the greatest possible degree of independence and autonomy;
- increase pupils' awareness and understanding of their environment and of the world;
- encourage pupils to explore, to question and to challenge;
- provide a wide range of learning experiences in age-appropriate contexts for pupils in each key stage.

These building-blocks are crucial to constructing a curriculum that is inclusive for all children. These principles should inform curriculum planning for the whole curriculum and enable all professionals in schools, including therapists and parents, to feel that their contribution is once more valued within a far-reaching overview. Common, group and individual needs can comfortably sit alongside each other knowing that a range of curriculum experiences will be available through which any of these needs can be met. What is clear is the recognition that the curriculum cannot remain static: it must be responsive to change and therefore it is a dynamic process in which teachers engage; and the outcomes of this process must be ultimately empowering to children as learners, prepared to accept their citizenship in an inclusive society (Carpenter 2001).

What does 'inclusion' look like? This is the question posed by many teachers. The following case-study illustrates inclusion in practice.

Children together: a case-study

Emily, Michael and Tim worked enthusiastically creating their information sheet on the town's historic church. This was part of a 'Tourist Office' project that Class 5 (9–10-year-olds) at Hilltown Primary School were engaged in. The town in which the school was located was full of local history, and often frequented by tourists.

The children in the class were asked to select a feature of the town (i.e. the church, market square, meadows etc.) that they would like to investigate. They were then grouped according to the feature of the town they wished to explore.

The class teacher was particularly keen to encourage collaborative group work amongst her pupils. She chose to try a jigsawing technique that she had read about (Rose 1991). Each child in a group was given a specific task to undertake; without the contribution of each group member the overall goal, in this case the creation of an illustrated tourist information sheet, would not be achieved.

On their visit to the church Emily chose to write down her thoughts and feelings about the church: that 'the windows were made of stained glass that shone like jewels'; that there was a high ceiling 'with stones in different shapes'. She decided to find a book in the school library about churches that would explain to her why the church ceiling was designed like this.

Michael's greatest pleasure was drawing. He took a variety of pencils with him to the church and sketched some of the objects he saw on the altar. He was particularly keen to do some rubbings of the old tombstone. His teacher obtained permission for him to do this and, with Tim and Emily holding the paper still for him, he set about taking a rubbing of a tombstone dating back to the sixteenth century.

Tim was fascinated by the size of the church, and walked around gently touching the various surfaces: the wooden pews with ornate carvings at each end; the tomb of the local landowner with a stone figure lying along it. As he explored each of these features, Tim recorded his comments with a small tape-recorder, and was not afraid to say exactly what he thought—'It's cold and it smells!'

Back at school, the three children pooled their findings about the church. Michael suggested that they use the computer to create their information fact-sheet. They discussed this idea with their teacher. The children took their idea one step further and decided to create an interactive information sheet. This involved using an A3 concept keyboard in conjunction with the computer.

Michael set about transforming his sketches and rubbings into an overlay, and with the help of the teacher blocked areas of the concept keyboard to correspond with each overlay picture.

Tim and Emily combined their written and oral observations into a description of various aspects of the church. They wrote up their findings directly onto the computer, using the 'Writing with Symbols' computer program (Detheridge and Detheridge 2001), which had a symbol accompanying each word in text. Emily thought this would be particularly good for foreign visitors who might not be able to read English but could decipher (or even guess) what the symbols meant.

Eventually their information sheet was complete. By pressing Tim's sketch of the altar on the concept keyboard, the description of the altar, compiled by Tim and Emily, came up on the computer screen. The contribution of each individual enabled the group to accomplish its task in a creative and innovative manner.

On the surface, Michael, Emily and Tim may appear like any nine- or ten-year-olds in a primary school, but when you delve deeply you discover that they each have unique individual needs.

Michael is on the Local Education Authority (LEA) Register of More Able Pupils. He has been nominated for his exceptional artistic ability. Once a term he is invited to attend a Saturday Art Workshop in a local secondary school. Local artists conduct the workshop, engaging the children in a variety of techniques and media. Michael meets other children of the same age who find art as exciting as he does. His teacher consults regularly with the LEA advisory teacher for more able pupils, and borrows resources for the classroom that match her schemes of work but which will challenge Michael and encourage him to use his talent.

Emily's mother died last year. Since then she has changed from an out-going girl at the centre of the group to a withdrawn child preferring her own company to that of others. Whilst her work in class has not deteriorated significantly, her teacher is concerned that Emily has become so withdrawn. The teacher talks to the school special educational needs (SEN) coordinator about Emily and has met with Emily's father, who is equally concerned about his daughter. They have agreed that the class teacher will keep an observational diary regarding Emily's behaviour over the next three months. As such, Emily is deemed to be at stage 2 of the Code of Practice under the 1993 Education Act (Great Britain 1994). If they are still concerned after this time then the SEN coordinator will ask the head teacher to make a referral to the Educational Psychology Team, which runs a counselling service: stage 3 in the Code of Practice.

Tim has Down Syndrome. He attends Hilltown Primary School for four afternoons per week. The remainder of the time he attends The Beeches, a neighbouring school for children with severe learning difficulties, which shares a campus with Hilltown and the local secondary school. Both schools are part of the Partnership network of schools that agree to support the integration of pupils from The Beeches into local mainstream schools.

Tim's placement at Hilltown is part of a shared learning project for several primary-age pupils from The Beeches. His involvement in this project has been planned jointly between his class teacher from The Beeches and the Hilltown Year 5 teacher. Tim used to be supported on his visits to Hilltown by a learning support assistant, but as he has grown in confidence this is no longer necessary.

Tim can write his name and a few other words. As his verbal skills are good, tape-recording his oral observations of the church was the most effective strategy. Also, as Tim could not read unfamiliar vocabulary such as 'altar' or 'font', Emily suggested that he use his symbols computer program. She has seen him using this in other lessons. As each word is accompanied by a pictographic symbol, Tim was able not only to access the text but to create sentences too.

Tim's involvement with the Year 5 class at Hilltown was planned on the basis of the targets set in his individual education programme (IEP). His teachers from the two schools examined these and asked, 'Which school environment is best able to facilitate each of these targets?' Consequently there was shared ownership of Tim's curriculum programme, with cross-school record-keeping strategies in place.

CONCLUSIONS

Education is the means by which society can prepare its future generations to respond to a rapidly changing world. If there are significant changes facing our typically developing children, then these changes are even more magnified for the child with learning difficulties. What will be the impact on them of continued globalisation of the economy and society, of the new work and leisure patterns, and the rapid expansion of communication technologies? The latter may bring welcome breakthroughs for many people with learning difficulties through greater access to areas of society that, to date, have been closed to them. What is important is that the citizenship of all children is recognised. Recent curricular developments in England and Ireland have enhanced this concept. Citizenship has been included as a statutory subject in the National Curriculum framework of England since 2002. The CSPE (Civic, Social and Political Education) programme in Ireland also addresses citizenship issues. These programmes, alongside Personal, Social and Health Education (PSHE), are essential to the holistic development of all of our children.

The challenge, then, for all teachers is to build an inclusive curriculum. An inclusive curriculum is fundamentally a framework for enabling pupils of all abilities to show what they know, understand and can do. It should enable a celebration of achievement for all pupils and provide, through careful monitoring and evaluation of pupil performance, information on continuity and progression. Most of all, if we are able to value the individual qualities and abilities of each and every one of our pupils, then the classroom must be pervaded by an atmosphere in which there is an expectation of success (Carpenter and Ashdown 2001).

The aspirations of inclusion should not cause consternation amongst teachers. They are a contemporary product of society. As such, inclusion is evolutionary; it is a pervasive approach intended to influence, develop and change not only schools but also society itself. Inclusion is a social valuing process: it states to each individual with disabilities, 'You are a welcome, valued and equal member of our community'. 'Inclusion is a process, not a location', states Rita Jordan (2001), and this is echoed in practice that is emerging in the UK and Ireland. Tomlinson (1982, 192–3) argues convincingly that the concept of inclusion should not be confused with integration:

> '[The] concept of inclusiveness is not synonymous with integration. It is a larger and prior concept. The first step is to determine the best possible learning environment, given the individual student and learning task. For those with learning difficulty the resulting educational environment will often be in an integrated setting and increasingly so as the skills of teachers and capacities of the system grow. Sometimes it will be a mixture of the integrated and the discrete. And sometimes . . . it will be discrete

provision. No apology is necessary for the paradox . . . that . . . the concept of inclusive learning is not necessarily coincident with total integration... into the mainstream'.

From integration to inclusion reflects society's determination to equalise opportunities for all of its citizens. We must, as O'Brien (2001) and colleagues argue, seek 'reality inclusion'. As we confront discrimination, then, schools and our children are the right starting-point.

REFERENCES

Avramidis, E., Bayliss, P. and Burden, R. (2002) Inclusion in action: an in-depth case study of an effective inclusive secondary school in the south-west of England. *International Journal of Inclusive Education* **6** (2), 143–63.

Bennett, J., Gash, H. and O'Reilly, M. (1998) Ireland: integration as appropriate, segregation where necessary. In T. Booth and M. Ainscow (eds), *From them to us: an international study of inclusion in education*, 149–64. London. Routledge.

Beveridge, S. (1996) Experiences of an integration link scheme: the perspectives of pupils with severe learning difficulties and their mainstream peers. *British Journal of Learning Disabilities* **24** (1), 9–19.

Buckley, D. (1999) Links between special and mainstream schools. Unpublished M.St. thesis, Trinity College, Dublin.

Butler, S. and Shevlin, M. (2001) Creating an inclusive school: the influence of teacher attitudes. *Irish Educational Studies* **20**, 125–38.

Carpenter, B. (1994) Shared learning: the developing practice of integration for children with severe learning difficulties. *European Journal of Special Needs Education* **9** (2), 182–9.

Carpenter, B. (2001) Inclusive societies: inclusive families. Lecture to the National Institute for the Study of Learning Difficulties, Trinity College, Dublin, April 2001.

Carpenter, B. and Ashdown, R. (2001) Enabling access. In B. Carpenter, R. Ashdown and K. Bovair (eds), *Enabling access: effective teaching and learning for pupils with learning difficulties* (2nd edn), 1–14. London. David Fulton.

Carpenter, B., Ashdown, R. and Bovair, K. (eds) (2001) *Enabling access: effective teaching and learning for pupils with learning difficulties* (2nd edn). London. David Fulton.

Commission on the Status of People with Disabilities (1996) *A strategy for equality: report of the Commission on the Status of People with Disabilities*. Dublin. Stationery Office.

Department of Education (1995) *Charting our educational future: White Paper on Education*. Dublin. Stationery Office.

DES (1978) *Special educational needs: report of the Committee of Inquiry into the*

Education of Handicapped Children and Young People (the Warnock Report). London. HMSO.

Detheridge, J. and Detheridge, M. (2001) *Literacy through symbols* (2nd edn). London. David Fulton.

DfEE/QCA (2001) *Planning, teaching and assessing the curriculum for pupils with learning difficulties.* London. DfEE/QCA.

Evans, J. and Lunt, I. (2002) Inclusive education: are there limits? *European Journal of Special Needs Education* **17** (1), 1–14.

Florian, L. (1998) Inclusive practice: what, why and how? In C. Tilstone, L. Florian and R. Rose (eds), *Promoting inclusive practice*, 13–26. London. Routledge.

Forest, M. and Pearpoint, J. (1992) Putting all kids on the map. *Educational Leadership* **50** (2), 26–31.

Gartner, A. and Lipsky, D. (1997) *Inclusion and school reform.* Baltimore, MD. Paul H. Brookes.

Government of Ireland (1998) *Education Act.* Dublin. Stationery Office.

Government of Ireland (2000) *Equal Status Act.* Dublin. Stationery Office.

Great Britain (1994) *Education Act 1993.* London. Sweet and Maxwell.

Howley, M. and Kime, S. (2003) Policies and practice for the management of individual learning needs. In C. Tilstone and R. Rose (eds), *Strategies to promote inclusive practice*, 18–33. London. Routledge Falmer.

Jordan, R. (2001) Equalising opportunities for people with autism. Paper to the British Institute of Learning Disabilities International Conference, Cork, Ireland, September 2001.

Lewis, A. (1995) *Children's understanding of disability.* London. Routledge.

Lynch, P. (1995) Integration in Ireland: policy and practice. In C. O'Hanlon (ed.), *Inclusive education in Europe,*. London. David Fulton.

McDonnell, P. (2000) Inclusive education in Ireland: rhetoric and reality. In F. Armstrong, D. Armstrong and L. Barton (eds), *Inclusive education: policy, contexts and comparative perspectives*, 12–26. London. David Fulton.

Mittler, P. (2000) *Working towards inclusive education: social contexts.* London. David Fulton.

National Council for Curriculum and Assessment (1999) *Special educational needs: curriculum issues.* Dublin. NCCA.

O'Brien, T. (ed.) (2001) *Enabling inclusion: blue skies . . . dark clouds?* London. Stationery Office.

Office of the Director of Equality Investigations (1998) *Employment Equality Act 1998.* Dublin. Office of the Director of Equality Investigations.

Read, G. (1998) Promoting inclusion through learning styles. In C. Tilstone, L. Florian and R. Rose (eds), *Promoting inclusive practice*, 128–37. London. Routledge.

Rose, R. (1991) A jigsaw approach to group work. *British Journal of Special Education* **18** (2), 54–8.

Sebba, J. and Ferguson, A. (1991) Reducing the marginalisation of pupils with severe learning difficulties through curricular initiatives. In M. Ainscow (ed.), *Effective schools for all*, 195–214. London. David Fulton.

Shevlin, M. and O'Moore, M. (1999) Schools' Link Programme: enabling strangers to meet. *REACH: Journal of Special Needs Education in Ireland* **12** (2), 102–9.

Shevlin, M., Kenny, M. and McNeela, E. (2002) Curriculum access for pupils with disabilities: an Irish experience. *Disability & Society* **17** (2), 159–69.

Skrtic, T. (1991) Students with special educational needs: artefacts of the traditional curriculum. In M. Ainscow (ed.), *Effective schools for all*, 20–42. London. David Fulton.

Special Education Review Committee (1993) *Report of the Special Education Review Committee*. Dublin. Stationery Office.

Steele, J. and Mitchell, D. (1992) Special links with mainstream. *Special Children* **55**, 14–16.

Thomas, G., Walker, D. and Webb, J. (1998) *The making of the inclusive school*. London. Routledge.

Tilstone, C., Florian, L. and Rose, R. (1998) Pragmatism not dogmatism: promoting more inclusive practice. In C. Tilstone, L. Florian and R. Rose (eds), *Promoting inclusive practice*, 1–9. London. Routledge.

Tilstone, C., Florian, L. and Rose, R. (eds) (1998) *Promoting inclusive practice*. London. Routledge.

Tilstone, C., Lacey, P., Porter, J. and Robertson, C. (2000) *Pupils with learning difficulties in mainstream schools*. London. David Fulton.

Tomlinson, S. (1982) *The sociology of special education*. London. Routledge.

Walsh, P.N., Shevlin, M., O'Moore, M., de Lacey, E. and Stritch, D. (1996) In-service training for teachers involved in link schemes: a consultative process. *British Journal of Special Education* **23** (2), 75–9.

7. ADULT RELATIONSHIPS AND SEXUALITY

SHAY CAFFREY

INTRODUCTION

The meeting had been arranged for some time and the author was the guest speaker. The topic was 'Sexuality and Intellectual Disabilities'. The audience was comprised of parents and staff. The setting was a centre for people with intellectual disabilities serving a catchment area in rural Ireland.

I arrived early. While driving up the avenue towards the carpark, I noticed small groups of people talking to each other. As I got out of the car I was approached and greeted by a small delegation. I had the distinct impression that they had been selected to 'check me out'. After pleasantries about the weather and some chit-chat, they got to the point: 'Are you the man who is giving the talk?' It was obvious that the word was out. 'What are you going to say?' I told them that the talk was about sexuality and relationships, and that I was talking to staff and parents. They already knew that. What they really wanted to know was 'What are you going to say?' They had an important stake in that. I explained briefly and they listened intently. Having gleamed the information that they needed, they returned to the other groups to report back. Slowly, small groups moved off to different parts of the campus, apparently satisfied with the information they had gathered.

However, one man in his early thirties approached me and introduced himself. He then said, with joy on his face, 'I have a new girlfriend'. I smiled and congratulated him, as he was obviously very happy. He was about to elaborate but I thought it might be a little inappropriate for him to divulge his heart to me, a complete stranger. I tried to explain this tactfully to him. He considered my point for a few moments but then went ahead. How often do you get a chance to tell someone who might understand about the joys of falling in love, or about the wonderful attributes of the love of your life? We talked for some minutes and he told me about his Niamh, and how he felt about her. After completing the conversation he shook my hand and then went off to another part of the campus. His happiness was obvious.

Later that afternoon, about halfway through my talk, I began to have the unpleasant feeling that the audience's interest was vanishing. It was an elderly audience, the vast majority of whom were in their mid- to late sixties. So I began thinking 'Oh no, they just don't want to think or talk about sexuality or relationships' . . . and other equally negative thoughts. At that point I decided to ask the question: 'Do you think your son/daughter should have education about sexuality and relationships?' To my pleasant surprise, almost 95% of hands went up immediately. But why was the audience losing interest? Was I boring? I posed other questions. Then one mother, expressing some frustration, said: 'We all know that our sons and daughters need education in the area of sexuality . . . we have known that for most of their lives . . . but when is it going to happen? . . . who is going to do it?' There were nods of agreement all round. The interest quickly reappeared. They wanted to know when it was going to happen. Who was going to do it? What was going to be taught?

This group were the same as the vast majority of parents of people with intellectual disabilities (90–95%). They want sexuality education for their son or daughter (Watson and Rogers 1980; Caffrey 1992). Over the past 25 years, people with learning disabilities have raised almost every conceivable issue regarding sexuality and relationships. Their concerns include going out together, longing for their loved ones, broken hearts, obsessed or radiant men and women, romantic men procuring money illegally to buy presents to impress, violence between partners, the longing to have a family, jealousy and fights, tempting and teasing, stringing along, unwanted pregnancy, house arrests in order to avoid men, embarrassing attempts to woo, *faux pas*, bewilderment, joy and excitement, giggling, tittering and embarrassment, cruelty, nasty comments and actions, sadness and hurt, passion and lust, fun, and last and sometimes least—love. All human life is there: the kaleidoscope of human experiences.

Arising from these experiences, one thing is abundantly clear: the vast majority of people with disabilities have a definite interest in sexuality and relationships.

VARIETIES OF RELATIONSHIPS

Up to this point we have focused on what are often categorised as romantic/loving relationships. There are of course many other types of relationships in which people with intellectual disabilities are involved. These serve to meet many of our human needs for understanding, intimacy and companionship, and can be engaged in at a multiplicity of levels. Some may take place at different levels of involvement, varying from casual to deep, and the frequency of contacts can also vary.

Our relationships are links with fellow human beings. They can provide us with support and help us to meet our personal needs. They can create a sense of familiarity, belonging and intimacy. In some cases they give a sense of direction to life and a purpose for living, and they can insulate us from loneliness. Relationships are profoundly important to human beings.

The main categories of relationships that people with intellectual disabilities are involved in are outlined below.

1. Family relationships

A whole series of family relationships exist, and the quality of each depends on many factors. Over time relationships change; some will grow deeper and stronger, whilst others will loosen or even evaporate. However, whatever the nature of the relationship, the kinship exists while the person is alive. Kinship relationships are of great importance to most people with intellectual disabilities. Often people with disabilities are animated when a long-lost relative, whoever it is, makes contact.

For many people with intellectual disabilities, particularly those living in residential services, relationships are transient owing to staff turnover. Staff may come and staff may go, but for many people with intellectual disabilities kinship relationships are a bedrock that will exist all their life. As mentioned above, the quality of this relationship may vary but the desire to maintain it is often striking. On occasions, despite lying dormant for many years, a strong desire to contact a relative can emerge.

In some cases staff are aware of the desire of the person to make contact with their relative but are concerned about the hurt the person may experience owing to further rejection. On other occasions the contact is a pragmatic task that needs to be arranged or facilitated.

One case was of a woman from a country town who was residing in Dublin and who wished to visit her family some 170 miles away. Her family did not have accommodation for her to stay overnight. This, coupled with the fact that the woman needed supervision to travel, had posed difficulties for many years. Following consultations, the staff came up with a number of solutions, which included a holiday visit to the area with a group of residents. Another solution that was implemented when resources permitted was that a staff member would go for a visit with the person to the town and they would stay in a local B&B. These visits have significantly added to the person's sense of family and of belonging to that family.

It is important to facilitate people in maintaining contacts with their families, taking into account safety issues. It may be necessary to structure time and contact with family members who have left the home and who may have other responsibilities. Spontaneous contact may be infrequent so a little planning may help. If contacts are to occur over time they must be manageable for both parties. 'Little and often' may be a wise policy.

If the person with disabilities is in residential care it is important to remember that staff may need to be continuously proactive and practical in facilitating these contacts. Sometimes staff feel that relatives should take more responsibility for maintaining the relationship with the person. However, it is still the responsibility of staff to facilitate the person with disabilities to maintain kinship relationships.

There are exceptional cases where it is not in the person's interest to be in contact with a particular member of the family, or indeed the family as a whole. In these cases the safety and welfare of the person with intellectual disabilities is paramount.

2. Educational/occupational relationships

Another great source of potential relationships are the activities we undertake in going about our daily lives. For the majority of people with intellectual disabilities this involves attending an educational facility, a place of work or a care/activation centre. There are, of course, others who do not attend these facilities and who stay at home or move about the community. It may be more difficult for them to form relationships as they are deprived of a potentially rich source of contacts and personal connections.

Attendance at the various facilities or work sites enables one to interact with a group of people with whom one is likely to form various relationships. These may be authority relationships, i.e. supervisor/boss to employee, or relationships with co-workers of either sex. Over time different levels of relationships may be formed, ranging from acquaintanceships to friendships, and on occasions to boyfriend/girlfriend relationships. This is a potentially fertile area for cultivating or facilitating the development of such relationships, and staff can play an active role in assisting the person to develop the competencies and skills needed to develop and maintain the relationships to which they aspire. Staff can also create the conditions for nurturing the development of various kinds of relationships.

3. Community relationships

In our interconnectedness with the community in which we live a whole series of interpersonal interactions take place. We shop in the local shop, say hello to our neighbours, recognise people but do not know their name, use the hairdresser's and dry-cleaner's, have a drink in the local pub and shout for local sports teams. As these and other activities take place regularly relationships usually develop. These may range from recognition to friendships, and sometimes to boyfriend/girlfriend relationships or even partnerships.

It is a truism to say we can only form relationships with people we meet. Let us look at some of the ways a person with an intellectual disability may come in contact with others.

A consumer of goods and services

Persons with disabilities may directly or indirectly purchase goods in community facilities. If they have the opportunity to be involved in these transactions they have more interpersonal interactions and increase the scope of their relationships. As the number of goods and services consumed are considerable, there are daily opportunities to meet different people in different ways. The local shopkeeper and staff at the fast-food outlet, dry-cleaner's, pub, coffee-shop, garage, vegetable shop and butcher's are all involved in these transactions. Some will be friendly, others less so, and some faces will change. Gradually patterns of acquaintance or loose friendships can be formed.

Participant in recreation and leisure
If people join in local recreational and leisure facilities over time they increase their opportunities to engage in activities with others. Possibilities include going to a gym or participating in exercise classes, arts and crafts courses, sports activities (as a participant or supporter), watching sports in a pub with friends, and specific hobbies such as model trains. The key is to choose an activity that brings people together on a regular basis over time. These interactions form the base on which to build relationships.

A citizen and neighbour
Very often people with disabilities are seen as objects of compassion or pity for whom things need to be done. Infrequently they are seen or encouraged to be citizens or good neighbours who contribute to community life. Yet the capacity of some people with disabilities to be helpful and useful to others is considerable, depending on the person's attributes and skills as well as local opportunities. Examples of these contributions include involvement in 'Tidy Towns' committees, neighbourhood support of the elderly, assistance in sporting organisations, involvement in parish activities, and acting as volunteers in community events and facilities. In addition to contributing to the welfare of others, these are useful ways of being in contact with a group of people on an ongoing basis and can also enhance a person's feelings of belonging to and contributing to the community.

4. Personal relationships
One's personal relationships are a result of the history of one's interactions with others. The nature and extent of these relationships will vary as a result of each person's capacities, skills and opportunities. People with disabilities may have a number of acquaintances of each sex, including peers with whom they work or with whom they are being educated. There may be a range of friendships, from close friendships to a partner.

Providing the person with intellectual disabilities with the skills and opportunities to maintain and enhance these relationships is the challenge. There is also the task of providing the skills and opportunities to facilitate people to form new relationships if they so choose.

The invisible norms and rules

Over the years we have all learned various hidden norms and rules, regulating how we behave in various relationships. We have learned about appropriate interpersonal standing distance. We have learned that this distance is dependent on the nature of the relationship between the people involved: too close and you are a space-invader, too far and you are aloof. We have learned about personal space and boundaries. When people are partners they are allowed through personal boundaries and into the other person's space. If they are acquaintances a different set of norms operate.

In the range of relationships there are different norms of acceptable interpersonal conduct regulating how people interact: who is allowed to touch whom, what type of touch is permissible, where on the body this touch can take place, what is acceptable in public and in private, etc.

There are hidden rules around touch, holding hands, and sexual touch of various parts of the body. One may have had the experience of a hand that lingered 4–5 seconds too long, an acceptable touch becoming one that caused the creeps. The same holds with kissing. Who is one allowed to kiss? What type of kiss is acceptable in the different relationships? How long should a kiss on the cheek last? How long is too long? Subtle, unspoken rules which if broken may cause unease or offence . . . the touch that lingered too long, the slightly extended kiss on the lips rather than a peck on the cheek. There are different rules for different relationships.

What is the difference between a one-second peck on the lips and a lingering 'television kiss', just a couple of seconds? But is there a vast difference in the level of intimacy and the nature of the relationship which permits those extra couple of seconds, or sometimes minutes, of lingering? Does a person with an intellectual disability necessarily know the significance of these extra seconds or the different relationships in which these different types of kisses are appropriate? Many do, but it is equally true to say that many do not.

What are the norms around hugs? What are the norms around sexual touch? What level of personal disclosure is appropriate to a casual friendship, to a person in authority, e.g. your boss, or between a husband and wife? Is it different in the different relationships? One of the difficulties in making these invisible rules visible is that they may vary somewhat from group to group, or from family to family. Different families may have slightly different rules in relation to touch, hugging and kissing. However, as the sexual contact becomes more intimate—i.e. passionate kissing, sexual touch and intercourse—the rules and the law of the land are clearer and more explicit.

There is another complication in this already complicated world for people with intellectual disabilities. Norms of acceptable or appropriate behaviour change as the person matures from a child to an adult. What is acceptable changes over time. The intimate hug that was cute at the age of six may cause discomfort at the age of sixteen, and be frowned upon at the age of 26. The same is true of kissing and other behaviours. The age-appropriateness of behaviour changes as the person matures. There is also the fact that the boundaries around touch and physical intimacy are often much less clear for people with intellectual disability than for their peers in the general population.

There are often hugs and levels of intimate contact accepted from people with intellectual disability that would not be tolerated from their non-disabled peers. It is also true that their peers would not seek, accept or tolerate these behaviours, as they are aware of the social norms governing these behaviours. We have absorbed these norms over the years to the point that we tend to follow the rules without being conscious of them. We 'just know them'. In fact, the only time we may become aware of these rules is when someone breaks them, creating a sense of unease.

People with learning disabilities need to know in as far as is possible what is appropriate or inappropriate, what is acceptable and unacceptable, in all of these relationships. It is important information to have in order to regulate one's behaviour in the different relationships. It enables one to interact in a socially acceptable manner and to be viewed as capable and competent in interpersonal interactions. It increases the likelihood of social acceptability and opens up greater opportunities for forming relationships.

WHAT NEEDS DO RELATIONSHIPS FULFIL?

What do people get out of relationships? Quite a lot, it would appear, as human beings continually strive to form relationships at different stages of their lives. It would seem that various layers of needs are satisfied in relationships, allowing people to grow and deal with the various tasks of life. However, as we are all aware, some relationships can have destructive or negative effects.

A significant majority of people with intellectual disabilities wish to have a loving personal relationship, a boyfriend or a girlfriend. The expectations and aspirations of this relationship will vary from person to person. For some it is to have a companion, someone to share intimacies with; for others it is about passion and sexual expression; for yet others it is a status symbol, a statement of their normality. Whatever the motivation, it is a live and vibrant topic for people with intellectual disabilities, their families and the staff who work with them. People with disabilities continually push it to centre stage; it would appear that indeed 'The Heart is a Lonely Hunter'.

In order to look at the needs that relationships fulfil in a systematic way, it is proposed to use four of Maslow's (1943) categories of needs. Although Maslow organised these needs in a hierarchical way, it is not proposed to do so in this chapter. Rather it is an attempt to enable us to understand the interplay of sexuality and human relationships in meeting human needs. Four of his categories are used to explore these needs and the different levels of personal fulfilment in relationships:

(i)   physiological needs;
(ii)   safety needs;
(iii)   love and belonging needs;
(iv)   esteem needs.

Level 1: Physiological needs

The first layer of needs to be met are bodily needs. In the area of sexuality and relationships this relates to sexual frustration and tension as well as stimulation and pleasure. These are the bodily urges, desires and pleasures which arise from touching, caressing or kissing various erogenous zones of the body. They include kissing, hugging, warming, comforting, sexual touching, masturbation and sexual intercourse. These activities are usually highly pleasurable and sought after. Because they are so pleasurable and reinforcing they are likely to be repeated. People with learning disabilities experience the same types of sensations, feelings and pleasures through their sensuous bodies as everyone else in the population. These experiences usually result in relaxation, physical well-being, comfort and feelings of release from tension.

Level 2: Safety needs

One of the next layers of human needs that are potentially met through a relationship is the desire for safety, both physically and at a personal–emotional level. When safety needs are met in a relationship, the person will usually have a feeling of comfort and security. There is frequently a sense of calmness, tranquillity and balance. However, when these needs are not met, the emotional consequences can be complex. Fear may be present, as well as a sense of yearning. There may also be a sense of loss. Within relationships people usually strive for comfort and security, to feel safe in a loving relationship. This is as true for people with intellectual disabilities as it is for the general population.

Level 3: Love needs

The need to be loved and cared for is universal throughout mankind. Our need to be loved may be met in many different ways in different relationships. There is a fundamental need to receive love and also powerful joy in giving love. In Western culture there is a primary emphasis on meeting a significant portion of these needs through a loving relationship with a partner.

The giving and receiving of love is a significant part of these relationships. Love involves an expression of various emotions and can produce a sense of wholeness and warmth. People with love regularly have a sense of growing together and a sense of life and strength. People who do not have someone to love or someone to love them frequently experience feelings of emptiness and loneliness. Feelings of being unwanted and worthless may follow. The vast majority of human beings search for love. There are many forms of relationship that meet these love needs, e.g. close friendships or the parent–child relationship. Although meeting love needs is not the exclusive preserve of romantic relationships, the latter are generally perceived as the usual ones for the purpose. This holds true for all people, with or without intellectual disabilities.

Level 4: Esteem needs

Esteem needs are met in many ways in our culture—through one's occupation, personal possessions, power and status, and personal achievements, to name but a few. Relationships also contribute to one's self-esteem needs. Having people who love you can enhance feelings of self-esteem. To feel that one is lovable and loved can have a favourable influence on self-evaluation. To have a partner may in itself add to one's social significance and prestige. The image of the recently engaged woman proudly displaying her ring to others springs to mind, or the bouquet of roses that arrives at the place of employment on St Valentine's Day.

Engaging in various forms of sexual expression can also enhance one's feelings of self-worth. With one's physical needs being met, feeling safe, loved and loving, a person may develop a sense of confidence and positive self-regard which is a very powerful feeling.

Feelings of inferiority and negative self-worth may also exist in relationships and are often a by-product of poor self-esteem which develops in intimate relationships.

Given the nature of the various needs that relationships meet, is it any wonder that people with intellectual disabilities express such an interest in this area? Often despite prohibitions and many negative experiences, the desire for a relationship with a partner burns in their hearts. They search for understanding, companionship and intimacy, and—like the rest of the population—many or most also search for passion. It is fitting that the next section explores the topic of love.

LOVE AND PEOPLE WITH DISABILITIES

Do people with intellectual disabilities experience love in all its splendour, turmoil and confusion in the same way as the love-struck general population? Are their emotions as intense? Are they as blind to the flaws in their loved ones? For many people with disabilities the answer is yes! However, only a small percentage of these people will go on to live with or marry the person with whom they fell in love.

The romantic love cycle

A romantic love cycle has been proposed by Masters, Johnson and Kolodny (1995). The first stage is seen as a love readiness stage, followed by falling in love. The state of being in love is next, and may or may not be followed by falling out of love.

Masters, Johnson and Kolodny (1995) believe that love readiness is made up of the following segments:

- love is seen as something desirable, something to be striven for;
- there is a longing for intimacy in interpersonal relationships;
- sexual desires and needs are present;
- a feeling of hopefulness that one will be loved exists.

So what are the components of this falling in love or being in love? There is such a wealth of literature on the topic, ranging from the metaphysical and poetic to the popular romantic novels of Mills and Boon.

Thankfully a theory has emerged that attempts to address the multifaceted complexity of the concept of love. Sternberg (1986) has articulated a three-part triangular theory of love: intimacy, passion and commitment/decision.

Intimacy

This involves a sense of closeness, warmth, acceptance and understanding in a relationship. People may express intimacy in three ways.

(a) Physical intimacy can be expressed through the various forms of touch, the giving and receiving of affection, and different sexual activities.

(b) Psychological intimacy may involve the sharing and exchanging of one's dreams, fears, hopes, feelings, aspirations and thoughts, resulting in a feeling of closeness.

(c) Social intimacy may be developed through sharing of recreational activities, involvement in family events, and shared friendships.

Passion

The second component of Sternberg's theory of love is passion. This involves heightened feelings of emotional arousal, increased sexual attraction and sexual arousal.

Commitment

The final component is commitment: a decision to remain in and maintain the loving relationship through time.

Family, friends and staff will all recognise these various components in people with learning disabilities. They all combine in different ways and in different strengths to produce the kaleidoscope of patterns of love in the population of people with learning disabilities.

Varieties of love

Sternberg (1986; 1988) combines these components of intimacy, passion and commitment in various ways to produce different varieties of love. He suggests that there are eight varieties: non-love, friendship, infatuation, empty love, romantic love, fatuous love, companionate love, and consummate love. The table below (source: Sternberg 1986) illustrates these varieties of love. Of course, it is not an all-or-nothing scenario in each component but rather a continuum of intimacy, a continuum of passion and a continuum of commitment. A person may be at different points on the various components.

VARIETIES OF LOVE	INTIMACY	PASSION	COMMITMENT
1. Non-love	−	−	−
2. Friendship	+	−	+
3. Infatuation	−	+	−
4. Empty love	−	−	+
5. Romantic love	+	+	-
6. Fatuous love	−	+	+
7. Companionate love	+	−	+
8. Consummate love	+	+	+

This table is a categorisation of different varieties of love. However, love is not a static thing. One variety of love may evolve into another—for example, romantic love may change to consummate love, or vice versa. The type of love may remain the same but grow or diminish in depth, as when friendships fade or grow in intensity.

It is interesting to reflect on people with learning disabilities and all the different varieties of love that they experience.

Non-love
Many of our casual acquaintances would fall into this category, be they at work or in the community. Such relationships do not involve intimacy, passion or commitment.

Friendship
This involves closeness and warmth, shared thoughts and feelings. There will be intimacy at different levels but not passionate arousal or permanence. It may, of course, evolve into another type of relationship, or evaporate, leaving only memories.

Infatuation
This variety is characterised by passion. It involves intense emotions, perhaps constantly thinking about the person, or sexual desire in relation to the person. There is a heightened arousal of various emotions.

Empty love
This involves people together without passion or intimacy. It is often seen after decades of marriage when all that is left to a couple is the commitment to stay together. Perhaps their star burned brightly at an earlier age but has long since faded.

Romantic love
There is passion and intimacy, living for the moment with intense physical and emotional intimacy, with or without sexual contact. The foundation of a holiday romance is often romantic love.

Fatuous love
Two people come in contact, their eyes meet across a crowded room, they get engaged, live together, and are married within the month. Passion and commitment, but little intimacy.

Companionate love
Passion may have faded but people are still intimate and committed. This is often seen in older couples. Another form of companionate love is seen in special long-term friendships which have endured through the years.

Consummate love
This involves all three components, intimacy, passion and commitment. It is seen as the ultimate or ideal form of love. It is interesting that Sternberg once observed that achieving consummate love is like losing weight: getting started is easy, but sticking to it over an extended period of time is much harder.

In the world of learning disabilities there are numerous examples of the different types of love outlined by Sternberg. Many people have witnessed the elation, joy and anticipation, as well as the sorrow, dejection and pain.

Some 25 years ago Michael and Ann Craft (1978), in dealing with the same topic of 'love and the mentally handicapped', wrote the following.

> 'We have tried to show that the range of emotion and feeling generated by interpersonal relationships varies greatly. That variety is not due to the degree of mental handicap, but to the different life experiences each partner brings to the interaction. Giving and receiving love, including physical satisfaction, is not the prerogative of those above a certain IQ level; being incapable of anything more than a superficial relationship is not an inherent feature of mental handicap. Love can raise some from apathy, others from despair or loneliness and give meaning to life to many who have lost it. We also feel it can decrease retardation.'

DIFFERENT PERSPECTIVES ON RELATIONSHIPS

There would often appear to be an implicit assumption that it is a positive thing for people with intellectual disabilities to have romantic relationships and that their development should be supported. But is that the case? There are different perspectives. Most parents would agree in principle, but what about the risks and dangers in practice? Many parents may think that certain types of relationships are fine, but others are not.

In research carried out by this author (Caffrey 1992) parents were found to be very positive about relationships for their son or daughter. They wanted their son or daughter to be happy, not to be lonely and to have someone special. However, it was at the point of sexual contact (touch and intercourse) that many became very cautious.

Parents' perspective

Research (e.g. Watson and Rogers 1980) has consistently shown that the primary concern of parents of people with intellectual disabilities is the protection of their son or daughter. This is quite understandable, given the potential consequences for the person with disabilities and the family itself. They wish to protect their children from sexual exploitation and sexual abuse. They wish to ensure their health and safety. They wish to minimise the hurt and loss that might occur in a relationship, and want to ensure that they do not cause concern in the community. They are also seriously concerned that their son or daughter might become a parent or they themselves surrogate parents.

Most people would agree that these are legitimate and reasonable concerns. But the danger in focusing only on protection is that people with disabilities may indeed be safe but miserable, the quality of their lives diminished, their aspirations unfulfilled and their human needs unmet. They become protected prisoners.

However, the vast majority of parents of people with intellectual disabilities also want their son or daughter to have friendships and relationships. They want them to love and be loved, and to experience affection and warmth. They do not wish them to be lonely, sad or isolated, but to be happy and to enjoy the humanness of being a man or a woman, and to have positive self-esteem.

Parents want the safety needs of their son or daughter met: this is primary. But they also want their love and belonging needs, as well as their self-esteem needs, to be met. If safety needs and love and belonging needs are counterpoised, parents usually opt for safety; they wish to take care of the safety needs first. However, in general, there are no good reasons why these two sets of needs should be counterpoised. Developing self-protection skills is a fundamental part of responsible education in the area of sexuality and relationships. In fact, in developing the safety skills of people with intellectual disabilities one helps to provide the basis upon which their love and belonging needs as well as their self-esteem needs can be met.

RIGHTS TO RELATIONSHIPS

We have been considering the concerns and aspirations of significant persons in the lives of individuals with intellectual disabilities. It is important to understand their perspectives as they have considerable power in the lives of such individuals. They can occupy many different roles (as we shall see below), and frequently have the power of censorship and repression. So often services, either consciously or unconsciously, give predominance to the initial wishes and perspectives of staff and parents. They may not take seriously the perspectives and aspirations of people with intellectual disabilities. This is frequently done with the best intentions, i.e. the person's safety. At other times it may be done with the intention of protecting oneself or the organisation: a case of a person agreeing with an idea in principle but not on *their* shift.

As far back as 1971 the United Nations issued a Declaration of Rights for people with intellectual disabilities. The first article read: 'The mentally retarded person has, to the maximum degree of feasibility, the same rights as other human beings'. Ann Craft (1987) translates this basic right into the area of sexuality and suggests that there are six rights pertaining to sexuality:

(i)   the right to grow up, i.e. to be treated with the respect and dignity accorded to adults;

(ii)   the right to know, i.e. to have access to as much information as they can assimilate about themselves and their bodies and those of other people, their emotions, appropriate social behaviour, etc.;

(iii) the right to be sexual and to make and break relationships;

(iv)   the right not to be at the mercy of the individual sexual attitudes of different care-givers;

(v)   the right not to be sexually abused;

(vi)   the right to a humane and dignified environment.

But do people with learning disabilities have these rights in the area of sexuality and relationships? In some cases the answer is yes in theory. It frequently is not the case in the reality of their lives.

From aspiration to perspiration

Most people will agree with the aspirations articulated by Ann Craft above. But how do staff and family members translate this into the lives of people with intellectual disabilities? The Eastern Health and Social Services Board in Northern Ireland produced what many consider to be a very useful set of guidelines in the directions they issued to staff concerning sexuality and relationships.

Statement of rights:
* 'The right to companionship and friendship in the same way as everyone else.
* The individual has the right to choose his/her friends. A consequence of this choice is the acceptance of the risk inherent in any relationship.
* The individual should have access to and opportunities to develop relationship networks and friendships within his/her local community.
* The individual should have access to training, which develops the social and interpersonal skills necessary for making relationships.
* The right to grow and be valued as adults.
* The right to knowledge of or access to as much information as he/she can comprehend about his/her own and other people's sexuality, including education and counselling in appropriate social behaviours.
* The right to be involved in making decisions about his/her lifestyle.
* The right to have protection against exploitation within an adult world. This will take account of the problems of intellectual, emotional and social impairment which may be a consequence of mental handicap.'

By using this set of guidelines staff can assess what they are doing in practice. It is possible to use these principles to evaluate whether the needs of a particular individual are being met. They can also be used to assess how a service is meeting these needs. They can develop new directions or provide additional services to people with intellectual disabilities, as the need arises. The guidelines can focus people's thinking and offer a direction to the development of programmes for specific individuals.

Competency and consent
When one reads the rights as articulated by Ann Craft and the guidelines for staff above, one imagines that the vast majority of people would agree that people with intellectual disabilities should have these rights and services, just like all other citizens. However, when one examines these rights in relation to specific individuals with learning disabilities, the picture may become more complex. A person may have a right to form relationships, but what if a particular relationship is judged to be detrimental to the person's welfare by those in positions of responsibility (e.g. family and staff)? Does the right to protection take precedence over the right to form a relationship?

The right to protection v. the right to choose
It could be argued that those in positions of responsibility tend to be protective and to err on the side of caution. The 'better safe than sorry' scenario frequently applies to relationships. In the non-disabled population this trend is counteracted by the natural push of young people towards independence and autonomy. This struggle is captured by Mark Twain's observation that 'parents

think that their son or daughter is two years younger than they are, and the son or daughter thinks they are two years older than they are'. This adaptive push–pull between parent and child produces its own equilibrium, which shifts towards independence and autonomy when the young person reaches maturity.

In the world of intellectual disabilities, the pull factors (stopping, restraining) frequently outweigh the push factors towards independence and autonomy. The normal tendency to rebel or subvert parental or staff authority is often not present. The person with intellectual disability frequently becomes a prisoner of our protection.

The question thus arises of whether there is any reasonable way to achieve a balance between these push–pull factors. Michael Gunn (1994) suggests that autonomy and self-determination are the generally accepted principles on which we base the practice of accepting adult decisions. Hence the more autonomous and self-determining a person is, the more their decisions are accepted as adult decisions. One may not, of course, agree with these decisions, but they are de facto accepted, even if sometimes reluctantly.

However, in the case of a person with learning disability, Gunn (1994) makes an interesting point: 'It makes little sense to espouse only the importance of the right to autonomy and self determination if an adult is not capable of making decisions. This is recognised in the first article of the United Nations' Declaration on the Rights of Retarded Persons 1971: "The mentally retarded person has, to the maximum degree feasible, the same rights as other human beings." Having recognised the impracticability of only relying upon the individual, the U.N. Declaration goes on, inter alia, to attempt to ensure that a "mentally retarded person" is provided with the supports she or he requires to achieve her or his full potential. This is a vital element of any approach to decision making. Resolving the problem about incapacity and consent or decision making is not merely about responding to a specific problem created by an individual's lack of capacity to consent, but it is also about enhancing and developing that individual's ability to make decisions and be independent.'

Therefore, by judging the competence of the person to be autonomous and self-determining, one might be in a position to decide the nature and level of consent the person is able to give. The task, then, for service-providers is to work to increase the level of competence in these areas so that the range of choices increases for the person with intellectual disability. As the knowledge base and the skills of people with intellectual disability increase, and as their decision-making abilities improve, they will be in a better position to make decisions about the type of relationships they wish to involve themselves in. In reality there may be differences of opinion about that decision. Are there any guidelines to assist when these divergences of perspective occur?

* The person with intellectual disability v. the parent(s), or
* The person with intellectual disability v. the staff, or

*   The parent(s) v. the staff.

The Law Commission in the UK (1991), recognising this dilemma, concluded that 'The aims of policy in this area may perhaps be summarised thus:

(i) That people are enabled and encouraged to take for themselves those decisions which they are able to take
(ii) That where it is necessary in their interests or for the protection of others that someone else should take decisions on their behalf, the intervention should be as limited as possible and concerned to achieve what the person himself would have wanted; and
(iii) That proper safeguards be provided against exploitation, neglect and physical, sexual or psychological abuse.'

Letting go
One of the implications of (i) above is that if the person with intellectual disability makes those decisions, then someone has to let go of some power in that relationship. It may be staff or it may be family. This involves surrendering some control and living with a tolerable level of ambiguity. It also means living with a certain level of risk. This may increase the anxieties of the carers concerned. Deciding on an acceptable level of risk is the key issue to be resolved, thus creating a balance between protection and autonomy.

Advocacy and self-advocacy
As mentioned above, there is a definite tendency to err on the side of caution, and in some instances unreasonable caution. This has on occasions placed people in very restricted environments, sometimes to the point of depriving them of basic human rights—the prison of protection. So, with regard to (ii), it would seem reasonable that the person with intellectual disability should have a representative who would explicitly represent his or her interests. A representative could be another family member, a key worker, or an advocate who does not have any affiliation with the service agency. This discussion on competence and decision-making leads us to an interesting phenomenon.

> **The KARE equation:** There is frequently a direct and inverse relationship between the competences of persons with intellectual disability to protect themselves in the area of sexuality and the carers' need to protect them. Thus, in general, as a person's safety skills increase over time, the carer's protectiveness decreases.

The seesaw of autonomy
It is interesting to think of this as a seesaw. As the competence of the person with learning disability goes up, the protectiveness of the carers goes down. This

seesaw process can go up and down depending on the contexts in which the person with learning disability finds himself or herself. He/she may be competent in a local club; hence the protectiveness of the carer is at a low level. However, if the person with intellectual disability were to go to a pub or disco, the protectiveness of the carer might initially go up, and later go down again as the safety skills of the person increase in these new contexts. Therefore by increasing the safety skills of the people with intellectual disabilities, we increase their potential for autonomy.

Ring of safety
Dave Hingsberger (1995) has an excellent way of presenting the whole concept of safety skills. He calls it the 'Ring of Safety'. There are various components to this ring, which if put in place will provide a protective shield for the person to help guard them against exploitation and abuse. It is like an invisible forcefield that repels potentially exploiting or abusing people. This ring is presented below.

Sexuality education
The goals of sexuality education are to ensure that people are informed about, and knowledgeable in, the area of sexuality. It is also important that they are fully aware of the consequences of their actions, and able to take responsibility for their sexuality.

Ability to non-comply
It is necessary to develop the person's level of assertiveness to the point where he/she can say 'no' in appropriate circumstances and stay safe.

Someone who listens
It is desirable to develop a confidant who will listen to the person's needs, hopes and aspirations, and be available if difficulties arise in their sexual world.

Understanding personal rights
It is important to make people aware of their rights vis-à-vis others, to be aware that they own their own bodies and may decline to participate in activities if they so wish. They should also be aware of their rights to live in a safe place in which their sexuality is respected.

Privacy awareness
It is useful to cultivate a sense of awareness of the privacy of their bodies, and privacy in the places where they live and work.

Healthy self-concept and self-confidence
It is necessary to develop a healthy and confident sense of self and to feel good about oneself.

Opportunities for healthy sexuality
It is important that people have the education, training and opportunities to meet their human sexual needs and aspirations in a constructive, healthy, human way. It is through knowledge, education, training and practice in real-life experiences that people with disabilities can develop the skills and competence to protect themselves from exploitation and abuse. Then they are in a better position to celebrate their human sexuality, and take their rightful place in their chosen relationships in the midst of their community. Education, training and counselling liberate people with intellectual disabilities. Ignorance and overprotection enslave them.

CULTIVATING RELATIONSHIPS

The majority of people with intellectual disabilities have significantly fewer relationships than their peers in the general population. This can result in social isolation and considerable loneliness. This is particularly true as they get older and other family members leave home to establish independent lives.

The reasons why people with intellectual disabilities tend to have fewer relationships are complex. There can be many causes. Some of these are to do with the nature of the disability itself, while others are due to the forms of services which are delivered to meet their needs. Family responses to disability can also be contributing factors, as can community reactions and attitudes. The lack of relationships is multi-causal, and each individual tells a unique story.

However, if we are to be proactive and constructive in enabling people to form relationships, we need to be aware of the obstacles. We also need to know the factors that facilitate forming relationships. Thus, by minimising or eliminating the obstacles and cultivating the factors that assist relationships, we will increase the likelihood of people with intellectual disabilities forming relationships that are personally satisfying.

Obstacles to forming relationships

1. Personal competence
The processes involved in establishing and maintaining relationships are quite complex. A number of skills are needed and these may vary from relationship to relationship. Often people with learning disabilities have deficits in the area of personal social competence. They may lack initiative and not be proactive in arranging events or dates, while some may be egocentric and have little awareness of the needs of the other person. Others may be very compliant and lack assertiveness skills. Articulating their thoughts and feelings or reading the emotions of others will pose difficulties for another group of people.

People with intellectual disabilities may also have gifts and competencies which they have been unable to utilise. Some have a great capacity to be affectionate and caring, while others are romantics in the grand style and long to be passionate lovers. Each person has a number of talents, yet to be unlocked. Very few programmes for adults with learning disabilities focus on the skills of relationship-building, however.

There is an overwhelming need to cultivate the talents of people with learning disabilities, to remedy their deficiencies and to teach them the norms of psychosexual interactions in relationships. There are a number of programmes available to assist in this area, and some publishing houses—e.g. Pavilion Publishers (Brighton, UK) and the Family Planning Association (UK)—produce materials specifically for use with people with intellectual disabilities.

2. Physical and social environment
There are many obstacles in the physical and social world which can inhibit the formation of relationships.

Segregation of the sexes. There are still a number of single-sex institutions in existence, though thankfully their numbers are decreasing gradually. There are also a number of institutions in which one sex significantly outnumbers the other, thus offering limited opportunities for a significant majority of that sex to form relationships. In other institutions a form of segregation of the sexes exists for many aspects of the person's life. These services tend to be long-established ones and are institutional in nature. At this point in time many such services are in transition. From a relationship point of view this is to be welcomed, as it is difficult to form relationships with the opposite sex if you have little or no contact with them.

Physical isolation. This can happen in any geographical area but it is a particular issue in a number of rural localities. This can restrict opportunities to socialise and interact with people. The inability to use public transport can also contribute to this physical isolation. In some cases this 'inability' is due to the fact that adequate training programmes have not been provided.

Social isolation. Very often people with intellectual disabilities can be quite isolated socially. Owing to lack of true integration into the community, many people with intellectual disabilities do not attend the various social, occupational or educational establishments that foster interactions and provide opportunities to develop relationships. Most people with intellectual disabilities do not have access to the loose social structures that their peers enjoy. They usually do not have permission to 'hang out' in the same way as their peers. The hours spent in apparently aimless wandering, sitting in coffee shops or pubs or other social amenities are not always available to people with learning disabilities. This breeding ground of many sexual fantasies, crushes, unrequited love, or passionate adolescent or adult romance is closed to them.

3. Families and staff

As mentioned earlier, the primary concern of parents is to ensure the safety of their son or daughter. This concern is very evident in the area of relationships. In general, staff members also operate with considerable caution in the realm of sexuality and relationships. This desire of parents and carers to protect young men and women as they move into adulthood has a natural antidote, known as 'adolescent rebellion'. This energy enables young people to become independent and autonomous and to form intimate personal relations. Autonomy and intimacy are the main tasks of emerging adulthood that need to be accomplished.

Many people with learning disabilities do not have this antidote of 'adolescent rebellion' in sufficient quantities to propel them towards autonomy. Thus many are safe and secure but not satisfied. Often parents and staff exercise their significant powers of benevolent censorship of information, activities, relationships and events relating to the sexuality of people with learning disabilities. This can, and in some cases does, constrict their lives and limits their opportunities in the area of sexuality and relationships.

Factors that facilitate relationships

Zgourides (1996) reviewed research on why people fall in love. A summary of some of his findings is presented below.

1. Attraction

What causes attraction between people? Is it love at first sight? Do opposites attract? Do birds of a feather flock together? As yet the research findings have not given definitive answers but they have provided some interesting perspectives. In the realm of attraction between people there would appear to be at least two significant components: personal characteristics and interactional factors.

(a) *Personal characteristics.* The personal characteristics that a person desires in a girlfriend/boyfriend or partner will of course vary from individual to individual. Most people have preconceived ideas of their desired partner. These ideas are usually influenced by their life experiences, family, peers and the prevailing norms in society. These desirable factors can range from being kind, considerate and wealthy to being tall, dark and handsome. There are, of course, gender differences in the choice of desirable attributes.

It is an intriguing experience to work with groups of people with disabilities and to enable them to work out the type of characteristics they would like in their boyfriend or girlfriend. Having established a list, it is instructive to order them from most important to least important. This provides fertile ground for the discussion of personal preferences and needs in relationships. It also enables the person to reflect on the attributes he/she desires in a partner, and to clarify what is essential and what is optional.

Let's consider Buss's (1985) work on ideal partners.

The ideal partner: desirable characteristics
CHARACTERISTICS PREFERRED BY MALES or BY FEMALES.
1. Kindness and understanding
2. Intelligence
3. Physical attractiveness
4. Exciting personality
5. Good health
6. Adaptability
7. Physical attractiveness
8. Creativity
9. Desire for children
10. College graduate
11. Good heredity
12. Good earning capacity
13. Good housekeeper
14. Religious orientation

Perhaps you, the reader, might rank-order the list, and/or add other attributes that you consider important.

(b) Interactional factors. For people to be attached to one another, they must somehow interact. In addition to the desirable attributes of a person, there are a number of interactive factors that facilitate attraction between people and assist in the formation of relationships.

(i) Proximity. This involves people sharing a common space for periods of time. It might be at work, on transport, at a regular social event, sitting close to a person, or living in the same neighbourhood, to mention but a few. Such situations provide opportunities to interact. In many cases this occurs spontaneously as one goes about daily life. But in others it may be necessary to cultivate proximity. There are various ways of doing this, such as organising outings, clubs, social circles, coffee groups, arranging meeting places, cinema groups, bowling groups, etc.

(ii) Familiarity. This develops from people meeting each other on a number of occasions and interacting with each other. These conditions are important for people to be attracted to each other, but frequency of contact and interaction do not necessarily lead to attraction. In fact, the opposite can also result, as in the phrase 'familiarity breeds contempt'.

(iii) Similarity. This factor refers to shared physical, emotional, attitudinal and

social characteristics. An interesting discovery is the fact that people who fall in love with each other tend to have similar characteristics. In general it would appear that couples tend to be similar in age, education, intelligence, social class, race, religion and physical health. They also tend to be similar in personality, attitudes and physical attractiveness. So, if one were to play Cupid and try to arrange the circumstances for people to fall in love, one would place similar people in close proximity, or arrange for them to be in close proximity on a sufficient number of occasions to become familiar with each other. Then the cherub with his arrow would do the rest. Alternatively, there is the bachelors' festival in Listowel!

(iv) Equity. While some people like to be swept off their feet and dominated just like in the movies, the vast majority wish to have an equitable relationship in which neither partner dominates. Some people with intellectual disabilities may well have skill deficits in this area. It may be that individuals will need to develop skills in sharing, in taking turns, in being assertive or in conflict resolution. It may be useful to address the cultural stereotypical view of gender roles and work to achieve a more balanced one that facilitates relationships.

(v) Self-disclosure. This is the process of sharing personal and intimate details about oneself with a person who is trusted. Usually attraction and self-disclosure increase as a relationship develops. Reiss (1960) developed the concept of the 'Wheel of Love', arguing that as rapport, self-disclosure and mutual dependency increased, so too did love. Again, people who have intellectual disabilities may have skill deficits in relation to self-disclosure, and it may be necessary to address this and to teach the person various aspects of appropriate self-disclosure.

2. Communication

In order to develop and maintain a relationship that is intimate and satisfying, clear and effective communication is needed. Communication will need to take place at different levels—at the personal emotional level as well as at the factual level. If a relationship is to be nurturing it is necessary to express affection and warmth, and to demonstrate this in reality. By so doing, people can relate to each other and feel attached.

Many people with intellectual disabilities have a need to develop competence in these areas of communication. It is not about developing an extensive vocabulary but about expressing who you are and how you feel in different ways, e.g. by words, gestures, touch, looks and caring acts. It is about taking account of the other person's thoughts and feelings. It is also about resolving problems and difficulties in a helpful way.

Good communication is fundamental to a relationship. The various skill areas will include effective listening allied to conversational skills, as well as non-verbal skills which are both expressive and appropriate, e.g. facial expression, eye contact, head movements, gestures and body language. There will also be the need to read and respond to different emotions, and to express one's emotional life in different ways.

3. Personal presentation

One of the biggest challenges for parents and staff is how to enable or facilitate people with learning disabilities to be sexually attractive to the opposite sex. To be sexually attractive is to send out messages to the opposite sex, or perhaps to particular members of the opposite sex. Choosing clothes that enhance, make-up or scents that embellish and jewellery that complements are the standard ways in which young—and not so young—men and women try to attract each other. Huge amounts of time, effort and money are spent on these mating rituals in the general population.

This is not always so in the world of people with intellectual disabilities. In many ways this enhancement of the sex appeal of people with intellectual disabilities runs counter to the primary concern of protection. If a person with an intellectual disability is sexually attractive, does this invite suitors, with the concomitant danger of sexual activities, of exploitation and abuse? Many people have decided that it does, and have either toned down or not enhanced the person's attributes (personal or physical) that contribute to this sex appeal. But a general rule of attraction applies: 'if you want to appeal, you have to have appeal'. This dilemma awaits solution.

4. Opportunities

One of the most important things that people with intellectual disabilities need in order to facilitate relationships is access to opportunities. It might be of interest to explore the various situations, activities and events that offer opportunities to form relationships. Take a person known to you who does not have a disability and make a list of those opportunities as they pass through a day in their lives, a week in their lives and a month in their lives. Then do the same for a person with intellectual disability. Contrast and compare.

Now make a list of seven ways in which you might increase the opportunities for forming relationships for the person with intellectual disability:

1.
2.
3.
4.
5.
6.
7.

WHAT CAN YOU DO?

Sexuality and relationship education is taking place each day, whether we have a sexuality education programme or not. Soap operas continually present relationship dilemmas; newspapers, magazines and television all carry information pertaining to relationships. Staff and family act as role models. Sexuality abounds in everyday life. We sanction or censor various conversations; we encourage or discourage different activities. In the wealth of everyday interactions families and staff adopt various roles in relationship education without realising it. Craft and Brown (1994) explored these roles and isolated eight. We will now explore these roles.

1. Role models
Bandura's (1977) social learning theory suggests that one of the principle ways by which we learn is observational learning. A person learns new behaviours by observing another person modelling them and then imitating the behaviour of the model.

In the area of sexuality and relationships, family and staff members are powerful models in the lives of people with intellectual disabilities. Much of this modelling takes place at an informal level, for example the way husband and wife interact, how male and female staff talk and act towards each other, and how staff relate to people with disabilities. *Gender roles* are also modelled and a variety of relationships may be observed—a brother with his girlfriend or a sister with her boyfriend. Television also models relationships. This modelling may be of positive, constructive male–female relationships or the opposite. Recognising this process of observational learning, staff and family can model constructive relationships and evaluate models that are conducive to forming relationships.

2. Educators
Frequently without realising it, staff and family members can act as educators in a multiplicity of ways. On occasions one may set about consciously teaching an item in a formal way, e.g. body parts or self-care at menstruation. However, more often than not the teaching takes place in an informal way. It may be a response to a question, or explaining something when a person looks puzzled. On other occasions it may occur when a person has done something that is inappropriate or is unaware of a social norm. Numerous opportunities present themselves as one goes about the activities of daily living: the girl next door getting married; a pregnancy; and being careful in particular contexts. All of these can be used to teach about the world of sexuality and relationships. Given that this is occurring already, it is a matter of a more systematic approach to looking at people's needs and more consciously utilising the activities in their lives to educate them about relationships.

3. Counsellors

Quite often people act as informal counsellors to people with intellectual disabilities in the area of relationships. This may involve 'the sympathetic ear', listening to the heartbreak or the joy and excitement that are occurring in the person's life. Again direction and advice will often be given, such as 'Stay away from . . .' or 'Well, why don't you ask . . .'. Sometimes it is about giving people permission to follow a particular course of action; at other times it may involve helping the person to clarify their own views or suggesting a particular course of action.

This active listening and allowing people to express their thoughts and feelings is a common phenomenon in most services. Imparting of information regularly occurs, as does the making of specific suggestions in the area of sexuality and relationships. The vast majority of staff know the limits of their competence and will remain within these limits. Many staff feel comfortable in the role of everyday counsellor, while others do not. Training in this area can be invaluable for staff to enable them to deal with the relationship issues that arise in everyday situations. People who need in-depth or psychotherapeutic counselling must of course be referred to specially trained professional counsellors, and staff must not go beyond the limits of their competence.

4. Liaison role

In this role a staff member may operate as a key worker liaising with various people involved with persons with intellectual disability. It may involve seeking out a sex educator or a relationship counsellor for the person, or consulting with the family. It may be encouraging or arranging social activities which involve meeting interesting others. Alternatively it may involve inviting others to events or activities. Another potential task might be linking with the person's place of employment, family or residential centre in order to facilitate continuity and development in the area of relationships in the person's life.

5. Protectors

Because many people with learning difficulties are vulnerable in the area of relationships it is important that staff and family alike are aware of the need to adopt this role. There is a clear responsibility for all those closely involved to be vigilant and proactive in preventing circumstances which significantly increase risk to people with learning disabilities. The task of early detection of exploitative or abusive relationships is also critical for staff and families. Training in this area is of the utmost importance.

6. Interveners

There may be occasions when it is considered wise to intervene, or indeed when *not* to intervene would be irresponsible or unprofessional. This intervention may be to protect the person or to prevent specific behaviours which are in serious conflict with society's norms or which are illegal. On other occasions it may involve a positive intervention to facilitate positive developments in a relationship. These interventions can be at different levels of seriousness. They may range from dialling a telephone number so that a person may talk to his girlfriend to being involved in making decisions concerning the availability or use of contraception by people in a relationship. The latter action would obviously only be taken after it had been carefully considered in consultation with the appropriate people.

7. Advocates and facilitators of self-advocacy
Staff and family members may find themselves in the role of advocate for a person with regard to that person's relationships. It may involve getting the necessary training, education or counselling in sexuality and relationships. It could be about defending the person's right to have a relationship or to healthy sexual expression. It might also involve pushing to ensure that the person has an input into decision-making. This role may involve the cultivation or facilitation of self-advocacy so that the person can express his or her own preferences and insist upon his/her rights in the area of personal relationships.

8. Staff as empowerers
Craft and Brown (1994) articulate this admirably: 'This sums up the staff role. It is about enabling individuals, by a process of encouragement, facilitation, and the imparting of skills, to exercise power over their own lives and to make their own choices at their pace'. In the realm of friendships, relationships and sexuality this is the essential goal for which we strive.

SUMMARY

In this chapter we have explored the following topics:

- The personal experiences of people with intellectual disabilities in the realm of sexuality and relationships.

- The various types of relationships that exist and their hidden rules.

- The human needs that relationships fulfil.

- The different types of love and people with intellectual disabilities.

- The different perspectives on relationships.

- The rights of people with intellectual disabilities in the area of relationships and sexuality.

- The issue of competency and consent.

- Factors involved in cultivating relationships.

- Roles that staff or families can adopt to facilitate relationships.

REFERENCES

Bandura, A. (1977) *Social learning theory*. New Jersey. Prentice Hall.

Buss, D.M. (1985) Human mate detection. *American Scientist* **73**, 47–51.

Caffrey, S. (1992) Sexual attitudes measured and sexual understanding explored. Unpublished Ph.D. thesis, Trinity College Dublin.

Craft, A. (1987) Mental handicap and sexuality: issues for individuals with a mental handicap, their parents and professionals. In A. Craft (ed.), *Mental handicap and sexuality: issues and perspectives*, 13–34. Costello. Tunbridge Wells.

Craft, A. and Brown, H. (1994) Personal relationships and sexuality: the staff role. In A. Craft (ed.), *Practice issues in sexuality and learning disabilities*, 1–22. London. Routledge.

Craft, M. and Craft, A. (1978) *Sex and the mentally handicapped*. London. Routledge and Kegan Paul.

Cramer, D. (1998) *Close relationships*. London. Arnold.

Gunn, M. (1994) Competency and consent: the importance of decision making. In A. Craft (ed.), *Practice issues in sexuality and learning disabilities*, 116–34. London. Routledge.

Hingsburger, D. (1995). *Just say know! Understanding and reducing the risk of sexual victimization of people with developmental disabilities*. Eastman, PQ. Diverse City Press.

Law Commission (1991) *Mentally incapacitated adults and decision making: an overview*. L.C. Consultation Paper No. 119. London. HMSO.

Maslow, A.H. (1943) A theory of human motivation. *Psychology Review* **50**, 370–96.

Masters, W.H., Johnson, V.E. and Kolodny, R.C. (1997) *Human sexuality* (5th edn). Boston. Addison-Wesley.

Reiss, I. (1960) *Premarital sexual standards in America*. Glencoe, Illinois. Free Press.

Sternberg, R.J. (1986) A triangular theory of love. *Psychological Review* **93**,119–35.

Sternberg, R.J. (1988) Triangular love. In R.J. Sternberg and M.L. Barnes (eds), *The psychology of love*, 119–38. New Haven. Yale University Press.

Watson, C. and Rogers, R. (1980) Sexual instruction for the mildly retarded and normal adolescent; a comparison of educational approaches, parental expectations and pupil knowledge and attitude. *Health and Education Journal* **39** (3), 88–95.

Zgourides, G. D. (1996) *Human sexuality; contemporary perspectives.* New York. Harper Collins.

8. PARENTS AND PROFESSIONALS—EXPLORING A COMPLEX RELATIONSHIP

BAIRBRE REDMOND

It may seem easier to make a clear distinction between the needs of an individual with intellectual disability and those of his or her family. However, the reality is that the level of adequacy of services offered to a person with intellectual disability has a considerable impact, either positive or negative, on that person's extended family. The reverse is also true, and the quality of response that families receive from service professionals also affects the overall well-being of the individual with disability. This chapter looks at the relationship between service professionals and family members, specifically parents who have children or young adults with intellectual disability (hereinafter referred to as 'parents'). It begins with a brief historical review of how professional attitudes towards families in general and parents in particular have evolved over the past 50 years. It also explores a typology of parent/professional relationships and examines the effect on parents of being perceived in different ways by the professionals who work with them. It concludes with a proposed new ontology for professionals that may allow them to work in a more appropriate and responsive manner with parents.

Having a child or young adult with an intellectual disability poses unique challenges for parents. How well parents cope with these challenges is significantly affected not only by overall service provision but also by the way in which they are treated by service professionals. Over the past twenty years major changes have occurred in the way we regard those with intellectual disability and in our views on the types of services that are needed in order to allow them to live more inclusive and dignified lives. Far fewer changes have occurred in the quality of work with parents and families. As the underlying trend has moved towards the creation of more inclusive, normalised lifestyles for those with intellectual disability, there is increasing uncertainty as to how to deal with parents who are neither as willing nor as able to embrace changes which seem so tantalisingly sensible and attractive to the professional. Parents are also becoming less willing to assume a stance of unquestioning gratitude towards service-providers. Many of them perceive—often correctly—that, rather than receiving recognition for their efforts, the longer families continue to care, the less is likely to be offered to them in the long term. Traditional 'support services' have offered welcome relief for many parents from the daily work of caring for someone with an intellectual disability, but these services have seldom addressed the more fundamental inequities and problems suffered by many parents.

HISTORICAL BACKGROUND

In general terms, up until the mid-twentieth century the care of those with intellectual disability was primarily considered to be best provided outside the family home. However, by the 1970s the conditions in many institutions caring for those with intellectual disability were beginning to come under public scrutiny. In Scandinavia, Kugel was comparing the conditions in institutions for those with intellectual disability unfavourably with those of animals in the zoo (Kugel and Wolfensberger 1969). In the United States in 1972 Geraldo Rivera, subsequently better known as a chat-show host, made a TV programme which exposed the appalling conditions of those with intellectual disability in two large institutions in New York State—Willowbrook State School and Letchworth Village. Ericsson and Mansell (1996) see Rivera's TV exposé, which attracted over two and a half million viewers, as the single most important event to give impetus to the decrease of institutional services in the United States.

Rivera's work was not unique in attempting to expose poor practice in residential institutions. John F. Kennedy's 1963 Community Mental Health and Mental Retardation Facilities Act had already done much to provide funding to improve the conditions for those in institutional care. In 1965, seven years before Rivera's exposé, Robert Kennedy had condemned Willowbrook State School for forcing its inmates to 'live amidst brutality and human excrement and intestinal disease' (Rivera 1972, 524). Joanna Ryan and Frank Thomas in *The politics of mental handicap* (1980; 1987) also present an arresting and often horrific account of the inhumanity and degradation suffered by many of those with intellectual disability being cared for in old-style 'mental handicap hospitals' in the United Kingdom at around the same time.

FAMILY VOICES

At this time the voices of families were beginning to be heard for the first time (Read 2000). Associations such as the National Association for Retarded Children in the United States were revealing that the problem of intellectual disability was not confined to the lower classes. In the United States this was tied in to a number of 'confessional' statements from well-known and affluent families who admitted to having a child in an institution but who were now fighting for better conditions for that child and for others (Trent 1994). One of the first couples to do so were Roy Rogers and Dale Evans, then well-known film stars, whose daughter was born with Down Syndrome and had died at home, aged two. Dale Evans Rogers's book about her daughter, although sentimental, showed the couple's determination to keep their daughter at home against what would have been typical medical advice at the time. The book, *Angel unaware* (Rogers 1953), was the third highest-selling book in the United States in 1953. Perhaps the most famous family to admit to having a member with intellectual disability, albeit after a long period of time, was the family of John F. Kennedy, whose sister Rosemary had an intellectual disability. As already discussed, both John and Robert Kennedy initiated change for those with intellectual disability at governmental level. Other members of the Kennedy family subsequently became significant figures in the development of new approaches to those with intellectual disability, such as the Special Olympics movement, not just in the United States but worldwide (Trent 1994). One result of such celebrity revelations was an easing of the stigma for parents in admitting that their child had a disability, and another was the feeling that there were other parents who might understand and appreciate their worries and fears.

Similar parents' movements were beginning in the United Kingdom in the early 1950s with the emergence of the National Association for Parents of Backward Children (now MENCAP, the Royal Society for Mentally Handicapped Children and Adults). In Ireland the National Association of the Mentally Handicapped in Ireland (NAMHI) was founded in 1961, at a time in the country when 'mental handicap was now ceasing to be regarded as shameful, something to be concealed and not publicly acknowledged' (Robins 1992, 53).

COMMUNITY CARE POLICIES

Running parallel with the growing public disquiet about conditions of care for those with intellectual disability in institutional care was the political pressure to move services, for both those with intellectual disability and those with mental health problems, out of institutions and into smaller, community settings. Such moves were not only in response to the demands for better-quality care; they were also related to the escalating costs of running large institutions and the belief that services could be provided at a lower cost within the community (Ericsson and Mansell 1996; Walker 1993).

Throughout the 1970s and 1980s the numbers of people with intellectual disability in institutional care dropped sharply; large institutions closed and care was provided in smaller units and houses based in the community (Emerson and Hatton 1994).

The cost-saving aspect of deinstitutionalisation was often achieved not because care in the community was, in itself, a cheaper option but because many of the services which were needed to adequately support those with intellectual disability in the community were not fully developed. Doyal (1993), writing in a British context, comments that for community care to operate effectively it is necessary for all individuals in that community to have access to adequate goods and services which allow them to flourish as persons in their own right and to participate as full citizens. He adds that none of the aims of community care can be achieved unless sufficient capital is made available and 'thus far this [finance] has not been forthcoming and there are good arguments for believing that it will not be forthcoming in the future' (Doyal 1993, 283).

The failure to develop adequate services in a community context had major implications for those with intellectual disability, as it became increasingly clear that without support their lives in the community could be just as limited and devalued as they had been in institutional care. The major difference was that within the community lay a source of care which was cheap, long-term and relatively reliable—the family. Policy statements, such as the 1990 report of the Review Group on Mental Handicap Services, recommend that those with intellectual disability should continue to live with their families 'without placing undue strain on parents or relatives' (Review Group on Mental Handicap Services 1990, 37). The reality for many families was that their role as long-term carers existed because no alternative to family care had been provided. This author's previous research has shown that none of the 78 parents interviewed in her study of parents of adolescents with intellectual disability had received any reassurance that accommodation other than family care would be available should they need it (Redmond 1996).

Inadequacies in policy-making embedded families, particularly parents, within the community care structure—as Walsh et al. (1994) say, 'making a virtue of a necessity'. Walker (1993, 220) noted that 'despite the rhetoric concerning the needs of carers, there are no proposals designed to ensure that their needs are taken into account. Furthermore, the fact that there might be a conflict of interest between carers and the cared-for is not recognised.' While it was often the stated wish of parents to keep the individual with intellectual disability living in the family home in the long term (McConkey 1989; Redmond 1996), the reality was that many families were coping without support either from the service agencies or from their own community. This also placed extra stress on professionals who were attempting to develop satisfactory services while not being given adequate finance to do so.

HOW PARENTS ARE PERCEIVED BY PROFESSIONALS—A VIEWPOINT PARADIGM

As major shifts in attitudes have occurred in how individuals with intellectual disability are perceived, interesting parallel changes have also occurred in the case of parents and families, most particularly in how they are appreciated by the professionals whom they encounter. A number of authors have looked at 'models' of the professional/parent relationship (Moroney 1986; Twigg and Atkin 1994; Dale 1996). A fundamental danger exists in trying to 'fit' parents into a specific category and the reality is that few parents stay neatly in one model. This section looks instead at the different standpoints that professionals have taken in regard to parents. These five professional 'viewpoints' have been drawn from a comprehensive review of the literature relating to parents from a number of different professional groups, including nursing, social work, psychology and medicine. It has also drawn from specific research that has recorded parents' experiences of their dealings with professionals (Redmond 2000).

1. Perceiving the parents as pathologically different
A significant feature of this type of professional view of parents stems from the perception that the birth of a child with disability is a tragedy that renders parents perpetually 'handicapped'. When taking this view, professionals tend to pathologise parents and to treat not only the individual with disability but also the entire family as 'ill' and in need of treatment. Dale (1996, 101) talks about how medical ideas of pathology have been extended to parents and families, who are expected to suffer adverse effects from having a child with disability: 'The birth of a disabled child was seen as a "crisis" or abnormal state and the concept of "crisis" was extended to the whole family'.

The notion of parents experiencing a predictable pattern of grief and bereavement, particularly following disclosure of the disability, is very relevant to this view of parents as misfortunates. There are a number of variations on the grief model (sometimes called a 'stage model' of grief) applied to parents. Cunningham's (1979) model of psychic shock is one of the most commonly used (Mittler and McConachie 1983; Dale 1996). This model takes the parents from shock through reaction and adaptation until they experience orientation and finally the crisis abates.

Such a stage model is useful, but only as a rough guide as to what some parents may experience at some stages of their lives. However, critics of the stage model find it too rigid and linear. Dale considers that not all parents necessarily go through the stages in a precise order; some will go through more than one stage at once, or go back and forth between stages (Dale 1996). One of the most problematic aspects of applying a stage model of grief is that it implies that if parents grieve *well enough* they should come to an acceptance of their child with disability. This ignores the individuality of each parent, each child and each family. It also makes the complex and individualistic reactions that all parents have to their growing children, disabled or not, into a series of emotional tasks to be accomplished before they can become 'good' parents. Goodey (1992) interviewed parents who had young children with Down Syndrome and found their reactions to their child's disability to be far from uniform and liberally leavened with humour and humanity.

The notion of chronic sorrow (Olshansky 1962) is probably more useful in helping to understand the complexities of emotions faced by parents. Olshansky suggests that 'the great stress professional workers tend to place on "acceptance" may suggest to the parent that he is expected to perceive his child from the point of view of the professional helper' (1962, 191). There is also a temptation for professionals to perceive that parents who continue to express sadness and anger in the long term may in some way be resisting professional help towards the 'cure' of acceptance. Olshansky (1962, 192) suggests that professionals will find it more helpful to view the parents' sorrow as a natural, rather than a neurotic, reaction. This concept allows for parents to experience periods of cyclical grief throughout their lives without being considered dysfunctional. 'Chronic sorrow and acceptance of a child's disability can coexist alongside each other as part of the normal long-term process of parental adjustment. A parent who continues to feel sadness about a child's disability can still be competent and caring' (Dale 1996, 58).

Olshansky's work on chronic sorrow may offer a less rigid approach to parents, allowing them to escape professional expectations that they will 'accomplish' the stages in a grief model. However, it is also possible that the notion of chronic sorrow has been overstated and that many families appear to experience little or no negative effects on a long-term basis. Quinn notes that a degree of self-fulfilment may well exist in the expectation of the grieving parent: 'depression and sadness need not be the expected response to learning that a family member has a disability, but when professionals anticipate such response, they will usually find it' (1998, xvi).

Finally, the use of a grief and bereavement paradigm poses considerable risks in offering professionals an easy way to misinterpret parents' reactions. By seeing anger and resentment as pathological components of a grief response, it becomes tempting for professionals to distance themselves from any responsibility for causing such emotion (Redmond 1996). Parents and families can be angry for many different reasons. Their anger may relate to their feelings about their child; equally, they may be angry and frustrated at having to cope with inadequate services, poor levels of communication and uncertainty about the short-term and long-term future of their child. Goodey (1992) felt that he had found far more reasons for anger in the parents in his study arising from their treatment at the hands of professionals than from any predetermined phase of grief and bereavement. To dismiss parental anger as being indicative of pathological sadness rather than as part of a legitimate frustration is one of the possible tacit professional presumptions about parents that the researcher will examine as part of her application of her reflective teaching and learning model.

2. Perceiving the parents as grateful recipients of professional expertise

It can be argued that most professionals have, on the whole, been treated with deferential respect and relatively high regard by their clients and by society at large. A refusal by clients to comply with professional expertise or to participate fully in service plans may, in effect, be a challenge to the professionals' position and expert powers (Dale 1996). There is strong evidence, in reviewing the professional literature in the field of intellectual disability, especially from the 1970s and early 1980s, that many professionals have found it hard to tolerate a lack of compliance by parents with their expertise.

By taking such an expert stance with parents, professionals do not allow for the parent to contribute any significant expertise. Essentially, in this viewpoint, professionals take total control, make all the decisions and select which information they consider to be of relevance to the family (Cunningham and Davis 1985). In this approach, the parents have little or no power, and compliance with the professionals' expertise is expected. In the field of intellectual disability, the professional as expert is very visible in the literature (Dale 1996). Whereas other viewpoints may suggest that parents fail to appreciate the wisdom of the professional owing to their grief-stricken state, parents in the expert view are described as defensive and over-protective if they fail to comply with professional advice. Note Blodgett's summation of the issue (1971, 79):

> 'we need to recognise that parent defensiveness often gets in the way of making the best use of available professional help . . . it is difficult enough to admit to yourself that you don't know how to cope with your own child; it is even more difficult to admit it to someone else. But if you can't say it, how can you expect help?'

By adopting this view of parents, professionals do make some acknowledgement that parents should be allowed to cooperate with them. However, there is a clear understanding that professionals, on the whole, are going to control the process. The use of parents as co-teachers or co-therapists is sometimes called a 'transplant relationship' with professionals (Dale 1996, 9). A significant feature of the transplant relationship is that parents can be trained to take part in programmes that are designed, initiated and evaluated by professionals. Mittler and Mittler (1983) describe the transplant relationship as one-sided; they do not find it surprising that many parents find it hard to tolerate its implicit assumption that professionals know best. Such a notion of alliance suggests that, while parents will collaborate with and acquiesce to professional expertise, professionals will not necessarily collaborate with or accede to parental proposals.

3. Perceiving the parent as a barrier to progress

As has already been discussed, the contemporary policy of care in the community has had a major impact on the nature of services provided in the area of intellectual disability. With its emphasis on normalisation, deinstitutionalisation and community integration, community care looked set to revolutionise systems of care which were custodial, demoralising and excluding—services whereby those with an intellectual disability were considered either unable or unacceptable to live in the company of 'normal' people. The ideal of care in the community, where those with intellectual disability could live a full, inclusive life nurtured by those around them, has never been fully achieved (Doyal 1993). The services that were needed to support such a system were never adequately developed and community care began to be synonymous with 'parent care', without the promised support and resources necessary for the system to function properly.

The development of community care, although imperfect, did bring with it a growing awareness of a rights perspective for those with intellectual disability. Although seldom enshrined in legislation or adequately supported, it began to be seen as important to recognise the rights of individuals to articulate choice in their lives in areas such as daily living, work and personal and sexual relationships. Such new approaches towards the 'empowerment' of individuals with disability sometimes created conflict for parents as they seemed to challenge the stability of home life which parents had often worked hard to achieve (Todd and Shearn 1996b). Such conflictual situations emerged as young people with intellectual disability moved towards a more adult lifestyle, either on their own initiative or with the encouragement of service professionals. Much of the literature on normalisation (Wolfensberger 1972; 1983), sexuality (Craft 1987; 1994), quality of life (Schalock 1990; Goode 1989; Felce 1996) and self-advocacy (Clare 1990) encouraged those with intellectual disability to live less restricted and more self-determined lives.

However, many families found the notion of facilitating these young adults to experience greater independence, particularly sexual independence, an alarming prospect (Craft and Craft 1982; Fairbrother 1983; McConkey 1989; Redmond 1996). Some writers can barely disguise their frustration at the seeming slowness of parents to embrace change, dismissing the concerns of parents as being a justification of their caring role. 'There is a danger that the emphasis on providing care may continue beyond its usefulness, thus encouraging dependence in children. In turn this dependency provides solace for the parents and verifies their ability to function as good parents' (Baker 1991, 61). Such attitudes fuelled a professional view that tended to dismiss these seemingly over-protective parents and simply to 'work around them'. In relation to this practice in their field of sex education, Rose and Jones (1994, 24) say: 'Whilst sympathetic to the aims of the principles of normalisation, the strategy of non-involvement of parents does not seem a sensible way of achieving them'.

The reality is that families are seldom supported, either practically or emotionally, to help a young person move into a more adult lifestyle. Brown (1996, 13) notes that parental conservatism can be linked to a lack of adequate resources: 'parents are scared to let go of traditional models if they cannot be sure these will be replaced'. The view of one mother, unhappy that the professionals working with her 20-year-old moderately disabled daughter were supportive of the girl's relationship with a young man with similar disability, illustrates this point:

> 'I look after my daughter on my own with no guarantee if there will be a service for her in one year . . . even in one month's time. I'll do that till I die. If she gets pregnant and has a baby will the staff who think this is such a good idea come around to do night feeds for me? Will they sit up and comfort her if she gets dumped? This is not their risk, they won't bear the consequences if it goes wrong, I will. So why am I so rotten to have an opinion in this matter?' (Redmond 2000, 80).

The concern of parents, especially in sensitive areas such as sexuality, may be intensified in the realms of self-advocacy or citizen advocacy. Parents may perceive that the professionals involved in advocacy groups or citizen advocacy will encourage young people with disability to engage in activities which they will not be able to handle, or which will lead them into danger. In this author's study it was shown that 80% of parents felt that by becoming more independent their daughter would be placed in jeopardy; their greatest fear was sexual exploitation or pregnancy (Redmond 1996). Simons (1995) sees how easily conflicts of interest arise between families who may emphasise safety and security and advocates who may be arguing for the right of the individual to take risks. It must be remembered that families have often been advocating for the rights of their child with intellectual disability for many years. A mother sums up the frustration expressed by many parents:

> 'We've had to fight for a lot for our daughter. I feel that she might not have got such a good service if the family had not made sacrifices' (Redmond 1996, 76).

Dilemmas occur when, with their growing maturity, the wishes of young adults with intellectual disability begin to differ from those of their parents. This is, of course, a normal part of growing up, and all families engage in the process of trying to protect their older children as they reach towards maturity and self-determination. The big difference occurs when parents perceive that, because of their intellectual disability, their child will never reach a level of maturity when they will be able to comprehend the implications of becoming more independent. In such cases conflicts may arise if professionals adopt an advocacy role to support and empower such young adults to express their own needs, seemingly against their parents' wishes.

In her work with adolescents and adults involved in an 'empowerment' programme and with their families, Monica Barnes (1997) comments that many of the parents with whom she worked were fearful of encouraging freedom and independence in a world they perceived as dangerous. Barnes (1997) also notes that none of the parents she talked to felt that service-providers were helping them to plan and prepare for their son or daughter's future. This highlights the importance of acknowledging and incorporating diverse opinions and concerns of both parents and individuals with intellectual disability if young adults are to become more independent and self-determined. 'Carers have their own legitimate concerns and user empowerment should never be seen as a reason for ignoring families' (Simons 1995, 173). The danger is that, unless different professional and parental opinions are fully acknowledged, parents and professional advocates will get embroiled in win/lose situations over the rights of the individual with disability. As Barnes (1997, 85) says, 'empowerment is too often viewed as a zero sum—empowering one person is thought to mean removing power from another'. Taking power away from parents is unlikely to be a helpful strategy in increasing the empowerment of people with learning disabilities; it is likely to result in both groups becoming losers in the end.

4. Perceiving the parent as a partner

The view of the parent as partner with the professional has been evolving gradually over the past fifteen years and has emerged partly as a result of pressure by a growing lobby of parents, dissatisfied with the treatment offered to them by professionals. Swan, a mother of a young woman with intellectual disability, expresses the feelings of many parents: 'In order to ensure that we as parents, and our children, have real choices and that these choices are seen as a right and not a charity, it is imperative that power is shared between parents and professionals. We can no longer be assigned to fund-raising—with no control in how that money is spent' (Swan 1995, 22).

Since the early 1980s the literature has suggested that working in collaboration with parents might be fruitful, yet much of this literature suggested collaboration of a kind which 'transplanted' knowledge from professional to parents (Cameron 1982; Daly *et al.* 1985; Cameron 1986). Mittler and Mittler (1983) asserted that parental participation in schemes designed and controlled by professionals could not be regarded as partnership. This is especially true when parents are not consulted about the rationale of the work, nor are the resources and abilities which individual families bring to the venture considered important. Turnbull and Turnbull (1982) considered that no 'typical' partnership relationship could exist but that each family would engage with professionals in ways determined by their own physical, emotional and practical resources: 'rather than mandating that all parents be equal participants, policy should tolerate a range of parental involvement choices and options, matched to the needs and interests of the parent' (Turnbull and Turnbull 1982, 120).

The need to appreciate this individuality of parents is essential to forming partnerships. Mittler and Mittler (1983, 11) feel that partnership calls for the recognition that parents of those with disability have no common characteristics: 'they come from all sections of society and represent the whole range of individual differences and personality'. Hewett et al. (1970) noted in their research that parents approached their parenting tasks in a very similar way to those with able-bodied children. Mittler and Mittler (1983) emphasise the importance of recognising and harnessing the parenting skills already achieved by many parents with their other able-bodied children. As Cunningham and Davis (1985, 26) point out, 'if we are to work in a respectful partnership with parents we have to accept the reality of their interpretations and not oppose or ignore them'.

At the heart of partnership is the notion of equality; Mittler and Mittler stressed that 'partnership can take many forms but it must be on the basis of equality' (1983, 11). However, McConachie (1983) cautions that professional workers do not adjust well to being equal partners. Educationalist Sheila Wolfendale (1983) sees that equality between professionals and parents only becomes possible when parents cease being treated as 'clients'. Wolfendale considers that parents become clients when they are dependent on professional opinion, when they are peripheral to decision-making, and when they are perceived as 'inadequate' or 'deficient'. For real partnership to occur parents must be:

- active and central to decision-making and its implementation;
- perceived as having equal strengths and equal expertise;
- able to contribute to, as well as to receive, services (reciprocity);
- able to share responsibility so that they and professionals are mutually accountable (Wolfendale 1992, 14).

In spite of the enthusiasm that many of the earlier writers on partnership brought to the topic, the notion of partnership has yet to be realised. McConachie (1994), writing eleven years after her first work on partnership, admits that, although partnership can be a good idea, it may be disappointing in practice. Many parents are aware that the services available to them and their child are limited and that professionals play a vital role in advocating for scarce resources on their behalf. Expressing criticism of a professional, even when that professional deserves it, may seem too risky an action for some parents who may be concerned that they will put their chances of being offered needed resources in jeopardy. Pleasing a professional may seem like a safer route for some parents than an open and frank exchange of views.

Lastly, professionals are ultimately and legally accountable to their employers, who also have control over how professionals use their time and resources. This fact considerably limits the ability of professionals to have a full partnership with parents. Dale (1996) also cites higher demands and expectation of parents, the shortfall between parental expectations and professional delivery, and greater divisions between and within professional agencies as all combining to increase the likelihood of conflict and mistrust. Thus, partnership may not have been as easy to achieve as seemed possible in the early 1980s. What writers like Mittler and Mittler (1982; 1983), Turnbull and Turnbull (1982) and McConachie (1994) did, however, was to introduce a concept which was truly mould-breaking at a time when professional expertise was considered to be all that a family might need in order to 'cope'. They challenged a powerful and value-ridden system and, for the first time, put forward the notion that not only are the opinions of parents worth hearing, but that professionals might even consider changing their practice as a result of hearing them. Like all new ways of looking at things, partnership did not provide the answer for everybody. What it did suggest was that there might be more than one answer, and that if parents themselves were included in policy- and decision-making, their expertise and knowledge could enhance, rather than thwart, the professional's work.

5. Perceiving parents as people in their own right

There is a danger when reviewing the literature of being seduced into the supposition that parents of a child with intellectual disability are qualitatively different to other parents. This is due to a number of causes, not least of which is that the vast majority of the literature on parents in this context is written by professionals. With the exception of writers who straddle the professional/parent divide (Mittler and Mittler 1983; Turnbull and Turnbull 1982; Shearer 1986; Russell 1985) most of the writing by parents comes into a 'non-academic' category, primarily in quite a personal, autobiographical style. The reality is that many families do not feel themselves to be different because they have a child with disability, but they may feel that the society in which they live treats them differently (Dale 1996, 117–18). If this is so, they may also feel that, because of a lack of support to help them take care of their child or young adult, their lives are forced to be different. In their evaluation of family supports offered as part of the All Wales Strategy, Felce *et al.* (1998) noted that the supports provided to families required a more complete understanding of the nature of care-giving and its association with other actual or potential aspects of parents' lives.

Ironically, in some of the literature on normalisation there is an underlying suggestion that parents may constitute a barrier towards individuals with intellectual disability becoming more normalised. However, if we apply many of the principles of normalisation to families themselves, we find that they, too, do not have normal lives. For example, Wolfensberger (1972) considered that personal and vocational normalisation could only be achieved if the individual was allowed to live and work in environments that encouraged the development of self-determination, independence and personal dignity. The reality for many parents is that taking care of someone with intellectual disability, without adequate support, may also rob them of some of their self-determination, independence and personal dignity. Consider the following points.

- Unlike other parents, parents of those with intellectual disability take care of their child with no parenting 'blueprint' and few recognisable reference points from the children and adults in the society around them (Redmond 1996, 81–2).
- Unlike other parents, parents of those with intellectual disability may have little choice in what school or day service their children attend. Their children may have to wait for a school place or receive part-time education, if, indeed, they are offered an educational service at all (Smyth 1988, 233; Oliver 1996, 81).
- Unlike other parents, parents of those with intellectual disability experience lives that defy the normal chronology of parenting. Many continue carrying out tasks associated with babyhood and early childhood into their middle and old age (McConkey 1989, 17; Seligman and Darling 1989, 9–12).
- Unlike other parents, in families taking care of someone with intellectual disability mothers are less likely to work, and some perceive that they will never be in a position to consider taking a job (Todd and Shearn 1996a; Shearn and Todd 1998; 2000; Lukemeyer et al. 2000; Redmond et al., forthcoming).
- Unlike other parents, parents of someone with intellectual disability are very likely to have an adult child live with them until they die. Most of these parents live into their old age without any reassurance about who will care for that person when they die (McConkey 1989, 30–2; Krauss and Seltzer 1993, 60; Redmond 1996, 47–50; Prosser 1997).

Moroney argues that part of this 'abnormalisation' of parents occurs because support services are directed primarily at the individual with disability rather than at the family: 'wheelchairs may be seen as appropriate expenditure for handicapped children, but not washing machines' (1986, 137). Furthermore, as the examination of other professional viewpoints has shown, it is also because of the professional tendency to look for symptoms in parents. These viewpoints imply something significant—that parents are grief-stricken, defensive, overprotective or uncooperative because they have a child with a disability. It can be just as valid to argue that parents may well behave in this way because the attitudes and services offered to them by professionals are inappropriate or inadequate.

Having a child with an intellectual disability means that many parents 'acquire' professionals in their lives, and they may soon discover that how well they can function as a family may depend on how well they get on with those professionals and what the professionals can offer them. The harsh reality is that there is little or nothing parents can do to change the disability their child has acquired, but they may discover that they, too, have lost much of their own self-determination. A mother of a 25-year-old man expressed such a loss in the following manner:

'Why do I need a professional to decide how money from the Government should be spent on my son? Why can't we, as a family, be given that money into our hands and we'll decide how best we can spend it. I'm damn sure I'd make a better fist of it—I know what he wants, I know what we need. It's really not that complicated' (Redmond 2000, 92).

ESTABLISHING A NEW ONTOLOGY FOR PARENTS AND PROFESSIONALS

Developing best professional practice with parents is not solely about the creation of practical support services; it is also about addressing the attitudinal and philosophical ethos inherent in the design and delivery of such services. The preceding discussion on professional perspectives gives some idea of how professional attitudes can either empower families or sideline them to the position of grateful recipients or obstructive hindrances. What seems to be needed is a way to help professionals to reappraise some of their traditional perceptions of the parent with whom they work. Such a reappraisal could then allow for the introduction of more responsive and collaborative professional practice that would be of benefit to parents and workers alike.

Donald Schön (1983; 1987) has pioneered this type of professional attitudinal reappraisal in what he termed 'reflective practice'. Schön considered that many professionals continually adopted a stance of 'technical rationality' with service-users, asserting that positivist knowledge could be applied to all human situations, providing clear and rational solutions. Craft (1994, 25) saw that such an approach 'consigned the person to a category of human defect that can only be understood and remedied by professional expertise'. Schön argued that, by continually adopting such a pose, professionals had created a crisis within many professions where service-users had become increasingly unwilling to tolerate attitudes from professionals that were patronising and paternalistic. He argued that the distant, arrogant professional stance of technical rationality needed to be replaced by a far more open, inclusive position whereby professionals devolved power back to clients/service-users, thus engaging them in real partnership. He called those who could achieve this change 'reflective practitioners'.

In Schön's work on the reflective relationship lies a clue as to how to address some of the difficulties caused by professional adherence to unhelpful perceptions of parents. Inherent in the reflective relationship is a respect for the opinion and expertise of the person with whom the professional works and a willingness to adapt and change according to that individual's unique situation. Schön argues that only by adopting a reflective position can professionals begin to learn that they do not hold fixed and superior knowledge. This then allows them to match their expertise to that of their client so that together the client and professional should produce the unique answer to their particular situation. Fook (1996) describes the reflective relationship as having four characteristics—inquiry, criticism, change and accountability, aspects frequently missing from the relationships that parents have with service professionals. In terms of intellectual disability, Schön's model has resonance not only for the professional/parent relationship but also for the dynamic three-way relationship between parent, professional and the person with intellectual disability (see Fig. 1).

The Reflective Relationship

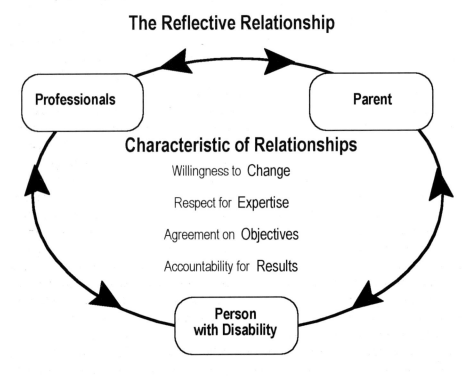

Fig. 1—The reflective relationship.

By fully including parents in a relationship that minimalises marginalisation, it is possible to create an atmosphere that encourages an appreciation of the abilities and expertise of others. Such an appreciation also has relevance for the relationship between parents and the person with intellectual disability. Nothing is more likely to produce uncooperative and defensive attitudes than a lack of communication and the attendant fear and suspicion it engenders. If professionals recognise the expertise of parents and provide clear short- and long-term commitments both to them and to the individual, then this can create an environment in which parents can better appreciate and support new initiatives for the person with intellectual disability. It is, of course, of vital importance that policy-makers also recognise this need and provide professionals and service-providers with adequate funds to design and implement secure and dependable services.

Reflective practice will not necessarily occur by itself, and professionals need time and space to review their practice attitudes and to judge how these affect service-users. Professional education and in-service training should incorporate reflective elements that encourage professionals to see their expertise as more than the acquisition of technical skills and academic knowledge. It must also facilitate professionals to learn to recognise and analyse the more fundamental perceptions that underpin their practice. Kember (2001) makes the point that effective reflection by professionals necessitates a change of deep-seated and often unconscious beliefs and leads to the creation of new belief structures. Reflective teaching and learning now plays an increasingly important role in professional training programmes in nursing (Jarvis 1987; 1992; Reed and Procter 1993), social work (Papell and Skolnik 1992; Gould and Taylor 1996; Fook 1996), occupational therapy (Sinclair and Tse 2001), teaching and education (Mezirow 1990; 1991; Jennings and Kennedy 1996; Brookfield 1995). Specific reflective teaching and training models for professionals in the area of intellectual disability are also being developed (Redmond, forthcoming).

Excellence and relevance in professional practice will only occur when professionals are encouraged to review their practice in a holistic manner and when service-users are treated as knowledgeable customers rather than fortunate recipients. By looking at the parents of those with intellectual disability from a systemic perspective, as this chapter has done, we can begin to appreciate that families have not, on the whole, been treated in ways that are equitable, encouraging or humane. For too long families have been perceived as, at best, a benign presence and, at worst, a disruptive and obstructive barrier towards change and improvement. By viewing families in terms of the philosophic and attitudinal systems in which they operate, we can begin to better understand their needs, their frustrations and their hopes for the future. Only by doing so can we hope to develop professional responses that not only cherish those with intellectual disability but also appreciate and consolidate the considerable strength of their families.

REFERENCES

Baker, P. (1991) The denial of adolescence for people with mental handicap: an unwitting conspiracy? *Mental Handicap* **19**, 61–5.

Barnes, M. (1997) Families and empowerment. In P. Ramcharan, G. Roberts, G. Grant and J. Borland (eds), *Empowerment in everyday life*, 70–87. London. Jessica Kingsley.

Blodgett, H. (1971) *Mentally retarded children—what parents and others should know.* Minneapolis. University of Minnesota Press.

Brookfield, S. (1995) *Becoming a critically reflective teacher.* San Francisco. Jossey Bass.

Brown, H. (1996) Reviewing respite services for adults with learning disabilities. *Tizard Learning Disability Review* **1** (2), 13–14.

Cameron, R.J. (1982) *Working together: portage in the UK.* Windsor. NFER-Nelson.

Cameron, R.J. (1986) *Portage: pre-schoolers, parents and professionals. Ten years of achievement in the UK.* Windsor. NFER-Nelson.

Clare, M. (1990) *Developing self-advocacy skills with people with disabilities and learning difficulties.* London. Further Education Unit.

Craft, A. (1987) Mental handicap and sexuality: issues for individuals with a mental handicap, the parents and professionals. In A. Craft (ed.), *Mental handicap and sexuality—issues and perspectives*, 13–34. Tunbridge Wells. Costello.

Craft, A. (1994) *Practice issues in sexuality and learning disabilities.* London. Routledge.

Craft, M. and Craft, A. (eds) (1982) *Sex and the mentally handicapped* (revised edn). London. Routledge and Kegan Paul.

Cunningham, C. (1979) Parent counselling. In M. Craft (ed.), *Tredgold's Mental Retardation*, 313–18. London. Balliere Tindall.

Cunningham, C.C. and Davis, H. (1985) *Working with parents: frameworks for collaboration.* Milton Keynes. Open University Press.

Dale, N. (1996) *Working with families of children with special needs—partnership and practice.* London. Routledge.

Daly, B., Addington, J., Kerfoot, S. and Sigston, A. (eds) (1985) *Portage: the importance of parents.* Oxford. NFER-Nelson.

Doyal, L. (1993) Human need and the moral right to optimal community care. In J. Bornat, C. Pereira, D. Pilgrim and F. Williams (eds), *Community care—a reader*, 276–86. London. Macmillan/Open University.

Emerson, E. and Hatton, C. (1994) *Moving out: re-location from hospital to community.* London. HMSO.

Ericsson, K. and Mansell, J. (1996) Introduction: towards deinstitutionalisation. In J. Mansell and K. Ericsson (eds), *Deinstitutionalization and community living—intellectual disability services in Britain, Scandinavia and the USA*, 3–11.

London. Chapman Hall.

Fairbrother, P. (1983) The parents' viewpoint. In A. Craft and M. Craft (eds), *Sex education and counselling for mentally handicapped people*, 95–102. London. Costello.

Felce, D. (1996) Quality of support for ordinary living. In J. Mansell and K. Ericsson (eds), *Deinstitutionalization and community living—intellectual disability services in Britain, Scandinavia and the USA*. London. Chapman Hall.

Felce, D., Grant, G., Todd, S. *et al.* (1998) *Towards a full life: researching policy innovation for people with learning disabilities*. Oxford. Butterworth-Heinemann.

Fook, J. (1996) The reflective researcher: developing a reflective approach to practice. In J. Fook (ed.), *The reflective researcher—social workers' theories of practice research*, 1–10. St Leonards, NSW. Allen and Unwin.

Goode, D.A. (1989) Quality of life and quality of work time. In W.E. Kiernan and R.L. Schalock (eds), *Economics, industry and economy: a look ahead*. Baltimore. Paul H. Brookes.

Goodey, C. (1992) Fools and heretics: parents' views of professionals. In T. Booth *et al.* (eds), *Learning for all: policies for diversity in education*, 165–76. London. Routledge in association with the Open University.

Gould, N. and Taylor, I. (eds) (1996) *Reflective learning for social work*. Aldershot. Arena.

Hewett, S., Newson, J. and Newson, E. (1970) *The family and the handicapped child*. London. Allen and Unwin.

Jarvis, P. (1987) *Adult learning in the social context*. London. Croome Helm.

Jarvis, P. (1992) Reflective practice and nursing. *Nurse Education Today* **12** (3), 174–81.

Jennings, C. and Kennedy, E. (eds) (1996) *The reflective professional in education: psychological perspectives on changing contexts*. London. Jessica Kingsley.

Kember, D. (2001) Reflections on reflection. In D. Kember *et al.* (eds), *Reflective teaching and learning in the health professions*, 167–75. London. Blackwell.

Krauss, M.W. and Seltzer, M.M. (1993) Current well-being and future care plans of older caregiving mothers. *The Irish Journal of Psychology* **14**, 48–63.

Kugel, R.B. and Wolfensberger, W. (eds) (1969) *Changing patterns in residential services for the mentally handicapped*. Washington DC. President's Committee on Mental Retardation.

Lukemeyer, A., Meyers, M.K. and Smeeding, T. (2000) Expensive children in poor families: out-of-pocket expenditures for the care of disabled and chronically ill children in welfare families. *Journal of Marriage and the Family* **62**, 399–415.

McConachie, H. (1983) Fathers, mothers, siblings: how do they see themselves? In P. Mittler and H. McConachie (eds), *Parents, professionals and mentally handicapped people—approaches to partnership*. London. Croome Helm.

McConachie, H. (1994) Changes in family roles. In P. Mittler and H. Mittler (eds),

Innovations in family support for people with learning disabilities. Chorley. Lisieux Hall.

McConkey, R. (1989) Our young lives: school leavers' impressions and those of their parents to life at home and their hopes for the future. In R. McConkey and C. Conliffe (eds), *The person with mental handicap: preparation for an adult life in the community,* 11–40. Dublin. St Michael's House.

Mezirow, J. (1990) How critical reflection triggers transformative learning. In J. Mezirow and associates, *Fostering critical reflection in adulthood: a guide to transformative and emancipatory learning.* San Francisco. Jossey Bass.

Mezirow, J. (1991) *Transformative dimensions of adult learning.* San Francisco. Jossey Bass.

Mittler, P. and McConachie, H. (eds) (1983) *Parents, professionals and mentally handicapped people.* London. Croome Helm.

Mittler, P. and Mittler, H. (1982) *Partnership with parents.* Stratford-upon-Avon. National Council for Special Education.

Mittler, P. and Mittler, H. (1983) Partnership with parents, an overview. In P. Mittler and H. McConachie (eds), *Parents, professionals and mentally handicapped people.* London. Croome Helm.

Moroney, R.M. (1986) *Shared responsibility: families and social policy.* Hawthorn, NY. Aldine.

Oliver, M. (1996) *Understanding disability, from theory to practice.* Basingstoke. Macmillan.

Olshansky, S. (1962) Chronic sorrow: a response to having a mentally defective child. *Social Casework* **43**, 190–3.

Papell, C. and Skolnik, L. (1992) The reflective practitioner: a contemporary paradigm's relevance for social work education. *Journal of Social Work Education* **28** (1), 18–25.

Prosser, H. (1997) The future care plans of older adults with intellectual disability living at home with family carers. *Journal of Applied Research in Intellectual Disabilities* **10** (1), 15–32.

Quinn, P. (1998) *Understanding disability—a lifespan approach.* Thousand Oaks and London. Sage.

Read, J. (2000) *Disability, the family and society: listening to mothers.* Buckingham. Open University Press.

Redmond, B. (1996) *Listening to parents—the aspirations, expectations and anxieties of parents about their teenagers with learning disability.* Dublin. Family Studies Centre, University College Dublin.

Redmond, B. (2000) Working reflectively with clients: a new teaching and learning model for professional training in the area of learning disability. Unpublished PhD thesis, University College Dublin.

Redmond, B. (forthcoming) *Developing reflective practice in health and social services: a model of teaching and learning for students and professionals.* Aldershot. Ashgate.

Redmond, B., Richardson, V. and Bowen, A. (forthcoming) Just getting on with it: exploring the perspectives of mothers who care for babies and young children with profound intellectual disability. *Journal of Applied Research in Intellectual Disabilities*.

Reed, J. and Procter, S. (1993) *Nurse education: a reflective approach*. London. Edward Arnold.

Review Group on Mental Handicap Services (1990) *Needs and abilities: a policy for the intellectually disabled*. Dublin. Stationery Office.

Rivera, G. (1972) *Willowbrook: a report on how it is and why it does not have to be that way*. New York. Random House.

Robins, J. (1992) *From rejection to integration—a centenary of service by the Daughters of Charity to persons with a mental handicap*. Dublin. Gill and Macmillan.

Rogers, D.E. (1953) *Angel unaware*. Westwood NJ. Revell.

Rose, J. and Jones, C. (1994) Working with parents. In A. Craft (ed.), *Practice issues in sexuality and learning disabilities*, 23–49. London. Routledge.

Russell, P. (1985) Portage—partnership with parents. In B. Daly, J. Addington, S. Kerfoot and A. Sigston (eds), *Portage: the importance of parents*. Oxford. NFER-Nelson.

Ryan, J. and Thomas, F. (1980) *The politics of mental handicap*. London. Penguin.

Ryan, J. and Thomas, F. (1987) *The politics of mental handicap* (revised and extended edn). London. Free Association Press.

Schalock, R.H. (1990) *Quality of life: perspectives and issues*. Washington DC. American Association on Mental Retardation.

Schön, D.A. (1983) *The reflective practitioner—how professionals think in action*. New York. Basic Books.

Schön, D.A. (1987) *Educating the reflective practitioner: toward a new design for teaching and learning in the professions*. San Francisco. Jossey Bass.

Seligman, M. and Darling, R.B. (1989) *Ordinary families, special children—a systems approach to childhood disability*. New York. Guilford Press.

Shearer, A. (1986) *Building community*. London. King's Fund.

Shearn, J. and Todd, S. (1998) Parental work. *Journal of Intellectual Disability Research* **41** (4), 285–301.

Shearn, J. and Todd, S. (2000) Maternal employment and family responsibilities. *Journal of Applied Research in Intellectual Disabilities* **13** (3), 109–31.

Simons, K. (1995) Empowerment and advocacy. In N. Malin (ed.), *Services for people with learning disabilities*. London. Routledge.

Sinclair, K. and Tse, H. (2001) Writing reflective journals. In D. Kember *et al.* (eds), *Reflective teaching and learning in the health professions*. London. Blackwell.

Smyth, F. (1988) Integration in special education: case proven or case dismissed. In R. McConkey and P. McGinley (eds), *Concepts and controversies in services for people with mental handicap*, 215–42. Galway and Dublin. Brothers of

Charity Services and St Michael's House.

Swan, R. (1995) In *Report of the 'Parents Forum' held in Cheeverstown House, 21st October 1995*. Dublin. NAMHI.

Todd, S. and Shearn, J. (1996a) Struggles with time: the careers of parents with adult sons and daughters with learning disability. *Disability and Society* **11** (3), 379–401.

Todd, S. and Shearn, J. (1996b) Time and the person: the impact of support services on the lives of parents of adults with learning disability. *Journal of Applied Research in Intellectual Disabilities* **9** (1), 40–60.

Trent, J.W. (1994) *Inventing the feeble mind—a history of mental retardation in the United States*. California. University of California Press.

Turnbull, A.P. and Turnbull, H.R. (1982) Parent involvement in the education of handicapped children—a critique. *Mental Retardation* **20** (3), 115–22.

Twigg, J. and Atkin, K. (1994) *Carers perceived: policy and practice in informal care*. Buckingham. Open University Press.

Walker, A. (1993) Community care policy: from consensus to conflict. In J. Bornat, C. Pereira, D. Pilgrim and F. Williams (eds), *Community care—a reader*, 204–20. Basingstoke. Macmillan.

Walsh, P.N., Conliffe, C. and Birbeck, G. (1994) Assessing the needs of family carers. In P. Mittler and H. Mittler (eds), *Innovations in family support for people with learning disability*, 176–88. Lancashire. Lisieux Hall.

Wolfensberger, W. (1972) *The principle of normalisation in human services*. Toronto. National Institute on Mental Retardation.

Wolfensberger, W. (1983) Social role valorisation: a proposed new term for the principle of normalization. *Mental Retardation* **21** (6), 234–9.

Wolfendale, S. (1983) *Parental participation in children's development and education*. New York. Gordon and Breach Science Publishers.

Wolfendale, S. (1992) *Empowering parents and teachers: working for children*. London. Cassell.

9. New Prospects: Ageing with Intellectual Disability

PATRICIA NOONAN WALSH AND CHRIS CONLIFFE

INTRODUCTION

Throughout the world, populations are ageing. This trend is more marked in the industrialised countries—much of Europe, for example—where life expectancy is longer and birth rates have declined (Council of Europe 1997). A parallel trend is the increasing lifespan of adults with intellectual disabilities, who are now more likely to live into middle and old age (Janicki 2001). They have emerged as a growing and more visible cohort. With trends toward greater community presence, it is important to understand the characteristics and experiences of these men and women as individuals, as members of society and as users of formal services.

Knowledge of the long-term developmental progress and life outcomes of individuals in this population is incomplete. Some are now middle-aged, representing the first wave of adults whose parents chose to keep their sons and daughters at home during the 1950s, when community-based services emerged in Ireland and other European countries. Others are the older, healthy survivors of harsher times when institutional living and lower levels of nutrition and of preventative health care took their toll (Seltzer and Luchterhand 1994). While some have lived in family homes in their communities, only a handful have worked in the open labour market. Virtually none of those with a moderate or severe level of intellectual disability ever married.

Service-providers must develop the capacity to support individuals for a longer lifetime than had perhaps been predicted. The greater presence of ageing and elderly people in the population of all persons with intellectual disability poses a challenge to those charged with providing support and services on their behalf. What happens when they reach the age at which most of their peers in the general population expect to retire from full paid employment? Which choice is optimal—generic services for the elderly, or special separate services for those with intellectual disabilities?

The rights of ageing individuals with intellectual disabilities command no less consideration than those of other adults (Herr and Weber 1999). Their needs should be identified in order to determine the shape of the supports they receive so that they can participate fully in society. According to the United Nations Standard Rules on the Equalization of Opportunities for Persons with Disabilities, the principle of equal rights implies that the needs of each individual are of equal importance and that these needs must be the basis for planning systems within society (United Nations 1994, 11).

This chapter adopts a perspective encompassing older people with intellectual disabilities on the island of Ireland. It presents a summary of the typical characteristics of older people with intellectual disabilities during their lifecourse; recent evidence on age-related developmental change; factors associated with well-being and vulnerability; family issues; promoting self-determination; and appropriate models of support. Finally, research priorities and strategies for good practice are proposed.

OLDER PEOPLE WITH INTELLECTUAL DISABILITIES

Older people with intellectual disabilities may be defined as a group not so much by inherent characteristics but rather as being the 'product of an interaction between their intellectual functioning and society's response to their level of ability' (Hogg 1997, 138). This contextual model of development places the individual in the centre of nested ecologies, with each person's life experiences at the core. Ties bind them to their families throughout their lives, regardless of age or level of disability. The principles of community inclusion suggest, for example, that an older person's home should be in a situation typical for other members of his/her community who do not have intellectual disabilities (Hogg et al. 2001). The outermost circles in this ecological model describe the social, economic and environmental contexts—national policy, regional issues, economic conditions, and any risks or benefits presented by the physical environment.

Ireland

Today, older people with intellectual disabilities in Ireland are veterans of vast changes marking Irish society during the past two decades. Since Ireland entered the European Community (then the European Economic Community) in 1973, parallel trends in policies and practices related to persons with intellectual and other disabilities have developed, many influenced by shifts in thinking at European level. European social policy aims at the pursuit of social inclusion for all citizens. Shifts in approach from a social care model to one framed in human rights have been reflected in recent disability-related policy (CEC 1998; Quinn and Bruce, this volume). In Ireland, for example, earlier government policy (*Towards a full life*, 1984) suggested that people with disabilities required kindness and understanding rather than anti-discrimination legislation. Just twelve years later, the authors of the *Report of the Commission on the Status of People with Disabilities* were forthright in declaring that 'People with disabilities are the neglected citizens of Ireland' (1996, 1). Subsequent policy changes in the equality, employment and disability sectors have advanced some of the Commission's priorities (Walsh 2003).

Northern Ireland

In Northern Ireland, policy trends have followed movements in the rest of Ireland and in the greater European Community. *People first* (DHSS 1990) set out standards for safeguarding the dignity and rights of people with intellectual disability and their carers and proposed an accelerated movement of people from special hospitals into the community. Recent government strategies established for the provision of caring services for people with intellectual disability have appeared in various policy documents: the Health and Personal Social Services (Northern Ireland) Order of 1991; the Regional Strategy for the Northern Ireland Health and Personal Social Services 1992–1997; and the *Review of policy for people with a learning disability* (DHSS 1997). These documents advanced a notion of care in the community that is firmly based on the twin philosophies of normalisation and integration into the local community. They assumed a mixed economy of care in which the statutory, voluntary and private sectors are invited to tender so that cost-effective, high-quality services can be developed.

While the strategic plans of Northern Ireland's four Health and Social Service Boards echo government policy, the special needs of older people with intellectual disability receive scant mention. This group is especially vulnerable as reliable data about their needs are absent. When the total population of persons with Down Syndrome in Northern Ireland was surveyed—identifying 2,124 individuals—it was found that 13% were not known to Social Services and a further 17% had only limited contact through their general practitioners. One fifth of all persons with Down Syndrome were deemed to be 'senior citizens' aged over 40 years (Conliffe 1998).

Parallel trends

Ireland remains relatively youthful by European standards, with a lower proportion of its population aged over 65 years than most of the other European countries (Walsh 1997). Rather, its share of middle-aged citizens is larger. This pattern is reflected in an increased proportion of adults with intellectual disabilities aged 35–54 and over 55 years (Table 1).

Lifecourse perspective

Group trends across decades may chart changing demography but say little about the lifespan experiences of men and women. Persons with intellectual

Table 1—Irish adults with moderate, severe and profound levels of intellectual disability by age group (%) (source: Health Research Board 1996; 2001).

Age group	1974	1981	1996	2000
20–34 years	26.3	31.6	32.6	31.6
35–54 years	19.1	18.4	28.2	32.1
55 years +	9.4	8.0	9.7	11.4

disability live their lives in a particular time and place. Each lives within a family as well as within shared political, social and economic contexts. Changes both in these environments and in individual life pathways—marriage, parenthood, career—influence the substance and course of human lives.

A lifecourse paradigm (Elder 1994) yields four key themes, each relevant to understanding the experiences of older people with intellectual disabilities. First, individuals live in *historical times*: their lives and times are interwoven. The resulting fabric resists any attempt to tease out the threads related to the personal capacity and preferences of individuals from those reflecting features of their personal history and the environment in which they currently live. Mature adults with intellectual disability now in their 30s, 40s and early 50s were among the first children to stay in the family home in Ireland and in Northern Ireland, and to avail of fledgling community-based services and state-funded medical care. Their lives today reflect their distinctive histories, the circumstances which prevailed when they were born and grew to be children and adolescents during the middle decades of the twentieth century.

A second theme is *social timing*, how and when individuals assume various social roles. Social timing refers also to our expectations of individuals—a judgement frequently linked to age. Typically, older people with intellectual disabilities have an impoverished history as self-determined adults. Few married, bore children, achieved an educational award, earned real wages, chose to migrate to another country, paid taxes or voted. In the past, expectations for what they might achieve were low, mirrored in their marginal, dependent social status. Many of today's older folk with intellectual disabilities spent years in residences or dayrooms where they were called 'boys and girls' long after these labels were appropriate. Custodial customs and practices, not always benign, linger in every country (Conliffe and Walsh 1999).

Linked lives is a third theme generated by the lifecourse paradigm, recognising that each human life is embedded in a network of social relationships across the individual's lifespan. Decisions and events in the lives of others are binding on the current well-being of older men and women with intellectual disabilities. For example, the parents—now long dead—of a son or daughter may have decided 30 or 40 years ago to keep their offspring at home.

Other parents of that time may have succumbed to the prevailing expertise of a generation ago and sought long-term residential care. Or perhaps an elder sister in a rural place bowed to unspoken family pressures and remained single as the lifelong care-giver of a youngest sibling—the two survivors forming a household on the family farm. Each choice left its mark on the lives of all family members and, in turn, their own friends, spouses and offspring.

Finally, *human agency* is expressed in the distinctive plans which individuals shape as they interact with their environment and make choices to construct their own lifecourse over time. No two individuals take the same pathway, no matter how similar their experiences may appear. The recent exploration of concepts such as self-determination (Wehmeyer *et al.* 1996) was launched late in the day for people with intellectual disabilities, who have only recently been perceived as autonomous decision-makers. Older people grounded in a lifelong habit of compliance are even less likely to take matters into their own hands and to act on their own behalf.

Sarah: an introduction

Today there is a notable growth in the proportion of all Irish persons with intellectual disabilities born between 1942 and 1961 in the Republic of Ireland (National Council on Ageing and Older People 2001). One of these citizens is Sarah. (See box on p. 148.)

INDIVIDUAL DEVELOPMENT

Although groups of people may share personal characteristics and social contexts as they grow and develop, individual differences always emerge over time. This is so for persons with intellectual disabilities as they enter middle and later adulthood. No two individuals, whether or not they have disabilities, will age in exactly the same way. Sarah is unique in her appearance, temperament, preferences, family history and a hundred other factors setting her apart from all other Irish women of her age, even from hundreds of other women who have Down Syndrome.

Age-related change

From the biological perspective, *ageing* refers to progressive changes that often reduce an individual's viability. Age-related physical changes accompany the years of middle adulthood: generally, seeing and hearing decline (Santrock 1995). Cognitive changes, such as a decline in long-term memory, may also be expected, although individuals typically adopt various strategies to reduce such deficits. Age-related changes in behaviour also occur among adults with intellectual disabilities. These include observed changes in cognitive performance, levels of adaptive behaviour and sensorial and physical functioning (van Schrojenstein Lantman-de Valk *et al.* 2002).

Sarah is an Irishwoman with Down Syndrome who was born in 1943. Until last year, Sarah lived with her older sister and brother-in-law in a suburb of Galway. Last year she moved to a group home which she shares with three women in their thirties. A member of staff in the voluntary agency which manages the home is always present, even at night. Sarah is just over five feet tall. She frets a bit about being a bit too plump for the fashions her co-residents admire and also about her skin, which is very dry. During the day Sarah attends a nearby sheltered work scheme—she is deft at assembling cardboard boxes and other packaging materials. Sarah enjoys her food in the evenings. Although quiet-spoken by nature, she has become an avid shopper since she began to share responsibility for the menu two days each week. Sarah especially enjoys the cinema and has taken up swimming after a good deal of encouragement. Many leisure experiences are novel for her as Sarah's parents were well into their forties when she was a small child and did not mix much socially themselves. They did not expect Sarah to live into adulthood, much less to middle age. Although they cared for her in every way until their deaths some years ago, they did not explore any alternatives to the meagre social services available to their family when Sarah was growing up.

Cognitive changes

The intellectual capability of adults who have developmental disabilities but who do not have Down Syndrome is likely to remain stable until age 65: thereafter, declines in IQ appear to be gradual (Zigman *et al.* 1994). Individual men and women may be expected to show diverse, even surprising, patterns of behaviour as they age. Fujiki and Brinton (1993) investigated the language ability of elderly adults (aged 55–77 years) with mild to moderate mental retardation (intellectual disability). They presented tasks designed to probe two aspects of communicative behaviour: (a) skills dependent on cognitive resources, such as the ability to follow verbal directions and story recall; and (b) skills crucial to social interaction—managing conversational requests and topics. Their findings did not support the hypothesis that young adults should perform better on both kinds of task. The authors concluded that 'the notion of plateauing levels of language skills must be questioned in light of the performance of the elderly subjects in this study' (1993, 88).

Among adults with Down Syndrome, a similar stability is evident until age 45–50, with some decline in performance thereafter. Age-related deficits in language among older people with Down Syndrome have also been reported (Young and Kramer 1991). Although older individuals performed more poorly in understanding spoken language and in self-help skills, there was no significant relation between age and expressive language. In a similar study, the expressive language skills of British adults with Down Syndrome were maintained until over 60 years of age, while comprehensive language was significantly lower for those aged over 40 (Cooper and Collacott 1995). Devenny *et al.* (1996, 219) reported that they followed 91 individuals with Down

Syndrome ranging from 30 to 63 years of age for six years and found that 'with only four exceptions, these individuals have essentially maintained their initial performance levels'. Those in their 50s showed test performance patterns suggesting precocious but 'normal' ageing. Hawkins *et al.* (2003) concluded that their longitudinal study of adults with Down Syndrome gave evidence of an age-related decline in functioning. The pattern of decline was similar to, but occurred later than, the pattern observed in the general population.

Adaptive behaviour

Over the long term, changes in patterns of adaptive behaviour—a core element in defining intellectual disability—are associated with the individual's age, level of functioning and type of residence. Declines in adaptive behaviour were identified among adults aged 50 years or more among 1020 Dutch residents with intellectual disabilities who took part in a prospective cohort study (van Schrojenstein Lantman-de Valk 1998, 22). Those aged over 70 showed significant declines. The author concluded that the changes observed were not influenced by the individual's level of intellectual disability (*ibid.*). Cohort differences may influence observed patterns of performance. For example, groups of older adults may show higher levels of adaptive behaviour than younger people simply because they entered a particular residential setting many years ago when institutional living was commonplace and was the norm for individuals who would today enjoy community living (Walsh *et al.* 2000).

Some evidence suggests that adults with Down Syndrome aged 50 years or older are at increased risk of a decline in adaptive behaviour (Seltzer *et al.* 1994). These authors point out that we cannot be certain whether this is due to precocious ageing or to the increased susceptibility of persons with Down Syndrome to the development of Alzheimer's Disease with increasing age. Evidence suggests that there is a decrease in adaptive behaviour among adults with Down Syndrome aged over 50 (Janicki and Dalton 1999a). These authors note, too, that any functional changes accompanying the onset and process of dementia will have a profound impact on every aspect of the individual's daily life and that of family members and professional workers offering support.

Physical health

Recent proliferation of interest in the physical health of adults with intellectual disabilities, health conditions and means of amelioration has helped to compensate for many decades of sparse knowledge (Prasher and Janicki 2002). Physical and sensorial age-related changes have been observed among older adults with intellectual disabilities in several studies carried out in the Netherlands, where until recently nearly all middle-aged and older persons with developmental disabilities lived in institutions (van Schrojenstein Lantman-de Valk 1998). Evidence from the Netherlands suggests that many older people in residential centres may have hearing loss that is unrecognised by the individuals themselves, by staff members and by general practitioners (Veraart and Bierman 1998).

Sexual and reproductive development

Sexual and reproductive development among older adults with intellectual disabilities has only recently been the focus of research and practice. Women with Down Syndrome seem to experience menopause at an earlier age, which suggests accelerated ageing for this population (van Schrojenstein Lantman-de Valk *et al.* 2002). Today's older men and women had no opportunity to learn about issues related to relationships and sexuality, whether through informal discussion or formal sex education programmes (Seltzer and Luchterhand 1994). While the rights of people with intellectual disabilities to have sexual relationships have increasingly been recognised, the need for appropriate education for them, their family members and professional workers has been given less attention (Walsh and Heller 2002). Further, many of today's adults are likely to have a history of sexual abuse (Walsh and Murphy 2002).

Life domains

Quality of Life has emerged as a sensitive, unifying construct to guide interventions on behalf of people with developmental disabilities and to measure outcomes for individuals in terms of impact on their health, living environment, relationships, work and leisure and other life domains. While it is obvious that Quality of Life will be applied differently to older men and women than to young children or adolescents with developmental disabilities, these desirable lifespan considerations present a challenge, as

> '. . . we lack an all-inclusive theory of normal development, even before adding the complexity and variation of each individual with mental retardation' (Stark and Faulkner 1996, 24).

Service-providers should acknowledge that the physical health domain, for example, is paramount in advancing the Quality of Life of older adults with intellectual disabilities (Schalock and Verdugo 2002).

Adults with developmental disabilities who live in the family home tend to rely on other family members, especially their mothers, in order to go out for any social activities at all. Their social networks tend to be small and dense, and to include fewer friends than their peers without disabilities. Cultures enrich and influence family life and care-giving as individuals age. Older mothers of adults with intellectual disability in Northern Ireland were found to share two thirds of the individuals named on their own social networks with their adult sons and daughters, compared to mothers in the United States and the Republic of Ireland, who shared just one half of theirs. Shared social support indicates greater social reliance of the adult on the mother (Seltzer *et al.* 1995; Walsh *et al.*

1993). The adults in Northern Ireland counted very much on their mothers for access to social supports. Often they shared nearly all of their mothers' friends and claimed few as their own friends. This familial pattern of social support is not typical for people in middle and older adulthood in the wider population.

In Ireland, people with intellectual disabilities are much less likely to live in a family setting as they age, reflecting a widespread age-related pattern of residence (Braddock *et al.* 2001). A quarter (24%) of those aged 55 years or older are living at home. It is striking that in the Netherlands, a country with a long-standing policy of congregate care, only 2–5% of people aged 50 or over live with their families (van Schrojenstein Lantman-de Valk 1998). Gender differences emerge in the pattern of residence among persons with intellectual disabilities. Men with intellectual disabilities in Ireland aged 55 years and over, for example, are much more likely to reside in psychiatric hospitals than are women of the same age (Mulvaney 2001).

Among persons aged 55 years or older, more men than women remain in sheltered work centres, even though women in this age group outnumber men. Today's pattern of daily activity for older people may reflect historical or geographical factors in the development of day services, or perhaps yesterday's expectations for gender roles, or some combination of these. Gender-sensitive studies of women with developmental disabilities, especially older women, are in their infancy (Walsh and LeRoy 2004). Most of the men and women with developmental disabilities aged over 55 years surveyed in an Australian study reported that they had never been employed. However, their attitudes to work were mainly positive. Many of those currently employed in sheltered workshops found it difficult to contemplate retirement (Ashman *et al.* 1995).

Community living

Participation in leisure and other community-based activities depends in part on the supports provided for older individuals, the initiative of family members and friends and the coverage available from specialist leisure services (Hogg 1997). At worst, sports and outings may be construed as time-fillers, particularly if adults have no paid employment. At best, sport and leisure activities matched to personal preferences serve to broaden social networks and to prepare individuals for retirement, just as they do for the wider population of middle-aged adults.

Out of step

Men and women do not mature and age in isolation. Each is a participant in the complex interplay of individuals with the social and physical environments available to them. Among adults with intellectual disabilities, satisfying social interactions potentially enhance competence in communication and other domains of everyday living. An individual's performance must be appraised and nurtured in a given context, as '. . . intellectual competence has social consequences, and inappropriate social conduct is often interpreted as intellectual deficit' (Kernan *et al.* 1989, 250). Many of today's middle-aged and elderly men and women with intellectual disabilities had sparse opportunities to take part in, and become skilled in, aspects of domestic and social life available to their peers.

WELL-BEING AND VULNERABILITY

Adults with intellectual disabilities experience the ageing process in much the same way as any other adults. Some may have particular vulnerabilities: for example, precocious ageing among men and women with Down Syndrome (Janicki and Dalton 1999b). Today's older people grew to adulthood at a time when many more of their peers lived in hospitals or large, special residential centres. Health targets were lower for the general population and much more elusive for people with developmental disabilities. Values shifted over the years. Today, physical health and well-being are highly valued, perhaps particularly among women (Government of Ireland 1997; Walsh and Heller 2002). Health is a core life domain which sensitively manifests changes in Quality of Life for all citizens, whether or not they have disabilities (Felce 1997). Medical care to ensure a healthier, better life is assumed to be a prerequisite if people with

---

Sarah had always lived with her parents until her father and then her mother died. An older sister—like so many Irish women of the time—had emigrated to England. Sarah lived for six years with her married sister before moving to a group home last year. She has no experience of living with men apart from her brother-in-law, who is some years older, and none whatever of living near or with children. By contrast, 68% of Irish women of Sarah's age married and about 31% are currently in paid employment: both percentages are low by international standards for women in the general population. Sarah attends a day activity centre which has one room designated as a 'sheltered workshop' where she helps to pack cardboard boxes for a supermarket chain a few hours each day if she chooses to do so. Most often, Sarah attends the workshop as her friend for many years, Larry, works there too, and they enjoy chatting to each other and listening to the radio together. Sarah looks forward to payday and spends some of her weekly wage of 15 euro on the cinema and face creams. Sarah is generally fit and active. She shows a few signs of slackening the pace with which she washes and dresses herself and helps with housework. Her remaining teeth are poor—in the part of the country where she lived in the 1940s and '50s, dental care was sparse and very little of it was allocated to people with intellectual disabilities. Her hearing has declined in the past years, her sister believes. Sarah has never had a gynaecological evaluation in her life, and although some talk she hears about it is on her mind, no one has spoken to her about the menopause.

disabilities, no matter what their age, are to enjoy equal opportunities for taking part in their society (United Nations 1994).

Even with closer understanding of the current health status of older persons with intellectual disabilities, it will prove difficult to generalise to other groups. First, today's younger adults with intellectual disabilities have had very different experiences of health promotion strategies, medical treatment and life in the community. Second, ageing persons may be the 'healthy survivors' of a cohort born 50, 60 or 70 years ago (Moss and Patel 1995; Beange 2002). Both of these effects—healthy survivor and cohort—make interpretation of cross-sectional results especially difficult in studies of ageing processes (Zigman *et al.* 1994). Yet recent evidence indicates that older people with intellectual disability have additional, distinctive health needs which are often unmet (Cooper 1998). These difficulties are even more daunting when the individuals who are growing older have, in addition, perhaps atypical personal histories of family life, and related health problems (Evenhuis *et al.* 2001).

Ageing brings not only changes in cognitive and other development but also an increased risk of disease. Particular threats to the physical health of adults with intellectual disabilities include a greater prevalence of heart defects, hypothyroidism, hearing impairments, obesity and diabetes (O'Brien *et al.* 2002). Age-related sensory loss occurs in the same way as in the general ageing population. However, progressive inner-ear hearing loss is found in most adults with Down Syndrome aged over 30, and other adults with developmental disabilities have greater frequencies and severities of hearing impairment (Evenhuis *et al.* 2001). While tooth loss is by no means a part of normative ageing, many older people with developmental disabilities are edentulous owing to a history of poor oral hygiene and generally lower standards for dental health over past decades (Malmstrom *et al.* 2002).

Mental health

Mental health difficulties, such as depression, may also arise among older adults (Moss and Patel 1997; Thorpe *et al.* 2001). In general, depression and other mental health disorders are prevalent among adults with intellectual disabilities, but more so as individuals age (Davidson *et al.*, 2003). Depression is more frequent among people with Down Syndrome than those with other aetiologies. Depression and other emotional symptoms have been found to occur in the early stages of dementia. Diagnoses of both conditions may be made in adults with intellectual disabilities. Gender differences in the prevalence and pattern of onset of these conditions are of great importance in this population, as in the general population (Lunsky and Havercamp 2002). Assessment is vital in order to distinguish between apparent changes due to dementia and those due to the onset of a mental health condition.

Dementia

As more people with intellectual disabilities live longer, they are at greater risk for age-related diseases such as dementia. Diagnosis of dementia requires documentation of cognitive decline that causes an impact on functioning. It is important that observed changes over time in functioning, such as activities of daily living, are measured against the individual's own baseline functioning.

In their study of a population of 111 British people with moderate levels of intellectual disability aged over 50, Moss and Patel (1997) found, generally, a loss of skills and chronic health problems which would be expected for any other group of similar age. But they found, in addition, that twelve of the subjects (11.4%) had dementia, and that five of these twelve individuals had Down Syndrome. The sufferers had more chronic health problems and physical disabilities and a lower capacity for self-direction. The authors concluded that, paradoxically, the most at-risk people are those with greater ability, as those with more severe levels of disability have a lower life expectancy.

Some groups—older people with Down Syndrome, or those adults with a family history of dementia—are more at risk (Janicki *et al.* 1996, 375). An international working group has prepared a protocol endorsing early and comprehensive assessment of older individuals so that baseline information may be recorded. Thus service-planners may readily identify changes in cognitive, emotional or adaptive behaviours as these arise over time for the individual.

Down Syndrome and dementia

Adults with Down Syndrome are a highly visible and much-studied group, not least because they show signs of earlier ageing than both adults with intellectual disabilities with other aetiologies and adults in the general population (Janicki *et al.* 1996). Individuals in this group have a disadvantage in life expectancy relative to the general population as well as to other adults who have intellectual disabilities but who do not have Down Syndrome. Evidence suggests that the neuropathy associated with Alzheimer's Disease, a form of dementia, is widespread among nearly all adults with Down Syndrome. However, clinical expression of this disease is by no means inevitable (*Face to Face* 1999). There are other causes of any observed changes in older adults in this group. Depression, reaction to bereavement and the effects of untreated hypothyroidism may each result in a decline in performance and well-being. Exploring the reasons for any observed decline of functioning in older adults with intellectual disabilities is of great importance. Recently, resource materials for family members and carers have been made more widely available, for example by the Rehabilitation Research and Training Center on Aging with Developmental Disabilities at the University of Illinois at Chicago (http://www.uic.edu/orgs/rrtcamr/azdintfactsaz.htm).

As part of a screening by clinicians in her service agency, Sarah was assessed by the psychologist recently. Her carers thought that she had slowed down of late and wished to know if there was evidence for an onset of dementia. They were aware of recent findings:

- Dementia is a major age-related impairment. The most common cause is Alzheimer's Disease, and this represents a significant risk factor for people with Down Syndrome (Janicki *et al* 2002).
- Not all persons with Down Syndrome develop dementia: while the neuropathy of Alzheimer's Disease may be universal among adults with Down Syndrome, its clinical expression is not.
- The adaptive behaviour of persons with intellectual disabilities, including those with Down Syndrome, may be expected to increase gradually up to about age 50.
- While adults with Down Syndrome experience normative ageing process, their ageing seems to be precocious.
- Comprehensive assessment with a protocol based on research evidence can help to identify individual needs today and also help to identify any changes in the person's behaviour which may arise over time.

FAMILY LIFE

Individual development must be understood within a family context—increasingly so as the proportion of individuals moving to institutions early in life continues to decline and older people continue to live in the family home or in a group home in the community.

Studies of family life, especially from the viewpoint of family care-giving, point to distinctive experiences for ageing adults with intellectual disability (Redmond, this volume). Overall, their social networks tend to have greater density than those of other adults of similar age in the same culture. They are likely to name fewer people as members of their social networks, and to name professionals or family friends as their own friends. Older residents of group homes or campus residential settings report smaller networks (Robertson *et al.* 2001). The social lives of adults living at home are often embedded with those of their parents or other carers, especially their mothers (Seltzer *et al.* 1995; Shearn and Todd 1997; Walsh *et al.* 1993). While the complex relationships which adults with developmental disabilities build with their brothers and sisters have begun to be explored (Krauss *et al.* 1996; Egan and Walsh 2001), there is much to learn about how these relationships, often lasting for a lifetime, will be expressed in unique households—perhaps two sisters-in-law—and in long-term care responsibilities.

As they have embraced a long-term, often lifelong, career, the carers themselves benefit from training and development. In Northern Ireland, workshops for carers and professionals working together have supported carers as partners in the delivery of care. The emphasis of the workshops is on practical help and advice tailored to individual needs, covering topics such as physical management at home, stress, epilepsy and positive support with behavioural problems. Carers have an opportunity to try things out and to share their personal experiences with others. Creating a working partnership among parents, professionals and those using services is an essential element of this scheme, *The competent carer* (ICPD 1998).

FREE TO CHOOSE?

Making choices about where and with whom to live, where to work, how to spend leisure time and how to stay healthy is widely recognised as a core element of an individual's quality of life. For older people with developmental disabilities, their decisions on how to grow old may reflect what services are available or what suits their families rather than personal choice. Choice lies at the heart of a new paradigm for supporting people with developmental disabilities so that they can determine the shape of their own lives. A good support or service is one which is effective in achieving this outcome for individuals, no matter how old they are. Self-determination is not age-limited. It means that the person acts as the primary causal agent in his or her life, reflecting autonomy, self-regulation, empowerment and self-realisation. Individuals sharing this disposition are more likely to make their own choices, solve problems and set goals for attainment (Wehmeyer *et al.* 1996). Not surprisingly, the self-advocacy movement promotes increased self-determination for people with developmental disabilities. But autonomy, or self-governance, is not a special characteristic of persons with disabilities: rather, it underlies the substance of human rights (Quinn 1995).

Having a home and personal security are basic human rights. A model of disability based on human rights, not only care, is current European policy (Quinn and Bruce, this volume). Equal opportunities for social participation—for living and working alongside fellow citizens—are an expression of these human rights (Conliffe and Walsh 1999). But equal opportunities are no more and no less than an extension of the social solidarity which we owe to each other and from which we all benefit (Quinn 1995). When Sarah and people like her find a chance to take an active part in society as they grow older, everyone stands to gain.

CHALLENGES FOR THE FUTURE

The future promises a widening population of old people with developmental disabilities, a success story founded on better health and opportunities. It must be recalled that in some parts of Europe there are few survivors of the deadly

Sarah has made few decisions about the course of her life. She was sheltered by her parents from birth through the school years, especially when their fears for her safety rose as she reached adolescence. Her mother shopped for clothes for Sarah so that she could try them on at home and a willing neighbour called in from time to time to cut her hair. Later, while she seemed contented enough with some contract work for the company and a little pocket money, Sarah never was offered vocational training or career development. Her only friends, she says, apart from her mother's elderly cousin, are some of the people she lives with now and two members of staff. She was transferred to the group home where she lives when a vacancy became available at the time when her brother-in-law had a heart attack which left him quite frail and dependent on care from Sarah's sister. Most Irish people of Sarah's age (aged 55 or older) with intellectual disabilities live in residential settings—perhaps in large special residences, or in a 'de-designated unit' on the grounds of a psychiatric hospital or in a hospital itself. Sarah is in the minority one-third who live in a family home or a group home. Sarah's sense of citizenship has only recently emerged. Although she had never voted, she was encouraged to register by a young houseparent in October 1997, and Sarah proudly voted in the presidential elections. Now a self-advocacy group is being formed in her service agency. Sarah likes the meetings, even though the facilitator, a member of staff appointed by the agency, seems to do most of the talking.

policies of 50 years ago which eliminated so-called imperfect individuals (Mitchell and Snyder 2001). Many are now living at home with their families, or in group homes. More and more, they expect to live longer and to stay healthy. But where will they live, and what will they do? These questions raise challenges for everyone—researchers, service-providers and policy-makers, as well as citizens everywhere (Hogg *et al.* 2001).

Who is old?

While countries vary in definitions and entitlement for services and benefits or pensions, the fact that many adults with developmental disabilities may age prematurely means that the criterion may need to be lowered for this population. Once identified, should older people with developmental disabilities be included in programmes dedicated to their peers, and excluded, for example, from day centres or sheltered workshops for persons aged over 18 years? How can each person's idiosyncratic characteristics and preferences be respected? Can insights from lifespan developmental psychology, gerontology and other disciplines usefully be applied to the experiences of older men and women in this group?

Separate and equal?

Should supports for older people with developmental disabilities be separate, tailor-made for them alone? Or should they avail of generic services for all older people in their communities? While integrated day and residential programmes for mixed groups of older people have achieved success in the United States (Janicki 1993) and in France (Fondation de France 1995), critics raise their concerns. If being old has devalued status, then supporting older adults with developmental disabilities to become old like everyone else in the wider population may place them in double jeopardy (Hogg *et al.* 2001).

Vulnerability
Although many of today's older adults had little education about sexuality, their needs, experiences and levels of knowledge should be acknowledged. Some may be at particular risk of abuse (Walsh and Murphy 2002). Guidelines for practice have been proposed in education for men and women, staff development and other changes at organisation level. Some service-providers have recently taken steps to ensure privacy and safety for women with intellectual disabilities in day services and residences, for example. Research can help to determine whether such initiatives bring benefits without placing limits on opportunities.

Health
The distinctive health needs of older people with developmental disabilities have recently been identified. Community living has brought a fresh focus on health promotion strategies targeted to particular groups (Lennox 2002). Increased longevity has highlighted increased risks for incurring age-related diseases. An international consensus on how to promote long, healthy life for everyone, including men and women with disabilities, is emerging (Walsh *et al.* 2000).

These are global issues, yet men and women live local lives. Sarah's future well-being may be interwoven with the strategic decisions of the WHO, the shifting shapes of government policies, the vagaries of management styles and the size of the annual budget allocated by her service-provider agency.

But the quality of her life in the years to come depends on the quality of her daily experiences at home, at work, in her town and wherever she goes. This chapter in her story is unfinished.

What does the future hold for Sarah?

REFERENCES

Ashman, A.F., Suttie, J.N. and Bramley, J. (1995) Employment, retirement and elderly persons with an intellectual disability. *Journal of Intellectual Disability Research* **39**, 107–15.

Beange, H. (2002) Epidemiological issues. In V.P. Prasher and M.P. Janicki (eds), *Physical health of adults with intellectual disabilities*, 1–20. Oxford. Blackwell.

Braddock, D., Emerson, E., Felce, D. and Stancliffe, R.J. (2001) Living circumstances of children and adults with mental retardation or developmental disabilities in the United States, Canada, England and Wales and Australia. *Mental Retardation and Developmental Disabilities Research Reviews* **7**, 115–21.

CEC (1998) *A new European Community disability strategy.* Document 98/0216 (CNS). Brussels. Commission of the European Communities.

Conliffe, C. (1998) *The Northern Ireland Down Syndrome Survey. Report of the first survey of the DS population in Northern Ireland, their families and carers.* Belfast. ICPD, Interpoint, 20–24 York Street.

Conliffe, C. and Walsh, P.N. (1999) An international perspective on quality. In S. Herr and G. Weber (eds), *Aging, rights and quality of life*, 237–52. Baltimore. Paul H. Brookes.

Cooper, S.-A. (1998) Clinical study of the effects of age on the physical health of adults with mental retardation. *American Journal on Mental Retardation* **102**, 582–9.

Cooper, S.-A. and Collacott, R.A. (1995) The effect of age on language in people with Down's Syndrome. *Journal of Intellectual Disability Research* **39,** 197–200.

Council of Europe (1997) *Recent demographic developments in Europe.* Strasbourg. Council of Europe.

Davidson, P., Prasher, V.P. and Janicki, M.P. (eds) (2003) *Mental health, intellectual disabilities and the aging process.* Oxford. Blackwell.

Devenny, D.A., Silverman, W.P., Hill, A.L., Jenkins, E., Sersen, E.A. and Wisniewski, K.E. (1996) Normal ageing in adults with Down's Syndrome: a longitudinal study. *Journal of Intellectual Disability Research* **40**, 208–21.

DHSS (1990) *People first. Community care in Northern Ireland in the 1990s.* Belfast. HMSO/DHSS.

DHSS (1997) *Review of policy for people with a learning disability.* Belfast. HMSO/DHSS.

Egan, J. and Walsh, P.N. (2001) Sources of stress among adult siblings of Irish people with intellectual disabilities. *Irish Journal of Psychology* **22,** 28–38.

Elder, G.H. (1994) Time, human agency, and social change: perspectives on the life course. *Social Psychology Quarterly* **57**, 4–15.

Evenhuis, H., Henderson, C.M., Beange, H., Lennox, N. and Chicoine, B. (2001) Healthy ageing-adults with intellectual disabilities: physical health issues. *Journal of Applied Research in Intellectual Disabilities* **14**, 175–94.

Face to Face (1999) Respectful coping with dementia in older people with intellectual disability. Working group on coping with dementia in people with intellectual disability—European Network on Intellectual Disability and Ageing (ENIDA). Available from Centre for Disability Studies, National University of Ireland, Dublin, Belfield, Dublin 4.

Felce, D. (1997) Defining and applying the concept of quality of life. *Journal of Intellectual Disability Research* **41**, 126–35.

Fondation de France (1995) *Pouvons-nous vieillir ensemble?* Paris. Fondation de France.

Fujiki, M. and Brinton, B. (1993) Growing old with retardation: the language of survivors. *Topics in Language Disorders* **13**, 77–89.

Government of Ireland (1997) *A plan for women's health*. Dublin. Stationery Office.

Hawkins, B.A., Eklund, S.J., James, D.R. and Foose, A.K. (2003) Adaptive behavior and cognitive function of adult with Down Syndrome: modeling change with age. *Mental Retardation* **41**, 2–28.

Health Research Board (1996) *Report on the Intellectual Disability Database 1996*. Dublin. Health Research Board.

Health Research Board (2001) *Report on the Intellectual Disability Database 2000*. Dublin. Health Research Board.

Herr, S. and Weber, G. (1999) *Aging, rights and quality of life*. Baltimore. Paul H. Brookes.

Hogg, J. (1997) Intellectual disability and ageing: ecological perspectives from recent research. *Journal of Intellectual Disability Research* **41**, 136–43.

Hogg, J., Lucchino, R., Wang, K.Y. and Janicki, M. (2001) Healthy ageing-adults with intellectual disabilities: ageing and social policy. *Journal of Applied Research in Intellectual Disabilities* **14**, 229–55.

ICPD (1998) *The competent carer*. Belfast. Institute for Counselling and Personal Development.

Janicki, M.P. (1993) *Building the future—planning and community development in aging and developmental disabilities*. Albany NY. CIPADD.

Janicki, M.P. (2001) Toward a rational strategy for promoting healthy ageing amongst people with intellectual disabilities. *Journal of Applied Research in Intellectual Disabilities* **14**, 171–4.

Janicki, M.P. and Dalton, A.J. (1999a) Dementia in developmental disabilities. In N. Bouras (ed.), *Psychiatric and behavioural disorders in developmental disabilities and mental retardation*, 121–53. Cambridge. Cambridge University Press.

Janicki, M.P. and Dalton, A.J. (eds) (1999b) *Dementia, aging, and intellectual disabilities: a handbook*. Philadelphia. Brunner-Mazel.

Janicki, M.P., Heller, T., Seltzer, G. and Hogg, J. (1996) Practice guidelines for the clinical assessment and care management of Alzheimer's Disease and other dementias among adults with intellectual disability. *Journal of Intellectual Disability Research* **40**, 374–82.

Janicki, M.P., McCallion, P. and Dalton, A.J. (2002) Dementia related care decision-making in group homes for persons with intellectual disability. *Journal of Gerontological Social Work*, **38** (1/2), 179–96.

Kernan, K.T., Sabsay, S. and Shinn, N. (1989) Lay people's judgements of storytellers as mentally retarded or not retarded. *Journal of Mental Deficiency Research* **33**, 149–57.

Krauss, M.W., Seltzer, M.M., Gordon, R. and Friedman, D.H. (1996) Binding ties: the roles of adult siblings of persons with mental retardation. *Mental Retardation* **34**, 83–93.

Lennox, N. (2002) Health promotion and disease prevention. In V.P. Prasher and M.P. Janicki (eds), *Physical health of adults with intellectual disabilities*, 230–51. Oxford. Blackwell.

Lunsky, Y. and Havercamp, S.M. (2002) Women's mental health. In P.N. Walsh and T. Heller (eds), *Health of women with intellectual disabilities*, 59–75. Oxford. Blackwell.

Malmstrom, H., Santos-Teachout, R.R. and Ren, Y.-F. (2002) Dentition and oral health. In V.P. Prasher and M.P. Janicki (eds), *Physical health of adults with intellectual disabilities*, 181–203. Oxford. Blackwell.

Mitchell, D. and Snyder, S. (2001) *A world without bodies*. Video. University of Illinois at Chicago. Author.

Moss, S. and Patel, P. (1995) Psychiatric symptoms associated with dementia in older people with learning disability. *British Journal of Psychiatry* **167**, 663–7.

Moss, S. and Patel, P. (1997) Dementia in older people with intellectual disability: symptoms of physical and mental illness, and levels of adaptive behaviour. *Journal of Intellectual Disability Research* **41**, 60–9.

Mulvaney, F. (2001) *Annual Report — National Intellectual Disability Database 2000*. Dublin. Health Research Board.

National Council on Ageing and Older People (2001) *Demography—Ageing in Ireland Fact File no. 1*. www.ncaop.ie/FF1demography.pdf

O'Brien, G., Barnard, L., Pearson, J. and Rippon, L. (2002) Physical health and clinical phenotypes. In V.P. Prasher and M.P. Janicki (eds), *Physical health of adults with intellectual disabilities*, 35–62. Oxford. Blackwell.

Prasher, V.P. and Janicki, M.P. (eds) (2002) *Physical health of adults with intellectual disabilities*. Oxford. Blackwell.

Quinn, G. (1995) The International Covenant on Civil and Political Rights and disability: a conceptual framework. In T. Degener and Y. Koster-Dreese (eds), *Human rights and disability*, 69–93. Dordrecht. Martinus Nijhoff.

Robertson, J., Emerson, E., Gregory, N., Hatton, C., Kessissoglou, S., Hallam, A. and Linehan, C. (2001) Social networks of people with intellectual disabilities in residential settings. *Mental Retardation* **39**, 201–14.

Santrock, J.W. (1995) *Life-span development*. Madison WI and Dubuque IA. WCB Brown and Benchmark.

Schalock, R. and Verdugo, M.-A. (2002) *Handbook on Quality of Life for human*

L160

service practitioners. Washington DC. AAMR.

Seltzer, G. and Luchterhand, C. (1994) Health and well-being of older persons with developmental disabilities: a clinical review. In M.M. Seltzer, M.W. Krauss and M.P. Janicki (eds), *Life course perspectives on adulthood and old age,* 109–42. Washington DC. AAMR.

Seltzer, M.M., Krauss, M.W. and Janicki, M.P. (eds) (1994) *Life course perspectives on adulthood and old age.* Washington DC. AAMR.

Seltzer, M.M., Krauss, M.W., Walsh, P.N., Conliffe, C., Larson, B., Birkbeck, G., Hong, J. and Choi, S.C. (1995) Cross-national comparisons of ageing mothers of adults with intellectual disability. *Journal of Intellectual Disability Research* **39**, 408–18.

Shearn, J. and Todd, S. (1997) Parental work: an account of the day-to-day activities of parents of adults with learning disabilities. *Journal of Intellectual Disability Research* **41**, 285–301.

Stark, J.A. and Faulkner, E. (1996) Quality of life across the life span. In R.L. Schalock (ed.), *Quality of Life Vol. 1. Conceptualization and measurement,* 23–32 Washington DC. AAMR.

Strategy for equality, A (1996) Report of the Commission on the Status of People with Disabilities. Dublin. Department of Equality, Justice and Law Reform.

Thase, M.E. (1982) Longevity and mortality in Down's Syndrome. *Journal of Mental Deficiency Research* **26**, 177–92.

Thorpe, L., Davidson, P. and Janicki, M. (2001) Healthy ageing-adults with intellectual disabilities: biobehavioural issues. *Journal of Applied Research in Intellectual Disabilities* **14**, 218–28.

Towards a full life (1984) Irish Government Green Paper. Dublin. Government Publications.

United Nations (1994) *Standard rules on the equalization of opportunities for people with disabilities.* New York. United Nations.

van Schrojenstein Lantman-de Valk, H.M.J. (1998) *Health problems in people with intellectual disabiity.* Maastricht. University of Maastricht and Unigraphic.

van Schrojenstein Lantman–de Valk, H.M.J., Schupf, N. and Patja, K. (2002) Reproductive and physical health. In P.N. Walsh and T. Heller (eds), *Health of women with intellectual disabilities,* 22–40. Oxford. Blackwell.

Veraart, M. and Bierman, A. (1998) Hearing loss in persons with intellectual disabilities in group homes. *NTZ* **1**, 3–13. [Cited by M. Haveman at the Scientific Conference on Intellectual Disability, Aging and Health, 6–9 December 2002, Tampa, Florida.]

Walsh, P.N. (1997) Old world—new territory: European perspectives on intellectual disability. *Journal of Intellectual Disability Research* **41**, 112–19.

Walsh, P.N. (2003) Gender and disability. In S. Quin and B. Redmond (eds), *Disability and social policy in Ireland.* Dublin. UCD Press.

Walsh, P.N. and Heller, T. (eds) (2002) *Health of women with intellectual disabilities.* Oxford. Blackwell.

Walsh, P.N. and LeRoy, B. (2004) *Women with disabilities ageing well: a global view.* Baltimore. Paul H. Brookes.

Walsh, P.N. and Murphy, G.H. (2002) Risk and vulnerability: dilemmas for women. In P.N. Walsh and T. Heller (eds), *Health of women with intellectual disabilities,* 154–69. Oxford. Blackwell.

Walsh, P.N., Conliffe, C. and Birkbeck, G. (1993) Permanency planning and maternal well-being: a study of caregivers of people with intellectual disability in Ireland and Northern Ireland. *Irish Journal of Psychology* **14**, 176–88.

Walsh, P.N. *et al.* (2000) Quality of life and social inclusion. In K. D. Keith and R.L. Schalock (eds), *Cross-cultural perspective on quality of life,* 315–26. Washington DC. AAMR.

Wehmeyer, M.L., Kelchner, K. and Richards, S. (1996) Essential characteristics of self-determined behaviour of individuals with mental retardation. *American Journal on Mental Retardation* **100**, 632–42.

World Health Organization (2000) *Healthy ageing—adults with intellectual disabilities.* http://www.who.int/mental_health and http://www.iassid.org

Young, E.C. and Kramer, B.M. (1991) Characteristics of age-related language decline in adults with Down Syndrome. *Mental Retardation* **29**, 75–9.

Zigman, W.B., Seltzer, G.B. and Silverman, W.P. (1994) Behavioral and mental health changes associated with aging in adults with mental retardation. In M.M. Seltzer, M.W. Krauss and M.P. Janicki (eds), *Life course perspectives on adulthood and old age,* 67–91. Washington. AAMR.

10. TRENDS IN EMPLOYMENT

PATRICIA NOONAN WALSH AND CHRISTY LYNCH

INTRODUCTION

The entry of Irish adults with disabilities into the ordinary workplace is scarcely a sea change: it is a real migration nonetheless. In the past, a few individuals grew to adulthood and found their feet in a workplace near home with help from relatives or friends—in garages and shops, farms and fisheries. For much of the twentieth century congregate residences sustained decades of silent, sheltered and often penniless industry by people with disabilities, the vulnerable and other men and women of no property. During the 1980s some adults with intellectual or other disabilities took up European grant-aided training aimed at promoting their vocational and social integration. Such grants often persisted for years, shoring up a segregated, long-term training industry and generating employment for thousands of trainers, rehabilitation workers and professionals. A few voluntary and statutory service agencies led the way by investing in supports for individual workers in ordinary jobs. As the twenty-first century opens there is a modest but steady flow of younger, middle-aged and older adults with diverse abilities into offices, supermarkets, gardens and a host of small and large enterprises throughout Ireland and other European countries. How did this migration begin? Why did it swell in numbers? And where will it lead?

This chapter identifies critical stages marking wider access to inclusive work experiences for Irish people with developmental disabilities. It examines the impact of two divergent pathways for adult occupation: traditional, sheltered day activity and open employment. The roots of more inclusive employment opportunities are traced. Current policy and practice are summarised within the context of a rights-based approach to disability in Europe. Strategies for research addressing the factors related to satisfying employment are suggested.

TRADITIONS

During the last century a traditional model of social care and protection for people with intellectual disabilities prevailed in Ireland. Since it was more convenient to care for groups, men and women lived and worked in separate, often rural, settings. Batches of contract work could be dispersed to large residential centres, influenced by earlier custodial traditions such as the workhouse, laundry, hospital farm or industrial therapy unit (McCormack, this volume). Workers activated token time clocks and earned token wages for performing contract work such as assembly and packaging, or for cleaning, cooking and gardening within the walls. The likelihood that they would complete a defined period of training or leave sheltered work to find jobs in the open labour market was negligible (McConkey and Murphy 1988).

In time, sheltered work generated its own buildings, personnel and administrative structures, and an institution took root. Thousands of Irish men and women worked for many years as 'trainees' or participants in 'pre-vocational' programmes. They worked for five or six hours, whether or not their tasks were genuinely productive. To fill production quotas, care staff or supervisors often worked alongside their charges. Investing years in a special training site removed from the ordinary labour market yielded a poor return, as virtual skills were unlikely to transfer to an actual workplace.

Other adults were excluded even from this sheltered work. An alternative, non-vocational occupation emerged as the default for those who could not use public transport independently or who failed to reach the criteria set by the provider agency on tests of manual dexterity or other performance measures. Congregate day services—variously labelled as day activity, day care, activation, pre-employment or special care—still flourish in Ireland, as elsewhere.

Mary

Mary was born at home in a country town in Ireland in 1952. Gradually it became apparent that she was slow to learn. Her parents took the best advice of the day from a local doctor and their neighbours. They agreed to send Mary to stay in St Martha's, a residential centre in the next county, when she was eight years old. Mary had very little formal education. She spent a good deal of her time walking around—although hampered a little by a slight limp—and learning to sew and to sing in the choir. Although well fed and cared for, dental treatment was poor and clothing was purchased in bulk: winter coats and boots were distributed from the seasonal supply or handed down from other residents. When she was seventeen, Mary was encouraged to spend most of the day in the centre's industrial occupation unit—a huge, draughty room where women aged from their teens into their sixties sat at long tables assembling soft toys for a local manufacturer. Staff members sat alongside and did much of this work. In time, Mary learned how to tack and glue from the older women at her table. She received a token wage—then a few shillings—at the end of each week.

In the 1980s and '90s awareness grew about the potential benefits of employment for people with disabilities. Productive work, even if unpaid, provides occupation, status, companionship and purposeful activity. For many the workplace is second in importance only to family life, the wellspring of social relationships and friendships (Chadsey *et al.* 1998). Paid work yields powerful economic incentives, especially when individuals perceive that they are much better off if they are working. In the industrialised countries, workers are most often motivated by the prospect of income or other financial benefits, such as extended social or health insurance. In the developing countries, especially if the social safety net is loose, work is essential for day-to-day livelihood and everyone who can do so contributes.

Whatever the shape of the work accomplished, its power to enhance the quality of life of people with developmental disabilities is widely respected (Schalock 1996; Felce 1997). Suitable employment confers a productive occupation, social status, personal satisfaction, companionship and other benefits in addition to earned income. Employment status helps to define the individual's personal and social identity and is thus linked to self-esteem and well-being. More widely, employment is construed as an indicator of social and economic integration which should be available to all citizens as a matter of right, particularly to those with disabilities. Rule 7 of the United Nations' *Standard rules* (1994) underscores the valued status of employment within the scope of universal human rights:

> 'States should recognise the principle that persons with disabilities must be empowered to exercise their human rights, particularly in the field of employment. In both rural and urban areas they must have equal opportunities for productive and gainful employment in the labour market.'

Michael

Michael was born in County Galway in 1964, the youngest of nine children. When he was six years old, Michael entered a special school 25 miles from home, spending three or more hours on the school bus each day. His family did their best to encourage him, as there was no other way for Michael to live at home and also benefit from an education. When Michael finished school at 18 years, his self-help skills and dexterity were found to be up to standard. Michael's widowed mother agreed that he could attend the new vocational training centre set up by St Blaise's, the agency that had managed Michael's special school. Since then, Michael has attended the workshop regularly. Some days he stays at home to keep company with his mother, who is getting on in years. At the workshop, trainees assemble and package farming supplies: Michael has learned to operate the heat-sealing press. Each Friday he receives €15 in wages. He buys a drink on Saturday night with his brother and his friend Jim, and is saving for a summer holiday.

Towards the end of the twentieth century, the service landscape in Ireland revealed well-entrenched sheltered workplaces for groups of adults with developmental or other disabilities, and for other marginal groups. But the seeds of change were germinating here and there, provoking new questions. If people with disabilities entered ordinary jobs, what wages should they earn? Could they change jobs, take training courses and plan for retirement, like their peers? As European citizens, should they not rightfully claim equal opportunities to take part in all aspects of social life, including employment (Commission of the European Communities 1996)? The conviction that people with developmental disabilities share basic human rights common to all—for example, the right to equal employment opportunities—steadily took root.

ROOTS OF INCLUSIVE EMPLOYMENT

Over time, the voices of professionals, family members and people with developmental disabilities themselves emerged. Some asked why the goal of social integration remained elusive. Most accepted that an unpromising economic climate prior to 1995 and fixed social attitudes made segregated employment resistant to change. Arguably, life outcomes for individuals were not satisfactory. After decades of sheltered work or day care, few showed lasting gains in competence, income or inclusion in their own communities. While no single event or law sparked the current critical environment in Ireland, a mix of internal and external factors helped to fuel change.

Social change

First, socio-economic change in Ireland was widespread, filtered through a refreshed European identity in the years following entry to the European Union (then the EEC) a generation ago, in 1973. Community living was embedded in government policy on people with disabilities (*Towards a full life* 1984). But even as hospital populations moved to special bungalows and group homes, anomalies were apparent. If it was desirable for a person with disabilities to move out of the shelter to a home in the community, then why did he/she not attend school with local children, and why not seek employment in an ordinary workplace? Men and women reaching adulthood in the 1990s were more likely to have benefited from special education: not surprisingly, their expectations for employment also rose. They echoed their counterparts in the United States, who were 'a new generation of persons who have experienced inclusive education and whose families have advocated for their rights' (Blanck 1996, 48).

Second, service-providers and policy-makers had access to a growing body of evidence showing that men and women with developmental disabilities could, with support, live satisfying, independent lives. Reports of successful innovations in the UK, the United States and the Scandinavian countries reached families and professionals in Ireland (Wehman and Walsh 1999). Less restrictive forms of education and community living were mirrored—most notably in the United States—by the growth of more inclusive employment opportunities.

Supported employment

Supported employment, the leading model, may be defined as real work with support for a real wage in an ordinary setting. Its key elements have been documented: placement in a suitable job, job site training, ongoing monitoring, advocacy and support for workers so that they may hold the jobs they find (Beyer and Kilsby 1998). It differs in substance from traditional, sheltered models of employment for people with developmental disabilities (Table 1).

Table 1—Supported and sheltered employment: a comparison.

Supported employment	Sheltered work
First, choose the job and take steps to get it	Spend years in pre- or vocational training with little chance of a job
Learn how to do the job with support on site	Continue to train in a special setting
Keep the job with the right supports	Training stops and is replaced by sheltered employment
Develop a career as preferences and opportunities change	Change jobs only infrequently
Aim at social inclusion in everyday life in the community	Social inclusion is possible but not an explicit aim

Candidates for supported employment need not meet any pre-set criteria of age, temperament or ability in order to enter employment. No one is excluded from the search for suitable employment, reflecting a policy of *zero rejection*. The approach does not dwell on the prospective employee's apparent deficits: rather, it addresses what people can do, in the workplace as in other domains of living. Everyone is encouraged to learn how best to interact with co-workers and supervisors, both within and outside the workplace, in order to enhance the employee's social competence and integration (Chadsey 1998).

Some key strategies to promote satisfying employment were developed:

- systematic instruction, adopting behavioural analysis and learning;
- job-coaching in the workplace;
- natural supports in the workplace;
- staff training—notably certification of training completed;
- building a positive role for employers;
- extension to other populations, such as people with traumatic brain injury, chronic mental illness or sensory impairments.

Focus on individuals

At first, practitioners aimed to place, train and maintain individuals in suitable employment. But the focus shifted from delivering services to offering suitable supports, with the prospective employee taking an active role. The person with developmental disabilities became the agent rather than the recipient. In this approach, he or she takes the central role in guiding a career path over the lifespan, so that each person may choose, get and then keep the job preferred. The language currently used expresses new thinking about the central role of people with disabilities in making decisions about their own lives. This shift in approach—from administering aggregate services already on the shelf to providing tailor-made individual supports—is at the heart of today's changed paradigm in human services for persons with developmental disabilities (Hardman *et al.* 1997). For example, government policy in the UK recently directed all service-providers to activate person-centred planning on behalf of people with developmental disabilities (Great Britain Department of Health 2001).

From the social policy viewpoint, supported employment was welcomed as it serves two related purposes (Lewis *et al.* 1998). First, it has the potential to have a positive social impact on the lives of individuals with developmental disabilities. Supported employment can increase levels of income, enhance personal status and vocational competence and thus promote social integration for adults with developmental disabilities, for example by setting the scene in which social interaction with workers who do not have disabilities may prosper (Ohtake and Chadsey 1999). Currently, the task of professionals such as employment specialists is to deliver whatever it takes to support individuals' needs to reach the outcomes they value.

Second, supported employment is justified because it brings economic benefits to society. If more people become gainfully employed, they are less likely to claim the benefits to which people who are not economically active are entitled. They are more likely to become productive taxpayers, although many people with developmental disabilities incur additional costs of living and thus a social safety net must be in place. This view has recently been endorsed by social policy targeted at unacceptable rates of unemployment and social exclusion within the European Member States. The Commission's employment strategy includes, for example, heightened efforts to raise employment levels among people with disabilities (European Commission 1998b, 11).

Jenny

Jenny is 26. She spent five years after leaving a special school in a sheltered workshop. Today, she works in a suburban office park ten hours each week. Jenny learned to use the paper-shredder in a small accountancy firm very quickly—much to the surprise of her mother, May, who had earlier held misgivings about how suitable a supported employment scheme might be for her only daughter. May was afraid that Jenny would be 'too giddy' and that other office workers might make fun of her. For years experts had told May that Jenny would never be capable of open employment. After May met office staff as well as Sarah, Jenny's job coach, she agreed that Jenny might begin a trial period. Within weeks it was clear that Jenny thrived in the lively office environment and that she only needed Sarah's help from time to time. Andrew, a junior accountant, supervises Jenny's work now. Sarah calls in to the office weekly to review progress and deal with any difficulties or new duties. The company is exploring ways for Jenny to increase her hours of work and to take part in a training course in health and safety with all other staff members. Jenny would like to earn more money but May worries lest her daughter risk losing entitlements—to the weekly Disability Allowance, for example.

EUROPEAN INFLUENCE

Only small pockets of supported employment were reported in most of Europe until the 1990s, when European initiatives proved to be the driving force behind its expansion in Ireland. A spirit of innovation in Irish voluntary agencies— leading providers of services for people with developmental disabilities—in combination with an open labour market and ease in finding partners in other countries ensured that the criteria for EU-funded initiatives such as HORIZON could readily be met.

A few initiatives deepened and were channelled by European funding aimed at the greater social and vocational integration of persons with developmental and other disabilities. In the midland region, the Midland Health Board and APT in Tullamore, Co. Offaly, collaborated in the HELIOS programme to extend employer-based training opportunities to people with disabilities (Walsh and Linehan 1995). The *Intogal* project was the source of community-based employment and residential initiatives in Galway (McConkey *et al.* 1993).

In Dublin, a three-year innovative project used a grant from the European Social Fund to develop supported employment for men and women with moderate or severe intellectual disabilities. This group had traditionally been excluded from vocational experience of any kind. The participants received services from St Michael's House, a large community-based provider agency in the Dublin region. The project, OPEN ROAD (1988–91), ultimately reached more than 80 individuals in newly established local day centres throughout Dublin city and county (Walsh, Rafferty and Lynch 1991). Twenty-four adults were successfully employed in fast-food outlets, shops, cafes, garages and small manufacturers, where they were trained and supported by job coaches and ultimately by co-workers. Overall, the supported employees maintained jobs and earned income for the first time: many improved daily living skills (Walsh, Lynch and De Lacey 1994; Lynch and Walsh 1997).

Each of these small-scale European-funded projects laid the foundation for a radically different approach to employment for people with more significant disabilities in Ireland. Later, projects such as *Connect* (Tinsley 1995) and *Challenge* (Kelly 1994) were funded through HORIZON. Substantial funding and evidence of positive early experiences led to replication of inclusive employment initiatives throughout Ireland, led by both statutory and voluntary service agencies.

HORIZON targeted people with disabilities while the Community Initiative on Employment targeted specific populations—those who were disadvantaged or otherwise removed from the labour market. A new policy in the European Commission was expressed in a document endorsing equal opportunities for all European citizens, particularly those with disabilities (Commission of the European Communities 1996). Reflecting this strategy, all mainstream intervention programmes were open to applications on behalf of people with disabilities. *Adapt* was aimed at the general workforce: a project aimed at developing shared worker skills training included workers with developmental disabilities (St Michael's House 1998). And a project identifying the needs of young people for a curriculum easing transition from school to adulthood was successfully funded through *Youthstart* (KARE 1997).

John Paul

John Paul was born in Dublin in 1979, a year when the number of babies born in Ireland reached its peak. His health in the early months was poor, but thanks to expert medical attention he not only survived but began to thrive. As he was her only child, John Paul's mother was eager for him to meet other children. At the age of three years, his difficulties in mobility and language were considerable. The voluntary agency which provided services in the area arranged for John Paul to attend a special pre-school for children with developmental disabilities in their clinic for two years. From the age of five, John Paul attended a day centre staffed by care-workers, nurses and other professionals. Later, a special teacher paid by the Department of Education visited to offer some hours of individual teaching each week. Now that he is 19, John Paul has outgrown the children's centre, and as he cannot use public transport he cannot enter a vocational training centre. John Paul's mother is anxious to explore all options for him, especially since she must go out to work all day. She has heard of a young man with disabilities who has started a part-time job nearby, where he is supported by a helper and his co-workers. She wonders whether a job might be an option for John Paul.

POLICY TRENDS

National policies on inclusive employment have been mixed. While the Irish government's Review Group on Services (*Needs and abilities*, 1990) recommended employment options for those able to benefit, it fell short of endorsing open employment as the preferred option for all adults. Voluntary and statutory service-providers varied in their enthusiasm for changing from sheltered to more open models of training and employment. A special report proposed to shift 30% of national resources away from segregated options such as workshops towards the expansion of inclusive options such as supported employment (NRB 1997). Others argued that open employment would remove individuals from the companionship and sense of belonging engendered by years of sheltered work. Large, segregated centres continue to thrive even as European policy and international consensus on good practice exert a pull towards greater inclusion.

Equality?

The Commission on the Status of People with Disabilities was established in Ireland by the (then) Minister for Equality and Law Reform in 1993. It reviewed all aspects of the lives of people with disabilities, including employment. Recognising the growth of the self-advocacy movement, which aims for individuals to have a greater say over their own lives and to participate fully in society, people with disabilities themselves were members of the Commission. The Commission's report, *A strategy for equality* (1996), presents 400 recommendations, a blueprint for services to achieve full citizenship and social participation.

One proposal was that governmental responsibility for the employment and vocational training of people with disabilities should be delivered through the Department of Enterprise and Employment or through FÁS, the national training agency. In response, FÁS launched a national pilot programme to promote supported employment. More than twenty consortia throughout Ireland with project managers and teams of job coaches assisted people with all types of disabilities to enter the labour market using supported employment strategies. Following an independent evaluation after the pilot phase, FÁS agreed to continue these projects. However, the Department of Health and Children remains responsible for rehabilitative training and sheltered workshops/occupational services.

Inclusion?

What has been the impact of EU-funded initiatives and government policies? One evaluation study concluded that an investment of millions had largely failed to achieve open employment, let alone social inclusion, for most of the people targeted (Department of Enterprise and Employment 1996). Only a minority of Irish people with intellectual disabilities spend their daytime hours in inclusive settings (Fig. 1). By 2000, just 957 of a total of 14,102 Irish adults with intellectual disabilities aged 20 or older recorded as receiving any form of day service were described as being in inclusive work settings—either open, enclave or supported employment (Fig. 1).[1]

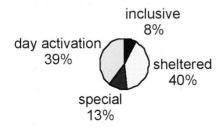

inclusive
8%

day activation
39%

sheltered
40%

special
13%

Fig. 1—Day settings: Irish adults with intellectual disability (Health Research Board 2001).

By contrast, 4585 adults aged over 20 were in sheltered work/long-term training centres, and a further 1724 in special vocational training centres (Health Research Board 2001). Nearly as many persons, 4681, were in day activation centres (some additional groups of adults were otherwise served).

Barriers

Despite the spread of good practice, a wealth of research evidence and the force of European and national policies, inclusive employment remains the option for few Irish adults with developmental disabilities. What barriers prevent this model from extending beyond time-limited demonstration projects into the mainstream of social and economic life? It seems that three key issues must be resolved.

First, how can resources flow towards individualised supports? More older adults, those with complex disabilities or additional mental health difficulties will enter the pool of prospective employees. Yet recent evidence suggests that these groups remain under-represented in supported employment services in the United States (Mank *et al.* 1998). There is no reason to expect a very different pattern of opportunity in Europe. It is a paradox that a model of employment devised a generation ago specifically for individuals with more severe levels of disability still eludes their grasp. One way to ensure that individual needs are reflected in supports is person-centred planning (Everson 1996). Rather than fitting people into existing service structures, this process places the individual at the centre of any decisions touching his or her life. The person is invited to chart a vision of the future, including a career path. Then the energies of family members, friends and other advocates are harnessed to make available whatever it takes to make the vision a reality.

Second, funding two parallel systems of employment support—segregated and inclusive—is untenable, especially when budgets are constrained. Traditional systems are likely to resist radical change fiercely. For decades, statutory and voluntary service-providers built stable systems of training and sheltered work. They have a vested interest in maintaining things the way they are. This sector is a distinctive industry with its own culture, employing thousands of care and supervisory staff. Family members may resist change if they expect that entry to vocational training at 18 or 19 years of age is the passport to a sheltered workplace for life: otherwise, they fear the loss of hard-won day services for their family members. Radical changes to service systems call for new organisational structures, new skills for professionals, moves away from large, factory-type buildings, and strategic alliances with mainstream employers.

In addition, social welfare systems may thwart efforts to involve more people with disabilities in the labour force. In Ireland, as elsewhere, benefits and income support often frustrate rather than advance steps towards more inclusive employment. For example, Irish adults who receive a weekly Disability Allowance may only earn income to a fixed ceiling. If they earn more, they risk losing what is for many a precious supplement of family income. Advocates bewail the loss of incentives.

While these three perplexing challenges may not be fully resolved, Ireland is likely to follow European trends towards mainstreaming the disability agenda and extending inclusive employment opportunities.

AGENDA: FUTURE DEVELOPMENTS

European Union membership permeates the working lives of all citizens. EU policy promotes mainstreaming of all services for people with disabilities as a matter of right. It has committed itself to addressing unacceptably high unemployment levels among European citizens with disabilities and to do so through mainstream, rather than special, interventions. The EU Employment Strategy stems from the Title on Employment in the Amsterdam Treaty, directing Ireland and every other member state to embed the employment needs of people with disabilities within that country's national action plan on employment. Action plans must be written in the context of a set of guidelines that have been developed by the European Commission to build capacity in the labour force, to be reviewed annually. There are four pillars:

- improving employability,
- developing entrepreneurship,
- encouraging adaptability,
- strengthening policies on equal opportunities.

European social funds have influenced fundamentally the growth of Irish training and employment services for people with disabilities. Regulations govern the allocation of these funds for a 5–7-year period, responding to the operational programme each country prepares. Important changes in the structural funds were included in the funding period extending from 2000 to 2006. Regulations will place greater emphasis on employment as well as training, and new policy guidelines for implementing new ESF regulations will be based on policy guidelines for the National Action Plans. Arguably, the future Operational Programme for employing people with disabilities in Ireland will be an integral part of the overall National Action Plan for Employment. The Commission sets the context through its guidelines on operational funding in an endeavour to translate an aspiration for the employment of people with disabilities into real employment in each member state.

To date, European countries have exerted various policies to assist citizens with disabilities in gaining employment. In Sweden and Denmark there are ombudsmen; in Belgium, Ireland, Spain and Italy there are quota systems, and in Austria, Germany and France quota-levy systems. Although some member states of the European Union have adopted anti-discrimination legislation, it is often more effective in gaining access to rehabilitation and vocational training than to jobs (European Commission 1997, 113). Increasingly, legislation is recognised as a powerful means for helping people with disabilities to gain employment. In the United States, the Americans with Disabilities Act of 1990 'has clearly done good work. More than 1m disabled people entered the workforce between 1991 and 1994. The work on offer is not just part-time' (*Economist* 1998, 47). A study carried out in the United States found that the average cost to employers of making arrangements to help an employee with a disability was more modest than expected (Blanck 1996).

Changes to the constitution and penal codes in many European countries have also supported rights for people with disabilities: Germany, France, Finland and Austria have taken such steps. The United Kingdom government recently passed legislation to eliminate discrimination in employment. In Ireland, the Employment Equality and Equal Status Acts were passed.

Arguably, the main criterion for measuring the impact of inclusive employment is the satisfaction of employees with their income and opportunities. Yet each year governments throughout Europe spend vast sums on interventions without any discernible outcomes for individuals with developmental disabilities being linked with investment. Can lessons be learned from the New World? In the United States, the states have begun to direct resources towards individuals and families. In five states, more than 20% of the total Mental Retardation/Developmental Disability resources are spent on individual and family support activities—supported living, supported employment, family supports. This stands in contrast to merely 7% in 1996 and just 4% in 1992 (Braddock *et al.* 1997).

Self-determination has emerged as an important construct in considering the quality of life of people with disabilities. It may be defined as 'acting as the primary causal agent in one's life and making choices and decisions regarding one's quality of life free from undue external influence or interference' (Wehmeyer and Schalock 2001, 2). Until recently people with developmental disabilities had little opportunity to take key decisions about preferred employment, or indeed any other aspect of their own lives. The self-advocacy movement has swelled as a political expression of this striving for autonomy. Gradually, men and women with disabilities have gravitated from the margins to the centre of decisions about where to live, with whom to spend leisure time and where to work. To participate fully in society, people with developmental disabilities need regular employment, earned income and a career path stretching into their future lives, just as other citizens do. In Ireland advocacy is still in its infancy. But this organisation reflects a world-wide trend towards self-advocacy led by the People First movement in the United Kingdom, Spain, the United States and other countries. Self-advocacy is likely to play an even greater part in developing employment opportunities and in measuring the outcomes of employment for individuals in the future.

SUMMARY

At the start of the twenty-first century, adults with developmental disabilities look back on a century of uneven progress towards full social inclusion. The model of disability endorsed by European social policy suggests that the tide has turned—from welfare to rights, from service delivery to matching appropriate supports, from special care to equal opportunities. Employment practices reflecting these waves of change have emerged and indeed prospered in Ireland and many other countries, offering many thousands their first experiences of the ordinary workplace. Research has yielded robust findings: properly supported, most adults who choose to work can do so productively and enhance their quality of life. By contrast, segregated training and employment continue to flourish for most, diminishing their chances of participation in society. Global and regional trends in policy have yet to trickle down to provider organisations. Their words may be inclusive, but the daily experiences they offer to service-users remain separate. Nevertheless, European policy is set on mainstreaming employment for people with developmental disabilities in their own countries, alongside other citizens. The next century will resonate to their voices clamouring for full social inclusion, nothing less.

REFERENCES

Beyer, S. and Kilsby, M. (1998) Financial costs and benefits of two supported employment agencies in Wales. *Journal of Applied Research in Intellectual Disabilities* **11** (4), 303–19.

Blanck, P.D. (1996) *Communicating the Americans with Disabilities Act.* Evanston ILL. Communications Policy Studies, Northwestern University.

Braddock, D., Hemp, R. and Parish, S. (1997) Emergence of individual and family support in state service-delivery systems. *Mental Retardation* **35** (6), 497–8.

Chadsey, J. (1998) Examining personal and environmental variables for social integration success in employment settings. In J.G. Chadsey and D.L. Shelden (eds), *Promoting social relationships and integration for supported employees in work settings,* 126–46. Urbana-Champaign ILL. University of Illinois Transition Research Institute.

Chadsey, J., Linneman, D., Rylance, B.J. and Kronick, N. (1998) Descriptions of close social relationships between workers with and without mental retardation. In J.G. Chadsey and D.L. Shelden (eds), *Promoting social relationships and integration for supported employees in work settings,* 24–48. Urbana-Champaign ILL. University of Illinois Transition Research Institute.

Commission of the European Communities (1996) *Communication of the Commission on Equality of Opportunity for People with Disabilities—a new European Community disability strategy.* Brussels. CEC, No. 96/0216 (CNS), 30-07-96.

Commission on the Status of People with Disabilities (1996) *A strategy for equality.* Dublin. Government Publications Office.

Department of Enterprise and Employment (1996) *Training for people with disabilities: summary report.* Dublin. ESF Programme Evaluation Unit.

Economist (1998) The halt, the blind, the dyslexic. *The Economist,* 18 April 1998, 47–8.

European Commission (1997) *Employment in Europe.* Luxembourg. Office for Official Publications of the European Communities.

European Commission (1998a) *From guidelines to actions: the national action plans for employment.* Luxembourg. Office for Official Publications of the European Communities.

European Commission (1998b) *Social action programme 1998–2000.* European Commission, Unit V/1. Luxembourg. Office for Official Publications of the European Communities.

Everson, J. (1996). Using person-centered planning concepts to enhance school-to-adult life transition planning. *Journal of Vocational Rehabilitation* **6**, 7–14.

Felce, D.·(1997) Defining and applying the construct of Quality of Life. *Journal of Intellectual Disability Research* **41** (2), 26–35.

Great Britain Department of Health (2001) *Valuing people: a new strategy for learning disability for the 21st century* [White Paper]. London. Stationery Office.

Hardman, M.L., McDonnell, J. and Welch, M. (1997) Perspectives on the future of IDEA. *Journal of the Association for Persons with Severe Handicaps* **22** (2), 61–77.

Health Research Board (1996) *Report on the Intellectual Disability Database*. Dublin. Health Research Board (www.hrb.ie).

Health Research Board (2001) *Report on the Intellectual Disability Database 2000*. Dublin. Health Research Board (www.hrb.ie).

KARE (1997) *The Bridge Project: a YOUTHSTART initiative*. Newbridge. KARE.

Kelly, S. (1994) *Report Challenge: final report*. Newbridge. KARE.

Lewis, D.R., Johnson, D.R. and Mangen, T. (1998) Evaluating the multi-dimensional nature of supported employment. *Journal of Applied Research in Intellectual Disabilities* **11** (2), 95–115.

Lynch, C. and Walsh, P.N. (1997) Local beginnings—global impact: the OPEN ROAD project. *Journal of Vocational Rehabilitation* **6**, 89–95.

McConkey, R. and Murphy, R. (1988) A national survey of centres and workshops for adult persons with mental handicap. In R. McConkey and C. Conliffe (eds), *The person with mental handicap*, 101–28. Dublin and Belfast. St Michael's House and Institute for Counselling and Personal Development.

McConkey, R., Walsh, P.N. and Conneally, S. (1993) Neighbours' reactions to community services: contrasts before and after services open in their locality. *Mental Handicap Research* **6** (2), 131–41.

Mank, D., Cioffi, A. and Yovanoff, P. (1998) Employment outcomes for people with severe disabilities: opportunities for improvement. *Mental Retardation* **36** (3), 205–16.

NRB (1997) *Employment challenges for the millennium*. Report of the NACTE Steering Group on Sheltered and Supported Work and Employment. Dublin. NRB.

Ohtake, Y. and Chadsey, J.G. (1999) Social disclosure among co-workers without disabilities in supported employment settings. *Mental Retardation* **37** (1), 25–35.

O'Toole, B. and McConkey, R. (1995) *Innovations for people with intellectual disabilities in developing countries*. Chorley. Lisieux Hall.

Race, D. (1996) Historical development of service provision. In N. Malin (ed.), *Services for people with learning disabilities*, 46–78. London and New York. Routledge.

St Michael's House (1998) *Shared training: report on an ADAPT project*. Dublin. St Michael's House.

Schalock, R. (1996) Reconsidering the conceptualization and measurement of quality of life. In R. Schalock (ed.), *Quality of Life—Volume 1*, 123–39. Washington DC. AAMR.

Sutton, B. and Walsh, P.N. (1999) Inclusion International's Open Project on inclusive employment. *Journal of Vocational Rehabilitation* **12** (3), 195–8.

Tinsley, B. (1995) *Project Connect: final report*. Dublin. St Michael's House Research.

Towards a full life (1984) Government Green Paper. Dublin. Government Stationery Office.

United Nations (1994) *Standard rules on the equalization of opportunities for people with disabilities*. New York. United Nations.

United Nations (1999) *Development Program Report 1999*. New York. UNDP.

Walsh, P.N. and Linehan, C. (1995) *RAPPORT II, an employment-based initiative: final report*. Dublin. St Michael's House Research.

Walsh, P.N., Lynch, C. and De Lacey, E. (1994) Supported employment for Irish adults with intellectual disability: the OPEN ROAD experience. *International Journal of Rehabilitation Research* **17**, 15–24.

Walsh, P.N., Rafferty, M. and Lynch, C. (1991) The OPEN ROAD project: real jobs for people with mental handicap. *International Journal of Rehabilitation Research* **14**, 155–61.

Wehman, P. and Walsh, P.N. (1999) Transition from school to adulthood: a look at the United States and Europe. In P. Retish and S. Reiter (eds), *Adults with disabilities*, 3–33. New Jersey. Lawrence Erlbaum Associates.

Wehmeyer, M.L. and Schalock, R.L. (2001) Self-determination and quality of life: implications for special education services and supports. *Focus on Exceptional Children* **33** (8), 1–16. [Cited in R. Schalock and Miguel Angel Verdugo Alonso, *Handbook on Quality of Life for human service practitioners* (Washington DC, 2002).]

Note

1 Percentages shown are based on a subtotal of 11,743 adults recorded as being in inclusive work settings, special vocational training, sheltered employment/work or day activation.

11. SPANISH AND IRISH IMAGES OF SPECIAL NEEDS: PERCEPTIONS OF INCLUSION

HUGH GASH, NURIA ILLÁN ROMEU AND JOSÉ ANTONIO LÓPEZ PINA

INTRODUCTION

The integration of pupils with a disability in ordinary schools is strongly recommended and accepted as a valuable goal; however, few studies examine the way integration works socially (Pijl and Meijer 1991). In the US this practice is called 'mainstreaming'; in Europe it is often called 'integration', though there has been a shift recently towards using the phrase 'inclusive education' to emphasise inclusion in the classroom and school. The aim of the present chapter is to examine attitudes and images relating to inclusive education programmes with a view to understanding more fully the socio-emotional context within which inclusion takes place. A number of elements are brought to bear on this issue. They include examination of variations in children's representations of intellectual disability and Down Syndrome, attitudes towards inclusive education and the issue of the validity of this type of attitude measure. Children in middle childhood are building their self-representations (Harter 1998), and we believe that representations of self and other develop together as youngsters mature. Further, there is good evidence that difficulties with peers place children at risk for developing psychological problems (Harter 1998).

In a series of classroom intervention studies the first author has investigated children's representations of their peers with special needs. Gender and grade level differences have consistently been found in these studies (Gash 1993; Gash and Coffey 1995; Gash 1996). Girls have been found to be more sociable, more socially concerned and more positive towards children with an intellectual disability than boys (Gash 1993). Older children have been found to be more socially concerned, more sociable and more positive towards integration (Gash 1993). Further, girls in a school with a special class were more socially concerned and sociable than peers in a similar school without this facility (Gash and Coffey 1995).

Two sets of linked studies are described in this chapter. The first set is based on the use of questionnaire techniques to examine children's attitudes towards intellectual disability and Down Syndrome. There are four studies in the first set. The first compares attitudes of samples of Irish and Spanish primary school pupils towards integrated or included pupils with intellectual disability. The second re-examines these cross-cultural findings through use of data requiring a more focused or restricted representation of intellectual disability, specifying Down Syndrome. The third provides evidence for the contextual validity of this attitude measure, and the fourth is an evaluation of a programme of integration at second level.

The second set of studies examines in more detail children's and parents' attitudes towards integration and Down Syndrome. The first of these is a qualitative assessment of Irish and Spanish primary school pupils' thinking about aspects of Down Syndrome, in particular inclusion of Down Syndrome children in their classrooms, and how pupils feel about socialising with peers with Down Syndrome. The second is based on a nationwide sample of 501 Irish farmers to assess their attitudes towards integration and its management in the Irish educational system. This provides data on adults' attitudes towards integration. It is important to note that these data were collected just prior to 1996 and so reflect the Irish primary system at that time. Subsequently there has been a dramatic increase in the educational services for children in difficulty in many Irish schools.

In the broader cultural domain the process of social identification is known to be important in the integration of minority groups into society (e.g. Lalonde *et al.* 1992). Learning to make friends and to have an identity in a group of friends is one of the tasks of childhood. A key element in the glue cementing a social group together is an individual's acceptance of the attitudes that this particular group considers important. If a child is different from other children this matching of attitudes may be more difficult. In the microcosm of classroom or school, attitudes play a central role in determining the success of integration and inclusion. Negative attitudes on the part of teachers or students towards a child with a disability may arise because of limited experience (e.g. Hegarty 1993). Whatever their origin, negative attitudes are likely to affect the quality of classroom and school life. Helen Keller is known to have said that the heaviest burdens of disability arise from difficulties in social relations and not from the disability itself. The present studies are concerned principally with two types of attitudes in children. The first is about sociable acceptance and concern, and the second is about acceptance of integration and inclusion. While these two are not identical, they are closely linked to the context in which friendships are formed in school. In turn, friendships support good outcomes across development in childhood (e.g. Hartup 1983; 1996).

STUDY 1: IRISH AND SPANISH ATTITUDES TO INTELLECTUAL DISABILITY

Ireland and Spain differ sharply in the emergence of inclusive practice, though both countries have similarly positive official policies towards it. An early official Irish view is that, 'except where individual circumstances make this impracticable, appropriate education for all children with special educational needs should be provided in ordinary schools' (Ireland 1993, 20). The Education Act (Ireland 1998) contains a similar qualification to provision of inclusion. The mechanisms planned to help teachers in integrated classrooms are only beginning to be put in place in Ireland, though some increases in promised finance have appeared (e.g. Ó Murchú and Shevlin 1995). In Spain the situation is different because since 1985 (e.g. Marchesi *et al.* 1991) there has been active promotion and facilitation of integration of children with special needs in selected Spanish schools. While there remains variability in the attitudes of Spanish teachers towards integration (Marchesi *et al.* 1991), it is likely that visible support for integration has played a role in making integration 'believable', as it was intended to do.

We were unable to locate studies on children's attitudes to integration and inclusion in Spain. The present study is the first that we are aware of in which national comparisons have been possible on these dimensions. Consequently, we feel it would be the safer strategy not to hypothesise about possible cultural difference but rather, following the example of Sundberg *et al.* (1991), to let the data speak for themselves and formulate hypotheses for later research.

Method

Subjects

The subjects were 136 Irish primary school urban children in ordinary (non-mainstreamed) schools at second class (approximately eight years of age) and fifth class (approximately eleven years of age), and 113 Spanish urban children in similar schools at the equivalent grade level (see Table 1).

Table 1—Subjects by nationality by gender and grade.

Mental handicap study

	Irish		Spanish	
	Girls	Boys	Girls	Boys
8-year-olds	38	37	23	18
11-year-olds	35	26	44	28

Down Syndrome study

| | *Irish* | | *Spanish* | |
	Girls	Boys	Girls	Boys
8-year-olds	28	30	9	18
11-year-olds	28	32	23	35

The questionnaire

The questionnaire used to investigate the children's attitudes towards children with learning disability has been described fully in Gash (1993). (The Spanish version is available from the first author.) There were three parts to this questionnaire.

(1) A 20-item attitude scale about a child with intellectual disability: 'I would like you to pretend that a new child came to your class this year. He or she has a mental handicap. Here are some questions for you to answer.' Responses to the items received one for 'yes' and two for 'no'. These 20 questions are presented in Table 2.

(2) A section to assess the child's experience of children with intellectual disability ('Are there any children with a mental handicap in your school/class, and do you know anybody who has a mental handicap?').

(3) A 34-adjective checklist: 'If you were describing him or her to your other friends which of these words do you think you would use?'

Results

The general strategy

In previous studies using this questionnaire (Gash 1993; Gash and Coffey 1995; Gash 1996) variables were constructed from two sources: first following a factor analysis of 20 attitudinal questions from the 791 pupils in Gash 1993 and by forming variables by summing scores on questions correlating highly on each factor, and second by constructing variables from the 34 descriptive words following an *a priori* categorisation of these words and then by creating a score based on the number of terms used by pupils in each of these categories.

Table 2—Items for factor analysis.

1. Would you smile at him/her on the first day?
2. Would you ask him/her to sit beside you?
3. Would you chat to him/her at break time?
4. Later on, would you tell him/her secrets that you usually keep for your friends?

5.   Would you make him/her your best friend?
6.   Would you invite him/her to your house to play in the evenings?
7.   Would you feel angry if he/she did not keep the rules of your games at playtime?
8.   Would you invite him/her to your birthday party with your other friends?
9.   Would you pick him/her on your team in a competition?
10. Would you ask him/her questions about himself/herself?
11. Would you care if other children made fun of the handicapped child?
12. Do you think the handicapped child could do the same maths as you?
13. Do you think that he/she could read the same books as you?
14. Do you think that he/she would have the same hobbies as the ordinary children?
15. Would you feel afraid of him/her because he/she is mentally handicapped?
16. Do you think mentally handicapped children should be taught in the same classroom as ordinary children?
17. Should mentally handicapped children have their own special classroom in your school?
18. Should mentally handicapped children have their own special school where all the children are handicapped?
19. Do handicapped children prefer other handicapped children as friends?
20. Can you tell if a child is mentally handicapped by just looking at his/her face?

The attitudinal factors and variables
A re-examination[1] of the original data (Gash 1993) provided support for the general strategy used previously with the 20 attitudinal questions but simplified the analysis by specifying two as compared to four composite variables (e.g. Gash 1993; Gash and Coffey 1995).

Composite variables were created by adding items which loaded at 0.40 or more on two factors. Items that loaded negatively on the factors were recoded (1=2 and 2=1) to contribute positively to each composite variable. In these studies item consistency, a form of reliability, was assessed using Cronbach's α on each composite variable.

The first factor dealing with sociability and social concern for the child with intellectual disability was made up of the following items: a willingness to smile at him/her (item 1), to sit beside him/her (item 2), to chat to him/her (item 3), to tell secrets to him/her (item 4), to have him/her as a best friend (item 5), to invite him/her home (item 6) or to a birthday party (item 8), to include him/her on their team (item 9), to be concerned if he/she were teased (item 11), and (not) to be upset if he/she broke the rules of a game (item 7 was recoded). Cronbach's coefficient α for this variable was 0.72 (Irish sample 0.65; Spanish sample 0.72). Recall that on all attitudinal items 'yes' scores one and 'no' scores two: low scores, therefore, imply a greater disposition towards social concern and sociability while high scores indicate less concern and unsociability.

The second factor concerned schooling. Items that loaded on this were about the child with intellectual disability being able to do the same maths (item 12), reading (item 13) and hobbies (item 14) as the other children, and the three items about schooling (16 to 18). Items 17 and 18 were recoded (1=2; 2=1), so a low score on this composite variable means that a child with intellectual disability should be taught in the same classroom (item 16), should *not* have their own special classroom in the school (item 17) and should *not* have their own special school (item 18). In other words, low scores on this variable imply an acceptance of total integration or inclusion and imply a belief in the ability of a child with intellectual disability to cope in ordinary classrooms. High scores indicate a focus on the serious difficulties a child with intellectual disability could experience in following the same academic programme in the same classroom. Coefficient α for this variable was 0.73 (Irish sample 0.72; Spanish sample 0.76).

The adjective checklist and variables

On this checklist each child was asked to indicate words he or she would use to describe a child with intellectual disability to their friends from a set of descriptors identified earlier in pilot tests. The 34 words were grouped into sets by consensus amongst student teachers who taught experimental classes in the original study. These included positive terms, negative terms and sensitive terms. We created three scales by summing the frequency of use of words in each category. Each scale indicates the salience of the dimension to pupils' ways of thinking about a child with intellectual disability.

The positive terms were as follows: clever, kind, friendly, lovable and happy; coefficient α for this variable was 0.69 (Irish sample 0.71; Spanish sample 0.67). The negative terms were: dirty, stupid, untidy, bold, dumb, rough, spa, crazy, geek, thick, simple, scary, dork, retarded, moron, twit, freak, idiot and nerd; coefficient α for this variable was 0.85 (Irish sample 0.87; Spanish sample 0.84). Finally, the sensitive terms were: special, sad, lonely, ashamed and unhappy; coefficient α for this variable was 0.52, and when the words 'special' and 'ashamed' were removed from the composite variable α rose to 0.63 (Irish sample 0.66; Spanish sample 0.60). High scores on each scale indicates the dimension's importance to the pupils' way of thinking about a child with intellectual disability. (The remaining terms were neutral or descriptive: neat, careful, different, shy and sloppy. These descriptive terms were not used in the present study as coefficient α was only 0.32.)

Irish–Spanish comparisons

Five separate three-way (nationality, gender and grade level) analyses of covariance[2] were undertaken with sociability, attitude to schooling and word use (positive, negative and sensitive words) as dependent variables.

Experience/inexperience of intellectual disability was used as a covariate since it has been shown to influence responses to these variables in previous studies. There were slight non-significant differences between samples in pupils who said they knew a child with intellectual disability (Spain 70%, Ireland 61%). Interaction effects were examined using post-hoc Scheffé contrasts ($p<0.05$).

The Spanish sample were more sociable towards children with intellectual disability than the Irish sample (Table 3) ($F(1, 230) = 59.84$, $p<0.001$). Girls were more sociable than boys ($F(1, 230) = 27.52$, $p<0.001$), and younger children than older children ($F(1, 230) = 11.19$, $p<0.005$). The simplicity of this picture is qualified by an interaction between nationality and gender, in which Spanish boys were only slightly less sociable than Spanish girls, whereas Irish boys were markedly less sociable than Irish girls ($F(1, 230) = 9.13$, $p<0.005$). Post-hoc Scheffé contrasts were used to examine the significance of mean differences between the four possible nationality–gender combinations. These contrasts showed that Irish boys were significantly less sociable than Irish girls and than both Spanish boys and girls; and that Irish girls were less sociable than Spanish girls. Irish and Spanish samples did not differ on the variable about schooling.

Table 3—Summaries of (un-)sociability in relation to intellectual disability by levels of country, and gender by country.

Variable	Value label	Mean	Std dev.	Cases
For entire population		12.30	2.13	239
COUNTRY	Irish	13.14	2.06	129
COUNTRY	Spanish	11.31	1.76	110
GRADE	Lower	12.15	2.03	110
GRADE	Upper	12.43	2.22	129
GENDER	Male	13.10	2.33	99
COUNTRY	Irish	14.25	1.91	56
COUNTRY	Spanish	11.60	1.97	43
GENDER	Female	11.73	1.78	140
COUNTRY	Irish	12.29	1.76	73
COUNTRY	Spanish	11.12	1.61	67

Irish pupils used significantly more positive terms than Spanish pupils (Table 4) ($F(1, 230) = 4.70$, $p<0.05$), and girls used significantly more than boys ($F(1, 230) = 31.15$, $p<0.001$). These findings are qualified by two interactions: first, a gender by grade interaction, in which with increasing age boys increased and girls decreased their use of positive adjectives ($F(1, 230) = 9.38$, $p<0.005$). Post-hoc contrasts showed that younger girls used significantly more positive words than both younger and older boys, and younger boys significantly less than older girls. However, these results must be interpreted in terms of the second interaction, gender by grade by nationality, which showed that only Irish boys increased their use of positive adjectives with increased age, whereas each of the other groups decreased slightly ($F(1, 230) = 4.57$, $p<0.05$). Post-hoc contrasts showed that the younger Irish boys used significantly less positive words than younger and older Irish girls and than younger Spanish girls; and younger Irish girls used significantly more than older Spanish boys.

Table 4—Summaries of use of positive adjectives in relation to intellectual disability by levels of country, gender by grade, and gender–grade and country.

Variable	Value label	Mean	Std dev.	Cases
For entire population		2.85	1.55	239
COUNTRY	Irish	3.02	1.57	129
COUNTRY	Spanish	2.65	1.51	110
GENDER	Male	2.23	1.60	99
GRADE	Lower	1.90	1.48	49
GRADE	Upper	2.56	1.66	50
GENDER	Female	3.28	1.36	140
GRADE	Lower	3.61	1.41	61
GRADE	Upper	3.03	1.28	79
COUNTRY	Irish	3.02	1.57	129
GENDER	Male	2.20	1.60	56
GRADE	Lower	1.66	1.33	32
GRADE	Upper	2.92	1.67	24
GENDER	Female	3.64	1.23	73
GRADE	Lower	3.92	1.26	38
GRADE	Upper	3.34	1.14	35

COUNTRY	Spanish	2.65	1.51	110
GENDER	Male	2.28	1.61	43
GRADE	Lower	2.35	1.66	17
GRADE	Upper	2.23	1.61	26
GENDER	Female	2.88	1.40	67
GRADE	Lower	3.09	1.50	23
GRADE	Upper	2.77	1.34	44

As might be expected from the results described above on use of positive adjectives, Spanish pupils used significantly more negative adjectives than Irish pupils (Table 5) ($F(1, 230) = 8.18$, $p<0.001$), girls used significantly fewer negative adjectives than boys ($F(1, 230) = 24.06$, $p<0.001$), and older children used significantly fewer negative words than younger children ($F(1, 230) = 4.91$, $p<0.05$). There was a significant interaction between nationality and age: with increased age Irish pupils used more negative terms while Spanish pupils used fewer negative terms ($F(1, 230) = 31.07$, $p<0.001$). The younger Spanish children were by far the greatest users of negative terms, and post-hoc contrasts showed that they differed significantly from each other in the grade–nationality group.

Table 5—Summaries of use of negative adjectives in relation to intellectual disability by levels of gender, grade, country, country by grade.

Variable	Value label	Mean	Std dev.	Cases
For entire population		2.53	3.27	239
GENDER	Male	3.57	4.05	99
GENDER	Female	1.80	2.33	140
GRADE	Lower	2.88	3.43	110
GRADE	Upper	2.23	3.10	129
COUNTRY	Irish	2.02	3.10	129
GRADE	Lower	1.56	2.42	70
GRADE	Upper	2.58	3.70	59
COUNTRY	Spanish	3.13	3.37	110
GRADE	Lower	5.20	3.72	40
GRADE	Upper	1.94	2.48	70

Table 6—Summaries of use of sensitive words in relation to intellectual disability by levels of country by grade.

Variable	Value label	Mean	Std dev.	Cases
For entire population		1.22	1.12	239
COUNTRY	Irish	1.40	1.15	129
GRADE	Lower	1.26	1.15	70
GRADE	Upper	1.58	1.13	59
COUNTRY	Spanish	1.00	1.04	110
GRADE	Lower	1.20	1.09	40
GRADE	Upper	0.89	1.00	70

Overall, Irish pupils used more sensitive terms than Spanish pupils ($F(1, 230)$ = 7.89, $p<0.005$). However, there was a nationality by grade interaction in which both national samples were similar at eight years of age; in the Irish sample the use of these terms increased with age, whereas in the Spanish sample use decreased with increase in grade (Table 6) ($F(1, 230)$ = 5.11, $p<0.05$). Post-hoc contrasts showed that the older Irish pupils used more sensitive words than the Spanish pupils.

Discussion

For two reasons it is wise to be cautious about these results. First, the samples are small and may not be representative of all Spanish and Irish children. Second, these comparisons are about children's perceptions of children with intellectual disability, so comparisons have not been made which reflect children's friendships in general in either culture. In fact, it is important to note that such judgements are unlikely to be made successfully with questionnaires like this, requiring children to respond to stereotyped images. The coefficients of internal consistency (Cronbach α) were sufficiently high, however, for us to be reasonably certain of the coherence of these data for this sample.

The Spanish sample differed from the Irish sample in a number of ways, though in each instance either gender or grade interactions were involved. The greater sociability of children in the Spanish sample was a striking difference. An interaction implied that Irish boys were less sociable than both Spanish boys and girls, and also than Irish girls; further, Irish girls were less sociable than Spanish girls. It is also noteworthy that Spanish boys and girls are very similar on this variable in contrast to the difference between Irish boys and girls.

How can the results be explained? We propose two related lines of argument. First, integration has been actively promoted in Spanish schools for a decade, so the idea of integration of children with intellectual disability has more public acceptance in Spain than in Ireland, where the policy to integrate is promoted and supported financially with less vigour. In the Spanish social context, therefore, it is reasonable to expect that more young children will be aware that children with intellectual disability go to school in some (integrated) primary schools. In Spain these integrated schools take in a small number of children with a special need into each entering class each year. In Ireland there is no policy of designating particular schools as integrated schools in this sense. While services are provided, at the time the data were collected over 50% of children with a specific disability in ordinary schools did not have access to a remedial teacher (Ireland 1993). On this line of argument, then, more Spanish children meet children with diverse forms of intellectual disability in schools. If some Spanish children have fears regarding children with intellectual disability, they express these fears early, as in this sample by younger children. We can argue that Spanish children are more sociable towards children with intellectual disability, especially in contrast to Irish boys, partly because the idea of socialising with them is not unexpected.

Second, because of their more varied experience, Spanish children's representations of intellectual disability may be less severe. In support of this, older Spanish children are less inclined to see children with intellectual disability as sad, lonely and unhappy because they are not like this in school. In contrast, older Irish children showed increased use of both negative and sensitive words, signalling that their representation of 'child with a mental handicap' is a rejected image. To examine these hypotheses in more detail, we compare data from a study focusing on children with Down Syndrome (Gash *et al.* 2000).

The main hypothesis is that sociability in Spanish pupils stems from the educational changes beginning in 1985 to promote integration. Consequently Spanish children have a more diversified and therefore less negative notion of intellectual disability than Irish children. If this is the case, differences between Irish and Spanish children in terms of socialising with Down Syndrome children may not exist.

STUDY 2: IRISH AND SPANISH ATTITUDES TO DOWN SYNDROME AND INTELLECTUAL DISABILITY

We believe that children's images of children with Down Syndrome are potentially less variable than images of children with 'a mental handicap'. Photographs of children with Down Syndrome were used to increase the homogeneity of understanding amongst the children. The questionnaire was the same as that used previously except that references to intellectual disability were replaced by references to Down Syndrome. The pupils selected from the Down

Syndrome data set were approximately the same grade (eight years old and eleven years old) and in non-integrated schools. There were differences between national samples in numbers of pupils who said they knew a child with Down Syndrome (Ireland 40%, Spain 64%) (2 (1) = 10.82, $p<0.001$). Total numbers of pupils are shown in Table 1. Internal consistencies of the five scales were checked and found to be essentially similar to those reported above for intellectual disability: for these data on Down Syndrome, the Cronbach's α for sociability was 0.70 (Irish sample 0.68; Spanish sample 0.74); for schooling 0.70 (Irish sample 0.73; Spanish sample 0.66); for use of positive words 0.69 (0.68 in both Spanish and Irish samples); for use of negative words 0.83 (Irish sample 0.84; Spanish sample 0.83); and for use of sensitive words 0.68 (Irish sample 0.61; Spanish sample 0.77).

Using these two data sets we investigated two questions. First, are children's responses to children with intellectual disability and Down Syndrome different using this questionnaire? Second, does this evidence support the idea that Irish and Spanish children differ in their responses? The analyses used to answer these questions followed the lines described above in the first study and are based partly on the data relating to Down Syndrome, and partly on the two data sets treated together. The strategy we adopted to answer these questions was first to analyse the data on Down Syndrome and then to repeat the analyses for the two data sets merged. We report summary analyses of covariance (levels of significance and F tests) for the five dependent variables for both the Down Syndrome data and the merged data set in Table 7, where for purposes of comparison we also show the parallel analyses for the study on intellectual disability just reported.

Table 7—Summary analyses of covariance (levels of significance and F tests) for the five dependent variables for both the Down Syndrome data and the merged data set.

	Both data sets	Mental handicap	Down Syndrome
	Sociability	Sociability	Sociability
DATABASE	$F(1,422)=4.01^*$		
NATION	$F(1,422)=39.61^{***}$	$F(1,230)=59.84^{***}$	
GENDER	$F(1,422)=13.52^{***}$	$F(1,230)=27.52^{***}$	
GRADE	$F(1,422)=16.18^{***}$	$F(1,230)=11.19^{***}$	$F(1,191)=6.41^*$
DATABASE X nation	$F(1,422)=14.65^{***}$		
DATABASE X gender	$F(1,422)=13.71^{***}$		
NATION X gender	$F(1,422)=3.89^*$	$F(1,230)=9.13^{**}$	

	Schooling	Schooling	Schooling
Database	F(1,416)=90.82***		
Nation	F(1,416)=3.91*		F(1,191)=5.09*
Gender	F(1,416)=4.54*	F(1,230)=8.71**	
Grade	F(1,416)=13.51***	F(1,230)=29.44***	
Database X gender	F(1,416)=5.00*		
Database X grade	F(1,416)=18.54***		
Nation X grade	F(1,416)=7.17**		F(1,191)=6.75**

Sociability and schooling

The answers to these questions are clearly affirmative in the case of sociability. We note first that in analysis of Down Syndrome data, grade level made a difference to mean sociability scores (eight-year-olds M 11.69; eleven-year-olds M 12.31), but country and gender had no effect. In other words, the greater sociability of Spanish children that we found towards children with intellectual disability disappears when attitudes of Spanish and Irish children towards children with Down Syndrome are compared. In terms of our interest in contrasting attitudes towards intellectual disability and Down Syndrome, we found that children were more sociable towards a child with Down Syndrome than towards a child with intellectual disability, though this difference depended on interactions described below. Comparative means and standard deviations of main effects and interactions are presented, beginning with Table 8.

Table 8—Summaries of (un-)sociability in the cases of both data sets by levels of database, nation, gender, grade, database by nation, and gender by database by nation.

Variable	Value label	Mean	Std dev.	Cases
For entire population		12.18	2.13	439
DATABASE	Intellectual disability	12.30	2.13	239
DATABASE	Down Syndrome	12.05	2.13	200
NATION	Ireland	2.74	2.12	244
NATION	Spain	11.49	1.95	195
GENDER	Male	12.52	2.32	211
GENDER	Female	11.87	1.90	228
GRADE	Eight	11.97	2.02	193
GRADE	Eleven	12.35	2.21	246

DATABASE	Intellectual disability	12.30	2.13	239
NATION	Ireland	13.14	2.06	129
NATION	Spain	11.31	1.76	110
DATABASE	Down Syndrome	12.05	2.13	200
NATION	Ireland	12.30	2.10	115
NATION	Spain	11.72	2.15	85
GENDER	Male	12.52	2.32	211
DATABASE	Intellectual disability	3.10	2.33	99
DATABASE	Down Syndrome	12.01	2.19	112
GENDER	Male	12.5	2.32	211
NATION	Ireland	13.23	2.32	115
NATION	Spain	11.67	2.02	96
GENDER	Female	11.87	1.90	228
DATABASE	Intellectual disability	11.73	1.78	140
DATABASE	Down Syndrome	12.10	2.07	88
GENDER	Female	11.87	1.90	228
NATION	Ireland	12.30	1.82	129
NATION	Spain	11.31	1.87	99

Total cases = 439

The interaction effects involving the database imply that mean scores for attitudes differed in the sample responding to questions concerning a child with intellectual disability as compared to the sample responding to questions about a child with Down Syndrome. There were interactions between database (intellectual disability or Down Syndrome data) and nationality, database (intellectual disability or Down Syndrome data) and gender, and between nationality and gender. Each of these interaction effects derives from differences in the intellectual disability data. The database–nationality interaction was due to a greater difference between the Spanish and Irish pupils in regard to their social attitudes towards a child with intellectual disability as compared to their social attitudes towards a child with Down Syndrome. Post-hoc Schaffé contrasts of this interaction showed that Irish pupils were less sociable towards a pupil with intellectual disability than towards a pupil with Down Syndrome and also less sociable than the Spanish pupils were to either group (intellectual disability or Down Syndrome). We note, however, that Spanish and Irish children's attitudes towards Down Syndrome did not differ, and further that the Spanish children's attitudes towards intellectual disability were not different from their attitudes to Down Syndrome. The database gender interaction arose because boys were less sociable than girls towards a child with intellectual disability. Post-hoc contrasts of the database–gender interaction showed that the boys' social attitudes towards a pupil with intellectual disability were less sociable than girls' attitudes, and also less sociable than boys' and girls' attitudes towards a pupil with Down Syndrome. The nationality–gender interaction depended on the interaction shown earlier in the case of attitudes towards intellectual disability and was due entirely to the strong unsociable sentiments of Irish boys in the intellectual disability data. These sentiments did not hold in the case of Down Syndrome, where boys and girls had virtually identical mean sociability scores in each national sample (Ireland: boys M 12.26, girls M 12.32; Spain: boys M 11.72, girls M 11.72).

While we noted earlier that there were no general differences between Irish and Spanish pupils in their perception of schooling and integration for pupils with intellectual disability, there were differences in the case of Down Syndrome (Table 9). This difference was robust and did not depend on the nationality by grade level interaction for the Down Syndrome data; post-hoc examination of means showed that this arose because the Irish eight-year-old pupils were significantly more favourably disposed towards integrated schooling than the Spanish eight-year-old pupils, or less aware of the difficulties. The scores of the Irish and Spanish eleven-year-olds were very similar.

Table 9—Summaries of attitudes towards inclusion for Down Syndrome data (only), nation by grade.

For entire population		7.52	1.68	203
NATION	Ireland	7.31	1.63	118
GRADE	Eight	6.98	1.28	58
GRADE	Eleven	7.62	1.87	60
NATION	Spain	7.81	1.72	85
GRADE	Eight	8.26	1.87	27
GRADE	Eleven	7.60	1.62	58

Total cases = 203

Pupils perceived greater difficulties in educating a pupil with intellectual disability versus a pupil with Down Syndrome in an integrated classroom (Table 10); Irish pupils were less aware of problems with integration than Spanish pupils; younger pupils were more wary of integration than older pupils, and boys more wary than girls. These significant differences depend on the interactions database by gender, database and grade, and nationality and grade. The difference between Irish and Spanish children overall depended on the views of the younger Spanish pupils, who perceived greater difficulties in integration than the older Spanish pupils and than the younger and older Irish pupils. The database–gender interaction showed that it was the negative attitudes of boys towards the integration of pupils with intellectual disability that contributed strongly to differences in attitude between intellectual disability and Down Syndrome; and the database–grade interaction showed a strong negative influence of younger children towards integration of pupils with intellectual disability.

Table 10—Summaries of attitudes towards inclusion in the cases of both data sets by levels of database.

Variable	Value label	Mean	Std dev.	Cases
For entire population		8.37	2.00	433
DATABASE	Intellectual disability	9.10	1.95	233
DATABASE	Down Syndrome	7.52	1.69	200
NATION	Ireland	8.22	1.99	240
NATION	Spain	8.50	2.00	193
GRADE	Eight	8.75	2.05	189
GRADE	Eleven	8.07	1.90	244
GENDER	Male	8.45	2.00	209
GENDER	Female	8.29	2.00	224
GRADE	Eight	8.75	2.05	189
DATABASE	Intellectual disability	9.83	1.69	106
DATABASE	Down Syndrome	7.37	1.61	83
GRADE	Eleven	8.07	1.90	244
DATABASE	Intellectual disability	8.49	1.96	127
DATABASE	Down Syndrome	7.62	1.75	117
GRADE	Eight	8.75	2.05	189
NATION	Ireland	8.38	2.00	123
NATION	Spain	9.44	1.98	66
GRADE	Eleven	8.07	1.90	244
NATION	Ireland	8.04	1.96	117
NATION	Spain	8.10	1.86	127
DATABASE	Intellectual disability	9.10	1.95	233
GENDER	Male	9.55	1.82	97

GENDER	Female	8.78	1.99	136
DATABASE	Down Syndrome	7.52	1.69	200
GENDER	Male	7.51	1.63	112
GENDER	Female	7.53	1.77	88

Total cases = 433

The general pattern reported above for the data on intellectual disability was repeated for the data on Down Syndrome in relation to the use of positive and negative words (Table 11). Only the results for the use of positive words will be reported here since the results for the negative words are very similar, though opposite, to the results for positive words. In relation to Down Syndrome children, Irish pupils (M 3.45) used significantly more positive words than Spanish pupils (M 2.72); there was no gender difference as there had been in the case of intellectual disability, but there was a difference between eight-year-olds (M 3.69) and eleven-year-olds (M 2.75). Children used more positive words to describe the child with Down Syndrome than a child with intellectual disability. All of these four main effects were robust in the sense that they did not depend on the interaction effects explaining ways in which these variables influence each other.

Table 11—Summaries of use of positive adjectives in the cases of both data sets by levels of database, nation, gender, grade, database by grade, database by gender, and nation by gender by grade.

Variable	Value label	Mean	Std dev.	Cases
For entire population		2.97	1.55	439
DATABASE	Intellectual disability	2.85	1.55	239
DATABASE	Down Syndrome	3.13	1.54	200
NATION	Ireland	3.21	1.53	244
NATION	Spain	2.68	1.53	195
GENDER	Male	2.65	1.60	211
GENDER	Female	3.28	1.44	228
GRADE	Eight	3.20	1.61	193
GRADE	Eleven	2.80	1.48	246
DATABASE	Intellectual disability	2.85	1.55	239
GRADE	Eight	2.85	1.67	110
GRADE	Eleven	2.85	1.45	129

DATABASE	Down Syndrome	3.13	1.54	200
GRADE	Eight	3.67	1.42	83
GRADE	Eleven	2.74	1.51	117
DATABASE	Intellectual disability	2.85	1.55	239
GENDER	Male	2.23	1.60	99
GENDER	Female	3.28	1.36	140
DATABASE	Down Syndrome	3.13	1.54	200
GENDER	Male	3.02	1.52	112
GENDER	Female	3.27	1.55	88
GENDER	Male	2.65	1.60	211
GRADE	Eight	2.69	1.64	95
GRADE	Eleven	2.61	1.58	116
GENDER	Female	3.28	1.44	228
GRADE	Eight	3.69	1.42	98
GRADE	Eleven	2.96	1.37	130
NATION	Ireland	3.21	1.53	244
GENDER	Male	2.76	1.65	115
GRADE	Eight	2.60	1.68	60
GRADE	Eleven	2.93	1.62	55
GENDER	Female	3.62	1.28	129
GRADE	Eight	3.98	1.16	66
GRADE	Eleven	3.24	1.30	63
NATION	Spain	2.68	1.53	195
GENDER	Male	2.52	1.54	96
GRADE	Eight	2.86	1.59	35
GRADE	Eleven	2.33	1.49	61
GENDER	Female	2.83	1.51	99
GRADE	Eight	3.09	1.73	32
GRADE	Eleven	2.70	1.38	67
DATABASE	Intellectual disability	2.85	1.55	239
GENDER	Male	2.23	1.60	99
GRADE	Eight	1.90	1.48	49
GRADE	Eleven	2.56	1.66	50
GENDER	Female	3.28	1.36	140
GRADE	Eight	3.61	1.41	61
GRADE	Eleven	3.03	1.28	79

DATABASE	Down Syndrome	3.13	1.54	200
GENDER	Male	3.02	1.52	112
GRADE	Eight	3.54	1.38	46
GRADE	Eleven	2.65	1.52	66
GENDER	Female	3.27	1.55	88
GRADE	Eight	3.84	1.46	37
GRADE	Eleven	2.86	1.50	51

Total cases = 439

There were interactions between the database (intellectual disability or Down Syndrome) and gender; between database and grade; between gender and grade; between database–gender and grade; and between nation–gender and grade. The boys used less positive words than girls in the case of intellectual disability, whereas there was less difference between them in the case of Down Syndrome. Post-hoc comparisons showed that boys in their judgements on intellectual disability were less positive than girls in relation to intellectual disability and to either boys or girls in regard to Down Syndrome. The eight-year-olds and eleven-year-olds used identical numbers of positive adjectives in the case of intellectual disability, whereas in the case of Down Syndrome younger children used more positive words than older children and more than their peers in the case of intellectual disability. The gender by grade interaction showed that the eight-year-old girls used more positive words than their peers; and the database-gender by grade interaction showed that both boys and girls used fewer positive adjectives when they were older whether they were describing Down Syndrome or intellectual disability, except in the case of intellectual disability where the older boys used more positive adjectives. The nationality by gender by grade interaction signalled that the tendency for older children to use fewer positive words held in each gender-grade combination except the Irish eleven-year-old pupils, who used more positive words than the eight-year-old Irish pupils. The eight-year-old Irish girls were the highest users of positive words.

Finally in this analysis we turn to the significant nationality by grade interaction in the use of sensitive words to describe the child with Down Syndrome (Table 12). Again post-hoc Scheffé contrasts show that this is due to the difference between the older Spanish and Irish children. However, in this case the direction of change is reversed. Now the older Spanish children use these sensitive words more frequently than the younger children, and the older Irish children use them less frequently than the younger Irish children. In the comparison of the images of intellectual disability and Down Syndrome we find a reversal of this trend: the older Irish children tend to use these sensitive words for children with intellectual disability, whereas the older Spanish children use these words more for children with Down Syndrome.

Table 12—Summaries of use of 'sad, lonely and unhappy' in the cases of both data sets by levels of gender, and database by nation by grade.

Variable	Value label	Mean	Std dev.	Cases
For entire population		1.11	1.10	439
GENDER	Male	1.20	1.06	211
GENDER	Female	1.03	1.13	228
DATABASE	Intellectual disability	1.22	1.12	239
NATION	Ireland	1.40	1.15	129
GRADE	Eight	1.26	1.15	70
GRADE	Eleven	1.58	1.13	59
NATION	Spain	1.00	1.04	110
GRADE	Eight	1.20	1.09	40
GRADE	Eleven	0.89	1.00	70
DATABASE	Down Syndrome	0.99	1.07	200
NATION	Ireland	0.90	.97	115
GRADE	Eight	.05	1.02	56
GRADE	Eleven	0.76	0.92	59
NATION	Spain	1.09	1.18	85
GRADE	Eight	0.63	0.97	27
GRADE	Eleven	1.31	1.22	58

Total cases = 439

Discussion

The data on Down Syndrome provide a number of interesting contrasts to the earlier data on intellectual disability. First, Spanish pupils had been found to be more sociable than Irish pupils towards a child with intellectual disability: however, here Spanish and Irish pupils did not differ from each other in regard to their social attitudes towards a child with Down Syndrome. Also the two samples of Spanish pupils did not differ from one another in their attitude to Down Syndrome as compared to intellectual disability. This is consistent with the view that the image of intellectual disability in the minds of the Irish pupils was more severe, but was more varied in the minds of the Spanish pupils. The image that Irish pupils have of the child with intellectual disability may be negative and unsociable for a number of reasons. It may be that it was an unspecified, unknown and possibly severe form of intellectual disability that led to the essentially negative social reaction of the Irish pupils. If this is so, it is important to note. It may also be that the Spanish pupils have a more varied view of intellectual disability because of the changes implemented in the Spanish system since 1985.

The possible influence of the Spanish integration project on the feasibility of inclusion as described in these data is interesting. The younger Spanish children were far more reticent about inclusion of a Down Syndrome child than their Irish peers. Generally in these studies older children tend to be more open to inclusion when the target is a child with intellectual disability handicap (e.g. Gash 1993; Gash and Coffey 1995). It may be the case that the Irish children are more sympathetic to Down Syndrome and less experienced. In Gash 1993 reference was made to the spontaneous goodwill expressed on this type of questionnaire by inexperienced Irish children towards a child with intellectual disability. This goodwill may be what lies behind the greater use of positive adjectives by Irish children in their descriptions of both a child with intellectual disability and a child with Down Syndrome.

Taking this further, in Study 1 we argued that Spanish children, through their experience, might learn by the end of primary school that pupils with intellectual disability are not sad, lonely and unhappy. In the present study on Down Syndrome, arguing again on the greater awareness of the Spanish pupils, we find that their image of Down Syndrome children at the end of primary school is indeed one of sadness, loneliness and unhappiness. Whether this is an accurate portrayal of the situation is a moot point. It may be that this says something very important about the pupils themselves and their relation to Down Syndrome children. A recent study made observations of the Irish experience of Down Syndrome children in integrated educational contexts (Bennett *et al.* 1998). In one school each morning there was an optional set-dancing class for interested pupils. One of the pupils with Down Syndrome who was ten years old at the time had ceased coming to the dancing class because she had noticed that the other children were becoming reluctant to dance with her. It may well be that the older Spanish children are more aware of rejection of some children with Down Syndrome in their age group.

It has long been known that attitudes to minority groups can be changed positively under appropriate conditions. It is most encouraging that in this sample the Spanish educational system has succeeded in promoting sociability towards children with intellectual disability in their school system. It is to be hoped that this finding is generalised in Spain because children with learning difficulties are often not well received in schools (Ochoa and Olivarez 1995).

THE VALIDITY STUDY

The research described in the first two studies has used questionnaires to assess children's attitudes. A frequently unexamined assumption in questionnaire research of this type is the relation between children's attitudes expressed on the questionnaire and their actual behaviour. Teachers frequently express the opinion that children are strongly influenced by social desirability in responding. This attitude may lead some to question the value of using questionnaires to assess children's attitudes. The present investigation was designed partly to assess the usefulness of this questionnaire and also as a tool to assess the effects of experience of integration on children's attitudes towards physical and intellectual disability in primary schools. Prior to the summer holidays two Dublin schools anticipated having a new included sixth class in September. A girl with a physical disability was to come to one school and a boy with Down Syndrome was to come to the other school. Both the process of integration and the questionnaire itself are evaluated here through use of qualitative and quantitative methods.

Method

Procedure
Questionnaires were given to all fifth-class children in the two urban schools in the summer term, and to the same children about nine months later just before Easter. Each school had more than one classroom at these grade levels and it was not known which would be the integrated class in each school until the school year began. In September, between these two assessments, a girl with a physical disability came to the girls' school and a boy with Down Syndrome came to the boys' school. The teachers who taught these integrated classes were interviewed after the school year had ended about their experiences during the year in their integrated class.

Sample
Pre-test and post-test questionnaires for children were matched for the data analysis. The matched sample in the girls' school consisted of 44 control children and 18 'integrated' children, and that in the boys' school comprised 28 control children and 30 'integrated' children. (A few children were missing on either pre-test or post-test dates.)

The questionnaires
The questionnaire used on the pre-test and the post-test was identical to that described earlier in this chapter except that references to physical disability replaced references to intellectual disability in the case of the girls' school.

Results

The attitudinal variables

Attitudinal variables were created with these data on the basis of factor analyses portraying aspects of sociability and views on schooling. In addition, variables were constructed from descriptive words by creating a score based on the number of words used in categories such as positive, negative and sensitive. On account of the different foci of these questionnaires (physical disability, Down Syndrome) results were analysed separately for girls and boys. Changes in the pupils' scores of five different measures (sociability, schooling, and use of positive, negative and sensitive words) were examined from pre-test to post-test. Repeated measures (pre-test and post-test) analysis of covariance[3] was used with experience/inexperience of intellectual/physical disability as covariate because this variable had been shown to influence children's answers in previous studies. Means are reported in Table 13 for girls and Table 14 for boys.

The first factor was about schooling. Items loading on this were about the child with intellectual or physical disability being able to do the same maths (item 12), reading (item 13) and hobbies (item 14) as the other children, and the three items about schooling (16 to 18). Items 17 and 18 were recoded (1=2; 2=1), as in the other studies. In other words, low scores on this variable imply an acceptance of total integration and of the ability of the child with intellectual disability to cope in ordinary classrooms. The reliability of each scale was assessed using Cronbach's α which was 0.69 for this variable (0.68 for boys, 0.71 for girls).

In the case of attitudes towards physical disability, girls changed their ideas about schooling from pre-test to post-test ($F(1,61) = 20.59$, $p<0.001$), but there was no significant difference between pupils in the control class and in the integrated classroom. If we look at the means we see improvement in attitudes towards integrated schooling on the post-test. In the case of boys and their attitudes to schooling of a child with Down Syndrome, pre-test and post-test scores also differed. The general pre-test to post-test change was not specific to either control or integrated classroom ($F(1,55) = 13.76$, $p<0.001$). However, in this case the direction of change is different. These pupils had understood difficulties with classroom inclusion and were noticing differences in ability and thinking more favourably about separate education options.

Table 13—Pre-test and post-test means and standard deviations in girls' attitudes towards physical disability.

Attitude to schooling

Variable	Label	Mean	Std dev.	Cases
For entire population pre-test		7.52	1.81	64
CONDITION	Control pre-test	7.41	1.62	44
CONDITION	Integrated pre-test	7.75	2.20	20
For entire population post-test		6.41	0.75	64
CONDITION	Control post-test	6.27	0.79	44
CONDITION	Integrated post-test	6.70	0.57	20

Sociability for girls

For entire population pre-test		9.41	1.56	64
CONDITION	Control pre-test	9.52	1.62	44
CONDITION	Integrated pre-test	9.15	1.42	20
For entire population post-test		7.86	1.92	64
CONDITION	Control post-test	7.61	2.12	44
CONDITION	Integrated post-test	8.40	1.27	20

Girls' use of positive words

For entire population pre-test		3.05	1.52	64
CONDITION	Control pre-test	2.93	1.53	44
CONDITION	Integrated pre-test	3.30	1.49	20
For entire population post-test		3.48	1.45	64
CONDITION	Control post-test	3.30	1.50	44
CONDITION	Integrated post-test	3.90	1.25	20

Girls' use of sensitive words

For entire population pre-test		0.97	1.10	64
CONDITION	Control pre-test	0.86	1.07	44
CONDITION	Integrated pre-test	1.20	1.15	20

For entire population post-test		0.47	0.85	64
CONDITION	Control post-test	0.45	0.70	44
CONDITION	Integrated post-test	0.50	1.15	20

The second factor dealing with sociability towards the child with an intellectual or physical disability was made up of items based on the following dispositions: a willingness to smile at him/her (item 1), to sit beside him/her (item 2), to chat to him/her (item 3), to tell secrets to him/her (item 4), to have him/her as a best friend (item 5), to invite him/her home (item 6) or to a birthday party (item 8), to include him/her on their team (item 9), to be concerned if he/she were teased (item 11), and (not) to be upset if he/she broke the rules of a game (item 7, which was recoded). Recall that on all attitudinal items 'yes' scores one and 'no' scores two: low scores therefore imply a greater disposition to sociability. The internal consistency of this scale for this sample was unacceptably low (0.31), so the scale was refined for boys and girls separately, subtracting items to increase α. An α of 0.61 was obtained with items 2, 3, 5, 6, 8 and 11 for boys, and an α of 0.52 was obtained for items 2, 3, 4, 5, 6, 8 and 9 for girls. We created separate variables for girls and boys by adding scores together on these items.

In the case of girls' attitudes towards physical disability there were increases in sociability from pre-test to post-test ($F(1,61) = 26.50$, $p<0.001$); in addition, attitudes in the control class changed more than in the integrated class ($F(1,61) = 5.25$, $p<0.05$). In the case of boys' attitudes towards Down Syndrome there were decreases in sociability from pre-test to post-test but no difference between control and integrated classes ($F(1,55) = 24.17$, $p<0.001$).

The descriptive variables
These variables were created as described in previous studies. The positive terms were as follows: clever, kind, friendly, lovable and happy; Cronbach's α was 0.70 for the sample (boys 0.68; girls 0.71). The negative words were: dirty, stupid, untidy, bold, dumb, rough, spa, crazy, geek, thick, simple, scary, dork, retarded, moron, twit, freak, idiot and nerd. Removing the words 'simple' and 'retarded' from this list boosted Cronbach's α to 0.78 for the sample (boys 0.73; girls 0.85). Finally, the sensitive words were: special, sad, lonely, ashamed and unhappy. Removing the word 'special' from this list brought Cronbach's α to 0.61 (boys 0.60; girls 0.62).

Boys describing a Down Syndrome pupil increased in their use of negative words from pre-test to post-test ($F(1,55) = 29.16$, $p<0.001$), and decreased in their use of both positive words ($F(1,55) = 10.19$, $p<0.002$) and sensitive words ($F(1,55) = 5.48$, $p<0.05$). There were no differences between control and integrated groups on these variables.

Table 14—Pre-test and post-test means and standard deviations in boys' attitudes towards Down Syndrome.

Attitude to schooling

Variable	Label	Mean	Std dev.	Cases
For entire population pre-test		7.17	1.63	58
CONDITION	Control pre-test	7.14	1.78	28
CONDITION	Integrated pre-test	7.20	1.52	30
For entire population post-test		8.21	1.96	58
CONDITION	Control post-test	8.50	1.95	28
CONDITION	Integrated post-test	7.93	1.96	30

Sociability for boys

For entire population pre-test		7.88	1.50	58
CONDITION	Control pre-test	8.18	1.68	28
CONDITION	Integrated pre-test	7.60	1.28	30
For entire population post-test		9.28	2.02	58
CONDITION	Control post-test	9.61	1.23	28
CONDITION	Integrated post-test	8.97	2.53	30

Boys' use of negative words

For entire population pre-test		0.72	1.36	58
CONDITION	Control pre-test	1.07	1.51	28
CONDITION	Integrated pre-test	0.40	1.13	30
For entire population post-test		3.57	4.35	58
CONDITION	Control post-test	3.43	4.41	28
CONDITION	Integrated post-test	3.70	4.36	30

Boys' use of positive words

For entire population pre-test		2.28	1.54	58
CONDITION	Control pre-test	1.93	1.46	28
CONDITION	Integrated pre-test	2.60	1.57	30
For entire population post-test		1.52	1.62	58
CONDITION	Control post-test	1.54	1.62	28
CONDITION	Integrated post-test	1.50	1.66	30

Boys' use of sensitive words

For entire population pre-test		1.33	1.21	58
CONDITION	Control pre-test	1.54	1.32	28
CONDITION	Integrated pre-test	1.13	1.07	30
For entire population post-test		0.86	0.93	58
CONDITION	Control post-test	0.89	0.83	28
CONDITION	Integrated post-test	0.83	1.02	30

Girls describing a pupil with physical disabillity increased in their use of positive words from pre-test to post-test ($F(1,61) = 5.29$, $p<0.05$) and decreased in their use of sensitive words ($F(1,61) = 9.95$, $p<0.002$). There were no differences between control and integrated groups on these variables.

Qualitative data

The teacher of the integrated class in the boys' school explained that he had 39 boys in his class. This is a large number by any standards. At the beginning of the year he told his pupils that Mike (not his real name) was a boy with Down Syndrome coming to their classroom; he spoke to the pupils about ways they might relate to Mike, and how he was different. For about one month there were no major problems, then some boys in a remedial group started to make things difficult. There were problems in a number of areas: Mike was taught some bad language; when the boys lined up to leave the room, Mike often wanted to be first in line and the others became less willing to allow this as time went on; in football games the others cooperated to allow Mike to play for about five minutes, and then he was ignored; finally, his manner of speaking was mocked. These problems did not seem to affect him as much as the teacher feared. At times Mike was upset, though mostly for little things like not being lent an eraser or a pencil sharpener. The boys would sometimes urge Mike to dance, which he did willingly but clumsily. This was malicious on the boys' part, but when Mike noticed them mocking him he seemed to interpret it as applause. He even bowed in thanks, and this infuriated the others! The teacher felt that it might have been easier to integrate Mike if he had arrived earlier into the school, and if the whole school had been involved in his inclusion. However, in spite of these difficulties the teacher reported that Mike's mother had learned important coping skills, and she was pleased with what Mike had learned. At the end of the year he moved on to a local comprehensive school.

In the girls' school the teacher of the integrated class talked about Susan (not her real name) to the fifth classes in June. She spoke about her primarily as a new girl, though her physical disability was mentioned in terms of her needing help on the stairs. Susan had a strong personality and did not like to be too dependent on others. When she fell she preferred to get up herself, and the girls rapidly learned to let her be independent. The teacher was surprised at how quickly the girls accepted her. Susan used to lend the girls her crutches and she laughed with them at their efforts to use them at break time. When Susan did need help on the stairs, the girls helped her without being prompted by teachers. Also, the girls found ways to include her in their activities. When they played rounders, she bowled and was given a chair so that she could do this. In many ways the school was unsuitable; it had stairs that had to be negotiated with some pain each day and which may have caused Susan physical problems. She came to the school to join a sixth class, which is late, and she also changed home at the same time, moving to the school's locality. This was partly so as to be near a suitable secondary school. Her experiences in this school were significantly better than they had been in her previous school, where she was sometimes teased and mocked.

Discussion

The most striking feature of these results is the difference between the experience of integration in the girls' school and in the boys' school. Secondly, these results provide strong support for the validity of the questionnaire as a measure of children's attitudes. In the case of the girls' school there were a number of positive effects, not specific to the integration class. Over the period of the study the girls became more positive about inclusion of children with a physical disability; they became more positive socially, particularly in the unintegrated classroom; and they used more positive words to describe a child with a physical disability.

In the case of the boys' school the differences between pre-test and post-test were in the opposite direction. On the post-test the boys used more negative words, fewer positive words, saw more difficulties with inclusive education, and were less sociable. This picture was confirmed by the qualitative data based on the teacher interview. In previous studies boys have shown more negative attitudes (e.g. Gash 1993; 1996). It is clear that in the present study these negative attitudes increased.

Finally, there was a decrease in use of sensitive words in both boys' and girls' samples. The children in each school seem to have learned not to think of these different pupils as sad, lonely, ashamed and unhappy. This is in itself encouraging and shows that there is a need to avoid stereotyping of children with special educational needs, such as learning to think of them as helpless and in need of babying.

This study also highlights the need to prepare carefully for integration. There are a series of well-documented steps that schools ought to follow prior to integrating pupils with special needs. These include explaining the new situation to all staff and pupils because the attitudes of the staff and pupils especially have implications for the success of integration.

AN EVALUATION OF INTEGRATION AT SECOND LEVEL

There are a series of primary schools in Ireland now with special classes, and increasingly there are pupils with special needs who attend primary school and are included in ordinary classrooms. The *Report of the Special Education Review Committee* (Ireland 1993; hereafter referred to as SERC) provides information about the numbers of pupils with different disabilities who receive their education in special schools and in special classes in ordinary schools, and a survey was undertaken to find out how many pupils with special needs were in ordinary classes. SERC reported that at that time there were nine special classes in ordinary National Schools for pupils with moderate intellectual disability, with an enrolment of 81. Data for the evaluation reported here were collected in the academic year 1993–4. There are few opportunities for children with moderate intellectual disability to be guaranteed a place in second-level schools. This is an issue being vigorously addressed in Spain at present. In Ireland at this time it seems that it is being dealt with informally between parents and schools rather than formally. More recently it has moved to the courts. In the present case a class of pupils with moderate intellectual disability moved to a second-level school in a small town in Ireland and so became the first special class at this secondary school. This was the first time this had happened in Ireland. It was possible to give the incoming group of ordinary pupils this questionnaire in September and then again in May to assess the effects of the experience of integration on these pupils. In some ways the present study was like the previous validation study, but in this case the purpose of the study was simply to check on the experience.

Method

The questionnaire was administered to the incoming class of second-level pupils. They were asked to use the questionnaire bearing in mind that it had been designed for primary pupils and so they might not find some questions entirely appropriate for their age level. Fifty-three pupils (44 boys and nine girls) completed the questionnaire on pre-test and post-test.

Results

The same methods of analysis were used as before (analysis of covariance with repeated measures on the same five dependent variables and using experience of intellectual disability as the covariate). There were significant differences between pre-test and post-test scores on sociability ($F(1,50) = 10.00$, $p<0.005$; pre-test M 13.96, post-test M 13.00) and sensitive words ($F(1,50) = 6.72$, $p<0.05$; pre-test M 0.88, post-test M 0.48). The other three dependent variables (attitudes to integrated schooling, and use of positive and negative words) did not change from pre-test to post-test.

Discussion

These results provide reassuring quantitative evidence of the success of this integration experience at second level. The change in the mean sociability scores, showing clear improvements in the levels of sociability from pre-test to post-test, is most encouraging. Similarly the decrease in the sensitivity score is welcome and provides reassurance. We note that decreases in frequency of the words 'sad, lonely and unhappy' during the year by the pupils show that the level of use of these words in September had halved by the end of the school year. This is a most encouraging sign. The informal evidence has also been supportive of the success of this experience and this special class continues in this secondary school at the time of writing.

A QUALITATIVE APPROACH TO PERCEPTION OF DOWN SYNDROME IN IRELAND AND SPAIN

Following on from the use of the present questionnaire in research in Ireland and Spain, a study on Down Syndrome was undertaken using an open rather than a closed approach. The purpose of the investigation was to further our understanding of two main dimensions in this questionnaire: (1) the ways in which children in each country think about socialising with Down Syndrome children, and (2) how children think about the inclusion of children with Down Syndrome in class at school. Eleven-year-old children were asked to write answers to questions about this in essay format. This age group was chosen as it corresponded to the highest age in Spanish primary schools. The first question was: 'Do you think children with Down Syndrome should attend ordinary schools?' A second question, asked only in Spain, was: 'What do you know about Down Syndrome children?' The third question was: 'If you know someone with Down Syndrome, how do you feel about relating with him or her?' In Spain one class in each of three schools participated; two schools (A and C) were integrated and one (B) was not. In Ireland one class in each of two unintegrated schools participated. There were approximately 25 pupils in each of the five classes sampled.

Generally there were three types of answers to the first question about integration: social reasons, principles and educational reasons. The social reasons included reference to the system of relations, together with positive and negative consequences. Principles and beliefs were either positive or negative valuations of the difference between Down Syndrome children and others. There were three types of educational reasons mentioned: limitations in regard to learning, reference to academic benefits in special educational opportunities, and reference to benefits in ordinary educational contexts.

There were five categories of answer to the question: 'What do you know about children with Down Syndrome?' There were the representations of a sick person, of someone less intelligent, of someone deformed physically, of someone kind-hearted or friendly, and of a clumsy person.

There were four major categories in response to the third question about how the pupils feel about social relations with Down Syndrome children. There were expressions of pity and sadness, the idea that feelings should not be different in relation to a child with Down Syndrome, feelings of satisfaction for helping a child with Down Syndrome together with feelings of personal growth in developing a relationship with a child with Down Syndrome, and finally the recognition of feelings of discomfort in oneself or in others.

Question 1: 'Do you think that children with Down Syndrome should go to ordinary schools?'
Category 1. Social reasons. Subcategory 1.1. Systems of relations.

Positive consequences

'If they went to ordinary schools they could communicate with the other children' 7a[4]

'Because they could relate to all the others' 15a, 19a, 3c, 4c, 15c, 17c, 21*, 42*, 43*

'Yes because they are great fun' 6*

'Yes because there is no need for them to be treated differently, or teased' 15*, 16*, 23*, 41*, 46*

'Yes they should go to ordinary schools, otherwise they would feel excluded' 29*, 38*

Negative consequences

'They should go to a special school because otherwise they would be teased' 9*

'They could not make friends in an ordinary school' 9b

'If they went to a special school they would feel better and have friends like themselves' 2*, 5*

Commentary

The benefits seen for integrated education in ordinary schools for children with Down Syndrome were noted by only certain pupils in the Spanish schools A and C and some Irish pupils (indicated thus *). Not one pupil in school B gave a response that could be classified in this subcategory. In the same way we notice that pupils from school B and some Irish pupils give the negative consequences. As you can see in the description given of the different schools in Spain, it is schools A and C that have the best reputation for the quality of teaching and educational practice. The essays of the Irish pupils (indicated*) in this category reflect their position against exclusion and show that they are very positive about inclusive education because this type of education will avoid children with Down Syndrome feeling different. The positive consequences cited by Spanish pupils from schools A and C were mainly about relations between children and about communication.

Question 1: 'Do you think that children with Down Syndrome should go to ordinary schools?'
Category 1. Social reasons. Subcategory 1.2. Systems of emotion and effect.

Positive consequences	Negative consequences
'One can give them more affection' 5a	'The other children insult them all the time' 18b
'They are treated better' 19a	'They would be intimidated and alone' 19b
'They have more friends' 11a, 16b	'If they went to an ordinary class they would be teased' 19*, 28*, 32*
'They can be helped to learn for life' 13*, 21*, 49*	

Commentary

Again Spanish pupils from school B and some Irish pupils gave the negative consequences. No pupil from schools A and C gave negative comments. On the contrary, the Spanish pupils from schools A and C maintained a position respecting the inclusion of children with Down Syndrome in ordinary schools. On this basis one can say that they value positively the inclusion of Down Syndrome children in ordinary classes because they are treated better there, and because they can be cared for by the other children.

Question 1: 'Do you think that children with Down Syndrome should go to ordinary schools?'
Category 2. Principles and beliefs.

Subcategory 2.1 Positive value placed on the difference

'They are our equals, they are like us' 14a, 22a, 12a, 15a, 16a, 17a, 20a, 10*, 12*, 13*, 15*, 17*, 18*, 23*, 26*, 30*, 40*, 44*, 45*

'They are people, not extraterrestrials' 14c

'They are not sick' 12a

'They are like us, though they have this horrible sickness' 18a

'They are like us though they have this grave defect' 4a, 4*, 35*

'They are like us though some people might be afraid of them' 50*

'I think that they themselves ought to decide which school to go to' 14*, 31*, 36*

Subcategory 2.2 Negative value placed on the difference

'They are not like us and so they should go to schools specially for them' 21a, 2b, 7b, 12b, 21b

'It should be that the others should be sick like him. Since they are sick they can't relate to their friends' 15b

Commentary

Again we note that the positive comments come from the same schools (A and C). All the negative comments come from school B. It is interesting to note that no Irish pupil made a negative comment about the difference.

Question 1: 'Do you think that children with Down Syndrome should go to ordinary schools?'
Category 3. Educational reasons.

Subcategory 3.1 Limitations in relation to learning	Subcategory 3.2 Academic benefits in special education contexts	Subcategory 3.3 Academic benefits in ordinary school contexts
'They are not capable of the school work' 17	'They need a special school, if in an ordinary school there are not teachers who can teach them, it is better they go to a school specially for them' 13a, 22*	'In an ordinary school one can teach them and they will learn more and better' 1a, 5a, 6a, 3c, 4c, 10c, 18c, 9*, 28*
'They could not do the work, they would complain about being left behind because they need a great deal of attention' 14b, 8*	'In a special school the teachers have more patience to teach them' 26b	'Although they need more things explained they should go to ordinary schools' 17a, 7*, 37*
'They do not understand anything' 11*	'They need special schools with specialist teachers who know how to teach them. If they go to ordinary schools the teachers do not know how to treat them' 1b, 3b, 25b, 6c	
	'They should go to a special school because in the ordinary class the teacher can not give them enough attention' 1*, 33*	
	'They could share their teaching between a special school and an ordinary classroom' 24b	

Commentary

The limitations to learning are only mentioned by the pupils in school B and by some Irish pupils. No responses occur in this category from schools A and C. If we look at the ideas expressed in Subcategory 3.2 on the benefits of special schools for children with Down Syndrome, they are largely expressed by pupils from school B and some Irish pupils (*). There are only two pupils—one from school A and the other from school C—who mention the benefits of a special school. (There were 22 pupils sampled from school A and 18 from school B.)

Question 2 (Spanish sample only):
'What do you know about children with Down Syndrome?'

Category I Image of a sick person	Category II Image of a less intelligent person	Category III Image of physical deformity	Category IV Image of an affectionate person	Category V Image of clumsiness
'They are children who unfortunately suffer a disease which makes them different from others' 1b	'They are less intelligent' 3b, 20b, 8c	'They are sick, they have bad eyes, nostrils, and arms...' 15b	'Although it is difficult to understand them, they never have bad intentions' 9a	'At times they shout because they can't help it, for me they are good friends' 4c
'They are sick in the head, they have not developed, they are missing something, bodily or mentally' 6b	'They do not understand things or how to reason' 9b, 18c, 16c, 10c, 7a	'They always have their mouths open' 16b	'They are really friendly, they like a lot to be with people' 13a	'They do things without thinking if what is going to happen is good or not' 6c
'They are born with a particular difficulty' 2b	'Those who are 20 years old have the intelligence of a 7 year old' 19b	'They are a little deformed and should be in special schools' 18b	'During the recreation they are good and bright, I like them a lot' 1c	'Lots of times they do not know what they are doing' 16a, 18a
'They are born with a problem, they say with a defect, the mother smoked or drank..., they needed air at birth' 7b, 12b, 13b, 25b	'They are not children that one can teach easily' 26b	'They do not have a well formed face' 20b	'They seem really nice to me, they do not talk much, but when you are near them they are kind' 2c	
'They are a little deficient, they have a handicap' 10b 23b	'They are a little more retarded than we are' 17c	'They find it hard to walk and talk easily' 21b	'Although nearly no one understands well what they say, they are better than other children without Down Syndrome' 3c	
		'They do not know that they do, they do not manage their hands feet or head well...' 18b	'These kids behave better than normal ones' 7c	
			'Their behaviour is playful and friendly' 14c	

Commentary

The pupils from school B make all the comments about children with Down Syndrome being sick or physically deformed. These data are consistent with the tendency we have noted of the negative representations of pupils in this school.

In the same way, the fourth category of comments reflecting the image of the child with Down Syndrome as a friendly or affectionate person all come from schools A and C; none of these positive comments are made by pupils from school B. Categories two and five contain comments from each of the three Spanish schools, though the numbers of responses from A and C are relatively low in each case.

Question 3: 'If you know someone with Down Syndrome, how do you feel when you relate with them?'

Category I. Emergence of feelings of sadness and pity

'I feel a little sadness and pity' 2a, 8a, 14a, 16a, 20a, 21a, 22a, 2b, 12b, 17b, 22b, 24b, 4c,11c

'You feel sadness for them and want to help, but most of the time you can't' 6a

'Sadness, because these children are not like others but certain persons treat them badly and this should not be like this, because I think they should be treated the same as others' 12a, 17a

'It makes me sad that in other ordinary schools they are not accepted as normal children, also because some people reject them' 7c

Category II. Non-emergence of different feelings in the context of a child with Down Syndrome

'They can participate in all activities like others' 2*, 12*, 17* 16b, 23b

'I like to be with them because they are not different' 5*, 15*, 33*, 37*

'I do not mind playing with them, it is all the same to me' 6*, 11*, 17*, 38*, 24b, 13c, 14c

'I do not feel tense, it is a person like any other, there is no reason to feel uncomfortable' 9*, 17c

'They are normal, so I like to play with them' 10*, 18*

'I would not mind, we can learn from each other' 13*

'I would not mind, although I need to have a little more patience' 32*

'I feel good, it is the same as if one was with another child' 7a, 11a, 16b, 23b

'I feel the same as for any person, like any companion close to me. I play with them and talk...' 2c

'I do not feel anything in particular if I am with him what I do is treat him well, you have to be happy, I also feel happy to be able to be with him' 3a

Category III. Emergence of feelings of satisfaction for help and self-development for building a relationship

'I believe you have to play with them, otherwise one could not be friends' 19*

'If a child with Down Syndrome asks you to play, you have to let him, it is good that they play with us' 21*, 34*, 35*, 36*

'I have played a number of times with a child with Down Syndrome. If my friends tease me I do not care. It is good to know them' 22*, 30*, 44*

'If we play with them we can know them more and tell our friends that there are not any problems. If we do this, these children can come to know more people' 23*, 46*

'If when I play with a child with Down Syndrome others tease me, I feel bad and cross because they are very inconsiderate' 26*, 28*, 42*, 43*

'It does not bother me to interact with them, people should be treated equally. If I have a friend with Down Syndrome and if he is teased I would help him' 29*, 47*

'I like to have relations with them and share their problems. If they are teased I would try to help' 31*

'I would like to be their friend because there are others who are cruel' 40*

'I feel a little more happiness, because I think that to help, is to make companionship' 3c

Category IV. Emergence of feelings of discomfort in them and others

'I feel uncomfortable, although I could go to their birthday, or shopping, or to their house...' 1*

'I feel uncomfortable, but that is all right' 3*

'I feel quite uncomfortable' 7*

'I do not mind, but others can feel uncomfortable' 25*

'It is unjust that they should be treated differently, at times I feel uncomfortable, because if I am with them my friends might tease me' 51*

'I do not mind playing with them or relating with them, but when I am beside them I feel uncomfortable' 16* 20*

Commentary

The responses to the question about sociability confirm some of the comments made in earlier studies using the questionnaire. In the series of articles using the questionnaire the first author has made comments in relation to the use of 'sensitive words', which is one of the major categories spontaneously used by the Spanish children in this study. The Irish children did not mention sadness in their spontaneous reactions to Down Syndrome children. This is entirely consistent with the nationality–grade interaction mentioned above in the quantitative analysis comparing Spanish and Irish children, where it was the older Spanish children who used the words 'sad, lonely and unhappy' with greater frequency than the older Irish children. While the Irish pupils did not feel sadness or pity, they did feel some discomfort while the Spanish pupils did not. So there is a curious balance here between the sadness and pity for the 'child with Down Syndrome' experienced by only the Spanish children and the 'personal' discomfort and embarrassment felt only by the Irish pupils in the presence of the child with Down Syndrome.

Curiously, too, the Irish children were far more likely to feel satisfaction and to experience self-affirmation for helping a child with Down Syndrome. Both Spanish and Irish children were concerned with equality and with coming to realise that a child with Down Syndrome is like other children in so many ways.

ADULTS' ATTITUDES TOWARDS INTEGRATION

The purpose of this research was to investigate the attitudes of adults towards integration of pupils with special needs in ordinary classrooms in Ireland. It was possible to assess the attitudes on this issue of a nationwide representative sample of 501 farmers with 20 or more cattle as part of another ongoing survey.[5] The data were collected by interview. A stratified sampling technique was used, based on the cattle herd size of the farmers questioned. (Details are available from the first author on request.) This survey was undertaken on foot of the SERC report which argued for 'as much integration as is appropriate and feasible with as little segregation as possible' (Ireland 1993, 22). The survey asked a number of questions relating to this policy position in order to examine the views of a sample of the general public in relation to this 'expert view'. Special needs were explained prior to the interview in terms of children who have special requirements for their education. These children have to be treated differently to other children because, for example, they have a physical disability or a mild intellectual disability.

The questions
The following questions were asked:
- To what extent would you agree with the idea of integrating pupils with special needs like these into ordinary classrooms?
- Why do you say that? (Interviewees probed but did not prompt.)
- To what extent would you be happy that the other children would learn to be tolerant of children with special needs if they were integrated into these classrooms?
- Do you think that special arrangements should be made in the classroom in which children with special needs are placed?
- Do you think that such classes should have fewer pupils?
- Do you think that such classes should have a helper to help the teacher?

- Do you think that parents of 'ordinary children' (not those with special needs) need advice on this issue?
- Why do you say this? (Interviewees probed but did not prompt.)
- To what extent would you agree with the idea of integrating pupils with Down Syndrome into ordinary classrooms?

Sample

A total of 501 farmers completed the interview. Five per cent were under 25, 16% were between 25 and 35 years of age, 35% were between 36 and 49 years of age, 24% were between 50 and 59 years of age, and 19% were over 60.

Results

Approximately two thirds of the sample were in favour of integration: this was made up of 21% who said 'to a great extent', and 38% 'to some extent'. Fourteen per cent were not in favour of integration, and 24% were not at all in favour of integration. The respondents were next asked for their reasons for their position. There were quite a variety of reasons expressed which are in many ways comparable to reasons given by the Irish and Spanish children in the qualitative study above. The idea that everyone is equal or that everyone should get the same chance or that children with special needs should not be segregated and made to feel different was mentioned by 23% of the sample. Nearly one fifth of the sample felt that it was good for the children with special needs to learn to compete with the other children in school. Other positive reasons given were: both sets of children can learn from each other (6%); integration helps to get rid of the stigma associated with a disability; it would help children with special needs when they are older; it is good for all children to go to school near their homes; and it would promote awareness of special needs generally. (Percentages below 5% are not given.) The first two negative reasons given were the most frequently given ones: children with special needs would get better attention in a special school (given by 30%); the special needs children might be bullied by the other children (10%); the teacher would have to spend too much time on the special needs children (9%); children with special needs would fall behind the other children (8%); they would hold the other pupils back (9%); children with special needs could be disruptive; and it would be unfair to both sets of children and would not work. A number of parents gave equivocal answers, saying that it would depend on factors such as the severity of the handicap (14%), the teacher, on where the school is situated, on the facilities and on the size of the class. A few said that children could go to both types of school (special and ordinary) at different times depending on their particular needs.

The overwhelming majority of parents felt that pupils would learn to be tolerant of children with special needs if they were integrated—to some extent (47%) or to a great extent (32%). This shows a generally positive attitude in the sample as a whole. However, in terms of the educational provision made for integration, very high proportions of parents also held the view that special arrangements ought to be made in classrooms for integration (84%), that classrooms ought to have fewer pupils (88%), that the classes should have a helper for the teacher (80%), and that the parents of ordinary pupils need advice about integration (77%).

Of the parents who felt that advice was needed, 59% of them felt that integration would be facilitated if the parents understood the situation so that they could help their children to be more tolerant of the child with special needs, 35% felt that there was a need to promote awareness and understanding of integration amongst parents, 8% felt that such awareness would help to prevent bullying, and 7% felt that parents would worry that their children might be held back. Smaller percentages felt that it was important to consult with parents, to make people aware of the difficulties of parents of children with special needs, and that consultation might help parents to become involved in helping children with special needs.

Of the parents who did not perceive a need for advice, 40% felt that most people were aware of the needs of the disabled, 14% felt that it was not a problem for parents, 12% felt that it was not their concern unless it impinged on their child's education, and 10% felt that it was a mistake to draw too much attention to the child with a disability. Smaller percentages of parents were against advice being given on the grounds that schools ought to advise children, that parents of children with a disability could make their own arrangements, that the government will decide anyway, that such children are better off in special schools, and that information is unnecessary as it will make no difference. A small number felt that advice was not needed because all children ought to have equal access to education and because children with a disability are no different from other children.

Finally, there was a big and statistically significant difference between the willingness of parents to agree to integration in the case of mild intellectual disability (59%) and in the case of Down Syndrome (33%).

Discussion

This survey of 501 farmers makes a number of points clear. First, the idea of integration is supported by a two-thirds majority in the case of mild intellectual disability. However, support for integration of children with Down Syndrome is only supported by about one third of the sample. Second, about 80% of those sampled said that particular educational recommendations should be made for integration. One can infer that this large proportion is not happy that the present educational arrangements are optimal for integration in our schools. Equally large numbers, in the region of 80%, felt that numbers ought to be lowered and that help should be provided for teachers in this situation. Having documented some of the difficulties in classes in which Down Syndrome children are included, we suspect that appropriate educational arrangements such as reduced numbers and help for the teacher might persuade parents that it is possible to provide excellent education for all children in integrated classrooms. Clearly on the basis of these data a high proportion of parents are not satisfied with the present arrangements. Third, the clear division between two-thirds approval for integration in the case of mild intellectual disability and two-thirds disapproval in the case of Down Syndrome suggests that there are serious doubts about the appropriateness of ordinary classes as currently organised as being in the best educational interest of all the children. Since such a large number of these adults (77%) felt that advice was needed about integration, this is an area in which such advice is clearly needed.

CONCLUSION

This chapter has presented a series of studies designed to examine attitudes towards children with intellectual disability or Down Syndrome and their education. The first two questionnaire-based studies compared Spanish and Irish primary school children, and the second two provided evidence for the validity of the questionnaire as an evaluative instrument. The Spanish children were more sociable towards children with intellectual disability than Irish children. A possible explanation is that integration has been actively promoted by the Spanish Ministry of Education since 1985, whereas in Ireland measures to help primary school teachers with integration were less prominent when these data were collected. In consequence the Spanish children may have had a less 'severe' representation of 'mental handicap' than did the Irish children in this study. Thus older Spanish children did not see children with intellectual disability as sad, lonely and unhappy because they were more used to them, whereas older Irish children did see children with intellectual disability in these terms.

The second study attempted to overcome this difference and to compare Irish and Spanish children under circumstances in which they would be less likely to have different representations, namely by asking them about their attitudes towards a child with Down Syndrome. In these conditions the difference in sociability between the two national samples disappeared but other interesting differences remained. There were differences between the Irish and Spanish samples in terms of their views on the feasibility of integration arising from the very positive attitudes of the younger Irish children towards integration of children with Down Syndrome, in contrast to the more negative attitudes of their Spanish peers at the same age level.

It may be that experience/inexperience plays a role in explaining these differences, and greater numbers of Spanish children did report knowing a child with Down Syndrome. There was additional evidence for the apparent greater experience of the older Spanish pupils (in contrast to the older Irish pupils) in their greater use of the sensitive words 'sad, lonely and unhappy' to describe a child with Down Syndrome, a finding which was reversed in the case of describing a child with intellectual disability. It may take further studies to understand whether these differences between the Spanish and Irish children are based on culture or experience, but for the present these findings provide teachers with some insight into the ways their pupils think about children with intellectual disability and Down Syndrome. It is well known that reduction of hostility and stereotyping depends on long-term contact, institutional sanctions and the organisation of groups with equal status and shared goals (Minuchin and Shapiro 1983). We hope that this work on attitudes will allow helpful insights into the effects of school policies on how children are actually thinking.

The qualitative study of Spanish and Irish pupils indicated a number of dimensions not included on the questionnaire. These included awareness of the benefits of being educated in both ordinary and special schools, and additional images such as those of a sick person, an affectionate person and a clumsy person. There were also differences between the Spanish and Irish pupils in that sadness and pity for children with Down Syndrome were expressed only by Spanish pupils and embarrassment and discomfort were expressed mainly by the Irish pupils. The emergence of feelings of satisfaction for helping a child with Down Syndrome together with feelings of self-development for building a relationship were also expressed far more frequently by Irish pupils. These differences invite a qualitative understanding of differences in the classroom contexts where the data were collected.

Finally, the Irish farmers strongly supported the idea of integration for reasons based on equality and recognition of the need for children with intellectual disability to be challenged in school. Clearly, though, they were not satisfied with the level of help given to teachers who taught integrated classes, and were not convinced that it made educational sense to integrate children with Down Syndrome. We hope that these diverse data will stimulate debate and inform discussion on these fundamental issues in special education. A question to monitor is whether Irish children's attitudes have changed with increased educational support for children in difficulty.

REFERENCES

Bennett, J., Gash, H. and O'Reilly, M. (1998) Inclusion and exclusion: Irish experiences. In Tony Booth and Mel Ainscow (eds), *From Them to Us: international voices on inclusion in education*. Routledge.

Gash, H. (1993) A constructivist attempt to change attitudes towards children with special needs. *European Journal of Special Needs Education* **8**, 106–25.

Gash, H. (1996) Changing attitudes towards children with special needs. *European Journal of Special Needs Education* **11**, 286–97.

Gash, H. and Coffey, D. (1995) Influences on attitudes towards children with mental handicap. *European Journal of Special Needs Education* **10**, 1–16.

Gash, H., Guardia Gonzales, S., Pires, M. and Rault, C. (2000) Attitudes towards Down Syndrome: a national comparative study in France, Ireland, Portugal, and Spain. *Irish Journal of Psychology* **21** (3–4), 203–14.

Hambleton, R.K. and Swaminathan, H. (1985) *Item response theory: principles and applications*. Boston. Kluwer Nijhoff.

Hambleton, R.K., Swaminathan, H. and Rogers, H.J. (1991) *Fundamentals of item response theory*. Newbury Park CA. Sage.

Harter, S. (1998) The development of self-representations. In W. Damon (gen. ed.) and N. Eisenberg (vol. ed.), *Handbook of child psychology. Vol. 3. Social, emotional and personality development* (5th edn), 553–618. New York. Wiley.

Hartup, W.W. (1983) Peer relations. In P.H. Mussen (ed.) and E.M. Hetherington (vol. ed.), *Handbook of child psychology. Vol. 4. Socialization, personality and social development* (4th edn), 103–96. New York. Wiley.

Hartup, W.W. (1996) The company they keep: friendships and their developmental significance. *Child Development* **67**, 1–13.

Hegarty, S. (1993) Reviewing the literature on integration. *European Journal of Special Needs Education* **8**, 194–200.

Hulin, C.L., Drasgow, F. and Parsons, C.K. (1983) *Item response theory: application to psychological measurement*. Homewood IL. Dow Jones-Irwin.

Ireland (1993) *Report of the Special Education Review Committee*. Dublin. Stationery Office.

Ireland (1998) *The Education Act* (http://193.120.124.98/ZZA51Y1998.html). Dublin. Stationery Office.

Lalonde, R.N., Taylor, D.M. and Moghaddam, F.M. (1992) The process of social identification for visible immigrant women in a multicultural context. *Journal of Cross Cultural Psychology* **23**, 25–39.

Lord, F.M. (1980) *Applications of item response theory to practical testing problems*. Hillsdale NJ. LEA.

Marchesi, A., Echelta, G., Martín, E., Bavío, M. and Galán, M. (1991) Assessment of the integration project in Spain. *European Journal of Special Needs Education* **6**, 185–200.

Minuchin, P.P. and Shapiro, E.K. (1983) The school as a context for social development. In P.H. Mussen (ed.) and E.M. Hetherington (vol. ed.), *Handbook of child psychology. Vol. 4. Socialization, personality and social development* (4th edn), 197–274. New York. Wiley.

Ochoa, S.H. and Olivarez, A. (1995) A meta-analysis of peer rating sociometric studies of pupils with learning disabilities. *Journal of Special Education* **29**, 1–19.

Ó Murchú, E. and Shevlin, M. (1995) The SERC report: a basis for change. *Reach* **8**, 85–94.

Pijl, S.J. and Meijer, C.J.W. (1991) Does intregration count for much? *European Journal of Special Needs Education* **6**, 100–11.

Sundberg, N.S., Latkin, C.A., Farmer, R.F. and Saoud, J. (1991) Boredom in young adults: gender and cultural comparisons. *Journal of Cross Cultural Psychology* **22**, 209–23.

Notes

1   There is an ample literature showing that factoring a matrix of phi coefficients is sensitive to differences in difficulty level between items (Hulin *et al.* 1983; Lord 1980; Hambleton and Swaminathan 1985; Hambleton *et al.* 1991). Therefore factor analysis was based on the tetracoric correlation matrix. The consistency of test items was analysed first. Coefficient $\alpha = 0.68$ and analysis of biserial correlations between items and total test score indicated that three items (15, 19 and 20) correlated less than 0.20 with the test and so were excluded from the factor analysis. When these three items were excluded, 47.5% of the variance was explained by two factors: factor 1 was about sociability and social concern, and factor 2 was concerned with schooling.

2   This form of analysis removes the variation due to 'experience' from the analysis. This is important because while we planned to have approximately similar numbers of boys and girls of each grade in the Irish and Spanish samples it would be very difficult to equate the children in terms of their 'experience' of intellectual disability.

3   In this analysis the effects of 'experience' are removed before mean differences between groups are compared.

4   The Spanish schools are identified as a, b and c, and the Irish pupils are identified with an asterisk (*).

5   Thanks are expressed here to Thomas Healy & Associates for their advice and help in piloting the questions used in the interview and their generosity in collecting the data.

12. BEHAVIOUR SUPPORTS

JOHN MCEVOY

INTRODUCTION

Despite advances in service provision for people with intellectual disabilities within Ireland and the UK (see this volume), there are still a sizeable number of people who, because of their problem or challenging behaviour, are excluded from services and community living (Hill and Bruininks 1984; Emerson *et al.* 1994). Aggression, destructiveness, self-injury, stereotyped mannerisms, tantrums, disturbed sleep and being socially over-withdrawn are just some of the problem behaviours displayed by children and adults with intellectual disabilities (Fleming and Stenfert Kroese 1993; Qureshi 1993). The impact of these behaviours on people's quality of life can be devastating and far-reaching (Emerson 1995; Jones and Eayrs 1993). Problem behaviours:

- put the person with intellectual disability at increased risk of social deprivation and neglect, physical restraint, excessive medication, admission to institutional care and physical abuse (Emerson *et al.* 1994);
- cause considerable anxiety and stress for families and carers (Quine and Pahl 1985; A. Carr and O'Reilly 1996);
- prevent individuals from learning new skills and performing daily living skills (Matson and Coe 1992; La Vigna and Donnellan 1986; Scotti *et al.* 1991);
- act as a barrier to the achievement of equal rights and self-determination for persons with intellectual disabilities (Wehmeyer *et al.* 1996; Wehmeyer 2001).

Attempts to cope with and minimise the effects of challenging behaviour must be practical, effective, highly individualised, represent value for money and last throughout the life-course (Mansell 1993; Psychological Society of Ireland 1998).

Much problem behaviour is learnt and results from the interaction between the person and his/her environment (Emerson 1995; Matson and Coe 1992). This chapter provides a brief overview of behaviour support for serious challenging behaviours. The first section briefly discusses the nature and risks associated with problem behaviour. The use of 'behavioural' principles has been highly successful in treating a variety of difficult behaviours (Emerson 1995; Mace, Lalli *et al.* 1991). Thus interpretations of problem behaviour using the ABC model and the limitations of the model are outlined in the second section. To achieve effective interventions, a more complex explanation of behaviour is required and the purpose of the problem behaviour needs to be understood (Iwata *et al.* 1982; Carr, Levin *et al.* 1994). This is outlined in the next section, along with the stages of the behaviour support approach, the planning of a support strategy and the evaluation of outcomes. A central theme throughout the chapter is that behaviour support is not simply a matter of eliminating problem behaviour. It involves teaching new skills, changing and enriching the environment, and providing increased choice (Lancioni *et al.* 1996). The chapter closes with a discussion of some of the implications of adopting behaviour support principles for carers and service-providers—not least that behaviour support plans should fit with the person's natural surroundings and should concentrate on broad lifestyle change (Albin *et al.* 1996; Carr 1997; Koegel *et al.* 1996).

CHALLENGING BEHAVIOUR

Substitution of the term 'challenging behaviour' for 'problem behaviour' attempts to place the focus on behaviours that challenge services rather than on individuals with problems (Blunden and Allen 1987). Challenging behaviour, therefore, refers to any behaviour which places an individual and those around him/her in any danger, is harmful or detrimental to an individual's quality of life, challenges staff and carers, and results in the denial of services, facilities or events (Zarkowska and Clements 1988; Emerson 1995).

Prevalence

Though estimates vary, challenging behaviour is frequent and persistent among people with intellectual disabilities (Emerson 1998; Jacobson 1982; Kiernan and Alborz 1996; Qureshi 1993; Stenfert Kroese and Fleming 1993). UK studies estimate that 12–17% of people with intellectual disability will display challenging behaviour at any one point in time (Emerson 1998; Kiernan and Alborz 1996), and that for a population size of 220,000, 90–136 people with intellectual disabilities show challenging behaviour (Emerson 1998). In an Irish context, a survey of 243 service-users in County Galway estimated that 29% of individuals had serious challenging behaviours (Walsh *et al.* 1995). Similarly, a Dublin survey of 1068 service-users found that 35% displayed challenging behaviours, with the highest levels reported in communal residential centres and adult day services for people with more severe categories of intellectual disability (Mulrooney *et al.* 1997). Physical attacks on others and socially or sexually unacceptable behaviours are viewed as the most difficult to manage and arouse the most concern (Qureshi 1993).

Risk factors for challenging behaviour

Certain individuals may be more at risk for developing challenging behaviour. Individuals who challenge are more likely to be males in the 15–34 age group. Additional personal risk factors include the degree or severity of intellectual disability, illness, physical disability, sensory and motor impairments, genetic syndromes and communication difficulties (Emerson 1998; Reed and Head 1993; Qureshi 1994). Developmental and historical risk factors include a history of abuse and/or neglect, living in an institution or exposure to a restrictive environment which encourages confrontation and conflict, and a lack of opportunity to learn skills (Mansell 1993). Finally, specific and immediate environmental variables can precipitate challenging behaviour. For example, making demands can 'trigger' an aggressive outburst. These 'onset factors' (Reed and Head 1993) are much more difficult to discover and are identified through careful analysis of the behaviour (Groden 1989; Sturmey 1996).

BASIC BEHAVIOURAL PRINCIPLES

Applied behavioural analysis has been the most popular intervention approach used in managing challenging behaviour (Emerson 1995; Haynes and O'Brien 1990; Matson and Coe 1992). Using 'operant' procedures (Skinner 1953; 1969), applied behavioural analysis focuses on the functional relationships between behaviour and the environment (Emerson 1995; Haynes and O'Brien 1990; Matson and Gardner 1991; Scotti et al. 1991). Put simply, an individual's reaction to circumstances in his/her environment will be determined by signals indicating whether that behaviour will result in a 'pay-off' or reward (Bijou et al. 1968). The term 'operant' highlights the fact that children and adults with an intellectual disability 'operate' to produce effects on their environment (behaviours) depending on the presence of environmental signals (antecedents) and whether they attain their goal or reinforcement (consequences of behaviour) (Leslie and O'Reilly 1999). Antecedents, behaviour and consequences are the constituent elements of the ABC model of behaviour.

The ABC model of behaviour

Intellectually disabled persons are sensitive to cues in their environment and use them to predict whether or not a particular consequence will follow their behaviour. These antecedents or 'discriminative stimuli' signal when certain consequences are more or less likely (La Vigna and Donnellan 1986; Leslie and O'Reilly 1999). The consequences that strengthen behaviours, making them more likely to occur, are known as 'reinforcers'. For an event to be reinforcing it must have some significance and must be 'motivating' for the person.

An interpretation of Jimmy's challenging behaviour using the ABC model proposes that the supervisor's demand or 'antecedent' (A) triggers Jimmy's

> ### Jimmy: an introduction
>
> Jimmy is 22 years old and lives in County Louth with his mother and two younger sisters. Jimmy is very attached to his family, though his mother reports frequent language problems, aggressive outbursts and difficult behaviour since childhood. The family have few visitors as Jimmy shouts and screams and bites his hand when his mother talks to friends even for a short period of time. Jimmy must have a particular shirt and colour of socks for each day of the week. If the correct clothing is not provided, Jimmy becomes verbally abusive, threatening towards his mother, and breaks cups and plates in the kitchen. Interestingly, he does not disrupt his own bedroom, which is neat and tidy with an orderly collection of music cassettes and videos. During the day Jimmy attends the local sheltered workshop, where he is engaged in an assembly line packaging task with a group of twenty other people with intellectual disabilities. Jimmy seems very anxious at work and though friendly with his co-workers is often on the fringes. He visits the gentlemen's toilets frequently throughout the day and has broken mirrors and windows on a number of occasions. He attends literacy, numeracy and relationship classes for three sessions a week. His concentration and behaviour in these classes is described as poor, and Jimmy is often sent back to the assembly area as he refuses to answer questions. Recently, following his return from a literacy session Jimmy was instructed to attend to his work. He punched his supervisor. He was referred to the clinical team for 'treatment', with a threat of exclusion from the workshop if his behaviour did not improve.

aggressive behaviour (B), and as a consequence (C) of his aggression Jimmy is able to escape the task.

Antecedent	Behaviour	Consequences
Supervisor makes a request	Jimmy hits his supervisor	Jimmy escapes from the task

Because the consequences of Jimmy's behaviour were rewarding (he avoided having to do the task), he is highly likely to continue his aggressive behaviour when his supervisor makes future demands.

Reinforcement, punishment and extinction

Reinforcement is related to behaviour in two ways. Positive reinforcement increases the probability of occurrence of a behaviour, whereas negative reinforcement increases the probability of behaviour when the consequences are withdrawn. Thus, instead of adding something to the situation to encourage behaviour, negative reinforcement involves the removal of something unpleasant (Leslie and O'Reilly 1999).

| Jimmy becomes aggressive | Supervisor removes request | Aggression stops |

Negative reinforcement should not be confused with punishment, which involves adding an aversive event in order to decrease behaviour (Leslie and O'Reilly 1999). In the past, punishment techniques were quite popular and included methods such as 'time out' and the use of noxious stimuli (Duker and Seys 1996; Dixon and Helsel 1989; Foxx *et al.* 1980; Matson and Taras 1989; Rojahn *et al.* 1987). However, the use of punishment as an intervention technique raises a number of serious ethical issues and frequently results in serious side-effects (Chadwick and Stenfert Kroese 1993; La Vigna and Donnellan 1986; Lovett 1996).

Extinction describes how previously learnt behaviours cease when the reinforcer maintaining the behaviour is removed or withheld (Leslie and O'Reilly 1999). Although extinction can be used to eliminate behaviours (Mace, Page *et al.* 1986), it is rarely used on its own as it may have side-effects. Withdrawal of reinforcement can result in an 'extinction burst', a temporary increase in the challenging behaviour and in increased aggression, and because extinction does not provide for the teaching of alternative behaviours the eliminated behaviour is often replaced by other challenging behaviours (Ducharme and Van Houten 1994; Iwata *et al.* 1993).

Internal consequences and physiological and bodily changes can also influence and maintain behaviour. For example, masturbation or scratching are maintained by 'automatic reinforcers' internal to the person (Michael 1982; Vollmer 1994).

Shortcomings of the ABC model

The ABC model is useful in explaining challenging behaviours as it demonstrates that such behaviours are measurable, can be triggered by people or events, and are maintained by environmental consequences. However, the model does have limitations.

- The model fails to account for the individual's thoughts or feelings (Samson and McDonnell 1990). Understanding the thoughts and feelings behind the behaviour is vital in determining the relevance of the challenging behaviours to the individual and the reasons why they occur (Sturmey 1996; Toogood and Timlin 1996).
- An ABC interpretation of challenging behaviour suggests simply focusing on controlling or eliminating the unwanted behaviour. Experience indicates that fairly soon another challenging behaviour will take the place of the eliminated behaviour. Such an approach is too narrow, pays little attention to people's wider environment or lack of skills, and provides little direction for the teaching of useful activities (Horner *et al.* 1993).
- 'Setting events', events not immediately present in the environment, have

been associated with problem behaviours and can act as precursors to diffi-cult behaviour later in the day (Carr, Yarbrough *et al.* 1997; O'Reilly *et al.* 1999). Touchette *et al.* (1985) describe a case of self-injurious behaviour always occurring in the presence of a particular staff member. The ABC model does not account for such occurrences.

To be really of use the ABC model requires further expansion to include a more thorough analysis of the personal and environmental factors influencing chal-lenging behaviour (Emerson and Emerson 1987).

Consider Jimmy's behaviour further:
- Can you speculate as to what Jimmy might be
    thinking
    feeling
    before hitting his supervisor?

- Can you speculate as to what Jimmy might be
    thinking
    feeling
    after hitting his supervisor?

- Can you speculate as to what Jimmy's supervisor might be
    thinking?
    feeling?

- Can you think of any 'setting events' which may have increased the likelihood of Jimmy hitting his supervisor?

- What might have been a better way for Jimmy to react and what skills do you think he needs to develop?

POSITIVE BEHAVIOURAL SUPPORT

Positive behavioural support (Koegel *et al.* 1996; Carr, Dunlap *et al.* 2002) is a practical extension of 'applied behavioural analysis' and incorporates the prin-ciples of 'normalisation' (Wolfensberger 1983) within a 'person-centred plan-ning' framework (Horner, Sprague *et al.* 1990; Meyer and Evans 1989; Vandercook *et al.* 1989). The principle of normalisation proposes that people with intellectual disabilities are devalued and ignored by society. Therefore serv-ices must work to enhance the individual's community presence, support him/her in assuming socially valued roles and provide him/her with every opportunity to gain the respect of fellow citizens (Wolfensberger 1983). Person-centred planning rests on the assumption that services should be individually tailored to the needs and wishes of the individual (Horner, Sprague *et al.* 1990; Meyer and Evans 1989; Vandercook *et al.* 1989). Applied behavioural analysis interprets challenging behaviour as 'operant' behaviour (Iwata *et al.* 1993), an attempt by the person to exercise control over his/her personal and environmental circumstances.

The effect of personal and environmental factors on the behaviour of persons with intellectual disabilities may be twofold. First, individuals may experience deficient environments in so far as they are exposed to poor training and support, uninteresting surroundings, limited access to resources and little choice in their lives (Carr, Levin *et al.* 1994). Second, a person's limited 'learning history' may result in poorly developed or maladaptive social, functional and communication skills (McGill and Toogood 1994). As a result, individuals with intellectual disabilities may experience high levels of frustration, may be ignored by those around them and may be segregated from the general public.

Positive behavioural support recognises this poverty of experience and is not just about eliminating challenging behaviour but rather advocates a lifespan approach to managing challenging behaviour. This involves rectifying environmental conditions so as to improve the person's level of social contact, quality of relationships, and communication, social and self-control skills. The need for people with intellectual disabilities to take a more active role in designing their own lifestyles is also acknowledged in that support plans reflect the preferences of the individual. A central aim is to increase achievements and in so doing develop the individual's self-esteem and sense of self-worth. This is achieved by employing training methods that strengthen positive acceptable behaviours (Carr, Dunlap *et al.* 2002).

Developing behavioural support plans

Behavioural support plans consist of four stages. Stage one, the gathering of information, includes a full developmental and behavioural history; the specification of antecedents and consequences; and information as to possible setting events and other variables which may govern the behaviour (Groden 1989). Stage two involves generating and testing hypotheses regarding the variables controlling the behaviour and determining the purpose the behaviour serves for the individual (Iwata *et al.* 1982; O'Neill *et al.* 1990). During the third stage a support programme is devised based on the findings from stages one and two. This includes removal of the causal event (antecedent) and withdrawal of the consequences (reinforcers) controlling the behaviour, with those consequences redirected towards teaching alternative, more appropriate behaviours. But more importantly, additional environmental and lifestyle changes are incorporated into the plan (Carr, Levin *et al.* 1994; Koegel *et al.* 1996). The final supportive stage is an evaluation of the outcomes and success of the plan, focusing on the extent to which the plan fits the person's natural context, lifestyle changes have been achieved and the challenging behaviour diminished (Koegel *et al.* 1996).

Understanding the purpose of challenging behaviour

Because people with intellectual disabilities can experience difficulties in expressing their thoughts and emotions they often resort to challenging behaviour as a way of getting their message across (Carr, McConachie *et al.* 1993; Carr, Levin *et al.* 1994). The five purposes usually associated with challenging behaviour are:

- getting attention ('look at me', 'talk to me'),
- escape or avoidance ('No', 'this is too difficult/easy/boring'),
- access to desired items or activities ('I want . . .'),
- sensory stimulation such as self-regulation or self-reward (hand-flapping or spinning objects), and
- play or entertainment (Iwata *et al.* 1982; Mace, Lalli *et al.* 1993).

The purpose of self-regulation or play is sensory rather than communicative. Such activities can be rewarding in themselves and may serve to regulate the person's internal state or avoid over-stimulation from the environment. The first three purposes can be viewed as substitutes for verbal communication (Carr, McConachie *et al.* 1993; Carr, Levin *et al.* 1994).

Planning implications of the 'communication hypothesis'

Viewing challenging behaviour as a way of 'getting your message across' or as a way of coping with one's environment has implications for support planning. First, problem behaviour should not be seen as unwanted behaviour to be removed as quickly as possible but rather as a clue or key to understanding the purpose of the behaviour. Once the purpose of the behaviour is understood, a communicative behaviour that produces the same or approximate effect as the challenging behaviour (i.e. 'functionally equivalent' behaviours) can be taught (Carr, Levin *et al.* 1994). Second, problem behaviour(s) can serve more than one purpose. For example, a simple behaviour, such as screaming, can be employed to gain attention or to avoid completing a task (Day *et al.* 1994). Third, problem behaviours compete with and displace 'good' behaviours because from the individual's point of view these behaviours are reliable in bringing about the desired consequences most of the time and are easier to perform (Horner and Billingsley 1988). Therefore intervention must concentrate on teaching more efficient and effective ways for the individual to get his/her message across (Carr, Levin *et al.* 1994). Fourth, the communicative purpose of challenging behaviour serves to highlight the nature and quality of the 'relationship' between the individual and his/her social and material environment. By engaging in challenging behaviour the person with intellectual disabilities is drawing attention to the reality that his/her wishes, desires and needs are being ignored (Mansell 1994).

FUNCTIONAL ASSESSMENT

Functional assessment is the process of identifying the personal, historical and environmental factors that have created and maintained the difficult behaviour, and guides the support plan design. However, before embarking on functional assessment it is important to be clear on the purposes of the assessment and the possible broader impact of the proposed intervention (Emerson 1995; 1998). Setting goals for the support plan requires identification of the challenging behaviours in clear observable terms. Next, priorities are determined and decisions about the starting-point based on the seriousness of the behaviour.

Gathering information

Functional assessment requires analysis of the person's total life circumstances, not just the challenging behaviour. Fundamental to the procedure is determining the underlying purpose of behaviour for the individual (Carr, Levin *et al.* 1994; Sturmey 1996). Usually three methods of data collection are employed, targeting as wide a range of settings and variety of sources as possible. This includes (a) a review of diagnostic and case records, (b) structured interviews with those who know the person well, and (c) direct observation of the challenging behaviour.

On receipt of Jimmy's referral the clinical team leader decided to contact all those regularly involved with Jimmy, including his family and workshop personnel. The team leader suggested forming an 'action' team to help Jimmy. Jimmy's mother was sceptical as Jimmy receives medication and has been on numerous 'behavioural programmes', particularly when a child. A number of workshop staff expressed the view that Jimmy was dangerous both at home and in the workshop and suggested referral by the team to a specialist service. However, despite initial misgivings, all agreed that urgent action was required. Following a lengthy and at times heated meeting an action plan was developed and various tasks delegated to the team members. These included:

- a review of all clinical and daily records;
- a medical and health check;
- talking to Jimmy about his life and current activities;
- interviewing family, staff and friends about Jimmy's life and his challenging behaviour;
- functional assessment, which included ABC charts and observing Jimmy in the workshop.

The team leader explained that the purpose of gathering the information was to consider what it was that Jimmy was trying to communicate through his behaviours and to develop a vision of what Jimmy's life might be like in the future.
Can you think of any other useful sources of information?

Defining target behaviours

Definition of the 'target' behaviour(s) in observable measurable terms, such as frequency, severity and duration, determines the goals and design of the intervention. There are a number of direct and indirect methods of measuring behaviours, including interviews with parents and carers, the use of questionnaires, checklists and rating scales, naturalistic observation and direct manipulation of those variables thought to govern the behaviour (Lennox and Miltenberger 1989; O'Reilly et al. 1999; Sturmey 1996). A combination of all methods is advised (Carr, Levin et al. 1994; Horner and Carr 1997; Yarbrough and Carr 2000). When interviewing, the use of clear, non-judgemental, open-ended questions is advisable (O'Neill et al. 1997).

Possible interview question to consider:
- What does the behaviour look like/sound like?
- How often does it occur?
- How intense is it?
- Is the behaviour dangerous or destructive?
- Does the behaviour prevent learning and social activities?
- Can you think of any other useful interview questions?

Observing the behaviour(s)

Direct observation takes place in the person's natural surroundings and typically involves interval or time-sampling using behaviour charts (Iwata et al. 1990; Thompson et al. 2000). Information is recorded using an ABC chart with three columns, each providing space for describing the antecedents (A), behaviour (B) and consequences (C) in a sequential manner. Information collected over several days or weeks is closely examined to determine patterns associated with the behaviour and the inter-relationships between antecedents, behaviours and consequences (Groden 1989; Sturmey 1996). Similarly, 'scatterplots', a grid based on the time of day and day of the month, offer an alternative method of recording behaviour (Touchette et al. 1985).

Developing hypotheses

The purpose of functional assessment is to provide evidence to allow for the development of hypotheses of possible functional relationships between difficult behaviour and environmental variables (Iwata et al. 1982; Sturmey 1996; Yarbrough and Carr 2000). Hypotheses are statements about the 'function' or purpose the behaviour appears to serve for the individual. Once developed, the hypotheses can be tested either formally or informally by systematically altering the circumstances surrounding the behaviour and recording the outcome (Durand 1990).

Developing hypotheses involves looking for patterns within the antecedents and consequences which best suggest when the behaviour(s) is most or least likely to occur (Mace, Lalli *et al.* 1991; O'Neill *et al.* 1990; Repp *et al.* 1990). There is usually an identifiable reason why a person carried out a behaviour and in generating hypotheses one should consider the communicative function of challenging behaviour (Carr, Levin *et al.* 1994; La Vigna and Donnellan 1986). Also, it is important to consider possible 'setting events', those conditions or circumstances altering the probability of the behaviour occurring. These include physical and medical conditions, and environmental and relationship factors (Carr and Smith 1995; Kennedy and Itkonen 1993; O'Reilly 1995; O'Reilly and Lancioni 2000).

At the next meeting the review of records revealed that Jimmy had a history of difficult behaviour and delayed language. Also, it was discovered that Jimmy had some reading ability but serious difficulties with numbers. He has had a long-standing interest in videos and music. There are frequent references to Jimmy being 'a bit of a loner' and 'autistic-like' behaviours throughout the files. Medical colleagues reported that tests revealed Jimmy as having Fragile X Syndrome (Dykens *et al.* 1994), thus providing a context for his social anxiety, hand-biting and autistic-like behaviours; this apart, Jimmy was in excellent health. Jimmy's family reported that Jimmy had spoken to them about 'wanting his own place' and 'a job' similar to John, his eldest sister's boyfriend.

Testing hypotheses

When generating and testing hypotheses, Carr, Levin *et al.* (1994) suggest describing the various situations in which the behaviour occurs and then grouping or 'categorising' this information according to whether the behaviour is attention-seeking, escape-motivated, seeking desired items and so forth. The person is then exposed to those situations in which the behaviour is suspected to be most likely to occur in order to 'verify' the function of the behaviour.

To summarise, a thorough functional assessment provides

- knowledge of the historical, developmental and contextual factors contributing to the behaviour (e.g. the biological influences and setting events);
- description of the challenging behaviour in clear and specific terms;
- an understanding of the link between antecedents and consequences;
- evidence for the function or purpose of the behaviour;
- information on the reaction of others to the behaviour and the impact of the behaviour on the individual and his/her relationships;
- an appraisal of the person's likes and dislikes, his/her skills and abilities and methods of communication;
- goals for intervention and the identification of what alternative behaviours might be taught;

Workshop staff reported that the ABC charts suggested that Jimmy went to the toilet prior to the literacy and numeracy group sessions. Significantly, Jimmy 'went missing' whenever his supervisor made work demands or changed Jimmy's routine. Guided by the team leader, the action group reviewed all the information in detail and agreed on the following points.

• Descriptions of Jimmy's behaviours

At home Jimmy shouts and bites his hand when visitors call. This happened on four occasions during the assessment period.

Jimmy goes to the lavatory and bangs doors and strikes the windows and mirrors with his fists. This occurs 5 to 6 times a day. It has been discovered that Jimmy will cease when asked to do so.

During group sessions Jimmy sits apart from the group. He does not make eye contact and shuffles and hand waves when asked direct questions. These behaviours were observed during all group sessions.

• The purposes of Jimmy's behaviours

Jimmy communicates that he is feeling anxious and insecure with visitors and groups by biting and flapping his hands.

Jimmy expresses his anxiety about the unpredictability of his work schedule by retreating to the toilet area.

Jimmy communicates his dislike of change by becoming verbally abusive and breaking objects.

Can you advise the team as to the next stage in developing Jimmy's support plan?

• a framework for partnership with parents and carers in implementing the intervention plan;
• identification of the necessary system-wide supports.

This information is used to determine the support priorities and design of the plan.

DEVELOPING THE SUPPORT PLAN

It is only when the likely functions of the behaviour have been identified that attempts should be made to design a behavioural support plan. The plan, aimed at long-term behaviour change, incorporates four elements: (a) a reactive strategy; (b) ecological interventions involving changing the environment or context of the behaviour (Donnellan *et al.* 1988); (c) positive programming, incorporating the teaching of functionally alternative behaviours (Carr, Levin *et al.* 1994); and (d) direct treatment.

Reactive strategies

Reactive management strategies involve an immediate response to a challenging behaviour aimed at ensuring the safety of all concerned. This may involve physical protection, brief restraint, removal, or ignoring and use of distraction techniques (Carr, Levin *et al.* 1994; Rolider and Van Houten 1993; McDonnell *et al.* 1994). It is important to plan the reactive response well in advance (Hill and Spreat 1987) and to provide training in 'breakaway' techniques (McDonnell 1997). However, reactive strategies can be disadvantageous as they may reinforce the unwanted behaviour or have aversive qualities (Rolider and Van Houten 1993). Although effective in crisis management situations (*ibid.*), reactive strategies do not constitute a comprehensive treatment package as their effects are transitory (Carr, Levin *et al.* 1994).

Reviewing Jimmy's situation, can you identify any potentially dangerous flashpoints? Can you help the action team to devise a reaction strategy?

- Who will intervene in a crisis?

- How will Jimmy's chain of behaviour be interrupted?

- How might you de-escalate potential flashpoints?

- What information needs to be collected and how best should it be recorded?

Altering environments

A person's environment may be deficient because there may be too few variables supporting positive behaviour and too many encouraging challenging behaviour. Two methods, avoiding the antecedents and providing extra support, may be employed to rectify these environmental deficiencies and to prevent challenging behaviour occurring.

Avoiding antecedents

An obvious intervention strategy is to identify and avoid 'triggers' or remove discriminative stimuli for the unwanted behaviour (Dunlap *et al.* 1991). In addition, changing the context by not reinforcing the challenging behaviour and consistently rewarding the desired positive behaviours is a necessary part of any support plan (Horner and Carr 1997; Iwata *et al.* 1993).

There is considerable evidence that broad influences in an individual's personal life, known as setting events, will influence how a person responds in certain environments (Carr and Smith 1995; O'Reilly 1995; O'Reilly *et al.* 1999; Kennedy and Itkonen 1993; Lalli and Casey 1996). Supporting the individual in avoiding such events or rearranging the environment to accommodate such events will reduce the occurrence of challenging behaviour (Carr, Levin *et al.* 1994).

Similarly, the clarity of instructions, length of task, relevance to the person and level of interest in the task should be carefully considered (Dunlap *et al.* 1991).

A number of authors recommend the use of 'non-contingent reinforcement', a technique requiring the provision of activities and items to the person with no conditions attached (Bird *et al.* 1989; Carr and Durand 1985; Carr, Levin *et al.* 1994; Durand and Carr 1991). This helps to build rapport and develops cooperation (Carr, Levin *et al.* 1994).

A useful technique known as 'embedding' or 'behavioural momentum' involves the reframing of difficult requests within the context of positive, easily achievable tasks (Carr, Levin *et al.* 1994). A series of requests known to have a high probability of compliance are issued prior to delivering a more difficult target request. This sets up a momentum for compliance, thus making compliance with the 'difficult' request more likely (Carr, Levin *et al.* 1994; Horner, Day *et al.* 1991; Mace, Hock *et al.* 1988).

Providing extra support

The provision of extra assistance will result in behaviour change (Dunlap *et al.* 1991). However, broad changes in activities and programmes should be considered: for example, how might participation in activities be increased, friendships developed and extended, and opportunities for choice provided (Carr, Levin *et al.* 1994)? Though some individuals with intellectual disabilities may have difficulties in making meaningful choices (Lancioni *et al.* 1996), expanding opportunities for choice has been observed to significantly improve social behaviour and decrease challenging behaviour (Carr, Levin *et al.* 1994; Dyer *et al.* 1990). The 'person-centred planning' format (involving assessment, goal-setting and review of progress) ensures that the person with an intellectual disability is centrally involved in decision-making about his/her needs and in establishing the levels of support he/she requires (Blunden and Allen 1987; Chamberlain 1990). By involving the person in meaningful, interesting activities his/her lifestyle can be enhanced, he/she develops more autonomy and choice, and challenging behaviour declines (Carr, Levin *et al.* 1994).

Although making appropriate changes to the environment will result in decreases in challenging behaviour, the 'function' of the behaviour still remains (Carr, Levin *et al.* 1994). Therefore the support plan requires further extension.

Teaching new skills

Positive programming (La Vigna and Donnellan 1986) focuses on inviting individuals to develop more skills so that they themselves can control their environment. Also, teaching individuals to meet their needs using positive behaviours will result in a decrease in frustration and in the use of challenging behaviours to gain desired goals as they learn that positive behaviours are more efficient in gaining reinforcement (Carr, Levin *et al.* 1994). Based on the hypothesis that challenging behaviour is an alternative to communication (*ibid.*), a more appropriate behaviour such as a sign, gesture or word is reinforced and substituted for the inappropriate challenging behaviour. Thus if an individual is aggressive in order to gain attention, he/she is taught to communicate his/her need for attention in a more appropriate manner. However, 'Functional Communication Training' will only be effective if the alternative behaviour is easier to perform and more efficient in gaining reward than the challenging behaviour. Thus the newly taught behaviour must be consistently honoured, otherwise it will lose its effectiveness and the challenging behaviour will return (*ibid.*).

Consider Jimmy's situation:

- What steps could be taken to increase and strengthen friendships and social support for Jimmy?

- How might Jimmy's participation in activities at home and at work be increased?

- What would increase Jimmy's choice-making opportunities and ability to exercise control?

- How might Jimmy's self-esteem be strengthened?

- What are the potential barriers to progressing Jimmy's support plan?

Direct treatment

People with intellectual disabilities frequently need to be taught self-management strategies and to be provided with opportunities for personal development as part of their behaviour support plan. This can be facilitated on an individual or group basis.

(1)   The use of self-management techniques with people with intellectual disability can be very effective (Jones *et al.* 1993). In some instances the simple act of monitoring one's own behaviour can be a sufficient intervention in itself and eliminate the problem behaviour (Gardner and Cole 1989). Self-instruction involves encouraging the individual to verbalise a series of statements when performing a task; this ensures generalisation and allows the person to guide his/her own behaviour, thus promoting independence (Hughes and Rusch 1989).

(2)   Behavioural relaxation training is commonly used with individuals who are disruptive or present with anxiety or restlessness (Lindsay and Morrison 1996). Over time the person is taught to relax to a cue word and to refocus his/her attention (Lindsay *et al.* 1994; 1996).

(3)   Increasingly people with intellectual disabilities are availing of psychotherapy and cognitive-behavioural therapy (Beail 1998; Beail and Warden 1996; Stenfert Kroese *et al.* 1997; Waitman and Conboy-Hill 1992). These approaches have been adapted to supporting individuals in identifying their emotions and in developing their own awareness of the factors underlying their behavioural difficulties. More recently the introduction of anger management training has shown some promising success in helping to reduce expressed anger and the frequency of challenging behaviour (Rose *et al.* 2000; Taylor 2002).

Evaluation
Behavioural support incorporates a battery of interventions in an attempt to bring about lifestyle changes. Thus reduction in challenging behaviour is no longer a sufficient outcome measure on its own (Durand 2001; Horner, Sprague *et al.* 1993). Quantifiable change in the person's lifestyle, such as relationships, inclusion and choice, are equally if not more important. Therefore the following measures should be included alongside the traditional data-based measures of behaviour change when evaluating behaviour support plans (Horner, Sprague *et al.* 1993).

*   Physical integration — the extent to which the person is carrying out activities such as shopping, travelling and working in his/her local community.
*   Social integration — the breadth of social networks and the degree to which the individual interacts with others in the community.
*   Preference — the level of autonomy and choice in the person's life.
*   Variety — the variety and level of interest of daily activities.
*   Social relevance — the extent to which the person participates in activities and role, which are practical to society and valued by the local community.

Following much discussion with Jimmy, his family and workshop personnel the following behaviour support plan was agreed upon.

(a) Reactive strategies:

All those in contact with Jimmy have been advised that Jimmy finds eye contact and group activities anxiety-provoking.

If Jimmy bites or waves his hands say: 'Jimmy put your hands down now.' 'Take a deep breath and relax. You're getting things under control now.'

If following a demand or a change in task Jimmy starts to go to the toilet area, ask him: 'Jimmy, are you telling me no, you don't want to do this?' 'Let's look at your diary.'

(b) Alterations to the environment:

Jimmy and his supervisor are to develop a visual daily timetable/diary of tasks. Jimmy's supervisor will carefully explain the job requirements of each task. Easy and difficult tasks are to be interspersed.

Jimmy is to be given his own workstation near his friends but with a visual screen to prevent distractions.

Jimmy's mother has agreed that whenever possible she will give Jimmy prior notice that a visitor will call. Jimmy can choose to sit and talk to the visitor should he so wish.

(c) Training skills:

Jimmy is to keep a visual record of the task he has completed, showing this to his supervisor at the end of each work session. Jimmy can choose to play his 'Walkman' or talk to his supervisor about music for a short period (5 minutes).

Jimmy's mother has agreed to support Jimmy in preparing his clothes at night before Jimmy goes to sleep. Jimmy is to lay his clothes on a chair where he can see them.

Jimmy is to be taught to manage his own laundry, laying out his fresh clothes and placing dirty clothes in the wash basket.

Jimmy is to be taught to hold up his hand to signal his anxiety.

Jimmy is to start a supported employment placement in a local music and record shop. In addition, Jimmy is to be taught how to use local transport to travel to and from the shop.

(d) Direct treatment:

Jimmy is to start relaxation classes, first on an individual and then on a small group basis.

Can you help the action team to generate further elements of Jimmy's behaviour support plan?

It is advisable to constantly review the behavioural support plan to ensure that outcomes are being achieved on all of the above measures.

IMPLEMENTATION ISSUES

A lifespan perspective

It is unfortunate that (as in Jimmy's case) many of the key decisions in the lives of people with intellectual disability are made as a result of a crisis. Behavioural support is not about 'one-off' interventions provided during crises. It is about support for life. In taking a lifespan perspective, positive behavioural support encourages a preventative approach to managing challenging behaviour and avoids crisis management responses (Carr, Dunlap *et al.* 2002). Behavioural support is a dynamic, reflexive process supporting the individual through transition and the different stages of life (Vandercook *et al.* 1989).

The childhood origin of challenging behaviour is increasingly apparent and these behaviours may be difficult to overcome in adulthood (Stenfert Kroese and Fleming 1993). As challenging behaviour is an attempt by the person to control aspects of his/her world, it would seem advisable to make the teaching of more socially appropriate behaviour available as early as possible.

Individual and team responsibilities

The role of staff and parents in developing and maintaining challenging behaviour via reinforcement has frequently been highlighted (Carr, Taylor *et al.* 1991; Hall and Oliver 1992; Hastings and Remington 1994). Greater awareness of our own perceptions and reactions to behaviours is required (Bromley and Emerson 1995; Wanless and Jahoda 2002). In addition, adoption of a team approach to behavioural support is essential. Functional assessment and support plan design cannot be carried out without the involvement of all those in contact with the service-user. Moreover, behavioural support plans must be practical, must fit with the person's daily routine and must be acceptable to parents, care staff and teachers (Horner, Sprague *et al.* 1993; Carr, Dunlap *et al.* 2002).

Service implications

Behavioural support encourages services to move away from caring in the community to providing people with real outcomes in quality of life. This goes to the heart of service culture and design and has considerable organisational implications, not least the guiding principle that people with intellectual disabilities increase control over their own lives. Behavioural support requires considerable leadership and skilful change management as it makes significant demands on services and necessitates the adoption of flexible models of resource provision and financial planning.

Training implications

As a result of staff shortages and the limited availability of specialist support service for the development of rehabilitative intervention plans, staff training has become a service priority (Grey *et al.* 2002). However, it is envisaged that

future training initiatives will move away from training 'experts' towards training groups of collaborators and community stakeholders. Emphasis will be on
training delivered in typical community settings, to inter-professional teams
which include parents and other stakeholders. Intervention teams will require
knowledge of resource allocation and access to decision-makers within the
broader service network (Carr, Dunlap *et al.* 2002).

SUMMARY AND CONCLUSION

Challenging behaviour is a function of the interaction between the person, their
life history and their current situation and acts as a significant barrier to learning and personal development. The approach to managing challenging behaviour described in this chapter advocates a combination of techniques and methods based on identification of the underlying cause of the behaviour, including
the cognitive and affective purposes of the behaviour for the person. Other
essential ingredients of the approach are an acknowledgement of the need to
move away from concentrating on the elimination of single behaviours to the
complexity of behaviour and the importance of collaboration with stakeholders,
including the person with intellectual disabilities.

Having identified observable and unobservable 'triggers' for the behaviour
and examined the behaviour from as many different angles as possible, one can
start to set goals for intervention. Skill deficits can be addressed by teaching
communication, social and self-control skills, in context. Poor motivation can be
tackled by making performance of appropriate behaviour more attractive and
worthwhile. The person's situation can be enhanced by making environmental
changes such as altering physical features, greater attention to the nature of
activities and providing extra support. Encouraging people with an intellectual
disability to take an active role in running their own lives is achieved by supporting the development of positive relationships and providing choices. The
inclusion of parents, teachers and others within a problem-solving framework is
crucial to the success of any plan.

To conclude, behavioural support is about a positive change in lifestyle. It is
about developing social relationships, personal satisfaction, self-determination,
social inclusion, meaningful employment and a happy life for people with intellectual disabilities.

REFERENCES

Albin, R.W., Lucyshyn, J.M., Horner, R.H. and Flannery, K.B. (1996) Contextual fit for behaviour support plans. In L.K. Koegal, R.L. Koegel and G. Dunlap (eds), *Positive behavioral support*, 81–98. Baltimore. Paul H. Brookes.

Beail, N. (1998) Psychoanalytic psychotherapy with men with intellectual disabilities: a preliminary outcome study. *British Journal of Medical Psychology* **71** (1), 1–11.

Beail, N. and Warden, S. (1996) Evaluation of a psychodynamic psychotherapy service for adults with intellectual disabilities. *Journal of Applied Research in Intellectual Disabilities* **9** (3), 223–8.

Bijou, S.W., Peterson, R.F. and Adult, M.H. (1968) A method to integrate description and experimental field studies at the level of data and empirical concepts. *Journal of Applied Behaviour Analysis* **1**, 175–91.

Bird, F., Dores, P.A., Moniz, D. and Robinson, J. (1989) Reducing severe aggression and self-injurious behaviours with functional communication training. *American Journal on Mental Retardation* **94** (1), 37–48.

Blunden, R. and Allen, D. (1987) *Facing the challenge: an ordinary life for people with learning difficulties and challenging behaviour*. London. Kings Fund Centre.

Bromley, J. and Emerson, E. (1995) Beliefs and emotional reactions of care staff working with people with challenging behaviour. *Journal of Intellectual Disability Research* **39** (4), 341–52.

Carr, A. and O'Reilly, M. (1996) Service needs of carers of people with developmental disabilities: profiles of high-need and low-need groups. *Irish Journal of Psychology* **17** (1), 48–59.

Carr, E.G. (1997) The evolution of applied behaviour analysis into positive behavior support. *Journal of the Association for Persons with Severe Handicaps* **22** (4), 208–9.

Carr, E.G. and Durand, V.M. (1985) Reducing behaviour problems through functional communication training. *Journal of Applied Behaviour Analysis* **18**, 111–26.

Carr, E.G. and Smith, C.E. (1995) Biological setting events for self-injury. *Mental Retardation and Developmental Disabilities Research Reviews* **1**, 94–8.

Carr, E.G., Dunlap, G., Horner, R.H. *et al.* (2002) Positive behaviour support: evolution of an applied science. *Journal of Positive Behaviour Interventions* **4**, 4–16.

Carr, E.G., Levin, L., McConachie, G., Carlson, J.I., Kemp, D.C. and Smith, C.E. (1994) *Communication-based intervention for problem behaviour: a user's guide for producing positive change*. Baltimore. Paul H. Brookes.

Carr, E.G., McConachie, G., Levin, L. and Kemp, D.C. (1993) Communication-based treatment of severe behaviour problems. In R. Van Houten and S. Axelrod (eds), *Behaviour analysis and treatment*, 231–67. New York. Plenum Press.

Carr, E.G., Taylor, J.C. and Robinson, S. (1991) The effects of severe problems in children on the teaching behaviour of adults. *Journal of Applied Behaviour Analysis* **24** (3), 523–35.

Carr, E.G., Yarbrough, S.C. and Langdon, N.A. (1997) Effects of idiosyncratic stimulus variables on functional analysis outcomes. *Journal of Applied Behavior Analysis* **30** (4), 673–86.

Chadwick, R. and Stenfert Kroese, B. (1993) Do the ends justify the means? Aversive procedures in the treatment of severe challenging behaviours. In I. Fleming and B. Stenfert Kroese (eds), *People with learning disability and severe challenging behaviour: new developments in services and therapy*, 235–59. Manchester. Manchester University Press.

Chamberlain, P. (1990) *Life planning workpack*. Birmingham. Plan Publications.

Day, H.M., Horner, R.H. and O'Neill, R.E. (1994) Multiple functions of problem behaviours: assessment and intervention. *Journal of Applied Behavior Analysis* **27** (2), 279–89.

Dixon, M.J. and Helsel, W.J. (1989) Aversive conditioning of visual screening with aromatic ammonia for treating aggressive and disruptive behaviour in a developmentally disabled child. *Behavior Modification* **13**, 91–107.

Donnellan, A.M., La Vigna, G.W., Negri-Schoultz, N. and Fassbender, L. (1988) *Progress without punishment: effective approaches for learners with severe behaviour problems*. New York. Teachers College Press.

Ducharme, J. and Van Houten, R. (1994) Operant extinction in the treatment of severe maladaptive behaviour: adapting research to practice. *Behavior Modification* **18** (2), 139–70.

Duker, P.C. and Seys, D.M. (1996) Long-term use of electrical aversion treatment with self-injurious behaviour. *Research in Developmental Disabilities* **17** (4), 293–301.

Dunlap, G., Kern-Dunlap, L., Clarke, S. and Robbins, F.R. (1991) Functional assessment, curricular revision, and severe problems. *Journal of Applied Behaviour Analysis* **24** (2), 387–97.

Durand, V.M. (1990) *Severe behavior problems: a functional communication training approach*. New York. Guilford.

Durand, V.M. (2001) Future directions for children and adolescents with mental retardation. *Behaviour Therapy* **32** (4), 633–50.

Durand, V.M. and Carr, E.G. (1991) Functional communication training to reduce challenging behaviour: maintenance and application in new settings. *Journal of Applied Behavior Analysis* **24** (2), 251–64.

Dyer, K., Dunlap, G. and Winlerhing, V. (1990) The effects of choice-making on the problem behaviours of students with severe handicaps. *Journal of Applied Behavior Analysis* **23** (4), 515–24.

Dykens, E.M., Hodapp, R.M. and Leckman, J.F. (1994) *Behaviour and development in Fragile X Syndrome*. Thousand Oaks CA. Sage.

Emerson, E. (1995) *Challenging behaviour: analysis and intervention in people with learning disabilities*. Cambridge. Cambridge University Press.

Emerson, E. (1998) Working with people with challenging behaviour. In E. Emerson, C. Halton, J. Bromley and A. Caine (eds), *Clinical psychology in people with intellectual disabilities*, 127–53. Chichester. Wiley.

Emerson, E. and Emerson, C. (1987) Barriers to the effective implementation of habilitative behavioural programs in an institutional setting. *Mental Retardation* **25**, 101–6.

Emerson, E., McGill, P. and Mansell, J. (1994) *Severe learning disabilities and challenging behaviours*. London. Chapman and Hall.

Fleming, I. and Stenfert Kroese, B. (eds) (1993) *People with learning disability and severe challenging behaviour: new developments in services and therapy.* Manchester. Manchester University Press.

Foxx, C., Foxx, R.M., Jones, J.R. and Riely, D. (1980) Twenty four hour social isolation. *Behaviour Modification* **4**, 130–44.

Gardner, W.I. and Cole, C.L. (1989) Self-management approaches. In E. Cipani (ed.), *The treatment of severe behavior disorders*, 19–35. Washington DC. American Association on Mental Deficiency.

Grey, I.M., McClean, B. and Barnes-Holmes, D. (2002) Staff attributions about the causes of challenging behaviours. *Journal of Learning Disabilities* **6**, 297–312.

Groden, G. (1989) A guide for conducting a comprehensive behavioral analysis of a target behavior. *Journal of Behavior Therapy and Experimental Psychiatry* **20**, 163–9.

Hall, S. and Oliver, C. (1992) Differential effects of severe-injurious behaviour in the behaviour of others. *Behavioural Psychotherapy* **20**, 355–66.

Hastings, R.P. and Remington, B. (1994) Staff behaviour and its implications for people with learning disabilities and challenging behaviours. *British Journal of Clinical Psychology* **33** (4), 423–38.

Haynes, S.N. and O'Brien, W.H. (1990) Functional analysis in behaviour therapy. *Clinical Psychology Review* **10** (6), 649–68.

Hill, B.K. and Bruininks, R.H. (1984) Maladaptive behaviour of mentally retarded people in residential facilities. *American Journal on Mental Deficiency* **88**, 380–7.

Hill, J. and Spreat, S. (1987) Staffing injury rates associated with the implementation of contingent restraint. *Mental Retardation* **25**, 141–5.

Horner, R. and Billingsley, F. (1988) The effects of competing behavior on the generalization and maintenance of adaptive behavior in applied settings. In R. Horner, G. Dunlap and R. Koegel (eds), *Generalization and maintenance: lifestyle changes in applied settings*, 197–220. Baltimore. Paul H. Brookes.

Horner, R.H. and Carr, E.G. (1997) Behavioural support for students with severe disabilities: functional assessment and comprehensive intervention. *Journal of Special Education* **31** (1), 84–104.

Horner, R.H., Day, H.M., Sprague, J.R., O'Brien, M. and Heathfield, L.T. (1991) Interspersed requests: a non-aversive procedure for reducing aggression and self-injury during instruction. *Journal of Applied Behavior Analysis* **24** (2),

265–78.

Horner, R.H., Sprague, J.R. and Flannery, B. (1993) Building functional curricula for students with severe intellectual disabilities and severe behaviour problems. In R. Van Houten and S. Axelrod (eds), *Behaviour analysis and treatment*, 47–71. New York. Plenum Press.

Horner, R.H., Sprague, J.R., O'Brien, M. and Heathfield, L.T. (1990) The role of response efficiency in the reduction of problem behaviours through functional equivalence training: a case study. *Journal of the Association for Persons with Severe Handicaps* **15** (2), 91–7.

Hughes, C. and Rusch, F.R. (1989) Teaching supported employees with severe mental retardation to solve problems. *Journal of Applied Behavior Analysis* **22** (4), 365–72.

Iwata, B.A., Dorsey, M.F., Slifer, K.J., Bauman, K.E. and Richman, G.S. (1982) Toward a functional analysis of self-injury. *Analysis and Intervention in Developmental Disabilities* **2** (1), 3–20.

Iwata, B.A., Vollmer, T.R. and Zarcone, J.R. (1990) The experimental (functional) analysis of behaviour disorders: methodology, applications, and limitations. In A. Repp and N. Singh (eds), *Perspectives on the use of non-aversive and aversive interventions for persons with severe disabilities*, 301–30. Sycamore. Sycamore Publishers.

Iwata, B.A., Vollmer, T.R., Zarcone, J.R. and Rodgers, T.A. (1993) Treatment classification and selection based on behavioural function. In R. Van Houten and S. Axelrod (eds), *Behaviour analysis and treatment*, 101–68. New York. Plenum.

Jacobson, J.W. (1982) Problem behaviour and psychiatric impairment within a developmentally disabled population 1: behaviour frequency. *Applied Research in Mental Retardation* **3**, 121–39.

Jones, R.S.P. and Eayrs, C. (1993) *Challenging behaviour and intellectual disability: a psychological perspective*. Clevendon. BILD.

Jones, R., Williams, H. and Lowe, F. (1993) Verbal self-regulation. In I. Fleming and B. Stenfert Kroese (eds), *Cognitive-behavioural therapy for people with learning disabilities*, 189–210. London. Routledge.

Kennedy, C.H. and Itkonen, T. (1993) Effects of setting events of the problem behaviour of students with severe disabilities. *Journal of Applied Behavior Analysis* **26** (3), 321–7.

Kiernan, C. and Alborz, A. (1996) Persistence in challenging and problem behaviours of young adults with intellectual disability in the family home. *Journal of Applied Research in Intellectual Disabilities* **9** (3), 181–93.

Koegel, L.K., Koegal, R.L. and Dunlap, G. (1996) *Positive behavioural support: including people with difficult behaviour in the community*. Baltimore. Paul H. Brookes.

Lalli, J.S. and Casey, S.D. (1996) Treatment of multiply controlled problem behaviour. *Journal of Applied Behavior Analysis* **29** (3), 391–5.

Lancioni, G., O'Reilly, M. and Emerson, E. (1996) A review of choice research with people with severe and profound developmental disabilities. *Research in Developmental Disabilities* **17** (5), 391–411.

La Vigna, G.W. and Donnellan, A.M. (1986) *Alternatives to punishment: solving behaviour problems with non-aversive strategies.* New York. Irvington.

Lennox, D.B. and Miltenberger, R.G. (1989) Conducting a functional assessment of problem behavior in applied settings. *Journal of the Association for Persons with Severe Handicaps* **14** (4), 304–11.

Leslie, J.C. and O'Reilly, M.F. (1999) *Behaviour analysis: foundations and applications to psychology.* Amsterdam. Harwood Academic Press.

Lindsay, W.R. and Morrison, F.M. (1996) The effects of behavioural relaxation on cognitive performance in adults with severe intellectual disabilities. *Journal of Intellectual Disability Research* **40** (4), 285–90.

Lindsay, W.R., Fee, M., Mitchie, A.M. and Heap, I. (1994) The effects of cue control relaxation on adults with severe mental retardation. *Research in Developmental Disabilities* **15** (6), 425–37.

Lindsay, W.R., Mitchie, A.M. and Marshall, I. (1996) The effects of behavioural relaxation training on adults with profound multiple disabilities: a preliminary study on treatment effectiveness. *British Journal of Learning Disabilities* **24**, 119–23.

Lovett, H. (1996) *Learning to listen: positive approaches and people with difficult behaviour.* London. Jessica Kingsley.

Mace, F.C., Hock, M.L., Lalli, J.S., West, B.J., Belfiore, P., Pinter, E. and Brown, D.K. (1988) Behavioral momentum in the treatment of non-compliance. *Journal of Applied Behavior Analysis* **21**, 123–41.

Mace, F.C., Lalli, J.S. and Lalli, E.P. (1991) Functional analysis and treatment of aberrant behavior. *Research in Developmental Disabilities* **12** (2), 155–80.

Mace, F.C., Lalli, J.S., Lalli, E.P. and Shea, M.C. (1993) Functional analysis and treatment of aberrant behaviour. In R. Van Houten and S. Axelrod (eds), *Behaviour analysis and treatment*, 75–99. New York. Plenum Press.

Mace, F.C., Page, T.J., Ivancic, M.T. and O'Brien, S. (1986) Effectiveness of brief time-out with and without contingent delay: a comparative analysis. *Journal of Applied Behavior Analysis* **19**, 63–78.

McDonnell, A. (1997) Training care staff to manage challenging behaviour: an evaluation of a three day course. *British Journal of Developmental Disabilities* **43** (2), 156–61.

McDonnell, A., McEvoy, J.A. and Dearden, R.L. (1994) Coping with violent situations in the caring environment. In T. Wykes (ed.), *Violence and health care professionals*, 189–206. London. Chapman and Hall.

McGill, P. and Toogood, S. (1994) Organising community placements. In E. Emerson, P. McGill and J. Mansell (eds), *Severe learning disabilities and challenging behaviours: designing quality services*, 232–58. London. Chapman and Hall.

Mansell, J.L. (1993) *Services to people with learning disabilities and challenging behav-*

iour or mental health needs: report of a project group. London. HMSO.

Mansell, J. (1994) Challenging behaviour: the prospect for change. A keynote review. *British Journal of Learning Disabilities* **22**, 2–5.

Matson, J.L. and Coe, D.A. (1992) Applied behaviour analysis: its impact on the treatment of mentally retarded emotionally disturbed people. *Research in Developmental Disabilities* **13** (2), 171–89.

Matson, J.L. and Gardner, W.I. (1991) Behavioural learning theory and current applications to severe behaviour problems in persons with mental retardation. *Clinical Psychology Review* **11** (2), 173–83.

Matson, J.L. and Taras, M.E. (1989) A 20 year review of punishment and alternative methods to treat problem behaviour in developmentally delayed persons. *Research in Developmental Disabilities* **19**, 85–104.

Meyer, L.H. and Evans, I.M. (1989) *Non-aversive intervention for behaviour problems: a manual for home and community*. Baltimore. Paul H. Brookes.

Michael, J. (1982) Distinguishing between discriminative and motivational functions of stimuli. *Journal of the Experimental Analysis of Behavior* **37**, 149–55.

Mulrooney, M., Harrold, M., Vandenberg, D. and Rogers, Y. (1997) A survey of challenging behaviour across a large Dublin-based organisation for people with learning disabilities. Unpublished manuscript, Psychology Department, St Michael's House, Dublin.

O'Neill, R.E., Horner, R.H., Albin, R.W., Storey, K. and Sprague, J.R. (1990) *Functional analysis of problem behavior: a practical assessment guide*. Baltimore. Brookes/Cole.

O'Neill, R.E., Horner, R.H., Albin, R.W., Sprague, J.R., Storey, K. and Newton, J.S. (1997) *Functional assessment and program development for problem behaviour: a practical handbook*. Pacific Grove CA. Brooks/Cole.

O'Reilly, M.F. (1995) Functional analysis and treatment of escape-maintained aggression correlated with sleep deprivation. *Journal of Applied Behavior Analysis* **28**, 225–6.

O'Reilly, M.F. and Lancioni, G. (2000) Response co-variation of escape-maintained aberrant behaviour correlated with sleep deprivation. *Research in Developmental Disabilities* **21** (2), 125–36.

O'Reilly, M.F., Lancioni, G.E. and Emerson, E. (1999) A systematic analysis of the influence of prior social context on aggression and self injury within analogue analysis assessments. *Behaviour Modification* **23** (4), 578–96.

Psychological Society of Ireland (1998) *Responding to behaviour that challenges*. Dublin. Psychological Society of Ireland.

Quine, L. and Pahl, J. (1985) Examining the causes of stress in families with severely mentally handicapped children. *British Journal of Social Work* **15**, 501–17.

Qureshi, H. (1993) Prevalence of challenging behaviour in adults. In I. Fleming and B. Stenfert Kroese (eds), *People with learning disability and severe challenging behaviour: new developments in services and therapy*, 11–42.

Manchester. Manchester University Press.

Qureshi, H. (1994) The size of the problem. In E. Emerson, P. McGill and J. Mansell (eds), *Severe learning disabilities and challenging behaviour: designing high quality services*, 17–34. London. Chapman and Hall.

Reed, J. and Head, D. (1993) The application of functional analysis in the treatment of challenging behaviour. In I. Fleming and B. Stenfert Kroese (eds), *People with learning disability and severe challenging behaviour: new developments in services and therapy*, 167–88. Manchester. Manchester University Press.

Repp, A.C., Singh, N.N., Olinger, E. and Olson, D.R. (1990) The use of functional analyses to test causes of self-injurious behaviour: rationale, current status and future directions. *Journal of Mental Deficiency Research* **34** (2), 95–105.

Rojahn, J., McGonigle, J.J., Curcio, C. and Dixon, M.J. (1987) Suppression of pica by water mist and aromatic ammonia: a comparative analysis. *Behaviour Modification* **11**, 65–74.

Rolider, A. and Van Houten, R. (1993) The interpersonal treatment model. In R. Van Houten and S. Axelrod (eds), *Behaviour analysis and treatment*, 127–68. New York. Plenum Press.

Rose, J., West, C. and Clifford, D. (2000) Group interventions for anger in people with intellectual disabilities. *Research in Developmental Disabilities* **21** (3), 171–81.

Samson, D. and McDonnell, A.A. (1990) Functional analysis and challenging behaviours. *Behavioural Psychotherapy* **18** (4), 259–71.

Scotti, J.R., Evans, I.M., Meyer, L.H. and Walker, P. (1991) A meta-analysis of intervention research with problem behaviour: treatment validity and standards of practice. *American Journal on Mental Retardation* **96** (3), 233–56.

Skinner, B.F. (1953) *Science and human behaviour*. New York. Macmillan.

Skinner, B.F. (1969) *Contingencies of reinforcment: a theoretical analysis*. New York. Appleton-Century-Crofts.

Stenfert Kroese, B. and Fleming, I. (1993) Prevalence and persistency of challenging behaviour in children. In I. Fleming and B. Stenfert Kroese (eds), *People with learning disability and severe challenging behaviour: new developments in services and therapy*, 43–55. Manchester. Manchester University Press.

Stenfert Kroese, B., Dagnan, D. and Loumidis, K. (eds) (1997) *Cognitive-behavioural therapy for people with learning disabilities*. London. Routledge.

Sturmey, P. (1996) *Functional analysis in clinical psychology*. Chichester. Wiley.

Taylor, J.L. (2002) A review of the assessment and treatment of anger and aggression in offenders with intellectual disability. *Journal of Intellectual Disability Research* **46** (Suppl. 1), 57–73.

Thompson, T., Felce, D. and Symons, F.J. (2000) *Behavioural observation: technology and applications in developmental disabilities*. Baltimore. Paul H. Brooks.

Toogood, S. and Timlin, K. (1996) The functional assessment of challenging behaviour: a comparison of informant-based, experimental and descriptive methods. *Journal of Applied Research and Intellectual Disabilities* **9** (3), 206–22.

Touchette, P.E., MacDonald, R.F. and Langer, S.N. (1985) A scatterplot for identifying stimulus control of problem behaviour. *Journal of Applied Behavior Analysis* **18**, 343–51.

Vandercook, T., York, J. and Forest, M. (1989) The McGill Action Planning Systems (MAPS): a strategy for building the vision. *Journal of the Association for Persons with Severe Handicaps* **14**, 205–15.

Vollmer, T.R. (1994) The concept of automatic reinforcement: implications for behavioural research in developmental disabilities. *Research in Developmental Disabilities* **15** (3), 187–207.

Waitman, A. and Conboy-Hill, S. (eds) (1992) *Psychotherapy and mental handicap.* London. Sage Publications.

Walsh, P.G., Hunt, O., Hunt, D. and Harsch, S. (1995) A survey of challenging behaviours exhibited by adults in centre and community based services in the west of Ireland. Unpublished manuscript, Brothers of Charity Services, Kilcornan, Galway.

Wanless, L.K. and Jahoda, A. (2002) Responses of staff towards people with mild to moderate intellectual disability who behave aggressively: a cognitive emotional analysis. *Journal of Intellectual Disability Research* **46** (6), 507–16.

Wehmeyer, M.L. (2001) Self-determination and mental retardation. In L. Masters Glidden (ed.), *International review of research in mental retardation, Vol. 24*, 1–48. San Diego. Academic Press.

Wehmeyer, M.L., Kelchner, K. and Richards, S. (1996) Essential characteristics of self-determined behaviour of individuals with mental retardation. *American Journal on Mental Retardation* **100** (6), 632–42.

Wolfensberger, W. (1983) Social role valorization: a proposed new term for the principle of normalization. *Mental Retardation* **21**, 234–9.

Yarbrough, S.C. and Carr, E.G. (2000) Some relationships between informant assessment and functional analysis of problem behaviour. *American Journal on Mental Retardation* **105** (2), 130–51.

Zarkowska, E. and Clements, J. (1988) *Problem behaviour in people with severe learning disabilities: a practical guide to constructional approach.* Beckenham. Croom Helm.

13. FAMILY THERAPY AND INTELLECTUAL DISABILITY

ALAN CARR

THE FAMILY LIFE CYCLE

The family life cycle is a useful framework within which to conceptualise the therapeutic needs of families containing children with intellectual disabilities. At transitional points within the life cycle, marked by events such as the birth of the child, entry into primary school, entry into secondary school, leaving secondary school and so forth, families face multiple stresses associated with having a child with a disability. They may, therefore, require episodes of intensive family therapy to help them manage the transitions between the stages of the life cycle. So let us begin with a working definition of the family before sketching a widely used family life cycle model.

With single-parenthood, divorce, separation and remarriage being common events, a narrow and traditional definition of the family is no longer useful (Walsh 1993). It is more expedient to think of the child's family as a network of people in the child's immediate psychosocial field. This may include members of the child's household and others who, while not members of the household, play a significant role in the child's life—for example a separated parent and spouse living elsewhere with whom the child has regular contact, foster parents who provide relief care periodically, a grandmother who provides informal day care, and so forth. In clinical practice the primary concern is the extent to which this network meets the child's developmental needs (Carr 1999; 2000).

Having noted the limitations of the traditional model of family structure, the most useful available models of the family life cycle are paradoxically based upon the norm of the traditional nuclear family, with other family forms being conceptualised as deviations from this norm (Carter and McGoldrick 1989). One such model is presented in Fig. 1. This model delineates the main developmental tasks to be completed by the family at each stage of development. In the first two stages of family development, the principal concerns are with differentiating from the family of origin by completing school, developing relationships outside the family, completing one's education and beginning a career. In the third stage

Stage	Tasks
1. Family of origin experiences	• Maintaining relationships with parents, siblings and peers • Completing school
2. Leaving home	• Differentiation of self from family of origin and developing adult to adult relationship with parents • Developing intimate peer relationships • Beginning a career
3. Premarriage stage	• Selecting partners • Developing a relationship • Deciding to marry
4. Childless couple stage	• Developing a way to live together based on reality rather than mutual projection • Realigning relationships with families of origin and peers to include spouses
5. Family with young children	• Adjusting marital system to make space for children • Adopting parenting roles • Realigning relationships with families of origin to include parenting and grandparenting roles • Children developing peer relationships
6. Family with adolescents	• Adjusting parent–child relationships to allow adolescents more autonomy • Adjusting marital relationships to focus on midlife marital and career issues • Taking on responsibility of caring for families of origin
7. Launching children	• Resolving midlife issues • Negotiating adult to adult relationships with children • Adjusting to living as a couple again • Adjusting to including in-laws and grandchildren within the family circle • Dealing with disabilities and death in the family of origin
8. Later life	• Coping with physiological decline • Adjusting to the children taking a more central role in family maintenance • Making room for the wisdom and experience of the elderly • Dealing with loss of spouse and peers • Preparation for death, life review and integration

Fig. 1—Stages of the family life cycle (after Carter and McGoldrick 1989).

the principal tasks are those associated with selecting a partner and deciding to marry. In the fourth stage the childless couple must develop routines for living together which are based on a realistic appraisal of the other's strengths, weaknesses and idiosyncrasies.

In the fifth stage, the main task is for couples to adjust their roles as marital partners to make space for young children. This involves the development of parenting roles which entail routines for meeting children's needs for

• safety,
• care,
• control, and
• intellectual stimulation.

Developing these routines is a complex process, particularly where couples have children with intellectual disabilities, and often difficulties in developing these routines lead to a referral for family therapy.

Routines for meeting children's needs for safety include protecting children from accidents by, for example, not leaving young children unsupervised, and also developing skills for managing the frustration and anger that the demands of parenting young children often elicit. Failure to develop such routines may lead to accidental injuries or child abuse.

Routines for providing children with food and shelter, attachment, empathy, understanding and emotional support need to be developed to meet children's needs for care in these various areas. Failure to develop such routines may lead to a variety of emotional difficulties.

Routines for setting clear rules and limits, for providing supervision to ensure that children conform to these expectations, and for offering appropriate rewards and sanctions for rule-following and rule violations meet children's need for control. Conduct problems or challenging behaviour may occur if such routines are not developed.

Parent–child play and communication routines for meeting children's needs for age-appropriate intellectual stimulation also need to be developed if children are to maximise their potential in the areas of emotional, language and intellectual development.

For families with youngsters who have intellectual disabilities the transition into primary school is a major challenge but essential for meeting the child's needs for intellectual stimulation. Negotiating an appropriate educational resourcing within the constraints of the available educational placement options and managing the impact of the transition to school on the child are major challenges that can tax the family's coping resources to the limit.

In addition to developing parental roles and routines for meeting children's needs, a further task of this stage is for the parents' parents to develop grandparental roles and for the family as a whole to realign family relationships to facilitate this.

In the sixth stage, which is marked by children's entry into adolescence, parent–child relationships require realignment to allow adolescents to develop more autonomy. Managing this process when youngsters have intellectual disabilities can be particularly challenging for all family members. Good parent–child communication and joint problem-solving skills facilitate this process, and skills deficits in these areas underpin many adolescent referrals for family therapy.

However, parents who find their families at this stage of development must contend not only with changes in their relationships with their maturing children but also with the increased dependency of the grandparents upon them, and also with a midlife re-evaluation of their marital relationship and career aspirations. The demands of grandparental dependency and midlife re-evaluation may compromise parents' abilities to meet their adolescents' needs for the negotiation of increasing autonomy.

The seventh stage is concerned with the transition of young adult children out of the parental home. Ideally this transition entails the development of a less hierarchical relationship between parents and children. Securing appropriate accommodation with adequate supports for young adults with intellectual disability is a major challenge for families making the transition into this stage of the life cycle.

During this stage the parents are also faced with the task of adjusting to living as a couple again, to dealing with disabilities and death in their families of origin, and of adjusting to the expansion of the family if their children marry and procreate.

In the final stage of this life cycle model, the family must cope with the parents' physiological decline and approaching death, while at the same time developing routines for benefiting from the wisdom and experience of the elderly. This stage of the family life cycle may be particularly challenging where parents have played a central role in supporting their adult offspring with intellectual disabilities. The question of how such parental support may be replaced as parents become unable to offer it must be addressed.

GRIEF PROCESSES AT LIFE CYCLE TRANSITIONS

Because most parents expect their children to be born without disabilities and to develop normally over the life cycle, the birth and growth of a child with a disability may be accompanied by a sense of loss—that is, parents of children with intellectual disability may experience a sense of having lost the opportunity to bring up a child without such a disability. In this respect, parents of children with intellectual disabilities may be involved in a process of grieving. Initially, when parents are informed that their child has an intellectual disability, the grief process may be set in motion. The grief process includes the sub-processes of shock; denial; yearning and searching; sadness and disappointment; anger; anxiety; guilt and bargaining; and acceptance. The way the news of disability is broken to parents affects their satisfaction with the consultation service received. The following factors are particularly important in breaking such news: the approachability of the clinician, the degree to which the clinician understands the parents' concerns, the sympathy of the clinician, and the directness and clarity of communication (Quine and Rutter 1994).

Throughout the life cycle at each transition the family is reminded of the loss of the able-bodied child that was initially expected and the grief process recurs, albeit in a progressively attenuated form (Goldberg *et al.* 1995). Life cycle transitions are particularly strong triggers for family grief processes since they entail unique features when compared with life cycle transitions associated with able-bodied children. For example, the transition to school may entail a higher

Grief process	Underlying theme	Adjustment problems
Shock	• I am stunned by the loss of the child I expected to have	• Complete lack of affect and difficulty engaging emotionally with others • Poor concentration
Denial	• My child has not got a disability or will grow out of his or her disability	• Not organising appropriate supports and educational provision
Yearning and searching	• I will find a miracle cure and retrieve my 'normal child'	• Experimentation with alternative medicine or faith healing
Sadness and disappointment	• I am sad, hopeless and lonely because I have lost the child I wanted	• Persistent low mood, tearfulness, low energy and lack of activity • Appetite and sleep disruption • Poor concentration
Anger	• I am angry because the child I needed has been taken from me	• Aggression • Conflict with family members and professionals in health and education systems • Leaving the family • Drug or alcohol abuse • Poor concentration
Anxiety	• I am frightened that some threatening event will occur to me or my child because I have been so angry	• Separation anxiety, agoraphobia and panic • Somatic complaints and hypochondriasis • Poor concentration
Guilt and bargaining	• It is my fault that my child has a disability so I should deserve misfortune	• Self-harming behaviour • Self-sacrificing behaviour
Acceptance	• I loved and lost the child I never had and now I must carry on without him/her while cherishing the disabled child that I do have	• Return to normal routines

Fig. 2—*Adjustment problems arising from grief processes in parents of children with intellectual disability.*

level of concern because of fears that the disability may prevent the child from forming peer relationships and fitting in. The 'leaving home' transition may occur later in life, if at all. The impending death of the parents may be a particular source of anxiety, since a major concern may be who will care for the disabled child when the parent has died. An important process in family therapy is to help families not only to mourn their disappointments but also to celebrate the achievements of their children with intellectual disabilities.

When parents of children with intellectual disabilities have difficulties coping with the demands of life cycle transitions or other challenges posed by rearing a child with a disability, it is sometimes the case that the parent is experiencing adjustment problems arising from grief processes. Some such grief-related adjustment problems are listed in Fig. 2. For example,   parents involved in the grief process of denial may have difficulties organising appropriate supports and educational placements to meet the special needs of their children with intellectual disabilities. Or parents involved in the grief process of anger may have problems cooperating with multidisciplinary teams and may engage in unproductive conflict. Where grief-related adjustment problems compromise their capacity to meet their youngsters' special needs, family therapy may offer a forum within which to address these issues.

THE PROCESS OF FAMILY THERAPY

Family therapy is one way of helping families to cope with the additional challenges of the life cycle entailed by having a youngster with an intellectual disability. The particular approach to family therapy outlined here is an integrative model which draws on ideas and practices from a variety of different traditions. A full account of the model is given elsewhere (Carr 1995; 1997; 2000).

When working with families where a youngster has an intellectual disability, it is useful to conceptualise the process of family therapy as occurring in time-limited episodes but within the overall context of an ongoing relationship between the family and the agency offering the therapy. At critical points in the family life cycle families may engage in episodes of therapy involving a limited number of sessions (e.g. six sessions) over a brief period (e.g. twelve weeks). Much longer periods of time (e.g. a year) may elapse between these episodes of therapy, during which family therapy input is superfluous. Family therapy offers a forum within which the family is helped to solve specific problems (e.g. managing behavioural problems) or address specific issues (e.g. dealing with disappointment and loss). Often these problems or issues arise at transitional points in the family life cycle.

Episodes of family therapy may be conceptualised as a series of stages using the framework set out in Fig. 3. In the first stage a plan for conducting the intake interview is made. The second stage is concerned with the processes of engagement, alliance-building, assessment and formulation. In the third stage, the therapeutic contract, the completion of a therapy plan and the management of resistance are the primary issues addressed. In the final stage, disengagement or recontracting for a further episode of intervention occurs.

Within the context of this stage-based model of consultation, family therapy is usefully conceptualised as a developmental and recursive process. At each developmental stage, key tasks must be completed before progression to the next stage. Failure to complete the tasks of a given stage before progressing to the next stage may jeopardise the consultation process and lengthen treatment unnecessarily. For example, attempting to conduct an assessment without first contracting for assessment may lead to cooperation difficulties if the child or parents find the assessment procedures arduous. Family therapy is an episodic

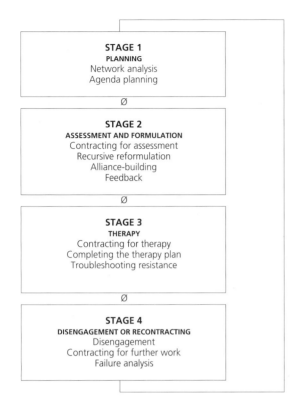

Fig. 3—Stages of therapy.

and recursive process insofar as it is possible to move from the final stage of one episode of family therapy to the first stage of the next.

STAGE 1. PLANNING

In the first stage of family therapy the main tasks are to plan who to invite to the initial assessment session and what to ask them.

Network analysis

There is often confusion about who to invite to an intake interview in cases where youngsters with intellectual disabilities have multiple problems, are from multiproblem families, or are involved with multiple agencies. In these cases a network analysis may be conducted. For network analysis it is essential to find out from the referral letter or through telephone contact with the referrer who is involved with the problem and tentatively establish what roles they play with respect to it. In some cases this will be straightforward: for example, where parents are concerned about a child's enuresis, it may be sufficient to invite the child and the parents. In other cases, where schoolteachers, hostel staff or social services personnel are most concerned about the case, the decision about who to invite to the first interview is less straightforward. In these complex cases it is particularly important to analyse network roles accurately before deciding who to invite to the first session. Most network members fall into one or more of the following categories:

- the *referrer*, to whom correspondence about the case should be sent;
- the *customer*, who is most concerned that the referral be made;
- the *child* or children with the problem;
- the legally responsible *guardians*, who are usually the parents but may be a social worker or other representative of the state;
- the primary *care-givers*, who are usually the parents but may be foster parents, residential child care staff or nursing staff;
- the child's main *teacher*;
- the *social control agents*, such as social workers or probation officers;
- *other involved professionals*, including the family doctor, the paediatrician, the school nurse, the parents' psychiatrist, etc.

Certain key network members constitute the minimum sufficient network necessary for effective case management (Carr 1995). These include the customer, the legal guardians, the care-givers and the referred child. Ideally, all members of the minimum sufficient network should be invited to an intake meeting. If this is not possible, then individual meetings or telephone calls may be used to connect with these key members of the network.

Agenda planning

In planning an agenda for a first family therapy meeting, a routine intake may be supplemented by questions which take account of the specific features of the case. The routine interview should cover the history of the presenting problems. This typically involves questions about the nature, frequency and intensity of the problems; previous successful and unsuccessful solutions to these problems; and different family members' views on the causes of these problems and possible solutions that they have tried or suspect may be fruitful to explore in future. In addition, the intake interview should inquire about the child's individual physical, cognitive and psychosocial developmental history and make an assessment of the family's development and functioning with particular reference to parent–child relationships, interparental relationships and the wider social network within which the family is embedded. Assessment of unique features of the case should be based on a preliminary formulation that contains hypotheses about possible antecedents, beliefs and consequences associated with the presenting problems. These hypotheses may be based on information given in the referral letter or phone call and the literature on the particular problem in question. For example, if a youngster presents with conduct problems or challenging behaviour, then an important hypothesis to consider would be the possibility that the parent and child are engaged in a coercive cycle of interaction (Patterson 1982). If a child, on the other hand, presents with social withdrawal at school, a hypothesis deserving consideration would be that the child is experiencing anxiety because of some threatening event which occurred within the school.

STAGE 2. ASSESSMENT AND FORMULATION

The more important features of the assessment and formulation stage, which may span one or two sessions, consist of establishing a contract for assessment; working through the assessment agenda and recursively refining the preliminary formulation in the light of the information obtained; dealing with engagement problems; building a therapeutic alliance; and giving feedback.

Contracting for assessment
Contracting for assessment involves the therapist, the child or adolescent and significant network members clarifying expectations and reaching an agreement to work together. The first task is to explain what assessment involves and to offer the parents, the child and each relevant member of the network a chance to accept or reject the opportunity to complete the assessment. With children and teenagers, misconceptions need to be dispelled. For example, some children believe that when referred for therapy they may be involuntarily admitted to hospital or placed in a detention centre. In some instances children may not wish to complete the assessment but their parents may be insistent. In others, parents may not wish to complete the assessment but a referring physician or social worker may forcefully recommend attendance. In such situations, the therapist may facilitate the negotiation of some compromise between parties. The contracting for assessment is complete when family members have been adequately informed about the process and have agreed to complete the assessment.

Recursive reformulation
The assessment phase of the overall consultation process involves conducting interviews to check the accuracy of the formulations and hypotheses made during the planning phase and modifying them in the light of the information gained in the interview or testing sessions. In practice, the first round of interviewing may not only lead to a modification of the preliminary formulation but may raise further hypotheses that need to be investigated through further interviews or tests. The process comes to an end when a formulation has been constructed that fits with significant aspects of the child's problems, with network members' experiences of the child's problems, and with available knowledge about similar problems described in the literature. This formulation should inform the construction of a treatment plan. Building blocks for treatment plans are described below. A formulation is a mini-theory that explains the way in which particular situational antecedents, beliefs about these, the

problem and related issues, and consequences for problematic behaviours maintain the presenting problem. A formulation may also highlight factors which predispose the child or adolescent to developing a particular presenting problem.

Here is an example of a formulation for a child with mild intellectual disability who presents with challenging behaviour. John is a five-year-old boy with a difficult temperament and this predisposes him to have difficulty with rule-following. In situations where he is tired, hungry or excited he has great difficulty following instructions from parents and teachers. He believes that such instructions are personal criticisms rather than requests for cooperative behaviour. At home and at school his parents and teachers typically respond to his uncooperative behaviour by either offering explanations and attention, which positively reinforces his lack of cooperation, or by withdrawing, which negatively reinforces his lack of cooperation by removing what he perceives to be an aversive stimulus, i.e. instructions and directions for rule-following.

Alliance-building

In addition to providing information, the process of assessment also serves as a way for the therapist, the child, the parents and members of the network to build a working alliance. Building a strong working alliance with the child and key members of the child's family and network is essential for valid assessment and effective therapy. *All other features of the consultation process should be subordinate to the working alliance*, since without it clients drop out of assessment and therapy or fail to make progress. The only exception to this rule is where the safety of child or family member is at risk, and in such cases protection takes priority over alliance-building. Key aspects of a therapeutic alliance are listed below.

- Warmth, empathy and genuineness should characterise the therapist's communication style.
- The therapist should form a collaborative partnership with the family.
- An invitational approach should be adopted in which family members are invited to participate in assessment and therapy procedures.
- The inevitability of ambivalence about change becoming an issue within the therapeutic relationship should be acknowledged.

The assessment is complete when the presenting problem and related difficulties are clarified; related antecedent situational factors, beliefs and consequences have been identified; a formulation has been constructed; possible goals have been identified; and options for case management or treatment have been identified and have been discussed with the family.

Feedback

Giving feedback is a psychoeducational process. Children and their parents and siblings are given both general information about the type of problem they face (such as the degree of disability and additional problems such as ADHD or encopresis) and specific information about the way this relates to the formulation of their own presenting problems. Simplicity and realistic optimism are central to good psychoeducation. It is important not to overwhelm parents and children with information, so a good rule of thumb is to think about a case in complex terms but to explain it to clients in the simplest possible terms. Put succinctly:

* *Think complex—Talk simple*

Good clinical practice involves matching the amount of information given about the formulation and treatment plan to the client's readiness to understand and accept it. A second important rule of thumb is to engender a realistic level of hope when giving feedback by focusing on strengths and protective factors first and referring to aetiological factors later. Put succinctly:

* *Create hope—Name strengths*

In providing psychoeducation about the general type of problem the family face, information on clinical features, predisposing, precipitating, maintaining and protective factors may be given along with the probable impact of the problem in the short and long term on cognition, emotions, behaviour, family adjustment, school adjustment and health.

The formulation is fed back to the family as a basis for a therapeutic contract. If the working alliance is the engine that drives the therapeutic process, the formulation is the map that provides guidance on what direction to take and what building blocks should be included in the therapy plan.

In some cases the process of assessment and formulation releases family members' natural problem-solving skills and they resolve the problem themselves. For example, some parents, once they discuss their anxiety about handling their child in a productive way during a family assessment interview, feel released to do so.

STAGE 3. THERAPY

When parents and their children have completed the assessment stage, have accepted the formulation, and are aware of the broad therapeutic possibilities, it is appropriate to progress to the therapy stage. The central tasks of this stage are contracting for therapy to achieve specific goals; participating in the completion of the agreed therapy plan; and troubleshooting resistance. If at this stage it is apparent that other family problems, such as parental depression or marital discord, require attention, referrals for this work may be made and it may be conducted concurrently with the child-focused family therapy programme.

Alternatively, addressing these problems may be postponed until after the child-focused difficulties have been resolved.

Contracting for therapy

The contracting process involves inviting parents and their youngsters to make a commitment to pursue a specific therapeutic plan to reach specific goals. This plan may be constructed from one or more of the building blocks outlined below. Clear, realistic, visualised goals that are fully accepted by all family members and that are perceived to be moderately challenging are crucial for effective therapy. Goal-setting takes time and patience. Different family members may have different priorities when it comes to goal-setting and negotiation about this is essential. This negotiation must take account of the costs and benefits of each goal for each family member. It is usually a more efficient use of time to agree on goals first before discussing the details of how they might be achieved.

The contracting session is complete when all involved members of the child's network necessary for implementing the therapeutic plan agree to be involved in an episode of consultation to achieve specific goals.

Therapy plans

Family therapy plans are constructed from the following building blocks:
- psychoeducation,
- establishing supports,
- redefinition,
- monitoring problems,
- communication training,
- problem-solving training,
- supportive play,
- reward systems,
- behavioural control systems.

The practices entailed by these building blocks will be detailed below with reference to examples.

Psychoeducation

The aim of psychoeducation in cases of intellectual disability is to help parents and other family members to understand their child's diagnosis and its implications for the child's development, and also to understand the nature and implications of formulations of secondary problems such as challenging behaviour, anxiety and so forth. Psychoeducation is not a once-only event. It is an ongoing process. It begins with feedback after the first comprehensive assessment and recurs in subsequent meetings. When children are reassessed periodically, feedback from these assessments provides further opportunities for psychoeducation.

It is very difficult for most parents to acknowledge and appreciate the implications of the diagnosis of intellectual disability when it is first mentioned, since the diagnosis violates their expectations associated with having a completely healthy child. Most parents experience shock and denial (two elements of the grief process described below). Clinicians on multidisciplinary teams have a responsibility to give parents and family members a clear, unified and unambiguous message about the diagnosis, since this is what the parents require to work through their denial and get on with the process of accepting their child's disability and dealing with it in a realistic way. The diagnosis should include information on the normative status of their child's cognitive abilities and adaptive skills; psychological and emotional status; biological factors; and supports necessary for the child to live a normal life. The way in which such supports may be accessed should also be clarified. These areas constitute the four axes of the diagnostic system developed by the American Association for Mental Retardation (AAMR 1992). The main pitfall in psychoeducation is to give parents ambiguous information which allows them to maintain the erroneous belief that their child has no disability or has a transient condition that will resolve with maturation. It is particularly valuable to offer psychoeducation within a family context, because it helps family members to develop a shared perspective and belief system concerning the youngster's intellectual disability.

At periodic reviews over the course of the life cycle, feedback sessions with parents and other family members are opportunities to continue the process of psychoeducation. In these sessions family members may be helped to develop accurate expectations concerning the strengths and limitations of the family member with intellectual disability.

Establishing support

Clinicians conducting family therapy may have a role in helping families to establish appropriate supports for themselves and their children with intellectual disabilities at various stages over the course of the family life cycle. For good practice in this area, the child and family's support needs must be clearly stated in concrete terms; the precise action plans for arranging supports must be agreed with the family and the professional network; the precise roles and responsibilities of members of the professional network in providing supports must be agreed; the way in which the provision of supports will be resourced financially must be agreed; and the timetable of periodic review dates must be drawn up. Central to this type of system is the concept of a key worker who holds administrative responsibility for ensuring that the child's support plan is implemented. Even the most robust system of this type will flounder without an organisational structure that requires key workers to take responsibility for coordinating the implementation of support plans. The terminology used to describe these individualised support plans varies from country to country, but the principles of good practice, outlined in Fig. 4, remain

SPECIFIC GUIDELINES	GENERAL GUIDELINES
• Assess support needs in a systematic way using a system that fits with the cultures of the agency and the family • State the child and family's support needs in concrete terms • Agree the precise action plans for arranging supports with the family and the professional network • Agree the precise roles and responsibilities of members of the professional network in providing supports • Agree the way in which the provision of supports will be resourced financially • Draw up a timetable of periodic review dates • Follow through on the plan and review it for effectiveness	• Include the family and other professionals who will be involved in providing support in some or all family meetings • Create opportunities for everyone to make a contribution to the meeting • When apparent disagreements occur between family members and professionals, clarify both sides of the conflict; don't take sides • Write down agreements and timetables • If the system is not working, do not criticise the family or colleagues; call another family–professional meeting and solve the problems

Fig. 4—Guidelines for establishing supports.

the same.

In family therapy sessions where the focus is on establishing supports, it is important to include both the family and other professionals who will be involved in providing support. Within these sessions, create opportunities for everyone to make a contribution. When apparent disagreements occur between family members and professionals, clarify both sides of the conflict and acknowledge that different people have different views. This is far more productive than taking sides or trying to establish who is right and who is wrong. When agreements about supports or schedules are reached, write these down and arrange to send copies to all present. If the system of supports is not working, do not criticise family members or colleagues. This will only make future cooperation problematic. It is more effective to call another family–professional meeting and use this as an opportunity to solve the problems that prevent the system of supports from working.

Redefinition
Commonly the definitions that children and their families hold of the problems and related issues that prompt them to seek professional help are of limited value in helping them to resolve their difficulties. Redefinition of presenting problems and related issues is central to family therapy. Separating the problem from the person is one way to achieve this. Here the child's difficulties are defined as distinct from the child's identity, and the child is described as being aligned with the parents and other network members in requiring a solution to the problem. Thus the child and parents may be described as a team who are working together to find a way to deal with a fiery temper, a difficult temperament, ADHD, anxiety, depression, encopresis, diabetes, addiction, or whatever the problem happens to be. With young children the problem may be

externalised and personified and the child and family's task defined as defeating the personification of the problem. For example, obsessive compulsive disorder may be personified as *Mr Too-tidy,* while enuresis may be personified as *Mr Wet-bed.* The parents' role is to support the child in defeating Mr Wet-bed or Mr Too-Tidy.

Monitoring problems
For most difficulties, it is useful to train parents to regularly record information about the main presenting problems, their antecedents, consequences, related beliefs and the impact of particular interventions. A monitoring chart for positive and negative target behaviours is given in Fig. 5. This may be used where the central difficulty is a child or adolescent's behaviour: for example, it may be useful for youngsters with conduct problems or sleep problems. When assessing a problem using this monitoring chart, events that typically precede and follow target behaviours are recorded in the second and fourth columns respectively. This information may suggest ways in which the frequency or intensity of negative target behaviours may be altered by inviting children and their parents to change the antecedent events that trigger problems or the consequences that reinforce them. The impact of these therapeutic interventions may be monitored using the same chart. Where the chart in Fig. 5 is used to monitor positive target behaviours, it may throw light on the antecedent events that trigger these positive behaviours and the consequences that reinforce them and so suggest ways in which the frequency of positive target behaviours might be increased.

Communication skills
Where parents and children have difficulties communicating clearly with each other about how best to manage the presenting problems, communication training may be appropriate. A common problem is that parents have difficulty listening to their children and children have difficulties clearly articulating their views to their parents. A second common communication problem is the difficulty parents have in listening to each other's views about how best to manage the child's difficulties in a non-judgemental way. In some instances parents and children have never learned communication skills. In others, good communication skills have been acquired but intoxication or intense emotions such as anger, anxiety or depression prevent parents and children from using these skills. Training in using communication skills is appropriate in the former situation, but in the latter the key problem to be solved is how to arrange episodes of communication which will be uninfluenced by intoxication or negative mood states. Communication skills may be artificially subdivided into those used for listening and those used for telling somebody something. These skills are listed in Fig. 6. Parents and children need, first, to be given an intellectual understanding of these skills. Then the therapist should model the

TARGET BEHAVIOUR TRACKING FORM

Fill out one line of this form when you have finished dealing with a situation in which any of the following target behaviours occur

1._____

2._____

3._____

This will help you to keep track of
- the types of situations which trigger these behaviours
- the consequences of these target behaviours
- the impact of these consequences on the intensity of target behaviours
- the frequency of these target behaviours

Day and time	What happened before the target?	What was the target behaviour and its intensity (1 = low 10 = high)	What happened after the target behaviour?	What was the intensity of target behaviour after this consequence? (1 = low 10 = high)

Fig. 5—Chart for monitoring antecedents and consequences of positive and negative target behaviours.

SPECIFIC GUIDELINES	GENERAL GUIDELINES
LISTENING SKILLS • Listen without interruption • Summarise key points • Check that you have understood accurately • Reply **COMMUNICATION SKILLS** • Decide on specific key points • Organise them logically • Say them clearly • Check you have been understood • Allow space for a reply	• Make a time and place for clear communication • Remove distractions and turn off the TV • Discuss one problem at a time • Try to listen with the intention of accurately remembering what was said • Try to listen without judging what is being said • Avoid negative mind-reading • State your points without attacking the other person • Avoid blaming, sulking or abusing • Avoid interruptions • Take turns fairly • Be brief • Make congruent *I* statements

Fig. 6—Guidelines for listening and communication skills.

skills for the clients. Clients should at this point be invited to try using the skills to discuss a neutral topic in the session. Let the episode of communication run for five or ten minutes, and take notes of various difficulties that occur. Then give feedback and, in the light of this, ask clients to complete the episode again. Typical mistakes include interrupting before the other person has finished, failing to summarise what the other person said accurately, attributing negative malicious intentions to the other person when they have not communicated that they hold such intentions, failing to check that the message was accurately sent, failing to check that the message has been accurately received, blaming and sulking. Once clients can use the skills to exchange views on a neutral topic, they may then be used to exchange views on emotionally loaded issues, first in the session and later at home. Communication homework assignments should be highly specific, to prevent clients from lapsing into poor communication habits. Thus specific members of a family should be invited to find out the other person's views on a specific topic. A time and place free of distractions should be agreed and a time limit of no more than twenty minutes set for initial communication assignments.

Problem-solving skills
When it is apparent that parents or children need to take a more systematic approach to resolving problems, problem-solving skills training is appropriate. Joint problem-solving training for parents is useful where parents have difficulty in cooperatively developing plans for solving children's difficulties. Joint problem-solving training for adolescents and parents may be useful where parents and teenagers are having difficulty negotiating about the youngster's increasing autonomy. Individual problem-solving training for youngsters may be helpful when children have specific peer group or academic problems that they repeatedly fail to solve, such as joining in peer activities without aggression or managing homework assignments set by their teachers. As with

communication difficulties, clients may have difficulties solving problems because they lack the skills or because intoxication, negative mood states or other factors interfere with the use of well-developed skills. Where such factors are present, therapy should focus on removing these obstacles to effective problem-solving. In problem-solving training, the sequence of stages described for communication training should be followed with a progression from explanation of the skills listed in Fig. 7 to modelling and to rehearsal in the session with the focus on a neutral topic. Feedback should be given during rehearsal until the skills are well developed. Then clients may be invited to use the skills to solve emotionally laden problems. When families are observed trying to solve emotionally laden problems, often the first pitfall they slide into is that of problem definition. Many clients need to be coached in how to translate a big vague problem into a few small, specific problems. A second pitfall involves trying to solve more than one problem at a time. A third area of difficulty is helping clients to hold off on evaluating the pros and cons of any one solution until as many solutions as possible have been listed. This is important, since premature evaluating can stifle the production of creative solutions. Often families need to be coached out of bad communication habits in

SPECIFIC GUIDELINES	GENERAL GUIDELINES
• Define the problem • Brainstorm options • Explore pros and cons • Agree on a joint action plan • Implement the plan • Review progress • Revise the original plan	• Make a time and place for clear communication • Remove distractions and turn off the TV • Discuss one problem at a time • Divide one big problem into a few small problems • Tackle problems one at a time • Avoid vague problem definitions • Define problems briefly • Show that the problem (not the person) makes you feel bad • Acknowledge your share of the responsibility in causing the problem • Do not explore pros and cons until you have finished brainstorming • Celebrate success

Fig. 7 — Guidelines for problem-solving skills.

problem-solving training, such as negative mind-reading where they attribute negative thoughts or feelings to others, blaming, sulking and abusing others. Where families with chronic problems successfully resolve a difficulty, a vital part of the coaching process is to help them celebrate this victory.

Supportive play

For children, particularly those with challenging behaviour, who have become embroiled in coercive problem-maintaining interaction patterns with their parents, an important intervention is to train parents in providing their children with support. Parents may be coached in joint sessions with their children in how to do this. The guidelines for supportive play set out in Fig. 8 are first explained. Next, the therapist models inviting the child to select a play activity and engaging in child-led play, while commenting positively on the child's activity, praising the child regularly and avoiding commands and teaching. Then the parent is invited to copy the therapist's activity and feedback is given to parents on what they are doing well and what they need to do more of. Finally, the parent and child are invited to complete a 20-minute daily episode of child-led play to increase the amount of support the child experiences from the parent.

SPECIFIC GUIDELINES	GENERAL GUIDELINES
• Set a specific time for 20 minutes of supportive play per day • Ask child to decide what he or she wants to do • Agree on an activity • Participate wholeheartedly • Run a commentary on what the child is doing or saying, to show your child that you are paying attention to what they find interesting • Make congruent *I like it when you...* statements, to show your child that you feel good about being there • Praise your child repeatedly • Laugh and make physical contact through hugs or rough and tumble • Finish the episode by summarising what you did together and how much you enjoyed it	• Set out to use the episode to build a positive relationship with your child • Try to use the episode to give your child the message that they are in control of what happens and that you like being with them • Try to foresee rule-breaking and prevent it from happening or ignore it • Avoid using commands, instructions or teaching • Notice how much you enjoy being with your child

Fig. 8 — Guidelines for supportive play.

Reward systems

Where the goal of treatment is to help children learn new habits such as complying with parental instructions, going to bed on time, taking medication, playing cooperatively with a sibling or coping with anxiety-provoking situations, reward systems may be used. Guidelines for using reward systems are presented in Fig. 9. It is critical that the target behaviour is clearly defined, is monitored regularly and is rewarded promptly, using a symbolic system of points, tokens, stars or smiling faces that is age-appropriate and acceptable to the child. An example of a smiling face chart is given in Fig. 10. The symbolic reward system must be backed by tangible rewards or prizes which are highly valued, so that the child may buy these with points or tokens after they have accumulated a sufficient number. When points systems are ineffective, it may be that some adult in the child's environment, such as a non-custodial parent in the case of children from separated families, is not committed to implementing the system. In other instances the target behaviours may be ambiguous or the number of points required to win a prize too high. Troubleshooting these difficulties is a routine part of coaching families in using reward systems.

SPECIFIC GUIDELINES	GENERAL GUIDELINES
• Define the target behaviour clearly • Decide when and where the monitoring will occur • Make up a smiling-face chart or points chart • Explain to the child that they can win points or smiling faces by carrying out the target behaviour • Ask the child to list a set of prizes that they would like to be able to buy with their points or smiling faces • Agree on how many points or faces are necessary to buy each prize • Follow through on the plan and review it for effectiveness	• Present the reward system to your child as a way of helping him or her to learn grown-up habits • All parental figures in the child's network should understand and agree to use the system • Use a chart that is age-appropriate. Smiling faces or stars are good for children and points may be used for adolescents • The sooner points are given after completing the target behaviour, the quicker the child will learn • Highly valued prizes lead to faster learning • Try to fine-tune the system so that successes are maximised • If prizes are not being won, make the target behaviour smaller and clearer or the cost of prizes lower and make sure that all parent figures understand and are committed to using the system • If the system is not working, do not criticise the child • Always keep the number of target behaviours below 5

Fig. 9—Guidelines for reward systems.

Behavioural control systems

There are two common behavioural patterns that may maintain aggressive or self-injurious behaviour (Oliver 1995). In the first pattern, a period of social isolation leads the child to a state of heightened need for social contact and challenging behaviour occurs. In response to this, the carer provides social contact until the child's need for contact is satiated. When the child's need for contact ceases, it is more likely that the child will engage in challenging behaviour again, since this has been positively reinforced by the carer's attention. It is also more likely that the carer will provide social contact in response to challenging behaviour, since giving attention leads the adult ultimately to experience relief (associated with negative reinforcement) when the challenging behaviour ceases. In the second pattern, the carer places demands upon the child and in response the child engages in challenging behaviour which leads the adult to cease placing demands upon the child. When the episode ceases, the child is more likely in future to engage in challenging behaviour when demands are placed upon him, because in the past this has led to a cessation of demands (negative reinforcement). The adult is more likely to stop making demands in response to challenging behaviour since this has led to a cessation of the child's challenging behaviour (negative reinforcement).

With both of these patterns, on the one hand children need to be coached in developing more appropriate ways of communicating their needs to their carers, and on the other there is a pressing need to help the youngsters to stop engaging in aggressive or self-injurious behaviour as rapidly as possible. Reward systems described in the previous section are useful in coaching youngsters to

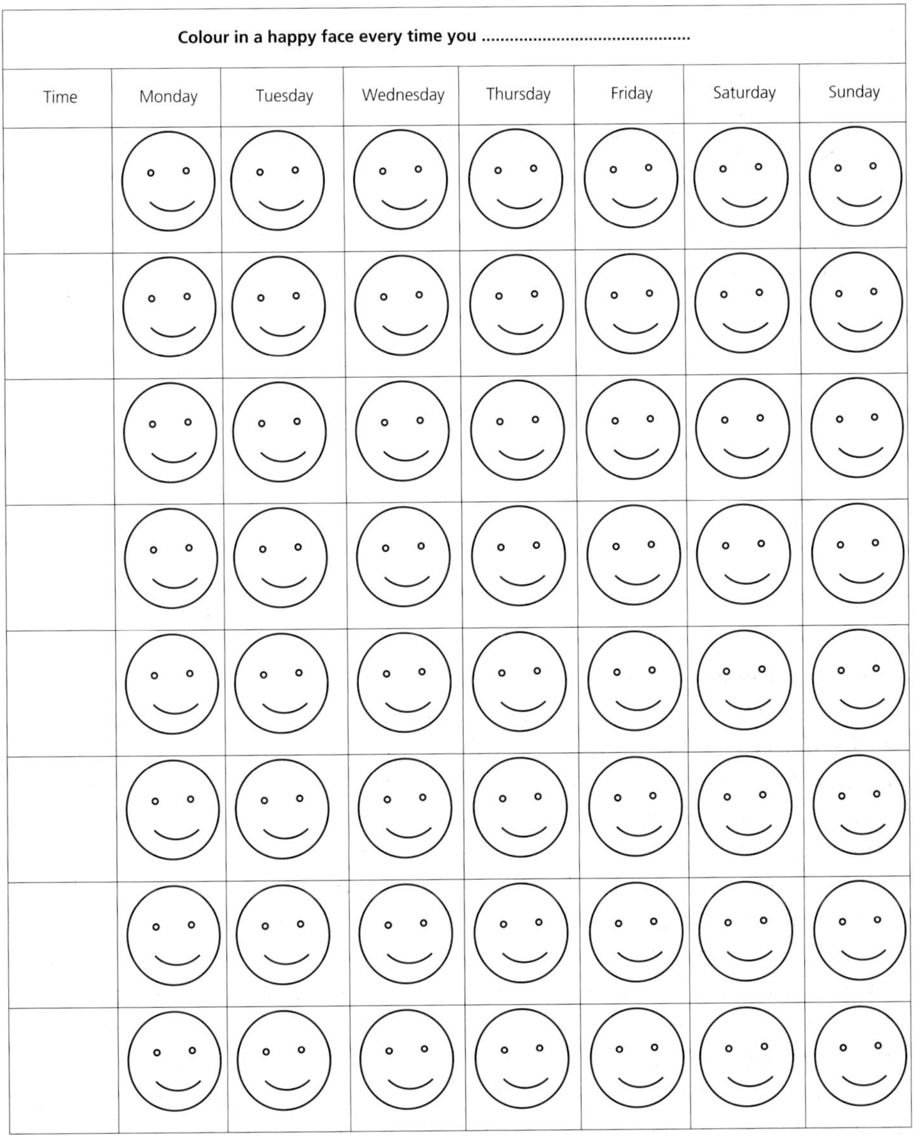

Fig. 10—Child's star chart for child reward systems.

communicate their needs more effectively. Behavioural control programmes, on the other hand, are a rapid way of dealing with aggression and self-injury. Guidelines for a behavioural control programme are set out in Fig. 11. The programme should be framed as a way for helping the child to develop self-control skills. Specific negative or aggressive behaviours are defined as targets for which time-out from reinforcement is given. When these behaviours occur, the parent gives a command to the child to stop, and this may be followed up by

SPECIFIC GUIDELINES	GENERAL GUIDELINES
BEHAVIOUR CONTROL PROGRAMME • Agree on a few clear rules • Set clear consequences • Follow through • Reward good behaviour • Use time-out or loss of privileges for rule-breaking • Monitor change visibly **TIME-OUT** • Give two warnings • Bring the child to time-out without negative emotion • After five minutes engage the child in a positive activity and praise him for temper control • If rule-breaking continues, return child to time-out until thirty seconds of quietness occurs • Engage in positive activity with child and praise for temper control	• Set out with the expectation that you can teach your child one good habit at a time • Build in episodes of unconditional special time into behavioural control programme • Frame the programme as learning self-control • Involve the child in filling in, designing and using the monitoring chart or system • Monitor increases in positive behaviour as well as decreases in negative behaviour • Do not hold grudges after episodes of negative behaviour • Avoid negative mind-reading • Avoid blaming, sulking or abusing • Ask for spouse support when you feel bad about the programme • Celebrate success

Fig. 11 — Guidelines for behaviour-control programmes.

two warnings. If children comply they are praised. If not, they are brought to time-out without any display of anger or any reasoned explanation being given at that time. The time for reasoned explanation is at the outset of the programme or when it is being reviewed, not following misbehaviour. During time-out, the child sits on a chair in the corner of the kitchen, the hall or their bedroom, away from family activities and interesting or reinforcing events or toys. Following a period of two to five minutes (depending on the child's age), the child is invited to rejoin family activities and is engaged in a stimulating and rewarding exchange with the parent. If children misbehave or protest aggressively while in time-out, they remain there until they have been compliant and quiet for 30 seconds before rejoining family activities and engaging in a stimulating interaction with the parent.

Running a behavioural control programme is very stressful for most families for the first two weeks. The normal pattern is for the time-out period to increase in length gradually and then eventually to begin to diminish. This pattern may be tracked using the time-out monitoring chart in Fig. 12. During this escalation period, when the child is testing out the parents' resolve and having a last binge of self-indulgence before learning self-control, it is important to help families maintain the unconditionally supportive aspect of family life. There are two important interventions that may be useful here. First, spouses may be invited to set aside special time where the focus is on mutual marital support. Second, parents may plan episodes of supportive play with the children. The important feature of spouse support is that the couple set aside time to spend together without the children, to talk to each other about issues unrelated to the children. In single-parent families, parents may be helped to explore ways of obtaining support from their network of friends and members of the extended family.

Troubleshooting resistance

Accepting the inevitability of resistance, and developing skills for managing it, is central to the effective practice of family therapy (Anderson and Stewart 1983). Clients show resistance in a wide variety of ways. It may take the form of not completing tasks between sessions, not attending sessions, or refusing to terminate the therapy process. It may also involve not cooperating during therapy sessions. For clients to make progress with the resolution of their difficulties the therapist must have some systematic way of dealing with resistance (Carr 1995). First, describe the discrepancy between what clients agreed to do and what they actually did. Second, ask about the difference between situations where they managed to follow through on an agreed course of action and those where they did not. Third, ask what they believed blocked them from making progress. Fourth, ask if these blocks can be overcome. Fifth, ask about strategies for getting around the blocks. Sixth, ask about the pros and cons of these courses of action. Seventh, frame a therapeutic dilemma which outlines the costs of maintaining the status quo and the costs of circumventing the blocks.

When resistance is questioned, factors that underpin it are uncovered. In some instances unforeseen events—'acts of God'—hinder progress. In others the problem is that the clients lack the skills and abilities that underpin resistance. Where a poor therapy contract has been formed, resistance is usually due to a lack of commitment to the therapeutic process. Specific convictions which form part of clients' individual, family or culturally based belief systems may also contribute to resistance, where the clients' values prevent them from following through on therapeutic tasks. The wish to avoid emotional pain is a further factor that commonly underpins resistance. Questioning resistance is only helpful if a good therapeutic alliance has been built. If clients feel that they are being blamed for not making progress, then they will usually respond by pleading helplessness, blaming the therapist or someone else for the resistance, or distracting the focus of therapy away from the problem of resistance into less painful areas.

STAGE 4. DISENGAGING OR RECONTRACTING

The process of disengagement begins once improvement is noticed. The interval between sessions is increased at this point. The degree to which goals have been met is reviewed when the session contract is complete, or before this if improvement is obvious. If goals have been achieved, the family's beliefs about the permanence of this change are established. Then the therapist helps the family to construct an understanding of the change process by reviewing with them the problem, the formulation, their progress through the treatment programme and the concurrent improvement in the problem. Relapse management is also discussed (Marlatt and Gordon 1985). Family members are

Date	Time going in	Number of minutes in time-out	Situation that led to time-out	Pleasant activity that happened afterwards

Fig. 12 — Time-out monitoring chart.

helped to forecast the types of stressful situations in which relapses may occur; their probable negative reactions to relapses; and the ways in which they can use the lessons learned in therapy to cope with these relapses in a productive way. In brief CBT disengagement is constructed as an episodic event rather than as the end of a relationship. It is recognised that further episodes of brief CBT may be required in the future to address other specific problems. If goals are not reached, it is in the clients' best interests to avoid doing *more of the same* (Segal 1991). Rather, therapeutic failures should be analysed in a systematic way. The understanding that emerges from this is useful both for the clients and for the therapist. From the clients' perspective, they avoid becoming trapped in a consultation process that maintains rather than resolves the problem. From the therapists' viewpoint it provides a mechanism for coping with burnout that occurs when intervention fails to lead to therapeutic goal attainment

REFERENCES

AAMR (1992) *Mental retardation: definitions, classification and systems of support* (9th revision). Washington DC. American Association on Mental Retardation.

Anderson, C. and Stewart, S. (1983) *Mastering resistance.* New York. Guilford.

Carr, A. (1995) *Positive practice: a step-by-step approach to family therapy.* Reading. Harwood.

Carr, A. (1997) *Family therapy and systemic practice.* Lanham MD. University Press of America.

Carr, A. (1999) *Handbook of clinical child psychology: a contextual approach.* London. Routledge.

Carr, A. (2000) *Family therapy: concepts, process and practice.* Chichester. Wiley.

Carter, B. and McGoldrick, M. (1989) *The changing family lifecycle. A framework for family therapy* (2nd edn). New York. Gardner Press.

Goldberg, D., Magrill, L., Hale, J., Damaskinidou, R., Paul, J. and Tham, S. (1995) Protection and loss: working with learning-disabled adults and their families. *Journal of Family Therapy* **17**, 263–80.

Marlatt, G. and Gordon, J. (1985) *Relapse prevention.* New York. Guilford.

Oliver, C. (1995) Annotation: Self-injurious behaviour in children with learning disabilities: recent advances in assessment and intervention. *Journal of Child Psychology and Psychiatry* **30**, 909–27.

Patterson, G. (1982) *Coercive family process.* Eugene OR. Castalia.

Quine, L. and Rutter, D. (1994) First diagnosis of severe mental and physical disability. *Journal of Child Psychology and Psychiatry* **35**, 1273–89.

Segal, L. (1991) Brief therapy: the MRI approach. In A. Gurman and D. Kniskern (eds), *Handbook of family therapy,* vol. 2, 17–199. New York. Brunner/Mazel.

Walsh, F. (1993) *Normal family processes* (2nd edn). New York. Guilford.

14. A GOOD PLACE TO LIVE: THE QUALITY OF RESIDENTIAL SUPPORTS

PATRICIA NOONAN WALSH, ERIC EMERSON AND JANET ROBERTSON

INTRODUCTION

Taking a global view, most people with intellectual disabilities live in the less affluent, still-developing countries and rely chiefly on family care (McConkey and O'Toole 2000). By contrast, Europe is a prosperous region where most countries have a tradition of formal, special services for people with intellectual disabilities. Where do people with intellectual disabilities live if they move away from their family homes? In Ireland, addresses like bungalow, unit, chalet, ward, hospital, hostel, group home and others describe an array of shelters. Some have a long history: they have dotted the service landscape for decades or centuries, embedded tightly within the surrounding community. Newer forms of residential support continue to emerge, such as flats or small houses where one or two persons choose to live as tenants. What do people and their families prefer? What indicates good quality and good outcomes for residents? What can service-providers afford to spend? If they spend more, will the outcomes be better? Today's questions are rooted in an institutional past, but the answers will help to shape the residential supports of the near future.

This chapter addresses briefly some issues involved in appraising the quality of residential supports for people with intellectual disabilities. First, it identifies current trends in patterns of residence. Next, it examines some measures of quality typically used in appraising outcomes for residents. It asks whether spending more necessarily means higher quality, drawing on evidence from recent studies. Finally, it discusses implications for both practice and policy in building supports that are likely to enhance the quality of residents' lives.

PATTERNS OF RESIDENCE

Globally, most people with intellectual disabilities live with their families. In the United States, for example, it is estimated that about 60% of people in this group do so (Seltzer and Krauss 2001). These authors comment that, although such families may incur additional expenditure with little guidance from a formal service system, more is known about the quality of life of individuals living in group homes or other residential settings. Drawing on cross-cultural data, Braddock *et al.* (2001) surveyed where people with intellectual disabilities currently live in five countries with developed service systems—Australia, Canada, England, the United States and Wales. Nearly all children and many adults in these countries lived in family homes, but the likelihood of placement outside the family home rose steadily with adulthood and progressively so as adults aged. These authors identified trends towards smaller, community settings, although many people with intellectual disabilities were living in larger groups than would be found among their peers in the general population. A further important finding was that all five countries reported that the availability of out-of-family residential provision was insufficient to meet current or future need or demand.

The recent past
Not very long ago, institutions were the leading form of out-of-family residential provision in many developed countries. In the United States, for example, institutions grew in size and number after the first establishments opened in the mid-nineteenth century: more than 11,000 were recorded in 1900 (Braddock and Parish 2001). But trends favouring greater presence in the community on the part of adults with intellectual disability have strengthened in the recent past. Government policy initiatives in many countries extended ordinary living opportunities to individuals who previously lived in institutional settings. Ideological changes swept across the five Nordic countries—distinct in culture but related by the thrust of their social welfare policies. Decades of change in providing supports for people with intellectual disability culminated in an overall enhancement of the quality of living environments for adults and widespread assent to the view that long-stay total institutions are neither desired nor needed (Tøssebro *et al.* 1996).

Trends towards deinstitutionalisation spread more widely by the end of the twentieth century. In the United States the population of residents in institutions fell by nearly a half (45%) between 1985 and 1996 as individuals moved to community settings (Stancliffe and Lakin 1998). In England the numbers of people with intellectual disabilities resident in state-operated institutions declined by 93% from 51,000 in 1976 to just over 3,500 in 2002. This reduction was accompanied by a corresponding increase in the number of people supported in smaller community-based residential services based on the use of domestic housing (Emerson and Hatton 1994; Kavanagh and Opit 1998).

Still, considerable variation in the size and form of residential supports persists in many European countries (Emerson, Hatton *et al.* 1996) with remnants of institutional provision (Walsh 1997). Even within countries, regional differences in the numbers of residential places and in the types of residential settings provided are apparent. In England deinstitutionalisation has not been a unified policy. There have been, and remain, significant variations over time and across localities in the ways in which these policy changes have been effected (cf. Bailey and Cooper 1997; Emerson and Hatton 1997; 1998; 2000). Leading up to 1980, deinstitutionalisation primarily involved the movement of those individuals with the least severe disabilities to a range of often pre-existing services, including hostels, semi-supported group homes, family placement schemes, bed-and-breakfast arrangements and independent living.

Since then, however, attention has switched to the development of community-based residential provision for people with more severe and complex disabilities. Initially such services were provided within purpose-built 20–24-place locally based hospital or community units to serve a defined geographical area (Felce et al. 1980). During the mid-1980s, however, these ideas gave way (at least in most areas) to services which provide staff support to people with severe disabilities within smaller domestic-scale dispersed housing schemes (Felce 1989; Lowe and de Paiva 1991). More recently, advocates of supported living—that is, arrangements where one or two individuals choose to live as householders—have questioned the appropriateness of group homes (Kinsella 1993; Simons 1995; 1997).

Village communities

Community-based residential supports are not, of course, the only alternative to traditional forms of institutional care. Other options include intentional or village communities—places where residents both with and without disabilities may choose to live. In the UK, the vast majority of people who live in intentional or village communities are relatively able and moved there from their family home or from residential special schools for children with intellectual disabilities. As such, the village community movement has developed independently of deinstitutionalisation. It has, however, been argued that village communities could be created out of state-operated institutions (Brook 1990).

However, a number of newly built state-operated residential campuses have been developed in the UK as a direct result of deinstitutionalisation. These are operated by National Health Service (NHS) organisations and provide residential support and centralised services on a campus site, typically supporting people with more severe and complex disabilities. None of these share the ideological underpinnings of village communities. Rather they represent a new wave of state-operated institutional provision.

Trends in Ireland

Ireland, with its population of 3.9 million persons, has for some years endorsed a policy of community living for people with intellectual disabilities. A government-led review group on services for this population recommended that sufficient family supports should be set in place so that adults might remain living in their own homes for as long as possible, and that any substitute home should '. . . have all the characteristics of a good family home' (*Needs and abilities* 1990, 38). This policy document described placement in a residential centre as the least-favoured option, envisaged as suitable chiefly for individuals with severe and profound levels of disability and/or complex needs.

But considerable variation in providing residential supports for Irish adults with intellectual disability was apparent within both statutory and voluntary sectors at the start of the twenty-first century. The demand for residential supports nonetheless shows no sign of abating. On the contrary, the Irish Department of Health and Children, the main funding body for residential supports for Irish people with intellectual disability, has documented a growing demand for full-time residential places from two distinct groups of adults. A first group is made up of those who presently live in another form of residential setting but who wish to transfer to community-based settings such as group homes. The second group comprises hundreds of adults living in the family home who urgently require full-time residential supports (Health Research Board 2001).

Group homes and campus residences, many traditionally managed by religious and other voluntary bodies (see Chapter 2 in this volume), are two dominant models of residential support currently provided for Irish adults. Of the 17,620 Irish adults aged 20 years or older recorded in the National Intellectual Disability Database in 2000, a total of 6594 received full-time residential services. Most lived in community group homes (2239) or in residential centres (3129), while a further 806 adults were living in psychiatric hospitals (Health Research Board 2001). The remaining adults received supported living services or lived in 'de-designated units'—separate buildings on the grounds of psychiatric hospitals dedicated to accommodating adults with intellectual disability. A few lived in intentional or village communities such as those managed by the Camphill Communities of Ireland. As the greying population of adults with intellectual disability continues to expand, the demand for residential supports will increase. By 2000, about 400 adults aged 20 years or older were on a waiting list for residential services (*ibid.*).

Measures of quality

Although supporting individuals to achieve a better quality of life is an aspiration widely endorsed in Ireland, there is as yet no agreed national standard of either service quality or user outcomes among the residential supports provided by an array of statutory and voluntary agencies. Many agencies develop their own sets of tools to measure quality, or perhaps commission external evaluators to appraise residential and other supports for people with intellectual disabilities. Other providers may adopt ready-made procedures such as *Personal Outcome Measures* (Council 2000) and train their staff to apply these.

Policy-makers in Ireland must plan appropriate supports in a new funding environment (Department of Health 1995). Until recently, service agencies providing residential and other services for people with intellectual disability were funded centrally by the Irish Department of Health. As a step towards implementing a national health strategy, regional health boards have assumed responsibility for funding voluntary agencies providing residential and other services to people with intellectual disability. While acknowledging that the existing practices for arriving at a dependency unit cost are not satisfactory, it has been recommended that '. . . Until a costed service methodology is developed, the annual allocation to agencies will continue to be based on the existing allocation process' (*ibid.*, 47). Currently there is no overall mechanism in Ireland to link service model and costs either with indicators of the quality of residential supports or with user outcomes.

In the next sections, some research findings related to the costs and the quality and outcomes for residents—for example, in terms of choice, level of risk, community participation or health—living in different residential settings in the UK and in Ireland are presented. While the two jurisdictions differ in size and in the structure of their health and social service systems, there are nevertheless common strands in current practice in providing residential supports for people with intellectual disabilities as well as in meeting the challenge posed by gaps in provision.

QUALITY AND COSTS: A STUDY IN THE UK

In 1998 a research team in the UK was commissioned to undertake a comparative cost-benefit analysis of community-based residential services (including supported living arrangements), village communities and NHS campuses. A parallel study, smaller in scale, took place in Ireland with support from the Department of Health and Children (Walsh *et al.* 2000, *inter alia*). Full details on the methods used to complete the studies have been reported elsewhere (Emerson, Robertson *et al.* 2000a; 2000b; 2000c; 2001; Gregory *et al.* 2001; Hallam and Emerson 1999; Hallam *et al.* 2002; Robertson *et al.* 2000a; 2000b; 2001a; 2001b; Walsh *et al.* 2001). Potential services in both jurisdictions were identified through a process of consultation with organisations and advocacy groups representing the interests of parents of people with intellectual disabilities, service-providers and the research and development community. The aim of the consultation was to identify services considered by key informants to be examples of 'good' or 'better' practice within that particular model of residential support.

Participants and residences

Ultimately, information was collected on 500 participants across seventeen services in the UK. These included 86 participants in three *intentional or village communities*, 133 participants in five *NHS campuses*, and 281 participants in ten community-based *dispersed housing schemes*. Of the latter, 63 people were identified as receiving *supported living schemes*.

The three *village communities* were operated by charities. None of these services had been developed as a direct result of the downsizing and closure of state-operated institutions. All expressed an aim of providing a partially self-contained community for their residents. The number of long-term residents supported on site ranged from 28 to 179. The mean number of residents per living unit ranged from seven to eight. In two of the village communities the majority of living units were free-standing buildings grouped in close proximity to centralised day and leisure facilities. In the third community, seventeen of the participants lived in a house for 25 people, the remainder living in houses for two to five people clustered around the central facility.

The five *residential campuses* were all operated by NHS organisations. They had all been developed as a direct result of the closure of NHS institutions for people with intellectual disabilities. The number of long-term residents supported on site ranged from 94 to 144. The mean number of residents per living unit ranged from seven to ten. In all five residential campuses the majority of living units were free-standing buildings grouped in close proximity to centralised day and leisure facilities.

Measures

Information about the setting in which participants were supported was collected by a combination of interview and ratings completed by research staff. They used a modified version of the Residential Services Setting Questionnaire (Emerson, Alborz *et al.* 1995), the Architectural Features Scale (Thompson *et al.* 1990), the Residential Services Working Practices Scale (Felce *et al.* 1995) and the Group Home Management Interview (Raynes *et al.* 1994). These scales provided information on the size and location of the setting; the age and gender of the participant served; the number and qualifications of staff employed within the setting; aspects of the physical environment; procedures implemented within the setting regarding person-centred planning, assessment and teaching, the planning of daily and weekly activity, arranging staff support for resident activity, and the training and supervision of staff; and the extent to which the setting embodied the cardinal features of 'total institutions' (block treatment, depersonalisation, rigidity of routines, social distance).

Information about the participants was collected by a combination of questionnaire and interview with a member of the participant's support team on: the abilities and skills of the person and the presence of additional physical and sensory impairments (Nihira *et al.* 1993, part 1); the severity of challenging behaviour (Aman *et al.* 1995); mental health (Moss *et al.* 1998); and autism (Howlin 1996).

Information was collected from key staff pertaining to a range of outcomes. These included involvement in leisure and community-based activities (a modified form of the Index of Community Involvement: Raynes *et al.* 1994); social networks (a modified version of the Social Network Map: Tracy and Abell 1994; Tracy and Whittaker 1990); smoking, alcohol use, diet and physical exercise (items from Bennett *et al.* 1995 and Turner 1997); the extent to which the person could exercise choice and control over key aspects of his/her life (Hatton *et al.*, in press); and level of risk of exposure to accidents and injuries, abuse and exploitation (Emerson, Robertson *et al.* 1999). For a small subsample of participants with severe and complex disabilities non-participant behavioural observation was used to collect information regarding participant engagement in constructive activity and staff support (for details see Emerson, Robertson *et al.* 2000b).

The views of UK participants were obtained through semi-structured interviews (Gregory *et al.* 2001). The views of relatives of participants in both the UK and Ireland were obtained through a postal questionnaire (Walsh *et al.* 2001).

Service costings

A revised version of the Client Service Receipt Inventory (Beecham and Knapp 1992; Beecham 1995) was completed for each participant to collect data relating to accommodation arrangements, income and expenditure, and use of services over the previous three months. The Residential Services Setting Questionnaire (Emerson, Alborz *et al.* 1995) was used to record information about managing agency arrangements, staffing levels within individual houses and the physical layout of each site. To allow facility-specific costs to be calculated, additional information was collected from analysis of facility accounts. In order to estimate the long-run marginal (opportunity) costs of building-based services, the cost implications of these buildings were included in the total accommodation facility cost. All capital costs were annuitised over an expected 60-year lifespan at a discount rate of eight per cent (Netten *et al.* 1998). Ten per cent of the annual figure was added as an estimate of the cost of replacement of fixtures and fittings.

Services received by clients independently of their accommodation arrangements were costed using national unit costs data (Netten *et al.* 1998). All hospital- and community-based services and day centres were costed in this way, as were education and training programs where these services were not included as part of the residential package. At the end of the costing process, the researchers had defined and costed a service package unique to each study participant: all costs relating to residential services, day activities and use of all other services were represented as their weekly contribution to the total cost of care.

Outcomes

Outcomes for residents were compared across different forms of residential settings in the UK (Emerson, Robertson *et al.* 2000a), identifying comparative advantages for residents in dispersed as opposed to congregate, campus-based housing. These included a more homely setting, more recreational opportunities, less institutional care, and a greater likelihood to name a person who was not a paid staff member, family member or another person with intellectual disability on their social networks. In village communities, residents were more likely to report health checks and contact with health professionals, more day activities and less risk of exploitation in the local community (Emerson, Robertson *et al.* 2000a). These authors suggest that variability in quality exists within any particular approach to providing residential supports and that service 'models' and costs have 'at best a tenuous relationship with indicators of service quality or user outcome' (*ibid.*, 15).

In summary, participants in dispersed housing schemes experienced relatively greater choice, more extensive social networks overall with both people with intellectual disabilities and local people, a more physically active life, fewer accidents in their home, and a greater number and variety of leisure activities. On the other hand, they can also expect to experience relatively greater exposure to crime and verbal abuse, and a shorter 'working week'. Participants in village communities experienced relatively more extensive social networks overall, less exposure to crime and verbal abuse, and a longer 'working week'. On the other hand, they can also expect to experience relatively less choice and a reduced number and variety of leisure activities. Participants in residential campuses experienced relatively less choice, less extensive social networks, a less physically active life, more accidents in their home, a reduced number and variety of leisure activities, greater exposure to crime and verbal abuse, and a shorter 'working week'.

Satisfaction

In the UK, participants in village communities and those in dispersed housing schemes reported similar levels of satisfaction overall in six of the seven domains assessed. But residents in village communities tended to express greater satisfaction with their friendships and social relationships (Gregory *et al.* 2001). Relatives rated the quality of supports received by participants across the three models in the UK or Ireland similarly (Emerson, Robertson *et al.* 2000a; Walsh *et al.* 2001). There were differences, however, in relatives' opposition to their family member's current placement, support from family and friends and statutory services.

When compared with small group homes, participants in supported living schemes experienced greater choice overall, greater choice as to where and with whom they lived, and a greater number of community-based activities. They also, however, had fewer hours and days per week of scheduled activity, were more likely to have had their home vandalised and were considered at greater risk of exploitation from people in the local community. When compared with large group homes, participants in small group homes had larger social networks, more staff in their social networks, more people in their social networks who were not staff or family and did not have intellectual disabilities, and were considered at less risk of abuse from co-residents. There were no statistically significant differences in any domain between the rated satisfaction of participants or their relatives in supported living schemes, small group homes and large group homes (Emerson, Robertson *et al.* 2000a; 2001).

Costs and outcomes

The researchers in the UK used two approaches to explore the relationship between costs and the outcomes which discriminated between the service models (Emerson, Robertson *et al.* 2000a; 2001). First, they controlled for the effects of adaptive behaviour and challenging behaviour and found that in village communities increased costs were only associated with increased performance on one of the thirteen quality indicators—physical activity. In residential campuses increased costs were associated with increased performance on three of the thirteen quality indicators—physical activity, number of recreational/community activities, and variety of recreational/community activities. In dispersed housing schemes increased costs were associated with increased performance on six of the thirteen quality indicators—choice, variety of recreational/community activities, total size of social network, number of 'others' in social network, number of days and hours of scheduled activity, and reduced perceived risk of exploitation.

The supports provided to people with the most severe and complex disabilities were analysed, also controlling for the effects of residents' levels of adaptive behaviour (Emerson, Robertson *et al.* 2000b). Increased total costs of residential supports for these individuals were associated with poorer procedures for assessment and teaching, less block treatment, greater variety of community-based activities, and greater amounts of praise.

Second, the researchers in the UK explored the relationship between resource inputs (e.g. cost, staff qualifications, user characteristics), service processes (such as internal management arrangements and institutional practices) and selected outcomes (Emerson, Robertson *et al.* 2000c; Robertson *et al.* 2000a; 2000b; 2001a; 2001b).

Benefits

A relatively clear picture of benefits for residents emerged from these results. First, across a range of measures of inputs and process and user outcomes (for example, residents' choice, activity, social networks, medication usage), residential campuses operated by the NHS offered a significantly poorer quality of care and quality of life than dispersed housing schemes. The researchers concluded that these deficiencies could not be accounted for by differences in the characteristics of people supported. They suggested that the additional costs associated with dispersed housing schemes (15% greater than residential campuses) may be justified when considered in light of the substantial benefits noted above.

Second, there appeared to be a distinct pattern of benefits associated with dispersed housing schemes (choice, size of social networks, social integration, recreational/leisure activities) and village communities (size of social networks, reduced risk of exposure to verbal abuse and crime, greater number of days and hours per week of scheduled day activities). These patterns are consistent with the ideological bases of these two approaches to providing residential support. The cost differential between the two approaches, the total adjusted costs of dispersed housing schemes being 20% greater than those associated with village communities, is of clear policy relevance given the growing level of unmet need for residential support for people with intellectual disabilities in the UK (Office of the Deputy Prime Minister and Department of Health 2003).

Third, size was an important factor even within dispersed housing schemes in that larger group homes were consistently associated with poorer outcomes than either smaller group homes or supported living schemes. When smaller group homes were compared with supported living schemes, different patterns of benefit were apparent (Emerson, Robertson *et al.* 2001). These results were consistent with those reported by Howe *et al.* (1998) in suggesting that, for similar costs, supported living schemes may offer distinct benefits in the areas of resident choice and community participation.

Fourth, there were no statistically significant differences in any domain between the rated satisfaction of either participants or their relatives (Gregory *et al.* 2001; Walsh *et al.* 2001). In general, and in common with previous research, participants tended to rate their satisfaction highly. Such high levels of expressed satisfaction are also common among studies which have solicited the views of relatives. This is consistent with previous research in the UK and elsewhere, indicating that discrimination in the views of service-users and/or relatives is only likely when it is possible for them to make comparative judgements (Stancliffe *et al.*, in press). Thus, for example, relatives typically rate the quality of care provided within traditional institutions very highly, and may often express considerable opposition to deinstitutionalisation (Tøssebro 1996). However, longitudinal studies have repeatedly demonstrated that, following their relation's move to community-based services, relatives rate these services highly and, in retrospect, tend to express preference for the new arrangements (e.g. Conroy 1996; Tuvesson and Ericsson 1996; Wing 1989).

Finally, the results of the project were also consistent in indicating that in multivariate analyses the costs of service provision were unrelated to outcomes. Again, these results are consistent with the existing UK literature that suggests that, while costs show moderate associations with indicators of participant need, they are largely unrelated to outcomes (Felce and Emerson, in press).

QUALITY AND COSTS: IRELAND

A companion study of quality and costs of residential supports took place in Ireland from 1998 to 2001 using the same protocol developed in the UK and described here (Emerson, Robertson *et al.* 2000a) Eleven service-provider organisations managing the residences where participants lived were invited to take part in the study. These organisations were considered to be exemplars of good and/or typical practice in providing either campus or group home residential supports in two regions of Ireland. Other forms of residential provision—supported living, adult foster homes, psychiatric hospitals or 'de-designated units' associated with hospital campuses—were not included.

Procedure
The procedure for data collection was similar for each of the eleven participating services in Ireland. A sampling frame was constructed comprising all adults (age 18+) receiving 24-hour long-term residential support (i.e. excluding people receiving short-term care or assessment and treatment on a residential basis). From this a random sample of potential participants was selected.

Informed consent was sought from each potential participant according to the practices of each provider organisation. If they were unable to give informed consent, agreement for participation was obtained from either (1) the user's independent advocate, (2) the closest family member who was in regular contact with the person, or (3) the chief executive or medical director of the provider organisation. If neither consent nor agreement were obtained, a further potential participant was selected from the sampling frame.

Participants
Ultimately, 65 Irish residents living in campus settings providing congregate care and 60 group home residents took part. The size of living unit was significantly larger in the campus residential settings. Residents in both forms of setting were similar in age and gender profiles (Table 1). However, campus residents were more likely to have previously resided in the family home and had spent longer in their current setting. Irish group home residents were, on the whole, more able than those living in campus settings: they reported significantly higher levels of ability on all subscales and total scores of the Adaptive Behavior Scale, part 1 (Walsh *et al.* 2000) (Table 1).

Copies of the instruments were distributed to members of staff who knew the participant. Following this, research staff visited the service and completed structured interviews with the participant (wherever appropriate) and a member of care staff who acted as key informant. Finally, researchers from the Institute of Psychiatry in the UK and/or the Centre for Health Economics at the National University of Ireland visited the service to obtain cost information from agency accounts.

	Group homes	Village communities	Test & stat. sig. *
Age (years)			
average age	40.6	35.8	n.s.
range	19–66	19–75	
standard deviation	10.8	14.4	
Gender			
% men	55% (n=33)	68% (n=44)	n.s.
% women	45% (n=27)	32% (n=21)	
ABS mean score1	222.6	113.2	p<.oo1 (t)

Table 1 — Age, gender and ABS (part 1) scores — Irish residents.

Choice	In general, group home residents were provided with significantly more opportunities to express choice on a range of day-to-day activities than campus residents.
Relationships with family	While group home residents lived significantly further away from family than campus residents, campus residents reported significantly more visits to and from family.
Extent of social network	Group home residents had significantly larger social networks than campus residents.
Health	No differences were reported between the two models regarding body mass index, level of physical activity, alcohol consumption, cigarette-smoking and diet. Both groups did, however, report marked differences from normative data.
Risks	Group home residents were more likely to have been the victim of a crime or to have experienced vandalism to their house, while campus residents were more likely to have experienced accidents within the residential home.
Work & education	Group home residents were more likely to engage in sheltered or supported employment while campus residents were more likely to attend day/social education centres. Group home residents engaged in significantly more scheduled activity per week than campus residents.
Day & leisure activities	Group home residents were more likely than campus residents to engage in a variety of daily activities such as shopping or attending a hairdresser. They were also more likely to have had a holiday in the preceding year.

Table 2 — Outcomes for residents in Ireland.

Outcomes

Outcomes for Irish group home residents (60) and those in campus residential settings (65) differed significantly in some domains (Table 2).

Summary of findings

The main findings of the Irish study are summarised below; a detailed discussion of methodology and results appears elsewhere (Walsh *et al.* 2000, *inter alia*).

- *Higher ability* of Irish residents was associated with their having more choices and work opportunities.
- *Homeliness* of the residential setting was associated with higher ability of the residents and more choice.
- Average weekly *costs* were higher for individuals residing in campus settings: these residences also had significantly higher scores on negative aspects of social climate, such as depersonalisation and block treatment of residents.
- Higher ability of residents was associated with *lower costs*, but this relationship was not linear.
- Finally, it was striking that the *costs* of residential supports did not predict *quality* of outcomes for residents, reflecting similar findings from the larger UK study.

Implications for practice and policy

Findings of the study were examined further to determine what factors predicted better outcomes for residents. These analyses yielded implications for those charged with providing residential supports for people with intellectual disabilities in Ireland:

- *Family contact* was more prevalent among residents with less ability who have moved from home more recently, suggesting that families retain a greater share in providing personal and instrumental support in the early years for residents in their new settings. Providers may wish to monitor levels of family contact over time, even while they actively nurture individuals in forming additional friendships and other social contacts.
- Residents' *personal characteristics* appear to have little predictive value in determining the quality of individual outcomes. While it is not surprising that higher levels of ability are associated with more choices and work opportunities, service-providers may wish to explore specific reasons why individuals with less ability appear to be removed from these opportunities.
- The *homeliness* of the residential setting was associated with higher levels of resident ability and higher levels of resident choice. It was striking that all residents in group homes in Ireland (Walsh *et al.* 2000) were of greater ability than their counterparts in campus settings, and that group home settings

were appraised as being significantly more homelike. It seems that people with higher ability have more opportunity to live in more homely, less institutionalised settings.

- In many cases, *health checks* for residents did not seem to take place at the levels appropriate for this population and fell short of the frequency suggested for the general population in Ireland. There are important implications here for providers of residential supports for individuals with intellectual disabilities, but also for those charged with responsibility for public health and health services generally (Prasher and Janicki 2002).

- Relatively few residents were engaged in work or leisure *activities* in inclusive settings. Providers of residential supports may usefully examine residents' patterns of activity to ensure that they are in keeping with other policy goals such as enhanced community presence and participation of adults with intellectual disabilities.

- Residents were most likely to have opportunities for making *choices* about details of their lives within residences, and least likely to decide where they wished to live, with whom, and with which members of staff to support them. It was striking that these issues of fundamental importance for most adults in Irish society were dormant for the adults with intellectual disabilities who took part in this study.

- High-quality individual planning, teaching and assessment on the part of professional *staff* members were associated with positive outcomes for residents. The implications of these findings for service-providers in the recruitment, development and retention of staff are potentially very great.

Practice

If residential supports set out to embody some of the findings reported here, what would they look like? Good practice based on the evidence of the studies outlined here would bear three indelible hallmarks. First, providers would focus resources and processes in residential supports on achieving *outcomes for residents*: good health, lowered risk, more choices, richer social networks, family contact, greater community presence. Then providers would be in a position to weigh these outcomes against the costs of supports and appraise their effectiveness in terms of benefits.

Second, providers would embed *individualised planning* as the guiding principle at the heart of the residential supports offered to men and women with intellectual disabilities. Enhancing quality here—specifically in staff development—is an investment likely to yield real benefits for residents. Perceived gains for individuals might in turn influence the performance and satisfaction of professional staff members: this is a potential benefit worthy of further research.

Third, wise providers and policy-makers would take heed of two forceful and unavoidable principles shaping society today: *demography and diversity*. For example, more adults with intellectual disabilities will live into middle and old age, and more will seek suitable homes in the community (see Chapter 9). They will experience the same functional declines associated with ageing as are apparent in the general population, and may also develop specific losses owing to illness or factors arising from their environment or life circumstances. Their distinctive needs, and those of other groups, must be taken into account when planning an array of residential supports suited to an increasingly diverse population.

SUMMARY

Generally, people with intellectual disabilities live at home. While family care is dominant, in the more developed countries such as the UK or Ireland people with intellectual disabilities tend to move out of home as they age. Less is known about patterns or outcomes for individuals living in the less affluent countries. Overall, trends towards deinstitutionalisation have swept across most countries in Europe, although variation in patterns of residence is apparent, even within countries. It is likely that all but a few countries hold fast to institutions. Diverse views on where men and women with intellectual disabilities should live have fuelled considerable debate. Researchers continue to address important questions about the quality and costs of residential supports. Two such studies were carried out in the UK and Ireland, brief reports of which appear in this chapter. They indicate that different forms of residential support yield different outcomes for residents, even when resident characteristics such as level of adaptive behaviour are taken into account. In both studies, smaller size of the living unit was associated with certain positive outcomes for residents. And in both studies the costs of residential supports did not predict quality or outcomes for residents. Future research should inform policies to shape residential supports that are more likely to yield measurable benefits for men and women with intellectual disabilities. In practice, this means supporting individuals so that they may lead satisfying lives in a setting that resembles 'a good family home' (*Needs and abilities* 1990, 38).

ACKNOWLEDGEMENTS

The authors acknowledge gratefully the cooperation of many participants, staff members, families and service organisations in the UK and Ireland. The research studies described here were funded by the Department of Health (UK) and Department of Health and Children (Ireland). The opinions expressed in this chapter do not necessarily reflect those of the funding bodies. Finally, the authors retain responsibility for any inaccuracies that may inadvertently appear.

REFERENCES

Aman, M.G., Burrow, W.H. and Wolford, P.L. (1995) The Aberrant Behavior Checklist—community: factor validity and effect of subject variables for adults in group homes. *American Journal on Mental Retardation* **100**, 283–92.

Bailey, N.M. and Cooper, S.-A. (1997) The current provision of specialist health services to people with learning disabilities in England and Wales. *Journal of Intellectual Disability Research* **41**, 52–9.

Beecham, J. (1995) Collecting and estimating costs. In M.R.J. Knapp (ed.), *The economic evaluation of mental health care*. Aldershot. Arena.

Beecham, J. and Knapp, M.R.J. (1992) Costing psychiatric interventions. In G.J. Thornicroft, C.R. Brewin and J.K. Wing (eds), *Measuring mental health needs*. London. Gaskell.

Bennett, N., Dodd, T., Flatley, J., Freeth, S. and Bolling, K. (1995) *The Health Survey for England 1993*. London. Stationery Office.

Braddock, D. and Parish, S. (2001) An institutional history of disability. In G.L. Albrecht, K.D. Seelman and M. Bury (eds), *Handbook of disability studies*, 11–68. Thousand Oaks CA. Sage Publications.

Braddock, D., Emerson, E., Felce, D. and Stancliffe, R.J. (2001) Living circumstances of children and adults with mental retardation or developmental disabilities in the United States, Canada, England and Wales and Australia. *Mental Retardation and Developmental Disabilities Research Reviews* **7**, 115–21.

Brook, M. (1990) Evolution from a mental handicap hospital into a village. In S. Segal (ed.), *The place of special villages and residential communities: the provision of care for people with severe, profound and multiple disabilities*, 29–38. Bicester. AB Academic Publishers.

Conroy, J.W. (1996) Results of deinstitutionalisation in Connecticut. In J. Mansell and K. Ericsson (eds), *Deinstitutionalisation and community living: intellectual disability services in Britain, Scandinavia and the USA*. London. Chapman and Hall.

Council (2000) *Personal Outcome Measures*. Towson MD. Council on Quality Leadership in Supports for People with Disabilities.

Department of Health (1995) *Enhancing the partnership*. Dublin. Government Publications.

Emerson, E. and Hatton, C. (1994) *Moving out: the impact of relocation from hospital to community on the quality of life of people with learning disabilities*. London. HMSO.

Emerson, E. and Hatton, C. (1996) Deinstitutionalization in the UK: outcomes for service users. *Journal of Intellectual and Developmental Disability* **21**, 17–37.

Emerson, E. and Hatton, C. (1997) Regional and local variations in residential provision for people with learning disabilities in England. *Tizard Learning Disability Review* **2**, 43–6.

Emerson, E. and Hatton, C. (1998) Residential provision for people with intellectual disabilities in England, Wales and Scotland. *Journal of Applied Research in Intellectual Disabilities* **11**, 1–14.

Emerson, E. and Hatton, C. (2000) Residential supports for people with learning disabilities in 1997 in England. *Tizard Learning Disability Review* **5**, 41–4.

Emerson, E., Alborz, A., Felce, D. and Lowe, K. (1995) *Residential Services Setting Questionnaire*. Manchester. Hester Adrian Research Centre, University of Manchester.

Emerson, E., Hatton, C., Bauer, I. *et al.* (1996) Patterns of institutionalisation in 15 European countries. *European Journal on Mental Disability* **3**, 29–32.

Emerson, E., Robertson, J., Gregory, N. *et al.* (1999) *Quality and costs of residential supports for people with learning disabilities: a comparative analysis of quality and costs in village communities, residential campuses and dispersed housing schemes.* Manchester. Hester Adrian Research Centre, University of Manchester.

Emerson, E., Robertson, J., Gregory, N. *et al.* (2000a) The quality and costs of village communities, residential campuses and community-based residential supports in the UK. *American Journal of Mental Retardation* **105**, 81–102.

Emerson, E., Robertson, J., Gregory, N. *et al.* (2000b) The quality and costs of community-based residential supports and residential campuses for people with severe and complex disabilities. *Journal of Intellectual and Developmental Disabilities* **25**, 263–79.

Emerson, E., Robertson, J., Gregory, N., Hatton, C., Kessissoglou, S., Hallam, A. and Hillery, J. (2000c) The treatment and management of challenging behaviours in residential settings. *Journal of Applied Research in Intellectual Disabilities* **13**, 197–215.

Emerson, E., Robertson, J., Gregory, N. *et al.* (2001) The quality and costs of supported living residences and group homes in the United Kingdom. *American Journal of Mental Retardation* **106**, 401–15.

Emerson, E., Robertson, J., Hatton, C., Knapp, M. and Walsh, P.N. (in press) Costs and outcomes of community residential supports in England. In R. Stancliffe and C. Lakin (eds), *Costs and outcomes: community services for people with intellectual disabilities.* Baltimore. Brookes.

Felce, D. (1989) *The Andover Project: staffed housing for adults with severe or profound mental handicaps.* Kidderminster. British Institute for Mental Handicap.

Felce, D. and Emerson, E. (in press) Community living, outcomes and economies of scale. In R. Stancliffe and C. Lakin (eds), *Costs and outcomes: community services for people with intellectual disabilities.* Baltimore. Brookes.

Felce, D., Kushlick, A. and Mansell, J. (1980) Evaluation of alternative residential facilities for the severely mentally handicapped in Wessex: client engagement. *Advances in Behaviour Research and Therapy* **3**, 13–18.

Felce, D., Lowe, K. and Emerson, E. (1995) *Residential Services Working Practices Scale.* Cardiff. Welsh Centre on Learning Disabilities Applied Research Unit.

Gregory, N., Robertson, J., Kessissoglou, S., Emerson, E. and Hatton, C. (2001)

Predictors of expressed satisfaction among people with intellectual disabilities receiving residential supports. *Journal of Intellectual Disability Research* **45**, 279–92.

Hallam, A. and Emerson, E. (1999) Costs of residential supports for people with learning disabilities. In A. Netten, J. Dennett and J. Knight (eds), *Unit costs of health and social care*. Canterbury. PSSRU, University of Kent at Canterbury.

Hallam, A., Knapp, M., Järbrink, K. *et al.* (2002) The costs of residential supports for people with intellectual disabilities. *Journal of Intellectual Disability Research* **46**, 394–404.

Hatton, C., Emerson, E., Robertson, J., Gregory, N. and Kessissoglou, S. (in press) The resident choice scale: a measure to assess opportunities for self-determination in residential settings. *Journal of Intellectual Disability Research.*

Health Research Board (2001) *Report on the Irish Intellectual Disability Database 2000.* Dublin. Health Research Board. <www.hrb.ie>

Howe, J., Horner, R.H. and Newton, J.S. (1998) Comparison of supported living and traditional residential services in the State of Oregon. *Mental Retardation* **36**, 1–11.

Howlin, P. (1996) *Autism Screening Questionnaire.* London. St George's Medical School.

Kavanagh, S. and Opit, L. (1998) *The cost of caring: the economics of providing for the intellectually disabled.* London. Politeia.

Kinsella, P. (1993) *Supported living: a new paradigm.* Manchester. National Development Team.

Lowe, K. and de Paiva, S. (1991) *NIMROD—an overview.* London. HMSO.

McConkey, R. and O'Toole, B. (2000) Improving the quality of life of people with disabilities in least affluent countries: insights from Guyana. In K. Keith and R. Schalock (eds), *Cross-cultural perspectives on quality of life,* 281–90. Washington DC. AAMR.

Moss, S.C., Prosser, H., Costello, H. *et al.* (1998) Reliability and validity of the PAS-ADD Checklist for detecting psychiatric disorders in adults with intellectual disabilities. *Journal of Intellectual Disability Research* **42**, 173–83.

Needs and abilities (1990) *Needs and abilities—a policy for the intellectually disabled.* Dublin. Government Publications.

Netten, A. , Dennett, J. and Knight, J. (1998) *The unit costs of health and social care.* Canterbury. Personal Social Services Research Unit.

Nihira, K., Leland, H. and Lambert, N. (1993) *Adaptive Behavior Scale—residential and community* (2nd edn). Austin TX. Pro-Ed.

Office of the Deputy Prime Minister and Department of Health (2003) *Housing and support services for people with learning disabilities.* London. Office of the Deputy Prime Minister and Department of Health.

Prasher, V.P. and Janicki, M.P. (eds) (2002) *Physical health of adults with intellectual disabilities.* Oxford. Blackwell.

Raynes, N.V., Wright, K., Shiell, A. and Pettipher, C. (1994) *The cost and quality of* community residential care: an evaluation of the services for adults with learning disabilities. London. David Fulton.

Robertson, J., Emerson, E., Gregory, N., Hatton, C., Kessissoglou, S. and Hallam, A. (2000a) Receipt of psychotropic medication by people with intellectual disabilities in residential settings. *Journal of Intellectual Disability Research* **44**, 666–76.

Robertson, J., Emerson, E., Gregory, N., Hatton, C., Turner, S., Kessissoglou, S. and Hallam, A. (2000b) Lifestyle related risk factors for poor health in residential settings for people with intellectual disabilities. *Research in Developmental Disabilities* **21**, 469–86.

Robertson, J., Emerson, E., Gregory, N., Hatton, C., Kessissoglou, S., Hallam, A. and Linehan, C. (2001a) Social networks of people with intellectual disabilities in residential settings. *Mental Retardation* **39**, 201–14.

Robertson, J., Emerson, E., Hatton, C., Gregory, N., Kessissoglou, S., Hallam, A. and Walsh, P.N. (2001b) Environmental opportunities for exercising self-determination in residential settings. *Research in Developmental Disabilities* **22**, 487–502.

Seltzer, M.M. and Krauss, M.W. (2001) Quality of life of adults with mental retardation/developmental disabilities who live with family. *Mental Retardation and Developmental Disabilities Research Reviews* **7**, 105–14.

Simons, K. (1995) *My home, my life: innovative approaches to housing and support for people with learning difficulties*. London. Values Into Action.

Simons, K. (1997) *A foot in the door: the early years of supported living for people with learning difficulties in the UK*. Manchester. National Development Team.

Stancliffe, R. and Lakin, C. (1998) Analysis of expenditures and outcomes of residential alternatives for persons with developmental disabilities. *American Journal on Mental Retardation* **102**, 552–68.

Stancliffe, R., Emerson, E. and Lakin, C. (in press) Residential supports. In E. Emerson, C. Hatton, T. Thompson and T. Parmenter (eds), *International handbook of research methods in intellectual disability*. Chichester. Wiley.

Thompson, T., Robinson, J., Graff, M. and Ingenmey, R. (1990) Home-like architectural features of residential environments. *American Journal on Mental Retardation* **95**, 328–41.

Tøssebro, J. (1996) Family attitudes to deinstitutionalisation in Norway. In J. Mansell and K. Ericsson (eds), *Deinstitutionalisation and community living: intellectual disability services in Britain, Scandinavia and the USA*. London. Chapman and Hall.

Tøssebro, J., Gustavsson, A. and Dyrendahl, G. (eds) (1996) *Intellectual disabilities in the Nordic welfare states*. Kristiansand. HøyskoleForlaget – Norwegian Academic Press.

Tracy, E.M. and Abell, N. (1994) Social network map: some further refinements on administration. *Social Work Research* **18**, 56–60.

Tracy, E.M. and Whittaker, J.K. (1990) The Social Network Map: assessing social support in clinical practice. *Families in Society* **71**, 461–70.

Turner, S. (1997) *The health needs of people using learning disability services in Tameside and Glossop*. Manchester. Hester Adrian Research Centre.

Tuvesson, B. and Ericsson, K. (1996) Relatives' opinions on institutional closure. In J. Mansell and K. Ericsson (eds), *Deinstitutionalisation and community living: intellectual disability services in Britain, Scandinavia and the USA*. London. Chapman and Hall.

Walsh, P.N. (1997) Old World—new territory: European perspectives on intellectual disability. *Journal of Intellectual Disability Research* **41**, 112–19.

Walsh, P.N., Linehan, C., Hillery, J. *et al.* (2000) *Quality and costs of residential supports for Irish adults with intellectual disability. Brief summary report*. Dublin. Centre for the Study of Developmental Disabilities, University College Dublin.

Walsh, P.N., Linehan, C., Hillery, J. *et al.* (2001) Family views of the quality of residential supports. *Journal of Applied Research in Intellectual Disabilities* **14**, 292–309.

Wing, L. (1989) *Hospital closure and the resettlement of residents: the case of Darenth Park Mental Handicap Hospital*. Aldershot. Avebury.

Note

1   Given the difference in levels of ability between residents in the two forms of support, levels of adaptive behaviour were taken into account when analysing differences observed between group homes and campus settings on any aspect of support provided. A detailed discussion appears in Walsh *et al.* 2000.

15. LAW AND DISABILITY IN IRELAND

SHIVAUN QUINLIVAN[1]

INTRODUCTION

Article 1 of the United Nations Declaration of Human Rights states:

> 'All human beings are born free and equal in dignity and rights' (UN
> General Assembly 1949, Article 1).

The use of human rights as a tool to engineer social change has long been
recognised in the context of gender, race and religious beliefs. Human rights
principles such as equality, autonomy and dignity can be applied as readily to
people with disabilities as they can to other groups. Despite that reality, Irish
law, until recently, provided the disabled community only with token charities.
The shift to a regime in which disabled persons are accorded legal rights and
entitlements is a slow and tenuous yet ongoing process.

In 1996 the Commission on the Status of People with Disabilities (1996)
published their report. This has been heralded as signifying the move from the
charity model of dealing with people with disabilities towards a rights
approach. The report has received all-party support and has been accepted as
'the blueprint for disability law reform in Ireland' (Quinn 2002). The
Commission made over 400 recommendations which have found their way into
various legislative enactments, such as the Employment Equality Act 1998 (see
Kimber 2001a; 2001b), the National Disability Authority Act 1999, the Comhairle
Act 2000, and the Equal Status Act 2000 (see Power 2000). While not part of this
package of reforms, there is also the related Mental Health Act 2001 (see Keys
2002).[2] There are still further reforms promised in the Disabilities Bill 2001 and
the Education for Persons with Disabilities Bill 2002.

While the move from charity to rights has received a certain amount of
recognition in legislation, it is questionable whether the Constitution, *Bunreacht
na hÉireann* (1937), is up to these developments. The Constitution takes
precedence over all other sources of law, with the exception of European
Community law.[3]

The Constitution establishes the state and its institutions and sets out the fundamental principles guiding the governance of the state. The Constitution forms the basis of the legal system and is amenable to interpretation by the courts. There are rights throughout the Constitution, with the majority of the personal rights contained in articles 40–44. Judicial interpretation of the relevant provisions of the Constitution, however, has not been kind to people with disabilities (*Draper v. Attorney General* 1984; *In the matter of Article 26 and the Employment Equality Bill 1996* 1997; *Sinnott v. Minister for Education* 2001). This is largely due to the weak wording of both the equality and education provisions contained within the Constitution.

CONSTITUTIONAL RIGHT TO EQUALITY

The equality provision, unlike other provisions within the Constitution, does not protect substantive rights. Instead, the purpose of Article 40.1 of the Constitution is to prohibit arbitrary and unreasonable or unjust discrimination (*O'B. v. S.* 1984) by the state. The equality guarantee does not guarantee equality in all circumstances, nor would this be desirable. Walsh J. stated of the equality guarantee that:

> 'It imports the Aristotelian concept that justice demands that we treat equals equally and unequals unequally' (*De Burca and Anderson v. Attorney General* 1976).

Accordingly, the state is entitled to make discriminations in favour of or against a particular category of persons on the basis of 'capacity, physical and moral, and of social function' (*Bunreacht na hÉireann* 1937, Article 40.1). It is only when these distinctions are deemed arbitrary, capricious or unreasonable that they will be deemed unconstitutional (*Dillane v. Ireland* 1980). The application of this relatively simple test has proven very difficult in reality. The Constitution Review Group, when discussing this point, contended that:

> 'Unfortunately, the second sentence has too frequently been used by the courts as a means of upholding legislation by reference to questionable stereotypes, thereby justifying discrimination . . .' (Constitution Review Group 1996, 228; see also *Lowth v. Minister for Social Welfare* 1999; *Norris v. Ireland* 1984).

The equality guarantee has failed to further the principle of equality in Irish law. Consequently, other constitutional rights have taken priority over equality, and legislative enactments proposed to enhance the equality agenda have been susceptible to constitutional challenge (*In the matter of Article 26 and the Employment Equality Bill 1996* 1997).

LEGISLATION

Traditionally in Ireland the equality agenda has been driven from Europe (Anti-Discrimination (Pay) Act 1974; Employment Equality Act 1977). During the early to mid-'nineties, the first attempts were made to introduce a new equality regime. The Oireachtas passed the Employment Equality Bill 1996 and the Equal Status Bill 1996 in March 1997, and in early April the president of Ireland referred the bills to the Supreme Court pursuant to Article 26 of the Constitution. Media reports of the time suggest that there was a concern that provisions in relation to religious discrimination were unconstitutional (Newman 1997). The Employment Equality Bill 1996 was deemed repugnant to the Constitution on three grounds: two of the three provisions were of a technical nature and the third related to the provisions on reasonable accommodation for people with disabilities. This in turn had an impact on the Equal Status Bill 1996, which was also deemed unconstitutional. Interestingly, the religious exemptions contained within the bill were upheld.

The Supreme Court took the view that requiring an employer to bear the costs of reasonable accommodation unless that cost gave rise to an 'undue burden' was a violation of the employer's property rights (*In the matter of Article 26 and the Employment Equality Bill 1996* 1997). The Supreme Court decision recognised the 'laudable aim of making provision for such of our fellow citizens as are disabled' (*ibid.*, 367) in accordance with the principles of social justice. However, this cost could not be placed on employers because of the Constitutional recognition given to private property (*Bunreacht na hÉireann* 1937, Article 43). Hamilton C.J. stated:

> 'the difficulty with the section now under discussion is that it attempts to transfer the cost of solving one of society's problems on to a particular group. The difficulty the Court finds with the section is not that it requires an employer to employ disabled people, but that it requires him to bear the cost of all special treatment or facilities which the disabled person may require to carry out the work unless the cost of the provision of such treatment or facilities would give rise to "undue hardship" to the employer' (*In the matter of Article 26 and the Employment Equality Bill 1996* 1997, 367–8).

Deputy Fitzgerald perhaps best summed up the situation when she stated:

> 'It is interesting to note that property rights have been found to have greater authority in our constitution than individual human rights' (*Dáil Debates* 1998, 466).

The property right at issue was the right of the employer to earn a profit. The

Supreme Court held that the right of employers to profit trumped the right of disabled persons to equality (O'Connell 1999). During its review of the reasonable accommodation provisions, the Supreme Court assumed that all reasonable accommodations would entail some level of cost and that the cost could be considerable. This assumed reality is not reflected in the US experience (Quinn *et al.* 1992). What is clear, however, is that the cost to the individual who is not accommodated is excessive. The decision can be criticised not only for ignoring the human cost but also for its refusal to ascertain what a reasonable accommodation involves. The legislation required the employer to do only what was reasonable, and even contained an 'undue hardship' provision. The Supreme Court was unwilling to allow a provision requiring reasonable accommodation to jeopardise the private property rights of employers.[4]

The result of the Supreme Court decision was that the provisions relating to reasonable accommodation had to be revisited and revised for the Employment Equality Act 1998 and the Equal Status Act 2000. There was no predecessor to the Equal Status Act 2000, which represents the first attempt by the Irish state to legislate for equality outside the sphere of employment. The Employment Equality Act 1998 continues to relate to employment, but the act does have an extended scope. The major consequences of these enactments have been the extension of the protected grounds, the introduction of the Equality Authority, and the ODEI—the Equality Tribunal.

EQUALITY ACTS

Equality regime
The Employment Equality Act 1998 and the Equal Status Act 2000 comprise what is known as the equality legislation in Ireland. The equality legislation prohibits discrimination on nine grounds (Employment Equality Act 1998, section 6; Equal Status Act 2000, section 3): gender, marital status, family status, sexual orientation, religion, age, disability, race and membership of the traveller community.

Disability
The definition of disability included in the Employment Equality Act 1998 is very broad, and it states at section 2(1) that:
> ' "disability" means —
> (a) the total or partial absence of a person's bodily or mental functions, including the absence of a part of a person's body,
> (b) the presence in the body of organisms causing, or likely to cause, chronic disease or illness,
> (c) the malfunction, malformation or disfigurement of a part of a person's body,

(d) a condition or malfunction which results in a person learning differently from a person without the condition or malfunction, or

(e) a condition, illness or disease which affects a person's thought processes, perception of reality, emotions or judgement or which results in disturbed behaviour,

and shall be taken to include a disability which exists at present, or which previously existed but no longer exists, or which may exist in the future or which is imputed to a person . . .'

The definition contained in sections 2 and 3 of the Equal Status Act 2000 is slightly different. It incorporates all elements contained within the above definition and also prohibits discrimination by association with a person with a disability.

The definition utilised is the medical model of disability with recognition of the role of society in disabling individuals and legislates accordingly. This social element prohibits discrimination against persons with a history of a disability, a possible propensity towards a disability or those imputed to have a disability. The legislative aim was that the definition should entitle all people with disabilities to the protection of the legislation and that no category of people with disabilities would be excluded by the definition (Employment Equality Act 1998, section 2).[5] In practical terms, the definition employed has not proven to be an evidentiary burden when taking a case (Employment Equality Act 1998, section 2 (1))[6].

Scope of the legislation

The Employment Equality Act 1998 relates to discrimination in the field of employment and/or occupation. Employment is broadly defined and includes pre-employment practices, conditions of employment, training or experience for or in relation to employment, promotion or regrading (Employment Equality Act 1998, section 8).

The Employment Equality Act 1998 prohibits discrimination in vocational training, advertising, collective agreements and employment agencies. It also sets several other specific guarantees of equal treatment. Section 29 promulgates an entitlement to equal pay for equal work. Like work is defined as: where two employees both perform the same work under similar conditions, or where their work is interchangeable, or where the work performed by one is of a similar nature to that performed by the other, or the work performed by one is equal in value to the work performed by the other. These general statements in sections 7 and 29 should be read in light of section 35 of the act. Section 35 allows employers to pay employees with disabilities different rates of pay if they are restricted in their capacity to do the same amount of work or to work the same hours as a person who does not have a disability. Finally, section 30 implies that all employment contracts contain an equality clause. Therefore, even where a person with a disability does not have a written contract, the act ensures that the guarantee of equal treatment is incorporated therein. On a general note, there is a requirement for a comparator. That comparator can be a person with a disability or a person with a different disability.

The Equal Status Act 2000 prohibits discrimination in the non-employment sphere. Among the activities covered by the legislation are the disposal of goods and the provision of services, the disposal of premises and the provision of accommodation, advertisements and the provision of education in any form of educational establishment. This act also prohibits discrimination in clubs, but the provisions in respect of clubs that discriminate differ from those in the aforementioned areas.

Discrimination
Both acts prohibit direct and indirect discrimination, as well as harassment based on any of the protected grounds (Employment Equality Act 1998; Equal Status Act 2000). The acts also require reasonable accommodation for persons with disabilities, provided that the accommodation does not engender more than a nominal cost. The acts are also permissive of the possibility of positive action if the purpose of that action is to eliminate the effects of discrimination within society.

Direct discrimination arises where one person is treated less favourably than another on one of the discriminatory grounds. In the interpretation of the term 'direct discrimination' under the Employment Equality Act 1998 the equality officers have relied on the European Court of Justice decision in *Finanzamt Koeln-Alstadt v. Roland Schumacker* (1995, 259), which held:

> 'It is also settled law that discrimination can arise only through the application of different rules to comparable situations or the application of the same rule to different situations'.

The equality officers have also relied on *Gillespie & Ors v. Northern Health and Social Services Board & Ors* (1996, 499), which held:

> 'It is well settled that discrimination involves the application of different rules to comparable situations, or the application of the same rules to different situations'.

While these European decisions initially related to discrimination based on nationality and gender respectively, they have been extended to cover discrimination based on a person's disability under the Employment Equality Act 1998 (see *Harrington v. East Coast Area Health Board* 2002).

Both acts also prohibit indirect discrimination. Section 31 of the Employment Equality Act 1998 prohibits the use of apparently neutral provisions where those provisions operate to the disadvantage of a group, or can be complied with by a substantially smaller proportion of people within that group and cannot be justified as being reasonable in all the circumstances of the case. Consequently, the employer must guarantee a basic level of equal treatment and an employer may actually discriminate or have discriminatory conditions where those conditions can be justified as necessary for the job in question. The complainant must show that the practice works to his/her disadvantage, and once a *prima facie* case is established the onus shifts to the employer to show that the provision is reasonable (*A Complainant v. Civil Service Commission* 2002). There is no requirement within this provision of an intention to discriminate—it is sufficient that discrimination in fact occurs. Equality officers are charged with investigating the complaints of discrimination. It is usually in the course of this investigation that the necessary statistical evidence is made available.

The definition of indirect discrimination in the Equal Status Act 2000 is slightly different. Indirect discrimination is deemed to occur where there is a precondition imposed that all must comply with equally, but with which able-bodied people are able to comply with greater ease. The precondition must be one that is capable of justification in all the circumstances of the case. There is no indication within the legislation as to what will be deemed a substantial number of persons. The courts have yet to give a precise interpretation of this amorphous term.

Both acts prohibit harassment. The Employment Equality Act 1998 covers harassment by the employer, other employees and clients of the employer. The provision also clearly places the onus on the employer to tackle harassment in the workplace. The Equal Status Act 2000 covers harassment by a person disposing of goods, accommodation or services and also by educational establishments. Harassment is defined broadly in both acts and involves subjecting a person to any unwelcome act, request or conduct, including spoken words, gestures or the production, display or circulation of written words, pictures or other material, which, in respect of the victim, is based on any discriminatory ground and could reasonably be regarded as offensive, humiliating or intimidating to him or her.

Two other points are worthy of mention. Both acts prohibit attempts to procure another person's doing anything that would amount to either discrimination or victimisation under the acts. One who commits such behaviour is deemed guilty of an offence. This, in effect, criminalises 'the conduct of a person who procured discrimination without criminalizing the conduct of the actual perpetrator of such discrimination' (O'Connell 1999, 32).

Reasonable accommodation
Both acts require reasonable accommodation to be provided to persons with disabilities, the non-provision of which will amount to discrimination. Within the Employment Equality Act 1998 the employer is not obliged to employ

anyone incapable of doing the job in question. A person with a disability will be deemed capable of doing the job if he can perform the functions of that job with or without special treatment or a facility. The employer is obliged to do all that is reasonable to accommodate the person with a disability, provided that this does not give rise to more than a nominal cost.[7]

The Equal Status Act 2000 declares that it will amount to discrimination to refuse or fail to do all that is reasonable to accommodate the needs of a person with a disability, if without that accommodation it would be impossible or unduly difficult for that person to avail herself of the service in question. This provision is also subject to the 'nominal cost' proviso.

While the legislation does not define the term 'nominal cost', the provision has been litigated under the Employment Equality Act 1998 in *An Employee v. A Local Authority* (2002). In this decision it was held that the term 'nominal cost' would mean different things to different employers. The equality officer stated that 'nominal cost' will depend on the size of the employer and the level of resources available, as well as whether the employer is in the public or private sector, and whether there were any grants or assistance available. In this instance the respondent did not reasonably accommodate the complainant, as the employer failed to examine the options available in respect of special treatment. FÁS, Ireland's national training and employment authority, provided the respondent with three options: an assessment of the complainant by an occupational therapist from the National Rehabilitation Hospital, the provision of a job coach or the adoption of the Employment Support Scheme, which is a financial support to employers who employ people with disabilities in certain circumstances. On the basis of the assessment that was carried out the equality officer determined that the complainant was clearly able and willing to do the job in question.[8] Ultimately, in determining the issue, the equality officer contended that it was reasonable to provide the assessment and a job coach for a period of up to three months for the complainant, and the failure to do so amounted to discrimination for a failure to provide reasonable accommodation. This is a broad interpretation of the term 'nominal cost', and this term will ultimately be superseded by the introduction of the Council Directive 2000/78 EC establishing a General Framework Directive on Employment and Occupation.

Positive discrimination
Both the Employment Equality Act 1998 and the Equal Status Act 2000 are permissive of positive action. The Employment Act permits positive action where the aim of those measures is to reduce or eliminate the effects of discrimination. There is also protection of any training or work experience programmes provided by the state for disadvantaged groups as a whole (Employment Equality Act 1998). Under the Equal Status Act 2000 preferential treatment is accorded to employers who undertake positive measures which are

bona fide intended to promote equality of opportunity for people who are disadvantaged or have special needs.

Derogations

The Equal Status Act 2000 does contain some specific derogations within the legislation that should be mentioned here. It is permissible to treat a person with a disability differently where he/she:

> 'could cause harm to the person or to others, treating the person differently to the extent reasonably necessary to prevent such harm does not constitute discrimination' (Equal Status Act 2000, section 4(3)).

Equally, the legislation states that it is acceptable in the context of education to discriminate against students with disabilities where:

> 'compliance with any of its provisions in relation to a student with a disability would, by virtue of the disability, make impossible, or have a seriously detrimental effect on, the provision by an educational establishment of its services to other students' (Equal Status Act 2000, section 7(4)(b)).

Other provisions

The Employment Equality Act 1998 created an enforcement mechanism for the equality legislation and also created two new bodies: the Equality Authority, who are charged with promoting equality in society, and the Office of the Director of Equality Investigations, known as ODEI—the Equality Tribunal, which is the enforcement body under the acts.

In the context of disability, the equality regime is quite new. Many of the terms and provisions within the legislation need to be clarified, litigated and expanded. This process has started, and that is a major development in the field of equality. The second area where there has been legal activity is in the field of education and the law. Again, the Constitution is the overarching document in the legal framework.

CONSTITUTIONAL RIGHT TO EDUCATION

The introduction of a right to education is an unusual inclusion within a modern constitution. The inclusion of this provision did not take place against the backdrop of a debate about the functions of education within society but rather about the role of religious denominations within education (Glendenning 1999). As the Constitution (Article 42) is silent about who is entitled to education and what education is for, it has been left to the courts to determine the issue. The text of the Constitution manifests a number of dimensions to education—religious, moral, intellectual, physical and social. Parents have the primary responsibility for ensuring that their children are educated in these various dimensions. The state has a duty to provide for a certain minimum education. In *Ryan v. Attorney General* (1965, 350) the courts were first required to look at the meaning of the word education. In the Supreme Court, O'Dalaigh C.J. stated:

> 'Education essentially is the teaching and training of a child to make the best possible use of his inherent and potential capacities, physical, mental and moral'.

This is a significant interpretation by O'Dalaigh C.J. in that it endeavours to ascertain the purpose of education in light of the Constitution. The definition is broad and, in the context of children with disabilities, inclusive. The issue of whether children with disabilities are entitled to benefit from a right to education was examined in *O'Donoghue v. Minister for Health and Ors* (1996). The plaintiff in this action sued the state for its failure to provide for free primary education. O'Hanlon J. was required to determine whether children with profound disabilities are educable or not. The constitutional right to receive free primary education could not be extended to those deemed uneducable. O'Hanlon determined that every child was educable and, in the process, further defined the term 'education'. O'Hanlon J. reiterated O'Dalaigh C.J.'s statement on education and posited that the task of education was to enable the individual:

> 'To make the best possible use of his (or her) inherent and potential capacities, physical, mental and moral—however limited those capacities may be' (*ibid.*, 62).

He also concluded that the state should respond to the rights of children with disabilities by 'providing for free primary education for this group of children in as full and positive a manner as it has done for all other children in the community' (*ibid.*, 66). This decision led the way for many parents to launch test cases and to force the state to respond to the rights of their children. The seminal test case is *Sinnott v. Minister for Education* (2001) (see also Quinlivan and Keys 2002).

  The *Sinnott* case also examined the state's obligation to provide education for those with a profound disability. The primary stumbling block in this action related to the age of the plaintiff. Jamie Sinnott was 23 at the time of the action. Barr J., in the High Court, rebuked the state for failing to meet its constitutional obligations to Jamie Sinnott and held that the determining factor when examining the extent of the right to education for 'the grievously disabled is "need" and not "age"' (*Sinnott v. Minister for Education* 2001, 584). The state appealed this aspect of the decision. The Supreme Court held that the right to free primary education only existed to the age of eighteen. Constitutionally, everyone in Ireland is entitled to free primary education, and persons with a disability may exercise that right until they are eighteen.

Education legislation

The Education Act 1998 establishes a framework for the provision of education in Ireland. The two most important elements are the commitment to mainstreaming and to support services for pupils with special educational needs.

The Education Act 1998 reflects a policy described in the legislation as 'maximum accessibility'. While no individual provision guarantees the right of access, the act enshrines as a goal the inclusion of children with disabilities. This legislation attempts to 'give practical effect to the constitutional rights of children, including children who have a disability or who have other special educational needs, as they relate to education . . . [and] to provide as far as is practicable . . . a level and quality of education appropriate to meeting the needs and abilities of students (Education Act 1998, section 6(a) and (b)). The first reference to access in the act is in the objectives, which require the system participators 'to promote equality of access to and participation in education' and 'to promote the rights of parents to send their children to a school of their parents' choice having regard to the rights of patrons' (Education Act 1998, section 6(c) and (e)). These guiding principles are insufficient to guarantee access. Accordingly, an examination of the more substantive provisions specifically set out in sections 9(m), 15(2)(d) and section 21(2) is required.

Section 9(m) states that a school shall, as far as resources permit, 'establish and maintain an admissions policy which provides for maximum accessibility to the school'. This has to be read alongside section 15(2)(d), which requires the board of management 'to publish . . . the policy of the school concerning admission to and participation by students with disabilities . . . and ensure that as regards that policy principles of equality and the right of parents to send their children to a school of the parents' choice are respected . . .'. Section 21(2) deals with the issue of a school plan, the purpose of which is to set out the objectives of the school in respect of 'equality of access to and participation in the school by students with disabilities'. The subsection also incorporates a requirement on the board of management of a school to delineate the measures employed to achieve access and participation for students with disabilities. Another important aspect of the act is the provision which states that the minister 'may make regulations in relation to . . . admissions of students to schools . . . [and] access to schools and centres for education by students with disabilities . . .' (Education Act 1998, section 33(g) and (j)). These provisions taken individually appear quite weak. However, taken together, they show a commitment to 'maximum accessibility'. While there is no right of access, it is clear that the principles of mainstreaming are guiding the legislature.

If the above provisions do not ensure access to a school, the act provides an appeal system to the secretary general. The appeals committee will deal with issues such as the refusal to enrol a student in a school. This section will require the school to ensure that a student is refused access only on grounds that can be substantiated. The school must act in accordance with the regulations, its public policy and in accordance with natural justice (Hogan 1997).[9] The legislation does not develop definitive rights of access to a school of choice, but schools are required to have a published policy that must be followed. This requirement serves to discourage schools from acting in an arbitrary manner in relation to access. At all times, the board of management are to be guided by principles of equality and 'have regard to the principles and requirement of a democratic society . . .' (Education Act 1998, section 15(2)(e)). If a student is successful in her or his appeal to the 'appeals committee', the appeal committee will make recommendations to the secretary general as to what action should be taken. The secretary general may give directions to the board to remedy the matter. It is important to note that the Education Act 1998 should now be read alongside the Equal Status Act 2000, which also applies to education.

For a student with disabilities who has gained access to a school, there are other relevant concerns. Foremost among them is the elimination of obstacles to learning for that student. The disabled student may need additional services and support to facilitate his/her full participation within the education system. A support service can include the assessment of students, psychological services and speech therapy, among other possibilities (Education Act 1998, section 291).

These support services ensure that students with disabilities have 'a level and quality of education appropriate to meeting the needs and abilities of that person' (Education Act 1998, section 7(1)(a)). The minister plans to accomplish this goal by coordinating the provision of support services and by funding both the schools and the students with special needs, if it is 'deemed appropriate'. The consequential question is how 'appropriate' is to be defined. This is answered in section 7(4)(b), where it is stated that the minister will make 'all reasonable efforts to consult with . . . such other persons who have a special interest in or knowledge of matters relating to education, including persons or groups of person who have a special interest in, or experience of, the education of students with special educational needs . . .'. Section 7(4)(b) therefore offers the professionals and parents of students with disabilities the opportunity to provide the information and the arguments necessary to show the minister what is necessary in terms of support services in order for students with disabilities to participate fully in their education.

The act requires the minister to make available a suitable education to persons with a disability resident in the state and, to that end, the concomitant support services. This section clearly utilises the language of rights without actually providing any enforceable rights to education or support services for students and their families, as regard is had to resources available. The reference to 'resources available' ensures that the provision of support services remains in the realm of ministerial discretion. Therefore there is no right to support services. The allocation thereof remains within the realm of state largesse.[10]

Access to primary and post-primary education in the Republic of Ireland is a complicated issue as the constitutional rights of the school patrons must be considered. There are, as has been described, 'internal tensions' within the system (Constitution Review Group 1996). However, the legislation reflects a demonstrable commitment to 'maximum participation' by students with disabilities. While schools are not required to admit all students, they must have an open, transparent and published admissions policy. The board of management are also required to give updates on how the school will achieve 'equality of access' to their schools (Education Act 1998, section 15). Should this not ensure access, the legislation has been given some teeth in the provision of both the grievance and appeals systems. The appeals system provides a legislative structure for those denied admission to challenge any such decisions. Overall, the education system, as a result of this legislation, should become more transparent and students with disabilities and/or their parents should become aware of the admission policies of schools. As a result, they may ascertain a school's relative position on the key issues of equality and access. Mindful of the aforementioned realities, the Education Act 1998 contains no right to education and has engendered a system wherein the parent who shouts loudest and longest is most likely to receive the support services necessary for their child to receive an effective education.

A number of new provisions have been introduced, one being the Education (Welfare) Act 2000. This act is concerned with school attendance and is focused on those children who have been educated at home or in alternative schooling at the request of their parents. It has some relevance to children with disabilities, but it is only a nominal interest. The act is to provide for the:

> 'Entitlement of every child in the state to a certain minimum education, and, for that purpose, to provide for the registration of children . . . the identification of the causes of non-attendance, on the part of certain students and the adoption of measures for its prevention'.

While on the surface this act may appear to be relevant, it is not geared towards those children who are absent from school by reason of disability. Section 10 is most relevant and delineates the functions of the Board:

> 'The general functions of the Board shall be to ensure that each child attends a recognised school or otherwise receives a certain minimum education, and to assist in the formulation and implementation of policies and objectives of the Government for the time being concerning the education of children . . .' (section 10 (1)).

The functions of the Board include the society-wide promotion of the benefits to be derived from education, the fostering of learning environments and the research of factors contributing to non-attendance. The act provides for a register of children who are receiving education in a place other than a school. A child will not be added to this register if he/she is receiving an adequate minimum education. The issue remains the education welfare officers' subjective determination of the adequate minimum with respect to children with disabilities.

UPCOMING PROVISIONS

The government has committed itself to acting on the recommendations laid out by the Commission on the Status of People with Disabilities (1996). They have suggested two enactments which further this intention, namely the Disabilities Bill 2001 and the Education for Persons with Disabilities Bill 2002.

It was envisaged that the Disabilities Bill 2001 would complete the non-discrimination agenda by addressing issues such as service provision, assessment of needs and accessibility. The Disabilities Bill 2001, when published, did not receive the support of the disability sector, who voiced strenuous opposition to it, eventually forcing the government to withdraw it, pending further consultation with the sector (see Quinlivan 2002). The Disabilities Bill 2001 did not endorse the rights-based approach. There were concerns over the enforcement, or lack of enforcement, mechanisms. The accessibility timeframes seemed to be extraordinarily long and at times contradictory. In the aftermath of the demise of the Disabilities Bill 2001 the government committed themselves to a further period of consultation. The disability sector awaits the 'Disabilities Bill, the Sequel'.

The second proposed enactment was entitled the Education for Persons with Disabilities Bill 2002. In the aftermath of the Sinnott case, the significance of the proposed legislation cannot be underestimated. This bill is drafted very much in the light of the Education Act 1998 and both provisions should work hand in hand. As the bill is still being negotiated, some corollary concerns are worthy of note. The first such concern is the definition of a child:

> '**Child** means a person not less than 3 nor more than 18 years of age'[11] (Education for Persons with Disabilities Bill 2002, section 1).

A child is, and should be regarded as, a child from birth. Most children with disabilities require the full range of educational facilities available to them from the earliest date possible. This definition indirectly absolves the Minister for Education and Science of responsibility for a child with a disability before that date. Equally, this flies in the face of the decisions in both *O'Donoghue* and *Sinnott*. Both cases recognised the different requirements with respect to children with disabilities, and while *Sinnott* did place an upper limit on the right to primary education there was no lower limit. Section 15 reiterates this principle where it states that the National Council for Special Education may accede to early intervention by the provision of education where they are requested to do so. There is, therefore, no right to education before the age of three. This provision is, at best, disingenuous and, at worst, unconstitutional in light of both *O'Donoghue* and *Sinnott*.

The second concern is in respect of education for adults with disabilities. The bill provides for the continuation of the person's education beyond the age of eighteen for a further year, where the new statutory body, the National Council for Special Education, deems it appropriate (section 16).[12] The focus of this bill is to develop the person's capabilities in order to benefit from training or employment services. Where a person will not be able to so benefit, provision may be made for that person to participate in a programme of continuing education and personal development. The decision as to who may continue in education lies with the National Council for Special Education and the Health Board. Clearly, the state will be required to provide for adults with disabilities and to establish necessary bodies under the act, but the fundamental issue remains unresolved. There is no guarantee of a right to education for an adult with a disability.

There is a clear preference set out in this bill in favour of mainstreaming. This should be the first choice, and only where mainstreaming fails should separate or special provisions be considered. The bill also makes provision for an individualised education plan.[13] The aim of such a plan is to ensure that the needs of students with disabilities are identified and tackled. Provision is made for the establishment of a National Council for Special Education, which has a number of functions, including advising the minister 'in relation to any matter relating to the education of children and others with disabilities' (section 19 (1)(1)). In giving this advice, the council must have regard for the 'resources, including the financial resources, available to the State in respect of the provision of education and to the practical implementation of that advice' (section 19 (3)(b)). This is a significant curtailment of the independence of the council. This limitation ensures that the council will not be in a position to advise the minister on best practice in this field, unless that practice does not give rise to resource concerns.

The primary problem with this bill has been noted in relation to the Education Act 1998—its reference to resources. The legislation expressly provides that the Minister for Education may only act with the consent of the Minister for Finance (Education for Persons with Disabilities Bill 2002). The legislation repeats the fundamental flaw of the Education Act 1998 by circumscribing any duties or obligations by the refusal to require funding of these elements.

CONCLUSION

In conclusion it is clear that we have moved away from the perception of people with disabilities as the recipients of charity. People with disabilities are right-holders within this society. While the rights ideology may have been accepted, the difficulty now lies in translating that ideology into enforceable legal rights. There are difficulties: the Constitution remains weak and only a constitutional change can alter this fact.

Ireland is beginning to change, and this is reflected in the new organisations that are working in this field: the National Disability Authority, Comhairle, the Equality Authority, ODEI—the Equality Tribunal and the Human Rights Commission. These organisations are a welcome development, but their existence does not alter the necessity for rights-based legislation. The present government has committed itself to acting on the recommendations made by the Commission on the Status of People with Disabilities (1996). This would involve completing the equality agenda, and they aim to do this by means of the Disabilities Bill and the Education for Persons with Disabilities Bill 2002. These provisions do not, as presently worded, commit themselves to enshrining rights for people with disability. The way forward seems clear: the Commission on the Status of People with Disabilities (1996) recommended the introduction of enforceable rights-based legislation. These recommendations were first made in 1996 by the government's own commission and they remain as compelling today as they were in 1996.

REFERENCES

A Complainant v. Civil Service Commission (2002) *Decision–Employment,* 15 (DEC–E–2002-015). (Available at www.odei.ie.)

An Employee v. A Local Authority (2002) *Decision–Employment,* 4 (DEC-E/2002/4). (Available at www.odei.ie.)

Anti–Discrimination (Pay) Act (1974) Dublin. Stationery Office.

Bunreacht na hÉireann (1937) Dublin. Stationery Office.

Comhairle Act (2000) Dublin. Stationery Office.

Commission on the Status of People with Disabilities (1996) *A strategy for equality—Report of the Commission on the Status of People with Disabilities.* Dublin. Stationery Office.

Constitution Review Group (1996) *Report of the Constitution Review Group.* Dublin. Constitution Review Group, Ireland.

Council Directive 2000/78/EC Establishing a General Framework for Equal Treatment in Employment and Occupation. *Official Journal of the European Communities,* L 303. (Available at www.europa.eu.int.)

Dáil Debates (1998) Volume 490, 29 April 1998.

De Burca and Anderson v. Attorney General (1976) *Irish Reports*, 38.

Dillane v. Ireland (1980) *Irish Law Reports Monthly*, 167.

Disabilities Bill (2001) Dublin. Stationery Office.

Draper v. Attorney General (1984) *Irish Reports*, 277.

Education Act (1998) Dublin. Stationery Office.

Education for Persons with Disabilities Bill (2002) Dublin. Stationery Office.

Education (Welfare) Act (2000) Dublin. Stationery Office.

Employment Equality Act (1977) Dublin. Stationery Office.

Employment Equality Act (1998) Dublin. Stationery Office.

Employment Equality Bill (1996) Dublin. Stationery Office.

Equal Status Act (2000) Dublin. Stationery Office.

Equal Status Bill (1996) Dublin. Stationery Office.

Finanzamt Koeln-Alstadt v. Roland Schumacker (1995) *European Court Reports*, I-225 (Case C-279/93).

Gillespie & Ors v. Northern Health and Social Services Board & Ors (1996) *European Court Reports*, I-475 (Case C-342/93).

Glendenning, D. (1999) *Education and the law.* Dublin, London and Edinburgh. Butterworths.

Harrington v. East Coast Area Health Board (2002) *Decision–Employment*, 1 (DEC-E/2002/001). (Available at www.odei.ie.)

Hogan, G. (1997) Constitutional issues raised in the Education Bill, 1997. *The Bar Review* **2** (6), 215–18.

In the matter of Article 26 and the Employment Equality Bill 1996 (1997) 2 *Irish Reports*, 321.

In the matter of Article 26 and the Planning and Development Bill 1999 (2000) *Irish Reports*, 81.

Keys, M. (2002) Mental Health Act 2001 annotated. *Irish Current Law Statutes Annotated*, 80.

Kimber, C. (2001a) Equality and disability (Part 1). *The Bar Review 2000–2001* **6** (9), 494–501.

Kimber, C. (2001b) Equality and disability (Part 2). *The Bar Review 2001–2002* **7** (2), 66–73.

Lowth v. Minister for Social Welfare (1999) 1 *Irish Law Reports Monthly*, 5.

Mental Health Act (2001) Dublin. Stationery Office.

Murtagh v. Board of Management of St Emer's School (1991) 1 *Irish Reports*, 482.

National Disability Authority Act (1999) Dublin. Stationery Office.

Newman, C. (1997) Bill's religious exemptions challenged. *Irish Times*, 1 May 1997.

Norris v. Ireland (1984) *Irish Reports*, 367.

O'B. v. S. (1984) *Irish Reports*, 316.

O'Connell, D. (1999) *Equality NOW: the SIPTU guide to the Employment Equality Act, 1998.* Dublin. Services Industrial Professional Technical Union, Equality Unit.

O'Donoghue v. Minister for Health and Ors (1996) 2 *Irish Reports*, 20.

Power, C. (2000) The Equal Status Bill, 1999. *The Bar Review* **5** (5), 267–71.

Quinlivan, S. (2002) Disabilities Bill, 2001. *The Bar Review* **7** (4), 37.

Quinlivan, S. and Keys, M. (2002) Official indifference and persistent procrastination: an analysis of *Sinnott. Judicial Studies Institute Journal* **2** (2), 163.

Quinn, G. (2002) Government needs to withdraw Disabilities Bill. *The Examiner*, 18 February 2002.

Quinn, G. and Quinlivan, S. (forthcoming) *Disability discrimination: the need to amend the Employment Equality Act 1998 in light of the EU Framework Directive on Employment.* Irish Centre for European Law / Equality Authority.

Quinn, G., McDonagh, M. and Kimber, C. (1992) *Disability discrimination law in the US, Australia and Canada.* Dublin. Oak Tree Press in association with the National Rehabilitation Board.

Ryan v. Attorney General (1965) *Irish Reports*, 294.

Sinnott v. Minister for Education (2001) 2 *Irish Reports*, 545.

UN General Assembly (1949) *Universal Declaration of Human Rights: final authorized text.* New York. United Nations. (Available at www.un.org.)

[Note: All legislation is available online at www.irlgov.ie.]

Notes

1 Lecturer in Law and member of the Disability Law and Policy Research Unit at the Faculty of Law, NUI, Galway. I wish to thank Mr Larry Donnelly of NUI, Galway, for his comments on this chapter.

2 This Act was introduced to bring Ireland into compliance with our obligations under the European Convention on Human Rights. Owing to time constraints we will not review this enactment; however, for more information see Keys 2002.

3 European Community law has supremacy over national law in its sphere of competencies as set out in the Treaties of the European Union.

4 The Supreme Court took a very different approach in the decision of *In the matter of Article 26 and the Planning and Development Bill 1999* (2000), I.R. 81.

5 'Family Status' is one of the protected grounds within the legislation and is defined as responsibility (a) as a parent or a person *in loco parentis* in relation to a person who has not attained the age of 18 years, or (b) as a parent or the resident primary carer in relation to a person of or over that age with a disability which is of such a nature as to give rise to the need for care or support on a continuing, regular or frequent basis, and, for the purposes of paragraph (b), a primary carer is a resident primary carer in relation to a person with a disability if the primary carer resides with the person with a disability (Employment Equality Act 1998, section 2).

6 Employment Equality Act 1998, section 2 (1). This definition has been

criticised for not adopting the social model of disability as used in the Americans with Disabilities Act 1990 and the UK Disability Discrimination Act 1995. For information on the difficulty that has been experienced with the social model of disability see Quinn and Quinlivan (forthcoming).

7   This is a result of the decision in *In the matter of Article 26 and the Employment Equality Bill 1996* (1997), where the Supreme Court determined that the duty to accommodate contained in the Employment Equality Bill 1996 was an unconstitutional interference with the property rights of employers.

8   Thereby complying with the Employment Equality Act 1998, section 16 (1).

9   The article raises the argument that the passage of this legislation will render schools susceptible to judicial review, thereby ensuring that schools must comply with the rules of natural justice, such as the rule against bias and the right to a fair hearing. See also *Murtagh v. Board of Management of St Emer's School* (1991).

10 The Education Act 1998 contains a myriad of other provisions which impose duties on the school and on the principal of the school to support access to and participation in education for students with disabilities. The act also provides for psychologists as inspectors.

11 For the purposes of this chapter, the version of the bill being relied on is Bill [No. 17b of 2002].

12 The council referred to here is the National Council for Special Education. This council consists of a chairperson and ten ordinary members appointed by the minister. These members may have a special interest in or knowledge relating to the education of 'children' with disabilities. There is no reference to representation from people with experience or special interest in adults with disabilities, nor is there reference to parental representation on the council.

13 The education plan is a detailed account of the nature and degree of a child's disability, stating how the disability affects his or her educational progress. The plan will review the level of educational performance of a child, the nature of his or her special educational needs, and the necessary support services to enable that child to benefit from education and participate in education. The plan should also set out any transitional supports that may be necessary during the child's education. The plan should contain goals for the child over the next twelve months, and should be regularly reviewed and must be updated at least once a year. Provision is also made for a review of the plan when a child is failing to achieve the goals within the plan. Additionally, provision is made for appeals of what is or is not contained within the said plan. (See particularly Education for Persons with Disabilities Bill 2002, sections 10, 11, 12.)

16. VISIBLE CITIZENS: HUMAN RIGHTS AND DISABILITY

GERARD QUINN AND ANNA BRUCE

Disability is a human rights issue! I repeat: disability is a human rights issue.

Those of us who happen to have a disability are fed up being treated by the society and our fellow citizens as if we did not exist or as if we were aliens from outer space. We are human beings with equal value, claiming equal rights . . .

If asked, most people, including politicians and other decision makers, agree with us. The problem is that they do not realize the consequences of this principle and they are not ready to take action accordingly.

—Bengt Lindqvist

INTRODUCTION

Recently, an approach to disability that is grounded in human rights rather than charity has gathered force. Individuals with disabilities, advocates and professionals have educated themselves about how human rights are defined and applied in society. But in many ways human rights activists need to be educated about the applicability of human rights standards in the context of disability. Conversely, disability activists need to see their struggle less in terms of interest-group agitation and more in terms of achieving justice and human rights for all. This chapter outlines the new human rights agenda in the field of disability, particularly how rights may be harnessed to enable people with disabilities to take their place in the mainstream. One focus for change is the UN International Covenant on Economic, Social and Cultural Rights. Reasons for moving towards a UN Convention on the Rights of Persons with Disabilities are presented. Finally, it sets current developments in Ireland within the global context of a human rights agenda.

DISABILITY AND RIGHTS

The application of the general human rights framework of reference in the field of disability is relatively new. This is curious, to say the least. One of the main attractions of human rights is their supposedly universal quality. Yet it seems that nearly every culture has no-go areas where logic and the rule of law don't apply, and are not even expected to apply. It is notable that most cultures experience no contradiction—no cognitive dissonance—in subscribing to high principle on the one hand and yet denying the benefits of these principles to particular sections of the population on the other.

The human rights revolution in the context of disability has to do with making the human being visible—the so-called 'visibility project' of human rights. A second goal is to make the benefits of the rule of law, human rights and democracy available to all and not just to some, or indeed to most. The application of human rights in the context of disability is not merely new—it is profoundly interesting for at least two main reasons. First of all, the case of disability tends to provide tangible proof of the interdependence and indivisibility of both sets of human rights—civil and political as well as economic, social and cultural. Both sets of rights are very deeply connected.

Rights and freedom

Disability reveals the links between both sets of rights clearly. Formal freedoms alone will not make life opportunities available for persons with disabilities. Some positive acts of social solidarity are also required to underpin the political economy of this new-found freedom. This is in fact true for all persons but only more obviously true in the case of persons with disabilities. The disability field shows how economic, social and cultural rights complement rather than undermine freedom.

Secondly, the application of economic, social and cultural rights in the context of disability brings out something often forgotten about these rights. Primed properly, they help to forge pathways into inclusive societies and economies. They help set the terms of access, entry and participation in the mainstream. In other words, they help to secure a system of freedom.

In this way, key goals of the disability rights movement are peculiarly modern and exemplify a new kind of human rights agenda. Perhaps one reason why persons with disabilities did not register on the radar screens even of human rights activists in the past has to do with the fact that human rights tended to have a particular mission over the past few decades since the catastrophe of the Second World War. True, human rights served the ultimate end of honouring human dignity. But they also served an instrumental purpose, by helping to inform, animate and underpin a new kind of post-war polity—one based on and bounded by high principle. Their chief mission was to protect people against power and to legitimate efforts by the international community to intervene in matters that were formerly considered the domestic prerogative of states.

This focus on the negative possibilities of power and on the need to afford adequate protections against the abuse of power was fully justified and continues to warrant the greatest possible attention. But it missed something of importance—something of double importance in fields such as disability. The fixation on power—and especially state power—meant that disability tended to register as a human rights issue only if potential abuses of state power were at issue. For quite a long time the most important human rights issue affecting persons with disabilities was deemed to be the reform of anachronistic civil commitment laws. This was and is important—but note that it misses substantive rights such as the right to health and the positive right to treatment. It misses the question of the status of persons with intellectual disabilities in society as distinct from the incarceration context. To this day, the reform of civil commitment laws tends to be inadequately tied to the more general rights revolution in the context of disability.

Rights and revolution

The relatively recent end of the Cold War is enabling us to see a more holistic role for human rights. Human rights are not just about protection against power—they are also crucially about restoring power to the person. This holds the key to the disability rights revolution. This revolution is not so much about protecting people against power. Nor is it about state largesse for its own sake. It is about the 'boundary problem' of every political community. It is about who gets defined as 'insiders' and 'outsiders'. It is about tackling the hierarchy of 'insiders' who are organised in nearly every culture in gradated and concentric circles of social exclusion. It entails a new orientation towards difference—in this case the human difference of disability. It views disability as something that complicates but does not ruin human existence or the basic incommensurable value of each human being.

Using human rights to re-engineer the terms of access and participation in the mainstream is generally a 'productive factor' in advanced market economies. One senses that this is often the real motor force behind much comparative disability law reform. But it is also a civilising factor in any society that treats no person as insignificant. This is of no small moment when market rationales give out in favour of persons with disabilities.

If the focus of human rights thinking has shifted away from protecting people against power and towards the development of more inclusive societies with power and choice restored to people, then what role do and can economic, social and cultural rights play? Set against the backdrop of using rights to restore power to people, economic, social and cultural rights have an enabling function—they provide a bridge whereby persons with disabilities can take their place as valued and often highly productive citizens. That is, such rights are not defendable (or not merely defendable) because they represent the least a state can do for the welfare of the individual. They are defendable because they facilitate freedom, because they enable people to take charge of their own lives. It is in this sense that economic, social and cultural rights enhance freedom.

LIMITS OF JUSTICE AND POLITICS

Disability issues do not get the proper airing they deserve either in the legal system or in politics. This is important for it underscores the need to move to the human rights framework of reference. Why has it taken so long for the disability issue to reach the human rights agenda? Justice is, of course, primarily a matter of principle. It should be a reflex built into any political system. But as we all know, this tells only part of the story. Justice also depends on politics—on numbers, on votes, on arguments, on bargains, on the visibility or invisibility of the person before the apparatus. On both of these scores—principle and politics—disability issues appear severely disadvantaged. Why is this so?

Invisibility
When justice is considered, three problems arise. First of all there is the inevitable gap between a state's 'myth system' and its 'operation system'. The myth system tells us that the legitimacy of our political system depends on the extent to which it honours the individual. The myth system tells us that no person is insignificant and that all are created equal. Yet each culture retains areas where such myths do not extend. Many have spoken of the phenomenon of 'invisible citizenship' in the context of the general debate about the status of persons with disabilities in society. Every culture faces challenges in opening up the system of freedom for all groups, including those who did not even appear on the radar screen.

Secondly, even when principles apply they seem to apply differently in the context of disability. For example, the right to liberty is one of the most treasured of rights in a liberal democracy. Yet the myriad of substantive and procedural rights available to a suspect in the criminal process greatly outweigh the comparable protections in the civil commitment field. The interesting thing is that the system appears to be saying that the 'normal' legal protections are only for 'normal' people. In this there is an implicit segregation of citizens—some with first-class status and others with no-class status.

Thirdly, the principles that do apply do not generally exhaust those that should apply in the disability field. You will find the principles embedded in our legal order of little use to you in this regard. For our legal orders tend not to place a high value on distributive justice. The net result is that the achievement of these rights is purely a matter of pressure politics and not a matter of principle.

Limits of politics

May citizens perceive justice as politics? The democratic marketplace is a tumultuous place. Ignorant armies do clash by night. Interest groups vie for advantage. There is nothing inherently wrong with this. By and large it serves us well. But there are problems here and they complicate the issue of disability.

First, there is the standing danger that the 'public interest' might simply be defined as the lowest common denominator—as the sum of competing vectors. Principle can be seen as something that can be bargained on or for, especially if it is not anchored strongly in the legal order. Right depends on might. Secondly, the political marketplace tends to favour those with most voice, or whose issues connect with priorities such as maintaining the economic viability of the nation. But what of those who have a muted voice or no voice at all? What of those whose concerns do not reflect economic or other policy priorities? They lack purchase power in the political market. They have demands but there is little supply to meet those demands. There is, in a sense, market failure, and no obvious corrective to that market failure unless one views the courts as that corrective.

RIGHTS AND EQUAL OPPORTUNITIES

The rights-based perspective is often contrasted with the so-called medical model of disability. Under the medical model the individual is objectified as the carrier of present symptoms and is not taken seriously as an end in him/herself. This is a parody of the true medical mission but nonetheless it contains at least a kernel of truth. What matters more than the attitude of the medical profession to disability is the way policy-makers have traditionally approached disability. A classic policy response stemmed from a control model, and aimed to restore the loss through rehabilitation or to compensate for the lack of opportunity to participate in life and fulfil one's own dreams. In short, people were perceived as problems to be managed.

One result of policies shaped by this model tended to be the formulation of segregated programmes to cater for the needs of people with disabilities. No matter how well-intentioned, they tended to cement in place a self-perpetuating cycle of social exclusion, low self-esteem and discrimination. By contrast, the rights-based perspective denies that people are problems and takes seriously the assertion that all persons are born equal and with inalienable rights.

Disability as a social construct

At the heart of this rights-based perspective lies a revolutionary new approach to human difference or the so-called 'social construct' idea. According to the 'social construct' idea people are not born different. Difference is not inherent in a human being. Rather, it comes into existence—or is socially constructed— when one person is compared to another or to an average or benchmark. The real problem is not the difference of disability but the way in which that difference is constructed. Obviously, the benchmark or average against which the difference of disability is created and measured is that of the able-bodied person. But the real question is why that average was selected in the first place. At one extreme it is often asserted that society disables people (Altman 2001).

The real value of the social construct idea is that it takes the analysis one step further. The point about averages or benchmarks is that they are not merely used to *mark* people apart but also to *keep* people apart. This is so because the lifeworld—the economy, culture, the provision of goods and services, and the structure of public services—is created to cater only for those who conform to the average. Thus anyone who fails to conform is marked and kept apart. The real problem from the 'social construct' viewpoint lies not in the person but in the way society treats difference.

From this perspective the main 'problem' in the disability field is not the disability itself but the way society treats the human difference of disability. In other words, the real problem is located outside the person and in the response of society to the difference presented by disability. Hence the disability rights movement is part of a broader movement that aims to develop inclusive societies where all persons are deemed entitled to play their part and assume their civil responsibilities like everyone else. While individuals are different, they are all equal in the eyes of the law. It follows that the core human right implicated by the civil rights perspective is equality. Creating a society that values difference and that does not use difference as an excuse for social exclusion is not easy. It means evaluating current programmes for their compatibility with respect for equality. It means undoing the inequalities inherited from the past. It means a sustained effort at ensuring genuine equal access to life opportunities for all.

Values and disability

International human rights law rests essentially on four connected basic human values: dignity, autonomy, equality and social solidarity. These values lie at the very basis of the legitimacy of this state. They animate a system of freedom—a system that provides protection against power but also space to assume power over one's own life. Consider these values in the context of disability.

Human dignity means that people are to be valued because they are people—not because they are economically or otherwise useful. How quickly we forget this in a utilitarian age. Autonomy means creating space for the flourishing of the human spirit. We have to constantly stress that this spirit lies within *all* of us, regardless of the difference of disability. Equality means creating a society that treats all equally and makes due and positive allowance for difference, including the difference of disability. We owe this to each other. Solidarity means helping those who cannot help themselves or whose capacity to do so is greatly diminished. Solidarity does not exist to make us feel good—

even less to dispense charity without any actual involvement. It exists because the system of freedom needs a substantive underpinning to allow people to use their capacities.

Putting these values together in the context of disability leads to a connected agenda: equality provides the core right. Equality can be rendered in three very different ways. At one extreme, equality is merely a formal right to exactly the same treatment as all others. This is of little avail to people with disabilities for it fails to take account adequately of the difference of disability. For example, to require that all persons would be admitted to a restaurant on exactly the same terms would be of little use to someone who must use a ramp to gain access. At another extreme, an insistence on exact equality of results for all regardless of ability or contribution would not appear to fit with the claim that people with disabilities should be treated on their individual merits. In between those two extremes lies the equal opportunities model.

The equal opportunities model insists that all persons be treated on their merits and that the task of law and policy is to open up opportunities to all on an equal basis. It rejects the formal equality model and instead insists that actors—employers, shopkeepers, etc.—take account of disability and 'reasonably accommodate' it in order to achieve genuine equality. A comprehensive equal opportunities model is one that tracks the typical life cycle of an individual. Its focus points can be clustered as follows.

- *Preparing* people with disabilities for participation: equal access to the preparatory processes for participation; inclusive education, vocational education and training.

- Guaranteeing *access* to the environment: equal access *within* the built environment, e.g. effective building regulations; equal access *to* the built environment, e.g. accessible public transportation; equal access *to* the communications medium—telecommunications policy.

- *Non-discrimination* law: clear and regularly enforced anti-discrimination law in the fields of employment and the provision of goods and services such as restaurants.

- *Mainstreaming* disability in the policy process: removing disability policy from specialist Health and Welfare ministries and mainstreaming responsibility into all general ministries—employment, training, civil rights.

- Re-styling *welfare and social supports* to achieve the goals of independence and participation: ensuring that welfare and other supports do not hinder participation but actively support it.

Harnessing rights

A comprehensive equal opportunities programme does entail the expenditure of resources. It does not rest exclusively on formal law. In actual fact many cost/benefit analyses of the above kind of measures generally result in positive findings. For one thing, it proves much more expensive for the taxpayer merely to maintain people passively than to invest in them so that they can secure their own future.

That is to say, a comprehensive equal opportunities policy in the context of disability requires extensive economic and social supports in order to prime people to become productive citizens and assume control over their own lives. These supports need to be thorough and integrated and tied to a model that sees the participation of the disabled person as a social and economic asset. Such support will need to be provided in the mainstream so as not to initiate or perpetuate a cycle of wasteful exclusion.

Obviously, women with disabilities experience the economic and social exclusion felt by all women, and indeed the impact is exacerbated for them. In turn, their overall status tends to be even lower than that of their disabled male peers (Walsh and Heller 2002). The application of economic, social and cultural rights for such women is therefore particularly important.

THE UN COVENANT

A core human rights document is the International Covenant on Economic, Social and Cultural Rights (ICESCR) ratified in 1966 (United Nations General Assembly 1966). Article 1 states:

> 'All peoples have the right of self-determination. By virtue of that right they freely determine their political status and freely pursue their economic, social and cultural development.'

A committee established seven goals on behalf of all states that are party to the UN Covenant.

(1)   The first goal is to ensure that national legislation, administrative rules and procedures, and practices are in conformity with the *rights and obligations* in the Covenant.

(2)   The state should *monitor* and gather information concerning the level of enjoyment of each of the rights in the Covenant.

(3)   States should show that they have adopted *policies and programmes* with a view to realising the rights in the Covenant.

(4)   States should encourage *public scrutiny* of government policies on a national level, across the economic, social and cultural sectors.

(5)   The fifth goal is to provide a basis against which the committee as

well as the state can *evaluate* the progressive realisation of economic, social and cultural rights over time.

(6)   The state should identify difficulties and *obstacles* to the realisation of economic, social and cultural rights (ICESCR General Comment 1, Third Session 1989).

(7)   Finally, the committee is to facilitate the *exchange of information* to develop a better understanding of the common problems faced by states as well as their solutions.

Obligations of states

Does the Covenant apply to people with disabilities? Although the Covenant does not specifically mention disability, ICESCR General Comment 5 (Eleventh Session 1994) insists that the terms prohibit disability discrimination. Further, the obligations of the states parties are firm and perhaps firmer than usual in the context of disability. Governments are obliged to do more than avoid taking measures that might have a negative impact on persons with disabilities. Rather, the obligation in the case of such a vulnerable and disadvantaged group is to take positive action to promote the objectives of full participation and equality within society. It is probable that additional resources will need to be allocated for this purpose and that a wide range of specially tailored measures will be required.

ICESCR General Comment 5 (Eleventh Session 1994) emphasises that the responsibilities of states encompass the structuring of the private as well as the public sector. No matter how productive voluntary service-providers may be, this does not permit governments to cede all responsibility.

ICESCR General Comment 5 (Eleventh Session 1994, paragraph 19) specifically mentions the equal rights of disabled women, noting that 'persons with disabilities are often seen as genderless human beings. As a result, the double discrimination suffered by disabled women is often neglected'. Also, 'even in times of severe resources constraint . . . the vulnerable members of society can and indeed must be protected by the adoption of relatively low-cost targeted programmes' (ICESCR General Comment 3, Fifth Session 1990, paragraph 12). Clearly, state obligations extend to taking positive measures, including affirmative action. According to the committee, 'there is no country in which a major policy and programme effort is not required' (ICESCR General Comment 5, Eleventh Session 1994, paragraphs 8 and 13). These efforts must include 'general, as well as specially designed, laws, policies and programmes and must be developed in co-operation with representatives for persons with a disability' (*ibid.*, paragraphs 6 and 14).

Non-discrimination

The specific measures to realise the rights of persons with a disability include 'the need to ascertain, through regular monitoring, the nature and scope of the problems existing within the State; the need to adopt appropriately tailored policies and programmes to respond to the requirements thus identified; the need to legislate where necessary and to eliminate any existing discriminatory legislation; and the need to make appropriate budgetary provisions or, where necessary, seek international co-operation and assistance' (ICESCR General Comment 5, Eleventh Session 1994, paragraph 13).

Countries must also make sure that agents in the private sphere do not hamper the enjoyment of rights by persons with a disability. Non-public entities, including private employers and private suppliers of goods and services, must 'be subject to both non-discrimination and equality norms in relation to persons with disabilities' (ICESCR General Comment 5, Eleventh Session 1994, paragraph 11). If states fall short of this, 'the ability of persons with disabilities to participate in the mainstream of community activities and to realize their full potential as active members of society will be severely and often arbitrarily constrained' (*ibid.*).

The committee notes that legal measures are not enough to ensure the equal enjoyment of rights for persons with a disability. It refers to *The Standard Rules on the Equalization of Opportunities for Persons with Disabilities* (United Nations 1994, Rule 1) by obliging states parties to 'take action to raise awareness in society about persons with disabilities, their rights, their needs, their potential and their contribution'. Further, the Covenant states that governments must guarantee that their people may exercise economic, social or cultural rights without discrimination on any grounds, including status—which, according to the committee, includes disability.

The committee embraces a broad concept of equality, granting each person with a disability what s/he needs in order to enjoy a certain right rather than just granting persons with a disability what able-bodied persons need to enjoy that right. These rights are to be enjoyed by equal participation in society.

Employment

While all the articles in the Covenant are relevant to persons with a disability, certain rights—to work and to just and favourable conditions of work—are not only relevant to the fulfilment of the correlating need but are instrumental for advancing a paradigm shift from institutionalisation to equal participation. Article 6 (1) proclaims 'the right of everyone to the opportunity to gain his living by work which he freely chooses or accepts'. The committee notes that the realisation of this right for persons with a disability will require the elimination of 'prominent and persistent' discrimination and of 'the physical barriers that society has erected in areas such as transport, housing and the workplace which are then cited as the reason why persons with disabilities cannot be employed'

(ICESCR General Comment 5, Eleventh Session 1994, paragraphs 20 and 22). It is the duty of states to actively support the integration of persons with a disability into the regular labour market, as well as to 'develop policies which promote and regulate flexible and alternative work arrangements that reasonably accommodate the needs of disabled workers' (*ibid.*).

States must also ensure that lack of access to transportation does not exclude persons with a disability from 'finding suitable, integrated jobs, taking advantage of educational and vocational training, or commuting to facilities of all types' (ICESCR General Comment 5, Eleventh Session 1994, paragraph 23). While sheltered employment may be suitable for some persons with a disability, confinement of categories of persons with a disability to a certain occupation or the production of certain goods may violate the right to freely chose or accept work. Similarly, the use of 'therapeutical treatment' which amounts to forced labour is a violation of the right to work (*ibid.*, paragraph 21).

Education

The rights in the Covenant, including the right to education, are equally applicable to persons with a disability. Disability-based discrimination is one of the forms of discrimination prohibited by the Covenant. In General Comment 5, dealing specifically with disability, the committee recognises that the general educational system is the best place for persons with a disability to receive the education to which they have a right. By reiterating *The Standard Rules on the Equalization of Opportunities for Persons with Disabilities* (United Nations 1994), the committee notes that 'States should recognize the principle of equal primary, secondary and tertiary educational opportunities for children, youth and adults with disabilities, in integrated settings' (ICESCR General Comment 5, Eleventh Session 1994, paragraph 35).

Implementing an integrated approach obliges states to educate teachers in regular schools and make available the necessary equipment and support in order to 'bring persons with disabilities up to the same level of education as their non-disabled peers' (ICESCR General Comment 5, Eleventh Session 1994, paragraph 35). For example, sign language should be recognised as a separate language and the children should have access to it. ICESCR General Comment 13 (Twenty-first Session 1999) states that technical and vocational education programmes are to be available to, *inter alia*, persons with a disability. Still, the committee recognises that 'education is the primary vehicle by which economically and socially marginalized adults and children can lift themselves out of poverty and obtain the means to participate fully in their communities' (*ibid.*, paragraph 1).

Access in the context of education has three overlapping dimensions: non-discrimination, physical accessibility and economic accessibility (ICESCR General Comment 13, Twenty-first Session 1999). While these dimensions are not explored in the context of disability, they are clearly relevant here. According to the committee, and consistent with the general obligations of states parties, the obligation to guarantee that the right to education is exercised without discrimination of any kind is of an immediate nature (*ibid.*). In addition, a 'minimum core obligation' is to ensure the right of access to public educational institutions and programmes on a non-discriminatory basis (*ibid.*, paragraph 57). According to the committee, temporary special measures designed to bring about *de facto* equality for disadvantaged groups in the context of education are not to be regarded as discriminatory provided they fulfil certain requirements. Exemplifying violations of the right to education, the committee mentions the failure to eliminate legal and *de facto* discrimination in the field of education and the failure to introduce, as a matter of priority, free primary education available to all.

States must also disaggregate educational data according to prohibited grounds of discrimination, implicitly including disability (ICESCR General Comment 13, Twenty-first Session 1999). States are also obliged to 'remove gender and other stereotyping which impedes the educational access of girls, women and other disadvantaged groups' (*ibid.*, paragraph 55). While the focus here is on gender, the obligation is highly relevant in the context of disability. Overall, the committee affirms that persons with a disability are best educated when integrated in the regular educational system.

Cultural life

Article 15 of the ICESCR recognises the right of everyone to take part in cultural life, as do *The Standard Rules on the Equalization of Opportunities for Persons with Disabilities* (United Nations 1994). To facilitate the equal participation of persons with a disability in culture, the committee urges states to inform and educate the general public about disability. Communication barriers must be eliminated if persons with a disability are to be able to take part in cultural life, adapting books and pictures suitably (ICESCR General Comment 5, Eleventh Session 1994).

In summary, states should review national legislation, administrative rules and procedures, and practices and report how these conform to the realisation of the economic, social and cultural rights of persons with a disability. They should report on a comprehensive policy envisaging how the rights of persons with a disability are to be realised, as well as identifying obstacles to such realisation. The actual situation of persons with a disability regarding each right should be monitored in these reports, and the progressive realisation of their rights should be evaluated against national benchmarks. States should seek help from representatives of persons with a disability in the creation of reports and should make these available to the public, especially to persons with a disability.

GLOBAL CONTEXT

Does the rights-based model of disability exert real influence? The UN General Assembly adopted the *UN Standard Rules on the Equalization of Opportunities for People with Disabilities* in 1993. The Rules did not contain legally binding rules, but did contain a monitoring mechanism that is more usually to be found in a treaty. Bengt Lindqvist, from Sweden, was the Special Rapporteur charged with responsibility for monitoring implementation.

The tide turned in favour of a binding treaty by the late 1990s. The enactment by the US of a civil rights statute in the context of disability—the Americans with Disabilities Act (or ADA) of 1990—underscored the power of the shift from welfare to rights. The ADA has inspired many parliaments around the world to follow suit, despite some recent setbacks in the US Supreme Court. Closer to home, the inclusion of disability as a ground for prohibited discrimination in Article 13 of the Treaty of Amsterdam pegged Europe to the rights-based model.

This shift of international opinion was first reflected in the UN system in the workings of the UN Commission on Human Rights, which passed a bi-annual resolution on human rights and disability. Ireland has been the main sponsor of this resolution since the late 1990s, and in 2000 Ireland tried to advance a treaty through this resolution. At that time Ireland was apparently thwarted by some of its EU partners, but it nevertheless deserves credit for its diplomatic efforts.

The Office of the UN High Commissioner for Human Rights under Mary Robinson commissioned Professor Theresia Degener (Germany) and Gerard Quinn (Ireland) to direct research on the current use and future potential of the six UN treaties on human rights in the context of disability. Their study (Quinn and Degener 2002) found that although the existing treaties had considerable relevance in the abstract, it was not likely to be realised under the existing system. The authors added to the arguments for a thematic treaty on disability—not as a way of creating new law but rather as a way of making explicit the relevance of the general standards in the specific context of disability.

In December 2001 the Mexican government had a resolution passed by the General Assembly in New York to the effect that an Ad Hoc Committee of interested states would begin the process of 'considering proposals' for the drafting of a treaty on disability. It organised a high-level seminar on the topic of a treaty in Mexico City in June 2002, unveiling its own draft text (Government of Mexico 2002). That seminar produced two important 'Outcome Documents': (1) a set of principles according to which the treaty should be drafted; and (2) an indicative outline of what the treaty might contain. The principles emphasised the need to ensure that the new treaty built on the existing general human rights standards and the importance of participation by non-governmental organisations.

A special Ad Hoc Committee of Member States of the United Nations began the process of drafting a legally binding treaty on the rights of persons with disabilities in 2002. The disability treaty would add a new thematic treaty—that is, a treaty that applies general standards to a particular group—to this body of law. While this process may last for up to five years, the very fact that it is under way testifies to the power of the emerging model of disability at the international level. Innovations were proposed: certain NGOs might be admitted to the proceedings as a matter of right; ordinary disability NGOs would be invited under certain conditions; and Human Rights Commissioners would be invited to all future sessions. The committee also recommended that persons with disabilities and other experts in the field of disability rights should be included on their delegations for coming sessions, and that there should be a series of regional meetings—in Europe, for example—on the treaty.

From a substantive point of view the first session of the Ad Hoc Committee achieved very little, which is not surprising at this stage in the process. Many states and some groups of states (e.g. the EU) outlined their initial positions on the substance of any new instrument. The EU, for example, issued important and generally positive statements in plenary on the arguments for a treaty, on the possible content of a treaty and on the enforcement mechanism that might be adopted. The next session should see the drafting process begin in earnest.

CONCLUSION

These groupings and processes may seem remote. How do they touch the lives of people with disabilities locally? It is worth bearing in mind that most of the world's 600 million people with disabilities live in developing countries. This process is as vital to them as it is to us. It is important that NGOs should learn about the UN process and the role they can play in it. What happens at the next session of the Ad Hoc Committee will ultimately have a powerful bearing on the enjoyment of rights by Irish people with disabilities. In sum, the current consultation exercise on the Disabilities Bill at home has a broader context. That context is the world-wide acceptance of the rights-based approach to disability. The challenge now is to translate that into something concrete at home and by so doing to recapture some of the high ground Ireland had already won for itself on the international stage until recently.

REFERENCES

Altman, B. (2001) Disability definitions, models, classification schemes, and applications. In G. Albrecht, K.D. Seelman and M. Bury (eds), *Handbook of disability studies*, 97–122. Thousand Oaks CA. Sage Publications.

Government of Mexico (2002) *Text of elements for a United Nations comprehensive and integral and international convention to promote and protect the rights and dignity of persons with disabilities.* (Available at http://www.sre.gob.mx/discapacidad/elements.htm)

ICESCR General Comment 1, Third Session (1989) *Reporting by states parties*, E/1989/22, paragraph 8.

ICESCR General Comment 3, Fifth Session (1990) *The nature of states parties obligations*, E/1991/23, paragraph 12.

ICESCR General Comment 5, Eleventh Session (1994) *Persons with disabilities*, E/1995/22, paragraphs 6, 8, 11, 13, 14, 20, 21, 22, 23, 35, 37.

ICESCR General Comment 13, Twenty-first Session (1999) *The right to education*, E/C.12/1999/10, paragraphs 1, 6, 16, 32, 33, 36, 37, 44, 45, 55, 57, 59.

Quinn, G. and Degener, T. (2002) *Human rights and disability*. New York and Geneva. United Nations. HR/PUB/02/1. (Available at http://www.unhchr.ch/)

United Nations (1994) *The Standard Rules on the Equalization of Opportunities for Persons with Disabilities.* New York. United Nations.

United Nations General Assembly (1966) *The International Covenant on Economic, Social, and Cultural Rights.* London. HMSO.

Walsh, P.N. and Heller, T. (eds) (2002) *Health of women with intellectual disabilities.* Oxford. Blackwell Science.

CONTRIBUTORS

Barry Carpenter is Chief Executive/Principal of Sunfield School and Honorary Professor at the University of Northumbria. His previous posts have included head teacher, school inspector, and principal lecturer (at Westminster College, Oxford). He has written extensively in the field of special educational needs and lectures internationally on his major research area of families of children with disabilities. He is the parent of Katie, a young woman with Down Syndrome.

Alan Carr, Ph.D., is Director of the Doctoral Programme in Clinical Psychology and Associate Professor of Clinical Psychology at University College Dublin. He is also a consultant clinical psychologist and marital and family therapist at the Clanwilliam Institute. He has published widely in the fields of clinical psychology and family therapy and has practised in Canada, the UK and Ireland.

Chris Conliffe, M.A., D.Phil., is Director of the Institute for Counselling and Personal Development (ICPD), *Interpoint*, 20–24 York Street, Belfast, and a clinical psychologist. He is also visiting professor and course director of the M.Sc. in Counselling Psychology at the University of Ulster. He has published widely in the field of learning disability and is actively involved in promoting peace and reconciliation in Northern Ireland.

Hugh Gash is Director of the Postgraduate Diploma in Education at St Patrick's College, Dublin City University. He is co-editor (with C. Rault and S. Molina García) of *Learning difficulties: what types of help?* (Paris, 2001). He is a Fellow of the Irish Psychological Society.

Stephen Kealy is Director of Psychology with the Sisters of Charity of Jesus and Mary, Moore Abbey, Monasterevan, Co. Kildare, which provides services for people with intellectual disabilities. Early assessment and intervention services are provided in partnership with the South-Western Area Health Board and the

Midland Health Board. He is Secretary of the International Association for the Scientific Study of Intellectual Disability (IASSID) and a Fellow of the Psychological Society of Ireland.

Christy Lynch trained as an occupational therapist. He managed *Open Road*, an EU-funded Supported Employment project (1988–2001), and subsequently founded the European Union of Supported Employment. He has consulted on inclusive employment initiatives throughout Europe and in Peru, Uruguay, Argentina, Russia, Botswana and South Africa. Actively involved with the European Disability Forum, Christy is Chief Executive Officer for KARE, an agency providing services in counties Kildare, Offaly and Wicklow, and is a member of the NDA.

Dr Bob McCormack is Director of Research and Service Development at St Michael's House, Dublin, and former Director of the Open Training College. He has published and presented widely on various aspects of learning disability. His current research interests include the prevention of abuse and the development of person-centred quality systems. He currently chairs the Outcomes Quality Network and the Research Subcommittee of the National Federation of Voluntary Bodies.

Dr John McEvoy, Senior Clinical Psychologist with the North-Eastern Health Board, lectures at University College Dublin and is a Research Associate at the Centre for Disability Studies there. He has over twenty years' experience in the field of developmental disability and has held a number of senior managerial and clinical posts in Ireland and the UK. His research interests include challenging behaviour and supporting people with intellectual disabilities through loss and bereavement.

Shivaun Quinlivan is a graduate of NUI Galway, King's College London and King's Inns, and currently works as a law lecturer in NUI Galway. Her research interests lie mainly in the field of equality and the law, with a particular interest in disability rights issues. She is a founder member of the Law Faculty's Disability Law Policy and Research Unit. She has also been appointed as the Irish national expert on the European Commission's Disability Discrimination Network of Experts.

Bairbre Redmond is Director of Social Work Training at University College Dublin, and previously worked as a social worker in the intellectual disability services. She has a particular research interest in the issues concerning parents who have children with a disability and in developing new, reflective teaching and training approaches for professionals working in the area of health and social care. She is the author of *Listening to parents* (1996) and *Reflection in action* (2004).

Patricia Noonan Walsh, Ph.D., is Professor of Disability Studies at University College Dublin. She is co-author (with Barbara LeRoy) of *Women with disabilities aging well: a global view* (Brookes, 2004), and is a Fellow of the International Association for the Scientific Study of Intellectual Disability (IASSID).

Michael Shevlin has taught in a secondary school in Ireland and was seconded to develop curricular links between mainstream and special schools. He subsequently joined the Education Department of Trinity College Dublin, where he is Senior Lecturer. He has taught Special Education courses at undergraduate and postgraduate level. He has written about the inclusion of young people with profound and complex learning needs in link programmes and also about the school and college experiences of young people with disabilities.

Eric Emerson is currently Professor of Clinical Psychology at the Institute for Health Research at Lancaster University. He previously held the chair at the Hester Adrian Research Centre (University of Manchester). He also worked as a clinical psychologist and in service development in the UK and Canada. He is a member of the English Department of Health's Ministerial Task Force overseeing implementation of health and social care policy for people with intellectual disabilities.

Janet Robertson, Ph.D., is a Senior Research Fellow at the Institute for Health Research, Lancaster University. She has specialised as a researcher in the field of intellectual disabilities, having been part of the Hester Adrian Research Centre from 1993 to 2000. She is currently involved in research on the impact of person-centred planning.

Dr Shea Caffrey is a senior clinical psychologist at St Michael's House, where he has worked for the last 25 years. He has worked in the areas of sexuality, teaching clinically, teaching and research. His Ph.D. was in the area of sexuality and disability. He also lectures, part-time, on personality and human sexuality in the Department of Psychology, Trinity College Dublin.

Dr Mark Mulrooney is a clinical psychologist working in the area of learning disabilities, with an interest in challenging behaviour, families, young children and individuals with severe and profound difficulties.

Dr Mark Harrold has been practising in the field of clinical psychology for the past sixteen years. He has extensive experience of working with people with learning disabilities and their families. He has been an active campaigner to establish rights for people with learning disabilities and has contributed to both print and broadcast media on the topic.

Anna Bruce studied at the University of Lund in Sweden and holds a postgraduate qualification in international human rights law. She is a member of the Disability Law and Policy Unit, NUI Galway.

Gerard Quinn is Professor of Law and Dean of the Faculty of Law at NUI Galway. He served as a full member on the Commission on the Status of People with Disabilities and has worked with the European Commission on its disability policy. He has published extensively on international and comparative disability law and has co-authored a major paper on global trends in disability law to mark the tenth anniversary of the Americans with Disabilities Act. He is a member of the Human Rights Commission of Ireland.